THIS IS MY BODY

THIS IS MY BODY

Representational Practices in the Early Middle Ages

MICHAL KOBIALKA

ANN ARBOR

THE UNIVERSITY OF MICHIGAN PRESS

Copyright © Michal Kobialka 1999
All rights reserved
Published in the United States of America by
The University of Michigan Press
Manufactured in the United States of America
♾ Printed on acid-free paper

2002   2001   2000   1999   4   3   2   1

A CIP catalog record for this book is available from the British Library.

Library of Congress Cataloging-in-Publication Data

Kobialka, Michal.
    This is my body : representational practices in the early
Middle Ages / [Michal Kobialka].
        p.   cm.
    Includes bibliographical references (p.   ) and index.
    ISBN 0-472-11029-2 (acid-free paper)
    1. Christian drama, Latin (Medieval and modern)—History and
criticism—Theory, etc.   2. Liturgical drama—History and
criticism—Theory, etc.   3. Body, Human—Religious
aspects—Christianity.   4. Lord's Supper in literature.   5.
Sacraments in literature.   6. Mimesis in literature.   I. Title.
PA8077   K63   1999
872'.03093823—dc21

99-6023
CIP

Contents

Preface

Whether or not we scholars think that medieval drama and theater originated in the Easter monastic practices in the tenth century depends on
how we understand the notion of representation as well as the conven-
tions that describe what drama and theater are. Postmodern historiography teaches us, however, that such an approach needs to be complemented by (1) the investigation of the past and present rationalizations
behind the practices that defined representation in the Middle Ages and
drama and theater in the twentieth century as well as (2) the analysis of
how these practices manifested themselves in different venues at different times. Rather than talking about our notion of representation or
drama and theater, I suggest that the medieval concept of representation
had little to do with a prevailing tradition in Western culture that considers representation in terms of (1) the imitation of nature (Aristotle
Physics 199a) or the process of doubling of the "one that becomes two"
(Plato *Phaedo*), delimited by hierarchism of optical geometry, that is, by
Leon Battista Alberti's 1435 rules of a single-point perspective ordering
a transfer of objects from a real space to an imaginary stage; (2) the
process of making the subject transparent to the monocular vision of the
identified community to which it belongs, that is, the nation, the city,
the ethnic group, and so on; or (3) in terms of today's taxonomies that
express the typology of Christ's passion as drama and theater. I contend
that the medieval concept of representation was enshrined in the interpretation of *Hoc est corpus meum* [This is my body]—the words spoken by
Christ at the Last Supper and repeated by a priest every time he cele-
brates the sacrament of the Eucharist during the Mass—and in establishing the visibility of the body that had disappeared both for women
at the tomb and for the faithful gathered on Easter Sunday for the
moment of resurrection:

Quem quaeritis? [Whom do you seek?]

Ihesum Nazarenum.

Non est hic. Surrexit sicut praedixerat. [He is not here. He has risen just as it was predicted.]

The medieval concept of representation (and its practices), however, was never stable but always in flux and always crossed by different modes of seeing until it was, as I argue in this book, stabilized by the constitutions of the Fourth Lateran Council in 1215. This book focuses precisely on this lack of homogeneity and on these moments when the idea of what it meant to represent was under discussion—the *Regularis concordia* (970x973), the Berengar-Lanfranc Eucharist controversy (1049–79), the ternary mode of the Eucharistic sacrament (twelfth century), and the Fourth Lateran Council (1215). By drawing attention to these epistemological fragments, I hope to disclose representational practices that might have been erased by us in the pursuit of objects caught in the mirror that we placed in front of ourselves.

Acknowledgments

This volume was rewritten many times; so that what is presented in it corresponds to the shifts and transformations in my treatment of the representational practices in the early Middle Ages. During this process, I encountered many people who encouraged me to continue the work. I would like to express my gratitude to all of them. Special thanks are due to Margaret Knapp and Charles Gattnig; Rosemarie Bank; Barbara Hanawalt; Donnalee Dox; Gary Williams; Kathy Biddick; Joanna and Andrzej Piotrowscy; Lynne Kirby and Neil Sieling; and Barbara and Vernon Sieling.

Also, I would like to thank Lance Brockman, chair of the Department of Theatre Arts and Dance, University of Minnesota, and the members of the University of Minnesota committees who provided me with the uninterrupted time to complete the research and writing of this book. This project was funded by the McKnight-Land Grant and the Bush Sabbatical Supplement Program.

Finally, I would like to thank LeAnn Fields of the University of Michigan Press for her continuing interest in the project; Alja Kooistra and Mary Meade of the Press for their professionalism in handling the production process; and Jill Butler Wilson for her sensitive, intelligent, and careful reading of my manuscript. It was my good fortune that I had the opportunity to work directly with them. I would also like to thank Malcolm Marjoram of the British Library for his professional handling of my requests.

Parts of chapter 3 appeared in my essay "*Corpus Mysticum et Representationem:* Hildegard of Bingen's *Scivias* and *Ordo Virtutum*," *Theatre Journal* 37.1 (May 1996): 1–22. Reprinted with permission.

Introduction

Identity freezes the gesture of thinking. It pays homage to an order. To think, on the contrary, is to pass through; it is to question that order, to marvel that it exists, to wonder what made it possible, to seek, in passing over its landscape, traces of the movement that formed it, to discover in these histories supposedly laid to rest "how and to what extent it would be possible to think otherwise."

—Michel de Certeau, *Heterologies*

As we are approaching the end of the second millennium, we are engaged in a systematic survey of the gains and the losses accrued in the twentieth century. The number of books that discuss this phenomenon is on the rise. The spectrum of the topics covered extends from the reevaluation of how we talk about history, politics, or culture to the impact of new technologies on the practices of everyday life and on gendered historical subjects. The tone of these investigations varies from exaltation to apocalyptic visions of despair. The strategies employed are multiple. Despite the differences between them, they tend to focus on the following questions: Who is speaking? What institutional site authorizes the investigation? What are the positions of the subject who is questioning, speaking, or listening? What are the modes of production, transmission, and dissemination of knowledge? How can we in the twentieth century think of the twentieth century? How can we think of these issues without conforming to *doxa,* complementarity, and polarization or without conforming to the political agendas that have dominated the economies of global capitalism or the academy?

Similar questions are asked by scholars in the field of medieval studies. "Word's out. There's is something exciting going on in medieval studies, and maybe in the Renaissance too. The study of medieval literature and culture has never been more alive or at a more interesting, innovative stage"—so hail the editors of the 1996 *Medievalism and the Modernist Temper.*[1] This "something exciting going on in medieval studies" is the formation of new research strategies by scholars who are not only well acquainted with the topography of the battlefields in what used to be known as hermetically closed or marginalized medieval studies but also well versed in the vagaries of postmodern theory. On the one hand, the scholars of medieval drama and theater have seen the changes in how medieval drama and theater were redefined to include both written texts as well as accompanying physical events. On the other hand, they brought in theoretical formulations that ruptured modernist critical agendas. In the 1990s, it is no longer possible to accept a historical practice that is grounded in the "verum ipsum factum" principle.[2] With questions posed about the relationship between subject (a historian) and object (a document; an event), historical investigations need to take into account the postmodern condition, that is, the notion that we can never speak of history without speaking about ourselves, and the emphasis on, for example, social negotiations (Said), the heterological practice of making the self acknowledge its historicity at the moment of speaking (de Certeau), the function of power in regulating and controlling bodies and spaces in the episteme (Foucault), decolonizing maneuvers (Spivak), local knowledge (Geertz), fatal strategies and simulacra that reduce events to sonorous and optical effects (Baudrillard), performative acts of gendered or sexed agency (Butler), reflexive sociology (Bourdieu), deterritorializing practices (Deleuze and Guattari), a textualization of what has previously been regarded as outside or beyond the text (Derrida), or cultural and symbolic anthropology (Geertz, Turner, Douglas).

The new medievalism, which emerged in 1991, seems to be open to these possibilities. It claims to interrogate both the internal history of the discipline (i.e., to what extent new discoveries change our understanding of the period) and the external history of the discipline (i.e., to what extent our own strategies and desires determine the questions we pose and the answers we give).[3] Using Stephen G. Nichols's metaphor, to what extent is the astrolabe an observing instrument and a mechanism crafted to reproduce the universe that it was meant to observe?[4] With this question posed, scholars in the discipline started to entertain the possibility that medieval studies had been determined by specific ideological or local, nationalistic or religious, and political or personal interests and not only by the arrangement of the available materials.[5]

Word is out. There is something exciting going on in the studies of medieval drama and theater. There have been many attempts at revising institutional as well as intellectual models that have dominated the field. *The Theatre of Medieval Europe* is a case in point. Published in 1991, the volume is a collection of reports prepared for and presented at a conference organized by the Department of Medieval Studies of Harvard University and held in October 1986. As the editor, Eckehard Simon, asserts, research on medieval drama and theater has grown considerably since the 1960s, not only in England and North America, but also on the European continent, so "it seemed appropriate to take the stock, to see where we stand, to share our concerns," and to stake out new directions for the research on medieval drama.[6]

Rather than using *The Theatre of Medieval Europe* as an iconic text of stocktaking, let me engage in a historiographic practice of positioning it vis-à-vis the most current changes in the field of medieval studies. In this book, the 1960s are identified as a threshold that divided the scholarship into two distinct and incompatible periods. On the one hand, there is the past whose historical itinerary was defined by the treatment of medieval drama as a philological or linguistic phenomenon and a special case of literature.[7] On the other hand, there is the present defined by once-the-avatars and now-the-mandarins, to use Norman Cantor's taxonomy, that is, by O. B. Hardison, who "returned to the liturgical drama, providing that the evolutionary approach reorganised the chronology of the plays to fit a theory"; by Glynne Wickham, who "had concentrated on details of performance"; and by V. A. Kolve, who introduced "the thematic study of the individual cycle."[8] Medieval studies can thus be an example of a differend par excellence. This differend implies the abyss between the two traditions in medieval studies that cannot be bridged because the conflict between the methodologies of research they represent cannot be equitably resolved for lack of a system that could be accepted by both traditions.[9] Therefore, even though each new generation of scholars may be indebted to, for example, Chambers and Young and their catalogues of the *Quem quaeritis* forms, it rejects the purpose, the scope, and the methodology used by Chambers and Young in their studies of the origins of medieval drama and theater. Hardison's "Darwin, Mutations, and the Origin of Medieval Drama" in his *Christ-*

ian Rite and Christian Drama in the Middle Ages speaks to this problem succinctly.[10]

The Theatre of Medieval Europe charts "the most significant advances in the research work undertaken in the past twenty-five years relating to theatre in the Middle Ages."[11] These "most significant advances," to use Glynne Wickham's words, are grouped into three categories—Latin drama, English drama, and Continental drama—and are explained and elaborated on in essays written by a select, eminent group of scholars in these fields.[12] The essays in the volume suggest that current medieval studies are open to new approaches toward archival research and to seeing medieval drama as performance rather than literary text. The emphasis on the internal history of medieval drama and theater merits a theoretical consideration.[13]

First, let us consider archival research. For historians who still reassert forcefully the validity of received dogmas under the guise of "progressive" and all-embracing thinking, the bifurcation between theory and history lies in a demonstrable attitude toward scholarly research.[14] As the volumes of *Records of Early English Drama* make us realize, the traditional research, which was grounded in "the old-style scholarship that tended to generalize, homogenize and patronize the religious drama of the late Middle Ages," focused primarily on the surviving records of dramatic activities.[15] Alexandra F. Johnston shows that this quest for the evidence of dramatic activity must be broadened to embrace a variety of other sources that have little or nothing to do with traditionally designated spaces for performance.

In the first decade of the twelfth century, the house of the sacrist of St Alban's, Dunstable burned to the ground. In 1200, a miracle was performed in Beverley Minster by a man later to be called St John of Beverley. In 1300, the prioress of Clerkenwell brought a suit for property damages against some citizens of London before the king. In 1345, the servants of the lord bishop of Carlisle and St Peter de Tilliol were cited before a royal commission in Carlisle for brawling in public.[16]

Even though, on the surface, these events have nothing in common, all of them contain a record of some kind of a dramatic performance: costumes were stored at the house of the sacrist of St. Alban's; two boys who wanted to see a saint play staged at the Beverley Minster fell to the floor of the nave from a great height and were revived by the saint; the prioress of Clerkenwell brought a suit against the citizens who had flocked to see a play presented by the clerks and who had destroyed her landscaping; the servants misbehaved at a performance given by clerks at the marketplace.

Consequently, research into the records of dramatic performances has been expanded to include the volumes and rolls stored at local and parish record offices as well as at the libraries of religious houses. They provide not only information about social and cultural values but also incidental information concerning costumes, the behavior of the audience, and the types of play staged, as well as information about patronage and the activities of the touring companies. There is no doubt that this evidence has increased our knowledge and understanding of the Middle Ages. On the basis of these pieces, historians have tried to create an image of mimetic activities that characterized the period.[17]

Closely connected with an image of mimetic activities is the concept of performance defined in medieval scholarship in terms of its opposition to text-centered research. Glynne Wickham is credited with repositioning the field that, until the middle of the twentieth century, accepted unquestionably the literary and linguistic critical position of the nineteenth century.[18] His *Early English Stages* contended that the medieval plays should be studied not as literary texts but as texts in performance. An entirely new understanding of, for example, cycle plays followed.[19] These studies have been aided by actual stagings of the cycles that not only showed a new appreciation for textual and paratextual humor and commentary but also forced the directors and designers to deal with the practical questions concerning the shape and size of a pageant wagon.[20] Thus, consideration of a performance covers the whole spectrum of activities describing the staging as well as information about the staging of a text. Consequently, the scholars unearthed evidence pertaining to the type of audience attending the staging of the cycle plays, financial data about the guilds responsible for the staging of plays, and materials concerning the behavior and status of those directly involved in staging. Even though the editor of *The Theatre of Medieval Europe* does not address the issue, it should be noted that the new attention given to the staging of the cycle plays opened up the possibility that the plays could be the loci of meanings defining the limits of the social body within an urban context and, with the help of a feminist criticism exploring medieval thinking about gender and the body, problematized the dominant myths about the ceremonial or festive social life in the late Middle Ages.[21]

The changes in our understanding of the nature of archival research, performance, and the social or gendered body prompt multiple questions, however. These questions are not necessarily about the records, the performances, or the intervention into a universalized notion of "body" but about the practice of putting together an image of the medieval past, medieval performance, and the specific meanings that male and female sexed bodies might have had to medieval audiences. While dealing with the notions of archival research, performance, and the social, gendered, or sexed body, should we not consider the challenges posed by Michel de Certeau, who argues that history is a discourse of facts shaped from conflicting imaginations, at once past and present; by Michel Foucault, who sees history in terms of monumentalizing the past; by Stanley Aronowitz, who observes that facts are not discovered but produced; by Pierre Bourdieu, who defines academics and their activity in terms of the externalization of a set of dispositions accepted and acceptable in their field; and by Joseph Roach, who modifies the notion of performance to embrace not only representation that can be rehearsed, repeated, and readapted (Richard Schechner) but also the performative practices of daily life (de Certeau) as they are constructed within historic cultures?[22]

These are some of the questions that this book on the early medieval drama and theater in general and this introduction in particular seek to address. Thus, the purpose of this introduction is to show how transformations in the concept of history and in the manner in which historians arrange information form the basis of current organization of knowledge about early medieval drama and theater.[23]

Anyone interested in medieval drama and theater is well acquainted with Chambers's theory of the evolution of drama, Young's literary analysis of the tropes, Hardison's theory of Christian rite, Dunn's studies of Gallican liturgy, Enders's study of the relationship between rhetoric and drama, Goldstein's Marxist interpretation of the origins of medieval drama, de Boor's *Textgeschichte,* and Smoldon's, Flanigan's, Norton's, and Hughes's studies of musical settings. They will be mentioned in the following section of this introduction to show the extent to which our perception of what constitutes drama, theater, or performance has constructed a homogeneous notion of representation in the Middle Ages. At the same time, I will offer a theoretical discussion of the concept of historiography that concerns itself with the notions of historical events and representational practices, both past and present, that made these events and practices worthy of notice and record.

In the sepulchre which the historian inhabits, only "emptiness remains." Hence this "intimacy with the other world poses no threat."

Historians never apprehend the origins, but all the successive stages of their loss.

—Michel de Certeau, *The Writing of History*

In his introductory essay "Darwin, Mutations, and the Origin of Medieval Drama," O. B. Hardison provides an excellent review of E. K. Chambers's and Karl Young's medieval scholarship, an in-depth analysis of major methodologies of research, and a general discussion of the patterns of criticism. He argues that Chambers's *The Mediaeval Stage* (1903) and Young's *The Drama of the Medieval Church* (1933) can indubitably be viewed as testimonies to their authors' knowledge of the subject matter but require a reexamination of the assumptions about both "cultural Darwinism" and the arrangement of the materials, because of the changes in historiography that occurred after the publication of Chambers's and Young's studies. These remarks are substantiated by a critical review of *The Mediaeval Stage* and *The Drama of the Medieval Church* that leads Hardison to conclude:

the standard historians of medieval drama have followed the procedure used by early evolutionary anthropologists in connection with the study of the myth. They have attributed present concepts and attitudes to the culture of the past. They have assumed that medieval man thought like nineteenth-century man, or ought to have done so. The result has been serious distortion. History has become teleological, interpreted both intentionally and unconsciously in terms of what texts anticipate rather than what they are. The texts themselves have been read as though they were intended for production under conditions vaguely foreshadowing Covent Garden and for audiences vaguely like the rowdies in the Victorian gallery.[24]

Instead of the standard procedure of distortion, Hardison proposes a methodology of research based on the analysis of documents in terms of what they are—that is, on contextual analysis (derived from Aristotle's *Poetics*)—and supported by literary and ritual theories (Frye, Murray, and Frazer), rather than in terms of how they fit into the evolutionary pattern defining the totality of a series. Such a particular methodology is selected to accommodate both the documents of the past and the methods of cognizance contemporary to Hardison.

Hardison's opening statement that "in the last fifty years literary criticism has experienced a series of major revolutions," which he made some thirty years ago, is also true today.[25] This is an unavoidable process, because the cognitive tools used to describe the research process, the parameters that delineate the scope and nature of historiography, and the definitions of the contemporary experience are constantly transforming or being transformed.

The historical investigations described by Hardison bring to the fore a historiographic modality that has several consequences. First, because history has been dominated in the twentieth century by the production of knowledge that will be recognized and validated as a real past by the discipline, it needed to invent a set of dispositions that would guarantee its legitimacy. This legitimacy has been secured by methodologies—by their normative, temporal categories, designed to establish the permanence of historical events/objects, and by their functional, ideological categories, devised to justify the presence or absence of such events/objects. In the 1967 essay "The Discourse of History," Roland Barthes challenges this dual system of specification and ponders the distinction between "the narration of past events, commonly subject in our culture, since the Greeks, to the sanction of historical 'science,' placed under the imperious warrant of the 'real,' justified by principles of 'rational exposition,'" and imaginary narration as can be found in the epic, in the novel, or in the drama.[26] According to Barthes, this distinction is grounded in the so-called reality effect, whose function is to verify that an event represented in history and as history has really taken place.

The prestige of *this happened* has a truly historical importance and scope. Our entire civilization has a taste for the reality effect, attested to by the development of specific genres such as the realistic novel, the private diary, documentary literature, the news item, the historical museum, the exhibition of ancient objects, and, above all, the massive development of photography, whose sole pertinent feature (in relation to drawing) is precisely to signify that the event represented has *really* taken place.[27]

This signification of the reality effect (*l'effet de réel,* "the effect of the real"), as a means of protecting consciousness from doubt, retains the possibility of a verification that can be done by scholars. In *The Names of History,* Jacques Rancière speaks about a maneuver that sheltered historical studies from the fables of opinions.[28] This maneuver was the establishment of historical science, which placed itself in opposition to fictionalized history and the historical novel. To maintain its position, history needed to escape literature, give itself the status of a science, and signify this status. This could only be achieved when the three procedures were articulated in a single discourse. Rancière refers to them as three contracts with the reality effect.

The first is the scientific contract, which necessitates the discovery of the latent order beneath the manifest order, through the substitution of the exact correlations and numbers of a complex process for the scale of the visible weights and sizes of politics. The second is the narrative contract, which commands the inscription of the structures of this hidden space, or of the laws of this complex process, in the readable forms of a story with a beginning and an end, with characters and events. And the third is a political contract, which ties what is invisible in science and what is readable in narration to the contradictory constraints of the age of the masses—of the great regularities of common law and the great tumults of democracy, of revolutions and counterrevolutions, of the hidden secret of the multitudes and the narration of a common history readable and teachable to all.[29]

With scientific, narrative, and political contracts in place, a reality effect entered the stage and became a general requirement. The degree to which this has been the case is best exemplified by the various theories and controversies that took place in the field of medieval studies over the position of a document in a historical investigation or over the question of the origins of drama and theater in the early Middle Ages—the publications by Chambers, Young, Hardison, Dunn, Goldstein, and Enders, to mention only the studies referred to in this introduction, can be used to substantiate this point.

In *The Mediaeval Stage,* published in 1903, E. K. Chambers proposes to "state and explain the pre-existing conditions which, by the latter half of the sixteenth-century, made the great Shakespearean stage possible." He claims, "The story is one of a sudden dissolution and a slow upbuilding."[30] Chambers's methodology can be seen in the arrangement of the material he deals with. His work is divided into two volumes and further subdivided into a set of four "books." Book 1, entitled "Minstrelsy," focuses on the Roman tradition of *scenici* (entertainers) from the third century B.C.E. to the thirteenth century C.E.[31] Book 2, "Folk Drama," discusses the *ludi* of the village feasts. Chambers analyzes numerous pagan rituals, especially those of the Teutonic tradition, and demonstrates how they were transformed to serve the needs of Christianity.[32] Book 3, "Religious Drama," examines liturgical plays and the process of secularization.[33] According to Chambers, as the service of the Mass evolved, it was seen as an actual repetition of Christ's original suffering, rather than as a metaphorical ceremony. This element of actual repetition further intensified the dramatic character of the Mass and of other observances (2:3–4). For example, the antiphon (usually a psalm whose successive verses are sung in alternation by two choruses) lends itself naturally to dialogue because of the element of repetition, and, Chambers writes, "it is from the antiphon that the actual evolution of liturgical drama begins" (2:7).

The *Quem quaeritis* illustrates the early stages of the evolution of liturgical drama. First, it was a plain chant that in the tenth century acquired the distinct form of a dialogue chant. Second, also in the tenth century, it ceased to be an Introit trope in the Easter Mass and became attached to the ceremony of the sepulchre.[34] The *Regularis concordia,* a monastic document from the tenth century, contains an example of the *Quem quaeritis* in which a dialogue chant and mimetic action are merged. Chambers cites the description of the Easter night office as evidence supporting the hypothesis of this merger.

While the third lesson is being read, four of the brethren shall vest, one of whom, wearing an alb as though for some different purpose, shall enter and go stealthily to the place of the "sepulchre" and sit there quietly, holding a palm in his hand. Then, while the third respond is being sung, the other three brethren, vested in copes and holding thuribles in their hands, shall enter in their turn and go to the place of the "sepulchre," step by step, as though searching for something. Now these things are done in imitation of an angel seated on the tomb and of the women coming with perfumes to anoint the body of Jesus. When, therefore, he that is seated shall see these things draw nigh, wandering about as it were and seeking something, he shall begin to sing softly and sweetly *Quem quaeritis:* as soon as this has been sung right through, the three shall answer together *Ihesum Nazarenum.* Then he that is seated shall say, *Non est hic: surrexit sicut praedixerat. Ite nuntiate quia surrexit a mortuis.* At this command the three shall turn to the choir saying *Alleluia. Resurrexit Dominus.* When this has been sung he that is seated, as though calling them back, shall say the antiphon, *Venite et videte locum.* [35]

Chambers draws attention to the phrases in this description that may be read as attempts at representing some form of action: the four brethren wear albs "as though for some different purpose"; their movements are done "in imitation of an angel seated on the tomb and of the women coming with perfumes to anoint the body of Jesus"; their responses are in dialogue form; and the exchange takes place in a well-defined setting. Therefore, Chambers is justified to maintain that, at that point, the first liturgical drama was, "in all its essentials, complete" (2:15).

The next stages of the evolution from simple to complex liturgical forms were marked (1) by the addition of scenes and free adaptations of the text of the Vulgate rather than by the further development of this trope; (2) by a slow process of secularization, that is, the contamination of the liturgical texts by secular elements introduced by *clerici vagantes* (wandering clerics); (3) by the appearance of the popular religious drama, that is, the cycle or mystery plays; and (4) by the development of morality plays, which, though religious in intention, were concerned with ethical or abstract concepts.

In the final book in *The Mediaeval Stage,* "The Interlude," Chambers concentrates on the social and economic implications of the emergence of a new class of professional players from the remnants of the minstrel tradition and on the growing impact of the classical model on vernacular interludes of the fifteenth and sixteenth centuries. He maintains, "These [were] precisely the dry bones which one day, beneath the breath of genius, should spring up into the wanton life of the Shakespearean drama" (2:225).

Like Chambers's *The Mediaeval Stage,* Karl Young's *The Drama of the Medieval Church,* published in 1933, left an imprint on medieval scholarship. The essential purpose of Young's book was "to assemble, in their authentic form, the dramatic compositions which were employed by the Church in Western Europe as a part of a public worship, and which are commonly regarded as the origins of modern theatre." [36] His theory rests on three axioms that delimit the boundaries and scope of his methodology of "cultural Darwinism": (1) medieval drama originated in the church; (2) dramatic development shows a logical transition from simple to complex forms; and (3) Latin liturgical drama developed independently, that is, separately from secular vernacular drama.

To validate his theory, Young focuses on the integral parts of the liturgy of the Roman Mass, the Canonical Office, and the ceremonies of the liturgical year and on their inherent dramatic aspects. These dramatic aspects of the Roman liturgy can be found in many liturgical utterances that take the form of dialogue, in the movements and gestures of the participants, and in the element of the symbolic impersonation of the Christ figure (1:79–80). Although the Mass and other observances (i.e., *Cena Domini, Depositio, Elevatio*) were, according to Young, often highly theatrical, they did not lead into the main current of dramatic development. They lacked the essentials of true drama: impersonation and setting. These two elements seem to have been reserved for the Easter trope, *Quem quaeritis,* which originally functioned as the Introit to the Easter Mass. The Easter trope of St. Gall (ca. 950) is viewed by Young as the simplest version, even though it is not the earliest one.[37] The trope contained a very important dramatic quality; that is, parts of a dialogue were assigned to specific actors. However, as long as this trope was a part of the service, it lacked an indispensable element for a full dramatic development, the setting. According to Young, once the trope was detached from the Introit and the Mass altogether, its dramatic potential was fully realized (1:231). When the *Quem quaeritis* was placed as a part of the Nocturns (now known as Matins), it achieved literary freedom and developed into an authentic Easter play, the *Visitatio Sepulchri* (which tells of the visit of the three Marys to the tomb where Christ was buried).[38] This independent dramatic ceremony recorded in the *Regularis concordia* possessed two crucial elements that fully classify it as drama: a setting (the sepulchre) and impersonation (of the three Marys and the angel). Young concludes, "The Mass, then, has never been a drama, nor did it ever directly give rise to drama" (1:85). Thus, the *Quem quaeritis* became drama after it was removed from the Mass and placed in the canonical hours services. The process of transformation and expansion of the Easter play followed the same pattern of development from simple to expanded forms that was characteristic for the tropes. Young thus differentiates three stages of the evolution of the Easter play. In the first stage, the dialogue between the three Marys and the angel was further elaborated on (1:239–306). In the second stage, a new scene and new characters (i.e., Peter and John) were added (1:307–68). In the third stage, the part of the risen Christ was introduced (1:369–410). As in the case of the evolution of the trope, Young's chapters concerning the development of the Easter play do not abide by the rules of chronological order. Young stresses the priority of his logical order, since the simplest forms are not always found in the earliest manuscripts but sometimes appear in later ones. Moreover, this methodology is deeply rooted in Young's attempt "to describe and interpret the texts rather than to implicate them in a web of theorizing as to *Urformen* and cross-influences" (1:ix).

In 1965, sixty-two years after Chambers's *The Mediaeval Stage* and thirty-two years after Young's *The Drama of the Medieval Church,* there appeared a third publication that altered contemporary perceptions and theories about medieval theater and drama: O. B. Hardison's *Christian Rite and Christian Drama in the Middle Ages.* It presents us with a new methodology of research that refutes the concept of evolutionary development and brings to the fore the anthropological, ritual, and literary theories. Hardison argues that the Christian liturgy should be perceived as ritual and that the Mass should thus be treated like other dramatic rituals that are universal in tribal societies and common among the various mystery cults that existed in the West between the first and fourth centuries.[39] In five chapters, called essays, he presents his theory of the interrelationship between Christian rite and Christian drama—that is, between religion (ritual) and literature (drama of the church)—to show that religious ritual was the drama of the early Middle Ages.[40]

To substantiate this claim, Hardison points to Gilbert Murray's classification of ritual forms in "Excursus on the Ritual Forms Preserved in Greek Tragedy" to draw parallels between the Mass and ritual forms preserved in Greek drama.[41] With the taxonomy provided by Murray's classification, the Mass becomes a two-act drama with definite roles assigned to the participants and with a plot that is based on the plan of redemption, through the re-creation of the life, death, and resurrection of Christ.

Having established the significance of all the elements of the Mass in terms of an agon, a pathos, a threnody, an anagnorisis, and a theophany, Hardison proceeds to the examination of the Easter liturgy. His analysis indicates that the Mass and the Easter liturgy have the same structure, the same emotional pattern, and the same historical association—

renewal and restatement of faith. They are restatements of the same drama in terms of two varieties of time: absolute (the Mass) and cyclical (the Easter ceremony). According to Hardison, therefore, the *Quem quaeritis* is not a trope, as it was perceived until his time, but a ceremony associated with the Easter drama (198). This ceremony was not assigned to one particular part of the Easter celebration; rather, its position varied. It could have been associated with the Easter Introit (a processional ceremony) or Matins (Nocturns; an extraliturgical or representational ceremony).

When considered from the point of view of dramatic structure, the *Quem quaeritis* (a representational ceremony) is a resurrection play because of its dialogue form. If one were to use the terminology provided in Aristotle's *Poetics* and Murray's "Excursus," the *Quem quaeritis* makes use of anagnorisis and peripeteia, that is, of the recognition and reversal of the Christian mythos when the lament of the three Marys turns into joy after the news of Christ's resurrection is announced by the angel guarding the sepulchre. Hardison therefore concludes that "as study of the Resurrection play shows, liturgical drama is the outcome of a search for representational modes which preserve a vital relation to ritual," rather than an accidental outcome of a haphazard mutation out of mimetic instinct; and it is not an isolated literary phenomenon of church origin (252).[42]

In a 1984 essay, "The Saint's Legend as *Mimesis:* Gallican Liturgy and Mediterranean Culture," Catherine Dunn seems to establish the origins of the medieval drama in "the public recitation of saints' lives in [the] early medieval liturgy of Gaul [that] was a form of drama in the Roman classical tradition."[43] The view she takes is that, in its substructure, Western Mediterranean culture—and Gaul and Spain in particular—remained pagan despite the imposition of Christian rule; Christianity was built on the existing values. As did Chambers, Dunn maintains that "[i]n the centuries following the fall of Rome, the complex population of Gaul, Spain, and Italy continued to live upon the cultural capital of the late Empire, sustained by the institutions and the wisdom of another day."[44] Having defined drama as a practice of presenting the "fictive impersonation of character through which a story is unfolded," rather than an imitation of an action, she discerns a whole spectrum of activities that could fall under the rubric, ranging from an enactment of physical combat to legitimate drama. She writes, "The whole tradition of Roman dramatic art as I see it, in late antiquity and in the early medieval centuries, was one of symbolic action involving performance by mimes and dancers rather than by actors of the legitimate theatre" (Barrol 17).

Dunn implies that one of the possible modes for a symbolic imitation of action is the confrontation between voices and characters that carry the action of drama. Such a pattern can be found in the recited or chanted saints' lives of the Gallican period. She supports her hypothesis by providing a description of the way a saint's day could have been celebrated in Gaul in the sixth century.

In the service books that have survived, the memorial of a saint permeates the whole liturgy of the day, and especially the Mass itself. The "Contestatio," a prayer corresponding to the "Preface" of the Roman Mass, would summarize the marvelous deeds of the saint, in a small-scale biography. A full-scale *vita* would probably be read in the solemn Matins service of the Divine Office and, in some cases, continued in the lections of the Mass. There might also be a procession honoring the relics of the martyr. (Barrol 19)

The saint's vita, according to Dunn, belonged not to dogmatic or theological explications but to the artistic heritage of classical literature, drama, and rhetoric. Here the nonrepresentational legend and the Roman dramatic practice came together. It was not, however, a play that could be seen on what she calls a legitimate stage; rather, it was a recited performance, projecting an interior world of emotions onto a series of words, melodies, and gestures. Dunn notes, "In this understanding of the legend's stylistics lies the richest possibility for the future study and analysis of the genre by critics and scholars, and perhaps the clearest way into the Carolingian Easter plays of a later century" (Barrol 24).[45]

The idea that a form existing within the confines of the church could be related to the classical heritage is further explored in Jody Enders's *Rhetoric and the Origins of Medieval Drama* (1992).[46] She recognizes the importance of Hardison's and Dunn's research and pays tribute to their intellectual thought.

Enders's argument is lucid: "I propose to show that the legal rhetoric of the courts in particular was the site of an ontological commingling of ritual and representation. . . . Characterized to a greater degree than the deliberative or epideictic rhetorical genres by such crucial protodramatic components as theatrical space, costume, staging, ritual conflict, audience participation, spectacle, dialogue, 'imitation of action,' and, most important of all, impersonation, legal rhetoric emerges as one of the very 'origins' of drama."[47]

Thus, when she approaches her subject, Enders is concerned with locating protodramatic elements in the theory and practice of rhetorical *actio* (delivery) that, she believes, "was the key to the performative register of discourse" (5–6). Her quest for dramatic rhetoric and rhetorical drama fully realizes itself in the degeneration of delivery into spectacle as noted by Lucian in his "Professor of Public Speaking" in the second century, in the mnemonic alphabet of dramatic images that could bridge the gap between rhetoric and drama that was perceivable each time classical and medieval orators used their voices to mediate between their mental pictures and their audiences, and in the introduction of dramatic impersonation into forensic rhetoric as recorded in Quintilian's *Institutio oratoria.* Having established a relationship between classical rhetoric and drama, Enders indicates a shift from legal ritual to dramatic representation that happened because of the so-called aestheticisization of rhetoric. This process is explained in terms of space, agon, and audience—the three crucial components of drama, according to Enders. To substantiate her hypothesis, she quotes a passage from Nicoll's 1949 *World Drama* asserting that the background was crucial for the emergence of drama from ritual. Enders argues, "A similar theatrical influence might have been exerted by the sacred space of law" (75). It follows, then, that medieval drama might have developed from forensic rhetoric. Further support is found in the forensic rhetoric's wars of words and in the function and the role that the audience played in the "space of law." Enders concludes, "By virtue of impersonation, conflictually structured plot, audience adaptation, and manipulation of pity, fear, and verisimilitude, rhetoric was an origin of drama" (124).[48]

The ideological aspect of medieval drama becomes a single focus in Leonard Goldstein's 1981 "On the Origin of Medieval Drama."[49] The article centers on the problem of the transition from ritual to drama as it was understood by Jane Harrison and that is now modified by a Marxist reading.[50] Goldstein explains that if the origin of tragedy was contingent on the change in the production relations, then the origin of drama in the period between the ninth and twelfth centuries will be also contingent on the change in the social structure whose institutions could not prevent a transformation from tribal toward individual property.

In his analysis of the feudal system, Goldstein provides a generalized pattern of changes: (1) the Carolingian model of a self-sufficient agricultural production unit on which a peasant is settled fails to produce a surplus; (2) second and third sons of the serfs are allowed to leave the manor to seek employment; (3) employment is found near military settlements and ecclesiastical centers; (4) the worker is able to sell his labor to a craftsman or a property owner for a wage; (5) there is increasing competition between the individual property owners to decrease the cost of production; (6) there is an organization of labor- and cost-saving centers—a division of labor in, for example, towns. Goldstein concludes, "This process means the creation of an urban bourgeoisie dominating a propertyless working class and a feudal landed aristocracy dominating a propertyless agricultural work force" (110).

Since the feudal system was incapable of supplying a unifying political system or a system of beliefs, the medieval church assumed this function; that is, as was the case with ritual defined by Harrison, when one structure loses its power to organize society, there is a need for another structure that would assume that function. Drama, in such a case, is the form that records changes in life itself and the manner in which these changes are experienced. In a ritual, all community members are equal. Drama presupposes a society divided within itself into the individuals competing for economic gains and those who are alienated from the means of production. Consequently medieval drama "does not develop directly out of liturgy," argues Goldstein, who continues:

It is, rather, that the newly developing relations find in the liturgy as *dromenon* a point of departure for the expression of something that is at bottom totally alien to it, namely, the competition of the new productive relations though the content of the plays is religious. A trope from which the drama emerges is not part of liturgy but an addition to it that can easily be dispensed with and indeed was. (111)

The church, thus, created a space for the alienated laborers and a sense of participation. It was an ideological surrogate where a conflict experienced in the market could be staged. In this sense, drama, which has nothing to do with the collective nature of ritual, is "the experience of the individualism and competition of private property estranged as an abstract representation, an enactment, and imitation of an action" (113).[51]

Even this brief discussion of the origins of medieval drama and theater indicates that there is no consensus among scholars concerned with the issue. The interpretations vary from nonecclesiastical to ecclesiastical origins, from ritual to literary origins, or from forensic discourse to Marxist labor relations. The studies mentioned here show, however, that the concept of the origin presupposes distancing to a past and a desire to recover what seems to be missing. Yet it tries to articulate the relationships that should mark the beginning of the process of accumulation of knowledge, that produce recognizable networks of designated experiences, or the relationships that no longer exist. One is tempted to agree with Jean-François Lyotard's comment that "the bulimia of Western thought is to have everything present."[52] What will the quest for the origins always reject from its discourse, what will it include, what is it aware of, and, finally, what does it say about itself in the process of reinterpreting the past?

These may be rhetorical questions. Since a document or a chant is shaped from conflicting imaginations, at once past and present, and since a historian can never be contemporaneous with the moment of the origin, he or she can only articulate himself or herself on the background where the past projected what it believed was worthy of record and safe-keeping. A historian thus shares the space with the "facts" that have previously been institutionalized. For this reason, the identity of the origin will always be inaccessible. Instead, there is what Foucault describes as

the surface he [the historian] traverses so innocently, always for the first time, and upon which his scarcely opened eyes discern figures as young as his own gaze—figures that must necessarily be just as ageless as he himself, though for an opposite reason; it is not because they are always equally young, it is because they belong to a time that has neither the same standards of measurement nor the same foundations as him.[53]

The lack of the same standards of measurement and the same foundations suggests that the origins will stay silent forever. The pursuit of the origins will only communicate our desires for "real" identity and the site from which we will be able to pronounce the statements authorized by the present organization of knowledge.

This brings us to the second consequence of the discussed historical investigations—the desire to construct an object of study. This object—in our case, the *Regularis concordia* or the *Quem quaeritis*—is perceived as a cipher that awaits deciphering to become a legible text. Its intelligibility is established through a relation to other elements in a group or a series. For this to happen, a group or a series needs to be developed by fixing its boundaries, by imposing on it the laws of systematic organization, and by specifying the relations that will unite or separate the objects. In this type of historical investigation, the concepts of influence, repetition, development, and tradition—the remains of the nineteenth-century positivist *doxa*—are used to construct what is relevant in the choice of the elements, before they are arranged according to the preselected principles safeguarded by a retrospective methodology.[54] A historical investigation is thus the process of exploring only "what must be understood in order to obtain a representation of a present intelligibility."[55] This present intelligibility is formulated with the help of normative and ideological categories—for example, the categories that frame how we think and talk about history: to mention a few, periods; centuries; social class; economic systems; gender relationships; mentalities; family structures; definitions of a village, town, city, region, and country; definitions of an individual, group, nation, and civilization; and characteristics of group and national identity. Within this framework, the object appears and is anchored to the operations, which give it permanence, and to the functions, which establish its relationship to other objects.

If the identity of, for example, a historical document is delimited by a historian, the process of knowledge production is the process of, first, selecting a document that is as yet undefined, at least as far as the historian is concerned; second, locating it within a series; and third, forming this document's "present intelligibility." To use a metaphor, a historical document is spoken to, and forced to respond by speaking, a language that is not its own but that belongs to the voice that framed its reality as well as present reality. The language of intelligibility may force a document to "speak," but it also homogenizes the moment when the nonhomogenized event took place. It does so by silencing different subjects, discourses, and practices that constituted the heterogeneity of the event. Alexandre Kojève may have been right when, some fifty years ago, he defined history as "the history of desired desires."[56] While discussing the praxis of philosophical investigations, Kojève stated that history is a process during which historians attempt to satisfy their desires for creativity, recognition, preservation, and conservation by dominating an object in their quest for the origins and in the process of ordering and translating the past into epistemological units. Nothing exemplifies this procedure better than subjecting a document—here, the *Regularis concordia*—to the workings of the procedures of legitimation at the historian's disposal in order to view it as the evidence for the origins of medieval drama and theater. Because of Chambers's and Young's interpretations, it has been accepted that the *Regularis concordia* houses the earliest extant example of what is believed to be "liturgical drama."[57] Wolfgang Michael's claim for the document typifies the way in which the consuetudinary is still considered.

It is no accident that the *Regularis Concordia,* the out-growth of the Winchester Synod, contains the first and the only early documentation for the drama in the Middle Ages; in short, that the author of the *Regularis Concordia* was the creator of medieval drama. After all, the *Regularis Concordia* was not just one of the innumerable ordinaries that contained the locally limited liturgical traditions. It was the rule for the entire Benedictine order in England, the order that mainly, and at first exclusively, performed religious drama.[58]

Thus, the *Regularis concordia* is the early documentation of drama and of the fact that the Benedictine monks became the actors who performed religious plays. Similar views are held by Hardin Craig, Smoldon, William Tydeman, and Wickham. Craig, for example, observes that "the full rubrics given in the *Regularis concordia* make it quite plain that the dramatic office is fully represented and understood."[59] Smoldon believes that the well-known Winchester document "is the earliest surviving example (or rather, examples) of a truly *dramatic* version of the Easter Sepulchre dialogue."[60] Tydeman agrees with Smoldon and suggests that "it has been argued that the *Visitatio Sepulchri* is an original piece of composition specially compiled by the authors of the *Regularis concordia.*"[61] Wickham, besides providing support for the accepted explanation of what the manuscript is and introduces, elicits not only its literary but also its theatrical aspect. He argues that the rubrics for the *Quem quaeritis* "give us a vivid picture of the style of acting and the means adopted to identify character and locality in this 'imitation of the angel sitting in the monument, and the women with spices coming to anoint the body of Jesus.'" He continues, "The result is liturgical music-drama, for which the theatre is the basilica itself, the occasion a festival of rejoicing. The style is Romanesque."[62] A similar attitude toward the manuscript is upheld by Mary Desiree Anderson, Sandro Sticca, and Axton.[63] Hardison deals with the *Regularis concordia* insofar as it illuminates his theory of the origins of medieval drama and theater.

This approach is evident in his essay "The Early History of the *Quem quaeritis*," where Hardison launches his thesis concerning the ceremonial character of the *Quem quaeritis*. His argument is that the *Regularis concordia* is the home of the "fullest and most attractive of all tenth-century texts of the *Quem quaeritis*," whose function is, "as the *Regularis Concordia* indicates, to instruct the 'unlearned common persons and neophytes.'"[64] He finds this element of "popular instruction" in the rubrics that "show a firm command of the significance of all parts of the ceremony, a sophisticated use of stage properties and dramatic gesture."[65]

Consequently, not only is the *Regularis concordia* viewed as a legitimate place for the origins of medieval drama and theater, but as the studies of the aforementioned scholars demonstrate, it assumed the position and function of "something more" than a monastic code. To paraphrase Michel Foucault, the *Regularis concordia,* a document of an event, which took place in 970x973, was transformed into a monument of history, which is written now. This particular transformation is, as Foucault observes, a mark of

history, in its traditional form, [which] undertook to "memorize" the *monuments* of the past, transform them into *documents,* and lend speech to those traces which, in themselves, are often not verbal, or which say in silence something other than what they actually say; in our time, history is that which transforms *documents* into *monuments.*[66]

Is it possible that Chambers, Young, Craig, Smoldon, Tydeman, Wickham, and Hardison "lend speech to those traces which, in themselves, are often not verbal, or which say in silence something other than what they actually say" on the pages of the books of these scholars?

The richer the material is, the more powerful are the forms of presentation that are invented to construct a text that produces the past.

The relation between the scientist's statement and "what 'nature says'" seems to be organized as a game without perfect information. The modalization of the scientist's statement reflects the fact that the effective, singular statement (the token) that nature will produce is unpredictable. All that can be calculated is the probability that the statement will say one thing rather than another. On the level of microphysics, "better" information—in other words, information with a higher performance capability—cannot be obtained. The problem is not to learn what the opponent ("nature") is, but to identify the game it plays.[67]

Thus, the relation between a historian's statement and "what 'a document says'" seems to be organized as a game without perfect information. All that can be achieved is a relative statement about what a document could have been and what it represented to diverse environments, including the historian's. Consequently, we may be forced to realize that the problem is not in determining what the *Regularis concordia,* or the *Quem quaeritis,* is but in identifying the "game" it plays—knowledge about the document can be made not in the form of a singular assertion but only as a modified assertion of the type of research methodology or strategy used by a scholar. The *Regularis concordia* "reveals" the information that "increases" its effectivity and use-value for medieval studies in the process of attracting the present (scholar's) language of intelligibility to some of its sections. Theater historians know about the *Regularis concordia* because it houses the *Quem quaeritis,* a liturgical drama. Why is it that only the *Quem quaeritis* section has been brought to our attention? What are the consequences of this "game" when identified?

The issue of identifying the "game" that is played becomes even more apparent and complicated when we acknowledge the possibility that there is no one definition of what the document, or the chant, is and that its definition will depend on how the one writing the *Regularis concordia* made it worthy of notice and how the one writing about the *Regularis concordia* made it worthy of record. To paraphrase de Certeau, the document, or the chant, that was recorded and is today assumed to be historically valid is shaped from conflicting imaginations, at once past and present.[68] Thus, what was true for the (past) scribe is not necessarily true for the (present) historian. Both, however, are engaged in the process of producing rationalizations and conditions that will cover up the possibility that the act of observation creates the reality and the representation of what is being observed. Is it possible that the document or the chant as represented by historical practice does not correspond to the document or the chant that emerged in the tenth century?

This question may be answered by the principle of cohesion—the third consequence of the discussed historical investigations. Foucault notes,

Such a project is linked to two or three hypotheses; it is supposed that between all the events of a well-defined spatio-temporal area, between all the phenomena of which traces have been found, it must be possible to establish a system of homogeneous relations: a network of causality that makes it possible to derive each of them, relations of analogy that show how they symbolize one another, or how they all express one and the same central core: it is also supposed that one and the same form of historicity operates upon economic structures, social institutions and customs, the inertia of mental attitudes, technological practices, political behavior, and subjects them all to the same type of transformation; lastly, it is supposed that history itself may be articulated into great units—stages or phases—which contain within themselves their own principle of cohesion.[69]

This manner of analysis was made possible by tools that historians either inherited or made themselves. The concepts of a linear succession of events, patterns of development, links between the phenomena, causal successions, establishment of continuities, significance of a group, cultural influence and tradition, hierarchy of importance, coherence, a single pattern of development, ordering phenomena to establish a unified horizon, a total history, periodization, or a system of relations have been used to isolate and establish the identity of an object. In the process of establishing links, patterns, and developments, an object is marginalized by the system of structures that organize its meaning using interpretative operations or referential systems. Take, for example, the attempts to establish the identity of the *Quem quaeritis* in the *Regularis concordia.* According to Chambers, the period from the ninth to the eleventh centuries was the time of liturgical elaboration and the time when the first tropes appeared in a written form. Chambers defines them as texts written for preexisting melodies. Several Introit tropes—for example, the ninth-century Christmas trope ascribed to Tutilo—take a dialogue form. However, the evolution of drama is closely connected only with the Easter trope, an adaptation of the story told by Matthew and Mark. Young defined the trope as a literary addition, "a verbal amplification of a passage in the authorized liturgy, in the form of an introduction, an interpolation, or a conclusion, or in the form of any combination of these."[70] Many tropes showed dramatic promise due to the dialogue form, but only one particular trope used for Easter made use of impersonation—an indispensable element for the further evolution of dramatic forms. Hardison rejects the assumption that the *Quem quaeritis* is a trope. According to him, it is "above all a resurrection play, and recognition of its context in Church ceremonial serves to dispel any notion that it originated by accident or through haphazard 'mutation.'"[71] Hardison suggests that the *Quem quaeritis* was created as a ceremony rather than as a trope whose content was a resurrection ceremony. Its aim was to instruct and prepare for the Vigil Mass. Helmut de Boor defines the *Quem quaeritis* in terms of the function it performed. It can be categorized as either a *Feier,* a part of the church ceremony (these forms were recorded in various types of liturgical books), or a *Spiel,* a representation that no longer is a part of a liturgical celebration proper.[72] William Smoldon and C. Clifford Flanigan perceive the *Quem quaeritis* as a trope that was a literary and musical embellishment for liturgical texts and liturgical actions.[73] David A. Bjork views the *Quem quaeritis* in the context of the geographic distribution of the various rites of the Easter liturgy rather than searching for its "inherent" dramatic qualities.[74] Michael L. Norton's "Of 'Stages' and 'Types' in *Visitatione Sepulchri*" demonstrates that the traditional divisions and classifications of the *Quem quaeritis*—that is, historical division of the repertory, arranging the sources to correspond to one or another historical development—are prime examples of alternating taxonomy with a methodological scheme, rather than an attempt to categorize the *Quem quaeritis.*[75] Finally, Andrew Hughes puts forth a hypothesis that the study of the musical settings, the structure, and the text of the *Quem quaeritis* creates the possibility that the tune was related to a responsory.[76]

Thus, to establish the identity of the *Quem quaeritis,* the scholars utilize seven different theatrical forms: (1) liturgical drama (Chambers), (2) play (Young, Sticca, Anderson, Axton), (3) play of a ritual drama (Hardison), (4) dramatic office (Craig), (5) liturgical music drama (Smoldon), (6) dramatic resurrection ceremony (Bjork), and (7) performance ceremony (Norton). In this process of naming, the *Quem quaeritis,* defined in terms of other forms that existed at the time, contrasted and compared to those forms, or categorized by proximity to, or analogy with, other forms, acquires functions by (1) exclusion (the *Quem quaeritis* is not a trope—Hardison), (2) rewriting (the *Quem quaeritis* is divided into a dialogue and descriptive parts—Chambers, Young, Hardison), (3) transfer and approximation (a theater taxonomy is imposed onto the *Quem quaeritis*), and (4) systematization (diverse, often contradictory arrangements of the existing versions of the *Quem quaeritis*—Young, de Boor, Norton, Rankin).[77]

Discourse is not life; its time is not yours; in it you will not reconcile
yourself with death; it is quite possible that you have killed God under

the weight of that you have said; but do not think that you will make, from all that you are saying, a man who will live longer than he. In each sentence that you pronounce . . . , in every sentence there reigns the nameless law, the blank indifference: "What does it matter who is speaking; someone has said: what does it matter who is speaking."
    —Michel Foucault, "Politics and the Study of Discourse"

Historiography is a contemporary form of mourning. Its writing is based on the absence and produces nothing but simulacra, however scientific. It offers representation in the place of bereavement.
    —Michel de Certeau, *The Mystic Fable*

The investigation of the theories of the origins of medieval drama and theater, of the production of an object of study, and of the principle of cohesion exemplifies the shifts and transformations in the internal history of the discipline that is now modified by the external history of the discipline—by a growing realization that medieval studies have always been determined by specific agendas, beliefs, and interests. Historians have reconciled themselves with the fact that they are no longer the empire builders. They "no longer aim at the paradise of global history, for nowadays [they] prefer to circulate about the acquired rationalizations of the past."[78] Current studies discuss local events and the records that thus far have been dismissed by the tradition that defined drama and theater in terms of written or literary texts. It is acknowledged that the writing of history is shaped by the system in which it is developed; that the history of *graphia* is bound to specifiable operations and defined by singular functions; that the archive is not a depository of information but a specific place organized by a particular group of people and categorized according to the practices that systematized this information according to preestablished rules; that what we used to consider as facts are not objective statements but statements that are theory laden (Aronowitz), linguistically linked to a privilege of being (Barthes), turned to images constructed and verified by science (Vattimo), or the designation of the relationship between an operation to be undertaken and the existing models (de Certeau); and that the process of writing history is a perpetual movement of reorganization and realignment.

If it is possible to fathom that history is a perpetual movement of reorganization and realignment, the function of a historian is to move around the past and present rationalizations that established the visibility of his or her object of inquiry. If this suggestion can compel consideration about history, the focus of a historical investigation might be on the manner in which history's objects are or can be thinkable, identified, or contrived—thus, represented; on the idea of a historical event, which is produced as a specific narrative according to this representational mode; and ultimately, on the challenges these present to a historian. Taking a cue from de Certeau, there is no question that the events occurred and that the documents were written. What is emphasized here is how these events are described, how they are made meaningful, and how they become worthy of record or notice by the past and the present. Since the focus is on the mode of historicity, rather than on history itself, this book contends that an event, or a document, cannot be governed by preestablished rules and categories that simulate its presence or materiality as the object of a historical investigation. Therefore, there can no longer be an equation mark placed between an event or a document and a historian's communicable experience of it.

With the focus on the mode of historicity, it is possible to acknowledge that traditional history, even though it signed a contract with science, narrative, and politics, is, as de Certeau notes, not "distinguishable from that prolix and fundamental narrativity that is our everyday historiography." De Certeau continues:

Scholarship is an integral part of the system that organizes by means of "histories" all social communication and everything that makes the present habitable. The book or the professional article, on the one hand, and the magazine or the television news, on the other, are distinguishable from one another only within the same historiographical field which is constituted by the innumerable narratives that recount and interpret events.[79]

These innumerable narratives that recount and interpret events are a part of the practices of interiorization of strategies that are made visible through the process of exteriorization of achievements. Pierre Bourdieu's *habitus* explains the relationship between the conditions of existence in a particular, specifiable, or elected field and the practices of scholarship. *Habitus* is a system of dispositions that structures the practice of individuals belonging to the same group; that is, it is "a system of internalized, embodied schemes which . . . are acquired in the course of individual history and function in their *practical* state, for *practice* (and not for the sake of pure knowledge)."[80] Accordingly, *habitus* participates in the proliferation of an assumed reality through the interpretation of observed and observable practices. These practices are engendered by a place that can be claimed by a historian as his or her own and that serves as a base from which to defend the place or prepare future attacks. This place, however, begets the ambiguity of the historian's position within the production of discourse, since precisely the (institutional) ownership of the place will either turn the uncertainties surrounding an event into a complete event itinerary or have a historian engage in a practice of a panoptic surveillance of knowledge.[81] This ambiguity will always be here even when it is erased or camouflaged by a scientific practice of verification or by what Rancière called a scientific contract, a narrative contract, or a political contract.

Following Barthes's argument regarding the "reality effect,"[82] modified by de Certeau's heterological procedures and Bourdieu's *habitus,* one may ask, however: How is it possible that a narrative form claims to produce not a fiction but a (past) event? How is it possible for a scientific practice and an institutional structure to constitute a type of writing that makes these conditions invisible to the reader? How is it possible to negotiate between a real event that speaks the truth (at least this is what we claim when observing it from a referential distance), another real event that lies (at least this is what we are told), and yet another real event that is effaced by those two other real events and that consequently loses its privilege of being? Through this stripping naked of the modern myth of writing and the resistance to representational effects, the event can expose the language of intelligibility that propels a historical investigation and promotes a selection between what can be accepted and what must be forgotten in the process of representing the event. However, as de Certeau notes, "whatever this new understanding of the past holds to be irrelevant—shards created by the selection of materials, remainders left aside by an explanation—comes back, despite everything, on the edges of discourse or in its rifts and crannies: 'resistances,' 'survivals,' or delays discreetly perturb the pretty order of a line of 'progress' or a system of interpretation"[83]—they make unsuspected depths visible.

If history, and to be more precise the writing of history, is a narrative that recounts and interprets events, the historian is challenged not to fall prey to countless practices of rearranging an aspect of a past reality—or should I say, its appearance—to give it an autonomy and independence that it never had. The challenge is to think about an event without conforming to schemes and sets of dispositions that legitimize one's position in a field.

There is no easy answer to this challenge. Postmodern theory, however, does provide us with a mode of thinking as doing rather than as an accumulation of information and the process of externalizing it as a system. Thinking as doing presupposes a movement through space, which, as current theoretical formulations suggest, is an open, dynamic field of specifiable relations and potentialities.[84] Within this field, it is possible to encounter a complex assemblage of events and to "marvel that it exists, to wonder what made it possible, to seek, in passing over its landscape, traces of the movement that formed it, to discover in these histories supposedly laid to rest how and to what extent it would be possible to think otherwise."[85]

If the medieval period is the landscape, historical practice is the practice of tracing how its representational practices were defined and circulated to organize its intelligibility. The representational practices scattered throughout the landscape of the medieval space of representation are the object of inquiry in this study. Rather than focusing on the concept of representation, which, since the early modern period, has been defined as the perspectival relationship between the subject and the object, this book argues that representation is a heterogeneous discursive practice, which was defined and redefined, disseminated and erased, and institutionalized and internalized within the dynamic field of the ever shifting relationships between theological, historical, metaphysical, social, political, and cultural formulations in the Middle Ages.

Consequently, no single concept of representation could be assigned to the Middle Ages. Rather, multiple representational practices labored to define a local reality and produce modes of thinking and expression that would implement it. Using the term *representational practice*—defined here as a dynamic field of enunciative possibilities rather than as the traditional (i.e., Aristotelian, Platonic, or post-Renaissance) perspectival concept of the relationship between life and art, thought and its material form, or what the subject is and what the object represents—I will ask the following questions: How can one talk bout these representational practices without destroying the technologies that governed their mode of functioning, expression, being, or action? How are these practices individualized from other practices, such as liturgical observation, political activity, social structure, economics, medicine, scholasticism, and architecture; or are they? What rules of formation for their objects, operations, concepts, and theoretical options are made visible or invisible? What are the conditions that must have been fulfilled in order for a particular representational practice to emerge? What are the conditions that alter it and the objects that appear in and disappear from its field of visibility? What networks or relations and correlations are established between the objects of a single formation and between different formations? What changes can be perceived within the space of representation, where the objects were put into a constellation, before a new departure takes place? And finally, how does what we consider today as medieval drama and theater execute these representational practices?

These questions not only replace the questions asked to determine the meaning of a historical event or document in theater or drama but articulate the mode of existence and functioning of representational practices that are never stable but always in flux. As a result of this instability, this historiographic practice is not epistemology but enunciation that concentrates on signification, institutionalization, and enunciative possibilities in a dynamic space where words, concepts, and objects can be situated but never classified. It is so because this space is never stable long enough to secure the classificatory grid of specification and meaning. It is a site of transformation. The objects in this space do not exist in a void but can be displaced or may morph as they move through or when they encounter other practices that interrupt the objects' trajectories and force them to assume new positions. Bereft of their empirical origins or epistemological signature, the objects may begin a different movement in a new location—that is, new time and space—and only their traces in the old time and space remain. Foucault observes:

And the great problem presented by such historical analyses is not how continuities are established, how a single pattern is formed and preserved, how for so many different, successive minds there is a single horizon, what mode of action and what substructure is implied by the interplay of transmissions, resumptions, disappearances, and repetitions, how the origin may extend its sway well beyond itself to that conclusion that is never given—the problem is no longer one of tradition, but one of division of limits; it is no longer one of lasting foundations, but one of transformations that serve as new foundations, the rebuilding of foundations.[86]

Succession and analogy become obsolete because they indicate linear, chronological progressions that lead to a single horizon. But there is no single horizon, no one meaning, no one ideology. Instead, there is a space of close-range vision where the eye performs nonoptical function: "no line separates earth from sky, which are of the same substance; there is neither horizon nor background nor perspective nor limit nor outline nor form nor center."[87] There is only a dynamic field of specifiable relationships, which reveals diverse practices in their complexity and density. In this sense, the analysis of representational practices operates within the space occupied by discourse. It does not explain or describe this space by contextualizing it, but it enunciates the systems of its formation as well as its modes of effectivity and action without destroying their materiality.

This book focuses on the practice of representation rather than on the history of medieval drama and theater as we know it today. I do not intend to argue for or against the upheld narratives describing medieval drama and theater. There is no question that the *Regularis concordia,* a monastic document of the Winchester Synod (970x973), is a record of a representational practice. I refrain from formulating its function by adding an adjective, either *theatrical* or *dramatic,* because such a formulation would immediately delineate the ways of seeing and of using a practice as a mimetic moment. Moreover, I would like to demonstrate that, because the concept of representation was neither homogeneous nor unified in the Middle Ages, medieval drama and theater need to be wrestled from the meaning given to them by our taxonomies. To substantiate this point, I will discuss four fragments in a historical *episteme:*

1. the *Quem quaeritis* chant in the tenth-century *Regularis concordia* (970x973) (the popular argument notwithstanding, I will suggest that this monastic code is not solely a record of the "earliest" extant description of some form of theatrical practice but a dynamic site where new monastic practices delimited how representation was defined in England at that time);

2. the shift in the practice of representation in the mid–eleventh century as exemplified by the Berengar-Lanfranc Eucharist controversy, Lanfranc's *Constitutions,* and the eleventh-century copy of the *Regularis concordia;*

3. the coexistence of the corporeal, spiritual, and ecclesiological discourse on the Eucharist in the twelfth century (by analyzing representational practices in Saint Anselm's *Cur Deus Homo,* Honorius Augustodunensis's *Gemma animae,* the theologies of the Eucharist [School of Laon and School of Peter

Abelard], Hildegard of Bingen's *Ordo Virtutum,* the Anglo-Norman *Jeu d'Adam,* and the twelfth-century versions of the *Quem quaeritis,* I will focus on the ternary mode of thinking in representational practices);

4. the stabilization of the concept of representation with the Fourth Lateran Council, which not only marked the disappearance of the ternary discourse and the emergence of a binary discourse of exclusion but also defined a standard for what was to be seen, how it should be seen, and where it should be seen (the Corpus Christi feast and the thirteenth-century versions of the *Quem quaeritis* will be discussed here to indicate how the dogma of transubstantiation was disseminated not only inside but also outside of the church).

The questions that I will be asking are the questions that view representational practices as a field of enunciative possibilities: How was representation inscribed into practices? What were the conditions that made them acceptable? How was representation defined? What aspects of representation were made invisible when representation was appropriated for the purpose of inscribing it into practices? What was altered every time the boundaries of representation were reterritorialized? What were the mode of existence and functioning of representational practices in their new position? What attributes did these practices possess that made them acceptable by institutions, ideologies, and other practices? How was the discourse on representation modified every time the language used to describe its practices was transformed?

Obviously, this book does not fall into the category of studies that primarily focus on medieval drama and theater. For the reasons I have enumerated here, I offer a historiographic practice that, rather than rearranging the internal history of the discipline with its external history, starts with the inquiry into representational practices in the early Middle Ages that established the rules for what has been made, seen, or done. These practices take on the properties of an event that did take place. I do believe that the investigation of their mode of functioning and existence will allow us to bring about new alignments and unexpected intensities made in response to the crystallization of a specific identity, without us providing a name for it.

What does this study have to do with drama and theater in the early Middle Ages? Not much if one decides to view drama and theater in the early Middle Ages in terms of their modernist definitions as a combination of dialogue, setting, and impersonation (with the emphasis on the external performative elements) or as a transfer from a real site to an imaginary site. I hope, however, that the following chapters will provide a different perspective.

I will focus on singular events that did take place in the period between 970x973 and 1215, which we perceive today as theatrical or dramatic, and I will suggest that they registered or labored to register the changing conditions of the practice of representing linked to the unstable interpretation of *Hoc est corpus meum* [This is my body]—the words spoken by Christ to the apostles at the Last Supper. By so doing, they show us that the notion of representation in the Middle Ages was heterogeneous and that it could morph or be morphed into different shapes once it entered a specific historical, cultural, or ideological constellation that attempted to form and to lay to rest the body that had disappeared a long time ago. I hope that, with this design in mind, this study will contribute to the scholarship that has chosen as its focus the gendered body of Christ and its visual/written manifestations in the late medieval culture and society.[88]

Also, I want to draw attention to a general dilemma of the theater person, one that centers on the issues of what it means to represent and on the consequences of this praxis. Both the meaning and consequences of representation suggest that technologies of power can be identified in the practices of representing in the early Middle Ages—in how and by whom the notion of representation was defined, how it was circulated within a specifiable field of distribution (monastic and ecclesiastic venues), and how it was disseminated into other fields and networks of relationships (culture and politics). Consider the exchange between the angel and three Marys on Easter morning, which we consider to be a liturgical drama.

> Quem quaeritis?
> Ihesum Nazarenum.
> Non est hic. Surrexit sicut praedixerat.

These words enunciated a complex assemblage of practices that revealed a singular mode of effectivity and action. This mode of effectivity and action, as the four chapters of this book will indicate, was changeable and produced different spaces where the exchange between the angel and three Marys as well as other exchanges were used to invoke what was to be seen/heard, where it was to be seen/heard, and finally, how it was to be seen/heard. The words and the actions had no other recourse but to link themselves onto and implicate the status of the reality of which they spoke, or, to express, with the help of representational practices, the complex theological thought and the institution that produced only this—and no other—social, institutional, and conceptual place where the body was to be seen.

CHAPTER I

The *Regularis concordia:* "Qui facit veritatem venit ad lucem"

What does one do when one is a historian, if not challenge chance, posit reasons—in other words, understand? Yet understanding does not mean flight to ideology, nor providing an alias for what remains hidden. It means having discovered through the very stuff of historical information what allows to be conceived.

—Michel de Certeau, *The Writing of History*

The changes in the field of medieval studies notwithstanding, the basic tenet of any theory of the emergence of drama and theater is that the signs of medieval drama can be found in the antiphonal dialogue of the *Quem quaeritis* trope that was a part of the Easter monastic ceremonies.[1] The support for this argument has been found in the *Regularis concordia,* which is treated as the earliest record of a theatrical representation in the Middle Ages and quoted as the irrefutable evidence of the transfer of the *Quem quaeritis* from the Introit of the Easter Mass to the Easter night office, or Nocturns (Matins, according to modern terminology). This transfer was of paramount significance. As part of the Easter Mass, the *Quem quaeritis* trope merely contained the signs of drama; however, the *Quem quaeritis* of the Easter Nocturns was a trope that had all the elements of drama, that is, dialogue, setting, and mimetic action.

I do not intend to argue for or against this hypothesis; however, I suggest that to say that the *Regularis concordia* chronicles events or examples of the tenth-century monastic beliefs and attitudes is to overlook that it also provides a place for vibrant conflicts, uncertainties, and ideologies. In the writing of history, though the makers of a document died a long time ago, we are left with their singular (t)exterior, that is, their visible, material narrative. It was believed to be a record of a verbal representation, a description of past events or of typical beliefs and attitudes that were to be remembered. The visibility of a document was established by a historian, who, in Michel de Certeau's words, from age to age, "always young and never tired, for thousands of years" roams the open road, "to take hold of the text of this traveler on foot." In his study of Michelet, a stand-in for a modernist discourse on history, de Certeau talks about Michelet's meetings with "'indulgence' and 'filial fear' in respect to the dead who are the inheritors of a 'strange dialogue,' but also with the assurance 'that never could anyone ever stir up again what life has left behind.'" De Certeau continues: "In the sepulchre which the historian inhabits, only 'emptiness remains.' Hence this 'intimacy with the other world poses no threat.'"[2]

The other world poses no threat because the writers of a document can neither speak to contradict us or do harm by refusing to accept the categories and taxonomies used to define them and their position: "These ghosts find access through *writing* on the condition that they remain *forever silent.*"[3] The silence of ghosts, to continue the metaphor, is what stirs up the strange dialogue between a historian and the writing in front of him or her. This dialogue is the very project of history. With the help of the institution and the narrative practices that lifted history from the domain of a discourse into the realm of a scientific discipline, it articulates history's possible objects of study, introduces various methods or procedures for studying them, and identifies a proper manner of speaking about them in order to construct the meaning of a document. De Certeau concludes, "The sole historical quest for 'meaning' remains indeed a quest for the Other, but, however contradictory it may be, this project aims at 'understanding' and, through 'meaning,' at hiding the alterity of this foreigner; or, in what amounts to the same thing, it aims at calming the dead who still haunt the present, and at offering them scriptural tombs."[4]

Once the scriptural nature of a historical investigation is acknowledged, some of the problems connected with the silencing of a document can be circumvented. This can be achieved when a document is seen as a material presence that brings to the fore, rather than answers, questions of the mode of writing in a culture and its relation to the "real" document as well as to the agencies of chance that made it possible for a document to be conceived in the past and to appear now in front of a historian. If such a proposition is tangible, documents will no longer be seen as the phantasms of historiography whose function was to illustrate constructs, truths, and iconographic lexicons encountered through the intimacy with the other world; rather, they will be commentaries that disclose the interplay between several simultaneous systems of significance. Documents will no longer be quoted to superimpose a unifying system on culturally disparate phenomena; rather, they will be treated as writings with their own generic designs, local positioning, and relations to governance or record making. Documents will no longer be cited uncritically; rather, they will be viewed as products of cultural technologies, the chief technology being the production and dissemination of distinctive forms of subjectivity and community: groups and individuals supported, intervened, or resisted the societal governmentality by defining themselves precisely as makers, users, and holders of documents. Documents will no longer be surveyed as the pieces calming the dead in their scriptural tombs; rather, their textuality, materiality, and tactile quality will articulate social forces by providing information about the circumstances of their production, dissemination, function, and reception.

This material narrative traverses, organizes, and registers the names of places, people, and events, as well as statements, all of which acquire the status of privileged elements—the place, the people, the event, the statement. Using words and sentences, the narrative selects and links these elements together, establishing the trajectories of that which will be enunciated. As de Certeau observes, however, this narrative not only registers but also erases the scribes and the conditions that made it possible for this narrative to exist.[5] On the one hand, it makes them visible by pulling them out of the obscurity of the past to give them life and permanence at the price of masking their alterity. On the other hand, it disseminates what is to be seen and specifies who is likely to be interested in seeing.

This double nature of a narrative is its seductive power. By giving permanence, it stabilizes the contours of the places, the people, and the statements as well as secures their acceptance. By organizing the act of dissemination, it circumscribes the locus "where we can [see] and where we can come to an understanding with others."[6] At the same time, it allows itself to be constructed by theoretical and methodological traditions, because that is its only way to protect the rights and the laws of the makers.

Can one be continuously aware of this double nature of a narrative? A possible answer is given by recent shifts and transformations in postmodern theory. These theoretical formulations enunciate the postmodern as the condition of existence (Lyotard), as an open field of specifiable relationships (Foucault), as a dynamic and open space of potentialities (Bourdieu), as a space of close-range vision (Deleuze), as a territory in which objects can be situated but never classified (de Certeau), and as a space where words, concepts, and objects need to be wrestled from their "proper" meaning or place (Spivak). They separate themselves from history and historiography, whose function is to produce schemata of thought and expression that describe events as part of a constructed representational model within an assumed reality. De Certeau may be right when he argues in *The Writing of History* that "[a] fact that has been recorded and is today assumed to be historically valid is shaped from conflicting imaginations, at once past and present."[7] Accordingly, the language of intelligibility, which propels a historical investigation, promotes a selection between what can be accepted and what must be forgotten in the process of representing the event. However, as de Certeau notes, "whatever this new understanding of the past holds to be irrelevant—shards created by the selection of materials, remainders left aside by an explanation—comes back, despite everything, on the edges of discourse or in its rifts and crannies: 'resistances,' 'survivals,' or delays discreetly perturb the pretty order of a line of 'progress' or a system of interpretation"[8]—they make these unsuspected depths visible.

Bearing these remarks in mind, I wish to suggest that the *Regularis concordia* is not necessarily only a record of a dramatic or theatrical representation of the visit of three Marys to the sepulchre where the body of crucified Christ was buried or an archival depository of the monastic practices. It also represents the labor to compose place, which will articulate the ensemble of movements and operations within it, and the labor to collate on the same plane heterogeneous places, that is, the configuration of positions, the order in accord with which the elements are distributed, and the identity of the practices, some received from tradition and some through the actions of historical subjects.[9] Seen as a practice of space identification and place production, the *Regularis concordia* discloses a moment when *a* space of representation was constructed and institutionalized as *the* place of representation in tenth-century England. That is to say, this specific labor to identify space and collate on the same plane heterogeneous places makes the *Regularis con-*

cordia a dynamic site delimiting how representation was defined in England at that time and describing the practices that were to solidify its identity.

To explore the possibility that the *Regularis concordia* is a dynamic site, rather than an archival repository, I will discuss both the document and other discourses that are linked or that link themselves to its surface. Thus, my own narrative regarding the *Regularis concordia* and its labor to compose and collate on the same plane different elements will be broken by this "other" narrative "discreetly perturb[ing] the pretty order of a line of 'progress' or a system of interpretation." This narrative, called a detour here, not only stops the flow of the argument but also reveals a site where a new realignment between thoughts and narrative practices can be established. Three detours from the order of a system of interpretation address specific issues in regard to the labor exemplified by and in the *Regularis concordia:* (1) a linguistic investigation into the historiographic practices implied by the term *concordia;* (2) a discussion of how the lives and hence the identities of the monks were constructed through various technologies, such as, the chapter or a daily confession; (3) an inquiry into the nature of the *Quem quaeritis* in the *Regularis concordia* and the possibility that its representational qualities were in flux and redefined its individuality each time the *Quem quaeritis* emerged in a liturgical manuscript or a network of ecclesiastic or monastic practices to which it was assigned. Ultimately, these three detours will shed some light on how representation was defined in England in the tenth century and on which of its attributes were accepted by a monastic institution and how they were made visible by the *Regularis concordia.*

Qui facit veritatem venit ad lucem.[10]
—Saint Augustine

The synodal Council of Winchester, at which English abbots and abbesses assembled, produced a document commonly known as the *Regularis concordia.*[11] Its full title, *Regularis concordia anglicae nationis monachorum sanctimonialiumque* (The Monastic Agreement of the Monks and Nuns of the English Nation), implies that the document is a written agreement that is monastic in nature. The term *monastic* also indicates that the rules were to be applied only to life in a monastery rather than to life in the town church.[12] This agreement was drawn up by and for the monks and nuns belonging to the growing ecclesiastical group in England who, judging from the words of the preface, called the *Proem*, were to abide by its regulations.[13] It was thus a consuetudinary, an ecclesiastic code, binding together the monasteries of Abingdon, Glastonbury, and Worcester, as well as the other, smaller monastic houses functioning in tenth-century England.[14]

On another level, the participants in the council were faced with the linguistic as well as political challenges contained in the term *concordia*. These challenges presented themselves on four interrelated and correlated levels. First, the term implies the quest for harmony within a particular group. Here, the group was the newly established community of the monks and nuns of the English nation, a community whose existence, as evidenced by history, could have been threatened by the change of the ruler or by a conflict between its different parties. The survival of the community depended on finding some kind of harmony between the diverse practices of monasticism as defined by the laws, customs, and codes that existed locally or regionally. Even though monasticism was based on the *Rule* of St. Benedict (ca. 480–550), its interpretations varied because of how it was disseminated and because of the changes introduced to manifest the local character and the individual forces shaping each and every monastic house, that is, climate, tradition, geographic location, and so on. Second, *concordia* signifies the quest for the harmony of ecclesiastical institutions, that is, the harmony between the organization, its function, and its social forms. Third, it suggests the quest for harmony of the spiritual and the corporeal body, a state indispensable for the essential execution of the other forms of harmony. Fourth, it implies that this quest for harmony was also the quest for the modes of control and power that would distinguish monastic institutions from other institutions and defend them from other social forms of existence.

The notion of a *concordia* leads to my first detour from my main narrative regarding the *Regularis concordia*. It will focus on a historical narrative describing both the transmission and dissemination of monastic practices and obligations in England as well as what we are to remember about this particular process of writing history that will culminate in a singular event, the Council of Winchester held in 970x973.

The available documents link the monastic revival in England to Athelstan, who came to the throne in 924.[15] He was the proponent of a close relationship between England and the Continent.[16] His political endeavors to advance the international prestige of the country led to and had its counterpart in the increase of ecclesiastical contacts at the time of the monastic revival in France, Germany, and Italy.[17] Thus, Bishop Cenwald of Worcester visited the monasteries of Germany in 929; Archbishop Oda of Canterbury, probably as bishop of Ramsbury, received the tonsure at Fleury in 936 while on a political mission in Francia; refugee monks from Flanders found their freedom in Bath; and Godelscalc, a foreign priest, lived in Abingdon.

This was the atmosphere in which three men, who are associated with the creation of the *Regularis concordia,* grew up and worked. They were Dunstan, some of whose family members were related to the English royal family and played a prominent role in the church; Aethelwold, who was born in Winchester; and Oswald, a man of Danish family whose two uncles were archbishops of Canterbury and York.[18]

Dunstan, born in or about 909, spent his first fourteen years in the village of Baltonsborough.[19] In 923, his parents allowed him to take the tonsure and he was admitted into membership in the community of Glastonbury. At that time, Glastonbury was still a religious community, a place of pilgrimage, and a center of learning. After taking the tonsure, Dunstan spent some time with his uncle, Archbishop Aethelhelm, who introduced him to King Athelstan.[20] It is difficult to state anything specific about the relationship between the royal household and Dunstan. We are told that he devoted his time mainly to studies and that this brought him into conflict with his young kinsmen at the court, who accused him of occult knowledge. As a result of this charge, Dunstan was expelled from the court.[21] He moved to the household of Bishop Aelfheah, known better as Aelfheah the Bald, in Winchester.[22] While in Winchester, as the story continues, a severe illness ended Dunstan's indecision over whether to get married or devote himself to the religious life. In 939, the last year of Athelstan's reign, Dunstan was ordained a priest. The new king, Edmund, gave him a place in the royal household, but because of the action of his enemies, Dunstan was dismissed. We are told by Auctore B that when Dunstan was getting ready to leave the country with the ambassador of a foreign prince whom the king was meeting in Cheddar, a strange accident happened—the king narrowly escaped death while hunting. He became convinced, through his narrow escape, that Dunstan should be brought back. Auctore B states that the king kept his vow and that Dunstan was recalled from exile and promoted to the position of the abbot of Glastonbury in 940.[23] The extant records about the observances at Glastonbury are too scanty to indicate what reforms Dunstan could have introduced there.[24]

Among those who joined Dunstan's community at Glastonbury was Aethelwold. Aethelwold's biographer Aelfric provides little information about his early life.[25] However, what can be gathered from the biography by Wulfstan of Winchester permits us to suggest that Aethelwold, who was born in Winchester during the reign of Edward the Elder, spent at least part of his youth at the court of Athelstan.[26] The king, as Aelfric explains, commended him to Aelfheah, who ordained him and Dunstan priests. Later on, Aethelwold became a monk at Glastonbury. According to Wulfstan, "He profited greatly by Dunstan's teaching, and eventually received the habit of the monastic order from him, devoting himself humbly to his rule."[27] He did not stay there long, however. Wulfstan tells us that Aethelwold wanted to go to one of the Continental reformed monastic houses to study but that Eadgifu, the queen mother, convinced King Eadred to give Abingdon to Aethelwold.[28] Dissuaded from leaving, Aethelwold accepted the task of restoring Abingdon in 954.

The monastery at Abingdon became a house of strict observance of the *Rule* and attracted both canons and monks from different parts of England.[29] To attract the religious men to Abingdon, Aethelwold brought monks from not only the mother monastery, Glastonbury (Osgar, Foldbriht, Frithegar), but also Corbie, a French monastery reformed under the guidance of Cluny, to instruct the community in chant and reading.[30] Aethelwold sent one of his monks, Osgar, to study the type of monasticism practiced at Fleury, which was already famous for its reforms as well as for its use of the *Rule* as a code regulating monastic life.[31] Wulfstan reports, "The king [Eadred] also gave his royal estates in Abingdon, the hundred hides, with excellent buildings, to the abbot and to the monks to increase their everyday provisions, and he gave them much monetary help from his royal treasury; but his mother [Eadgifu] sent them presents in an even more lavish scale."[32]

Aethelwold is said to have exercised a strict discipline by admonishing and reprimanding the monks.[33]

In 955, King Eadred died. The new ruler, Eadwig, was under the influence of those who resented the power of Dunstan. As a result of their plottings, on the day of coronation the abbot was exiled and had to take refuge at the monastery of St. Peter of Ghent in Flanders to escape the king's anger.[34] The words used by Pope John XII in his letter to Edgar confirm that Eadwig was against the church and monasticism.[35] Eadwig's hostile attitude toward the church and monasticism manifested itself through his actions of confiscating their property and establishing decrees hostile to both institutions.

Eadwig's rule lasted only four years and ended with a revolt in Mercia—an act of opposition to Eadwig's marriage to Aelfgifu, his relative. In the summer of 957, Eadwig's younger brother, Edgar, was elected the king of the country north of the Thames (Mercia and Northumbria).[36] Because of various political maneuverings, Eadwig recalled Dunstan from exile and allowed him to live in Edgar's kingdom. In 959, Edgar became the king of the whole country after Eadwig's death.[37] He appointed Dunstan to the vacant see of Worcester, London, and Canterbury.[38] Edgar also revoked Eadwig's decrees against the church.[39] Edgar's reign, from 960 to 975, was the period of the greatest extension of the movement whose demarcation lines are established by (1) Dunstan's return from exile at Ghent and (2) the *Promiso Regis* (975), the document guaranteeing the king's support for Christians.[40] During this time, as the biographers diligently assert, episcopal sees were cleansed from canons and filled with monks, secular clerks were removed from many of the old religious foundations and their place was taken by monks, and new religious houses were established or old religious houses were restored all over the country by the efforts of Dunstan, Aethelwold, Oswald, and their disciples.

Auctore B notes that Dunstan was against the unlawful marriages of clerks, their corruption, and their immoral lifestyle.[41] The testimony of his biographer focuses on the abominations that became commonplace in many of the monasteries in England. We are told that only Glastonbury and Abingdon were inhabited by monks.[42] The other monastic houses had fallen into ruin or were inhabited by the secular clergy with their wives.[43] The standard of morality must have been very low, if we accept the statements reproving not only marriages but also systematic bigamy.[44] Dunstan introduced the ideal of monastic reform, which could have been constructed during his stay in Ghent, into the monasteries in Bath and Westminster and into five others, all of which he kept under his rule.[45]

Aethelwold's reforming activities gained full strength when he became the bishop of the Old Minster in Winchester on November 29, 963.[46] In the following years, he completely changed the management of this cathedral. One of his first acts was the substitution of the monks from Abingdon for the secular canons who resided in the Old Minster and, according to Wulfstan, were involved "in wicked and scandalous behavior, were victims of pride, insolence, and riotous living to such a degree that some of them did not think fit to celebrate mass in due order." Wulfstan reports, "They married wives illicitly, divorced them, and took others."[47] The degree to which the excess in this description is justifiable and adequate can only be speculated.[48] Obviously, such behavior could not have been accepted. Sometime in 963, Pope John XII granted permission for the ejection of the secular canons from the Old Minster.[49] Wulfstan reports the consequences that occurred on February 20, 964 (Saturday, the beginning of Lent).

When the monks from Abingdon were standing at the entrance to the church, the clerics were finishing mass chanting the *communio*, "Serve ye the Lord with fear, and rejoice unto him with trembling: embrace discipline, lest ye perish from the just way," as if to say: "*We* have not wished to serve God or keep his discipline: but *you* must do so, lest like us you perish from the way which opens the kingdom of heaven to those who preserve justice." Hearing this, the brethren were glad, for they perceived that their journey had been speeded by the Lord and that it was God's will that this psalm had been sung, because they were there. They straightway applied to themselves the order given by David, for Osgar exhorted them thus: "Why are we wasting time outside? Let us do as the clerics encourage us. Let us go in, follow the way of justice, and serve the Lord our God with trembling and joy, so that 'when his wrath is kindled in a short time' we may deserve to share with those of whom the psalm goes on to say: 'Blessed are all they that put up their trust in him.'"[50]

To make the ejection not only a monastic matter but a state business, King Edgar sent Wulfstan of Dalham, one of his principal thanes, with Aethelwold and his monks. The canons were given an alternative: they could either give the place to the monks or take the monastic habit. The canons left the minster. Three of them—Eadsige, Wulfsige, and Wilstan—were converted later, however.[51] There are no records of how the ejection was viewed by the canons. But Wulfstan's description of "How the Holy Man [Aethelwold] Drank Poison and, Set Alight by the Heat of his Faith, Overcame the Lethal Draught" suggests that the secular canons must have taken at least some counteraction.[52]

Nevertheless theirs was a lost battle. Monasticism in England was institutionalized not only with the papal approval but also with the approval of secular powers defending monasticism against both the attacks of the canons and landowners fighting for their *saecularium prioratus* (secular domination) as well as against robbing God of the possessions that rightfully belonged to him.[53] In about 963, after the pestilence of 962, King Edgar promulgated a code consisting of a religious section, a secular section, directions about the circulation of the code, and a conclusion in which he promises to be a good ruler. It is suggested that the code was specifically addressed to the Danish area but that the regulations concerning ecclesiastical dues and punishments for not paying the prescribed tithes were to be respected in all parts of the kingdom.[54] Thus, for example, the following articles of the prologue enjoin that the document is a remedy for the pestilence that oppressed and reduced the number of people through the whole dominion.

[1] First, namely, that it seemed to him and his councilors that a calamity of this kind was merited by sins and by contempt of God's commands, and especially by the withholding of the tribute which Christian men ought to render to God in their tithes. . . .

[1.7] And those servants of God who receive the dues which we pay to God, are to live a pure life, that through that purity they may intercede for us to God.

[1.8] And I and my thegns shall compel our priests to that which the pastors of our souls direct us, namely our bishops, whom we should never disobey in any of the things which they prescribe for us for God's sake, that through that obedience with which we obey them for God's sake we may merit the eternal life to which they draw us by teaching and by example of good works.[55]

Aethelwold continued his activities. The Old Minster assumed the function of a monastic cathedral, a concept that would become a specifically English trait.[56] In Winchester, a monastic house was no longer located in an isolated place, as was the case in Cluny, for example; rather, it functioned within the town limits both as a monastery and a community church. It catered to thanes and townspeople alike during important religious festivals.[57] It was the location of some of the most lavish burials of rural elites.[58] Aethelwold combined in one person the office of bishop and that of abbot of the Old Minster.[59] There is enough evidence to assert that Aethelwold was a strict spiritual father. "Indeed," writes Wulfstan, "he was terrible as a lyon to malefactors and the wayward."[60] The description of the ejection of canons from the Old Minster, when contrasted with how other monastic communities—for example, Oswald's Worcester *familia*—seemed to be organized and functioned, is a poignant case of Aethelwold's monastic policy.[61] It is probable that the Old Minster was patterned after Abingdon, where Aethelwold ruled and trained his disciples for some ten years. The new community included monks from Abingdon, who had practiced the monastic norms as they were defined by the *Rule* and modified by the customs of Corbie and Fleury.[62]

In the following years, Aethelwold practiced also the art of governmentality that extended beyond the physical boundaries of the Old Minster. To secure the earthly existence of the monastic cathedral, he enjoyed a close relationship with Edgar and Aelfthryth. In 964 or 965, Edgar married Aelfthryth. Aethelwold seems to be very supportive of the queen. That had its benefits. Aelfthryth helped Aethelwold recover various lands and privileges for the Old Minster, as the "Renewal of the Freedom of Taunton by King Edgar" indicates; persuaded Edgar to sell him an estate at Stoke; gave him estates for the monastery at Ely; convinced Edgar to reform Peterborough; and defended Aethelwold's interests after the king's death.[63] In return, Aethelwold offered her "fifty mancuses of gold for her help in his just mission" (i.e., the renewal of the freedom of Taunton); made her the protectress of the nunneries, a position parallel to Edgar's position as the patron of monasteries; helped to advance the position of her son Edmund; and supported her other son, Aethelred, in his claim to the throne in the conflict with Edward after Edgar's death in 975.[64]

Aethelwold's skills helped him to gain Edgar's support for the reformation of the New Minster in 964.[65] The canons were driven away, and their place was taken by monks who were obliged to live according to the *Rule* of St. Benedict. Their spiritual father was Aethelgar, a monk, who was Aethelwold's pupil in Abingdon.[66] The event was solemnized by the "New Minster Charter," King Edgar's privilege for the New Minster, which was probably written by Aethelwold himself.[67]

At the same time, the Nunminster, the third cathedral in Winchester, was reformed. Wulfstan says: "[Aethelwold] established here flocks of nuns, placing over them Aethelthryth. Here the procedures of life according to the Rule are followed to this day."[68]

The solemn ceremonies of the reformation of these houses provided an occasion for the granting of lands. The rearrangement and extension of the sites of all three minsters, which were in a close proximity, led to a conflict between the Old Minster and the Nunminster.[69] The already mentioned "New Minster Charter" sheds some light on the relationship between the three houses and, especially, on their land exchange practices, which were or needed to be arbitrated by King Edgar himself.[70]

After the redefinition of the boundaries, the three monastic churches were brought into a single enclosure marked by ditches, fences, and walls. Inside of this "fortification" were three communities that were to live in spiritual as well as temporal concord. Even though they were supposed to lead individual lives, at least in terms of the feudal system of land acquisition and lease, they were controlled by Bishop Aethelwold, who was said to be living in the royal palace (located immediately west of the Old Minster and south of the New Minster cemetery) in the 970s at least.[71]

Whereas the physical existence and power of the three monastic houses were guaranteed by land accumulation and various injunctions as well as anathemas against those who would try to repossess the land or to introduce canons, the spiritual prestige of the Old Minster was increased by the translation of the remnants of St. Swithun into the cathedral on July 15, 971.[72] The implications of this translation cannot be overstated. Wulfstan, for example, draws attention to a direct correlation between the spoken words of Aethelwold and a spiritual manifestation of these words in the miracles of St. Swithun once the translation was accomplished.

Aethelwold's preaching was greatly aided by the holy bishop Swithun's being at this time marked out by signs from heaven and the gloriously translated to receive a proper burial within the church. So it was at one and the same time two lamps blazed in the house of God, placed on golden candlesticks; for what

Aethelwold preached by the saving encouragement of his words, Swithun wonderfully ornamented by display of miracles.[73]

Alan Thacker argues that Aethelwold used the cult of relics to recall the past and especially the time of a strict observance of the *Rule*.[74] Beyond and above the religious functions, the enhancement of the role of saints could have been politically motivated. As "An Account of King Edgar's Establishment of Monasticism" and the iconography contained in the *Benedictional of St. Aethelwold* unequivocally indicate, Aethelwold seemed to have been aware that to achieve his goal on a national and broadly based political scale, he needed to gain the support of King Edgar and Queen Aelfthryth for his activities.[75] The cult of the relics can be seen as a precise operation aimed at enlisting local support (i.e., the support of the social elite) and as a tool for pacifying the opponents of the reforms. This mode of operation was already in existence. Recall, for example, the cult of the Devotion to the Holy Cross in Abingdon. During the Danish invasion, the crucifix came to life and, with its arms, extracted stones from the walls of the monastery and drove the Danes away.[76] During the council that considered the expulsion of clerics from monasteries and that took place sometime between 964 and 969 (otherwise known as the Easter council), the Christ figure on the Holy Cross came to life and announced to the solemn gathering of abbots and abbesses that the expelled clerics' complaint against Dunstan was to be condemned because Dunstan's actions to restore destroyed monastic churches were exemplary and right.[77]

The translation of the remnants of St. Swithun enhanced the prestige of the Old Minster in Winchester. Until 971, the tomb of St. Swithun was located outside the west end of the minster. The message that St. Swithun wanted to be buried inside the minster was first revealed to a smith, who was supposed to pass it to Eadsige, one of the canons ejected from the Old Minster and Aethelwold's kinsman, who was to deliver the message to Aethelwold. The bringing of the remnants inside the church played a double function. On the one hand, the physical and spiritual presence of St. Swithun exemplified the true nature of the word of the Lord. On the other hand, the physical and spiritual presence of St. Swithun legitimized Aethelwold's actions of the renewal of monasticism in England by showing (1) that St. Swithun, a cleric himself, rather than a monk, could become an emblem for the monastic revival and (2) that some of the expelled canons recognized and reached for the true ecclesiastical life. (Eadsige was given the function of the sacrist of St. Swithun's shrine.) As the records presented here show, despite the support of the king and queen, Dunstan's and Aethelwold's controversial methods of conversion must have been challenged. Only the intervention of the figure of Christ (come to life) and the obvious parallel in the translation of St. Swithun could reestablish the authority of the leaders of the movement and the connection with the monarchy.[78] Therefore, it is not surprising that St. Swithun is featured in the *Benedictional of St. Aethelwold.* In the miniature, he is likened to a symbolic column supporting and strengthening the arch-shaped edifice of the *Ecclesia.*[79]

Aethelwold's power extended beyond the walls of the Winchester complex. He founded and introduced his monastic ideal through his pupils into the houses of Milton Abas; Chertsey; Ely, which he bought from the king, as Wulfstan indicates; Peterborough, which he reformed with the help of Aelfthryth and the support of the king, and which he endowed with twenty-one manuscripts and "enriched lavishly with estates nearby," that is, estates in Huntingdonshire and Northhamptonshire; and Thorney, which he also purchased. Wulfstan reports, "And so it came about, with king's agreement, that thanks both to Dunstan's counsel and activity and to Aethelwold's unremitting aid, monasteries were established everywhere in England, some for nuns, governed by abbots and abbesses who lived according to the Rule."[80]

The third reformer was Oswald. He was brought up by his uncle, Oda, archbishop of Canterbury. It was Oda who provided Dunstan with the means to purchase a church in Winchester that, at the time, was occupied by clerks. Oswald was made a canon and dean there. However, he found the community irreformable because of their lax style of clerical life and decided to leave the Winchester church and go abroad to join a small monastic community. "Had he been a Wessex man," writes J. Armitage Robinson, "he would have found what he sought under Abbot Dunstan at home. But there was another strain in his blood, and the archbishop himself had, it is said, received the monastic habit from the reformed monastery of Fleury."[81] Oswald stayed there until recalled by his uncle in 958. On his arrival in England, Oswald learned that Oda had passed away and that Dunstan had been nominated the new archbishop. In 961, Dunstan induced Edgar to make Oswald bishop of Worcester. Once the nomination took place, Oswald began to take a significant part in the monastic movement. He recalled Germanus from France to join him in Worcester. Also, following Aethelwold's practice in Winchester, he attempted to assign monks, instead of secular clerks, to his cathedral. This incident is recorded in the charter granted by King Edgar to Oswald on Holy Innocent's Day, Wednesday, December 28, 964, which confirmed the ejection of the recusants who refused to part with their wives and transfer all their rights and possessions to the newcomers.[82] Even though the new laws were very strict, it seems that their execution and strict observance were not Oswald's first priorities.[83] In his study of the witnesses shown on the seventy-one leases from Oswald's episcopate, P. H. Sawyer comes to the conclusion that Oswald's community must have been less monastic than has been maintained.

Both the witness lists and these grants to members of the community suggest that Oswald was indeed a gentle reformer. At no point was there any change that can reasonably be called a purge and it is hard to see what difference Oswald actually made at Worcester. Several of the leading members of the "reformed" community were witnessing leases in 962 and 963, and some were there in 957. Wulfric, who had been the head of the unreformed community, continued to head the witness lists for at least the first seven years of Oswald's episcopate, and when Wynsige returned to become the new leader, Wulfric was merely pushed into second place. . . . The members of the community were much more frequently called clerks than monks in the leases that they granted, despite the reformer's hostility to clerks.[84]

Even though the community grew in size during Oswald's tenure, the nature and the character of the reformed community are difficult to assess. The information gained from the leases provides the names of the witnesses and the data concerning the economic infrastructure of the monastery, rather than insights into its spiritual life.[85] Oswald's monastic reformation thus seems to differ considerably from Aethelwold's activities in Winchester in 963–64. In 962, Oswald established small monastic offshoots in Westbur-on-Trym and, later on, in Ramsey, Winchcombe, and Pershore and in four monasteries whose names are not known to us.[86]

This detour into the monastic revival in England in the years immediately proceeding the Winchester Synod discloses the elements that are linked or that link themselves onto the narrative surface of the *Regularis concordia*. First, there is the epistemic space of representation where the political events, ecclesiastical and monastic maneuvers, and economic factors encountered one another. They were represented by three speakers, Dunstan, Aethelwold, and Oswald, all of whom pursued a monastic ideal by espousing different political causes. Their position was never stable within the space of this formation, however. Consider Dunstan's and Aethelwold's relation to the royal family and, specifically, to the marriage between Eadwig and Aelgifu, or consider Dunstan's and Aethelwold's position in the battle for the throne after Edgar's death. Their involvement in secular politics was possible because of their position both in terms of their relation to the royal family and because of their status in society as well as the creation of the specific sites, both ideological and physical, from which they could pronounce their judgments. Dunstan, Aethelwold, and Oswald needed to acquire the institutional site from which their discourse derived its legitimacy. The revived monasticism offered such a possibility. Unlike the Continental monastic houses, the institution of the English monastic cathedral (Canterbury, Winchester, Worcester) facilitated a place for both secular politics and ecclesiastical control. Oswald was the abbot of Worcester but lived in Ramsey; Aethelwold was the abbot of Peterborough, Ely, and Thorney while he ruled in Winchester; Dunstan was the abbot of Glastonbury and archbishop of Canterbury. Such a situation was possible because of the role the three reformers played in the political life of England. Edgar needed them as his advisors and promoters of royalist propaganda; they needed Edgar to protect them and to reform the church and its servants.

This pluralism of positions is also inscribed into a topography of physical spaces. For example, during the reform period, Winchester was the seat of the royal and episcopal places as well as the place of the three monasteries. The Old Minster, with its shrine of St. Swithun, was immediately opposite the royal palace. Royal burials took place in the cemetery underlying the west work.[87] The New Minster was a royal mausoleum and, also, a burial church for important townspeople.[88] The Nunminster appears to have been established on an urban estate belonging to Ealhswith, Alfred's queen.[89] Edgar's charters and regulations articulate the labor to arrange on the same plane the close relationship between the royal family and the ecclesiastical community headed by Aethelwold.

Thanks to this relationship, Aethelwold's controversial actions were not questioned. The documents that describe them construct the past that, in the process of legitimizing itself, obfuscated—almost erased—the existence of this "other" past. The positions of Aethelwold, Dunstan, and Oswald were secured not only by the relation of these men to the crown but also by how they defined the boundary between the canons and the monks. The boundary was a line that established the binary opposition between the canons and the monks, a location where the struggle between two factions took place. But it was also a site of resistance and compliance, as brief statements in the relevant documents indicate. Even though the narratives of the events suggest a clear-cut division between the canons and the monks, the mapping out of the individual practices of the three reformers points in the opposite direction: these boundaries were not stable; they were the fields of struggle.

At the same time, when the materiality of borders was produced, their material form was multiplied, for each of the reformers had a different vision of English monasticism and its practices. Even though monastic movement was in the hands of Dunstan, the reformed houses constituted three individual groups that were dominated by the ideals introduced by Dunstan, who had spent some time in Ghent; Oswald, who had visited Fleury; and Aethelwold, who had been a proponent of strict monasticism. Although the *Rule* was the primary code of monastic life, its interpretation by the three leaders seems to have varied in different places. Moreover, each of the monastic houses was practically independent in its observances of the code. Therefore, to prevent a great diversity of practice among the many religious houses that then existed in England, the need arose for the unification of the whole movement.[90] This need for unification resulted in a call for a synodal council, which significantly was held in Winchester's Old Minster, and which produced the *Regularis concordia*.

Only two texts of the *Regularis concordia* are extant. One of them, Faustina B III, is from the late tenth century; the other, Tiberius A III, is from the second half of the eleventh century.[91] The document, which is in medieval Latin, is divided into a preface, twelve chapters, and an epilogue. It is generally accepted that Aethelwold was the author of the document, even though the *Regularis concordia* does not have an attestation that could provide the necessary information about the authorship the way, for example, the New Minster charter does.[92] The *Proem* says:

Edgar the glorious, by the grace of Christ illustrious King of the English and of the other peoples dwelling with the bounds of the island of Britain, from his earliest began to fear, love and worship God with all his heart. For while he engaged in the various pursuits that befit boyhood, he was nevertheless touched by the divine regard, by being diligently admonished by a certain abbot who explained to him the royal way of the Catholic faith. (1; 69)[93]

Michael Lapidge draws attention to the phrase "a certain abbot" and asks who that abbot could be and why his name is withheld. As far as the identity of the abbot is concerned, it can be suggested that it was either Dunstan or Aethelwold. It is quite possible that both of them tutored Edgar. Symons implies that Dunstan was the most likely person to be responsible for the education of the prince in the period from 949 to 956 and that Aethelwold may have assumed this responsibility when Dunstan was exiled.[94] Barbara Yorke notes: "From Byrhtferth's *Vita Oswaldi* we learn unambiguously that Edgar had received his instruction from Aethelwold . . . ; given this information, it becomes clear that Aethelwold had refrained from naming himself as Edgar's instructor out of simple modesty. The *Regularis concordia,* then, was written by Aethelwold."[95] Some thirty years later, Aelfric, in a letter known as "Letter to the Monks of Eynsham," tells the community that the *Regularis concordia* had been "put together from various sources and 'imposed' on all the monasteries" by Aethelwold and his fellow bishops and abbots. He makes no reference to the Council of Winchester, however.[96] Seventy years after Aelfric penned his letter, Saint Anselm wrote to Archbishop Lanfranc: "I have heard that St. Dunstan drew up a rule of monastic life: I should like, if it be possible, to see the Life and *Instituta* of so great a father." This suggests that, in the course of a hundred years, the *Regularis concordia* had come to be looked on as Dunstan's.[97]

The *Regularis concordia* was, as Aelfric informs us in his letter, "put together from various sources." "Deeply moved by the wise advice of this excellent King [Edgar], the bishops, abbots and abbesses were not slow in raising their hands to heaven in hearty thanksgiving to the throne above for that they were thought worthy to have so good and so great a teacher" (3; 72). They assembled at the Council of Winchester "for the advancement of the rude English Church," to gather customs from eminent monasteries and embody them "in this small book [for] regular observance" (3; 72). The document combines in itself both foreign and native elements. This twofold nature of the sources is due to the fact that the English monks brought back certain traditions from their trips to the Continental monasteries of Ghent and Fleury.[98] The monks from these two monasteries were invited to participate in the synod.[99] Numerous references to the Benedictine *Rule,*[100] the customs of Fleury,[101] Cluniac[102] and Lotharingian codes,[103] and the *Ordo qualiter* and the *Capitula* of Aachen are intertwined with solely English traditions, such as, for example, the prayer for the royal family or a fire in winter. The consuetudinary is a combination of native liturgical and devotional practices and customs usually introduced by such phrases as "as is the custom," "according to custom," and "goodly religious customs of this land," on the one hand, and, on the other, customs of Continental origin. The latter can be further divided into those that were consonant with early Benedictine usage,[104] those copied from the documents of the Anianian reform,[105] and finally, those that indicate a close relationship between the *Regularis concordia* and stereotyped observances contained in other consuetudinaries of the tenth and eleventh centuries.[106]

The *Regularis concordia* begins with a moderately long preface, the *Proem,* explaining the reasons for the meeting at Winchester, which was instigated, according to the document, by King Edgar.

When therefore he [King Edgar] learned that the holy monasteries in all quarters of his kingdom, brought low, and almost wholly lacking in the service of our Lord Jesus Christ, were wasting away and neglected, moved by the grace of the Lord he most gladly set himself to restore them everywhere to their former good estate. Wherefore he drove out the negligent clerks with their abominations, placing in their stead for the service of God, throughout the length and breadth of his dominions, not only monks but also nuns, under abbots and abbesses. . . . Exceedingly delighted with such great zeal the aforesaid king, after deep and careful study of the matter, commanded a Synodal Council to be held at Winchester (1–2; 69–70).

The resolutions and recommendations made by the assembly and approved by the king constitute the remaining part of the preface. We are told that, though the communities of monks and nuns were unified in faith, they were not unified in the manner of monastic usage (2; 71). Consequently, one of the resolutions states that the monks and nuns were obliged to obey and openly observe the ordinances of the *Rule* to "avoid all dissension" and "for the advancement of the rude English Church" (3; 72) and for the glory of the king's benefactors.

And this one thing we have thought ought to be looked to by the faithful who live under the yoke of the Rule, namely, that those prayers of intercession which, following the usage of our fathers before us, we are accustomed to say for the king and benefactors by whose bounty, under Christ, we are maintained, shall not be chanted at excessive speed lest rashly we provoke God to anger, which God forbid, instead of wisely beseeching Him to forgive us our sins. (5; 74)

Not only is this advancement of the church limited to spiritual practices, but a special emphasis is laid on the instructions regulating the behavior of monks and nuns, with the special emphasis on obedience and humility. Dunstan, "the noble archbishop moved by the spirit of prophesy," ordered, in the interest of discipline, that monks not enter or frequent the places visited and inhabited by nuns (4; 73). They were not to chant the prayers with excessive speed, for the prayers should be "chanted distinctly so that mind and voice agree" (5; 74). The assembly proclaimed, "In order that the most acceptable fruit of obedience be acquired and the pride of arrogance be brought low and that degree of humility, set forth in the Rule . . . let none henceforth dare rashly to hold any custom that has not been sanctioned by this Synodal Council" (5; 74). Moreover, the assembly forbade possession of private property, "which might lead to utter loss and ruin as it did in the past" (7; 75–76), and it forbade the monks and nuns from meeting with laymen, either within or outside of the monastery, for the purpose of feasting together. Other regulations put forth by the assembly referred to the behavior of brethren who while on a journey "will not waste time in idle talk but shall busy themselves with psalms or, at the proper time, speak on necessary matters" (7; 76).

Rules also were made regarding general comportment.

In the monastery moreover let neither monks nor abbots embrace or kiss, as it were, youths or children. . . . Not even on the excuse of some spiritual matter shall any monk presume to take with him a young boy alone for any private purpose but, . . . let the children always remain under the care of their master. Nor shall the master himself be allowed to be in company with a boy without a third person as witness. (7–8; 76–77)

Another decision of the synod concerned the election of abbots and abbesses, which should be carried according to the teaching of the *Rule* and, with the consort of the assembly, was subject to royal prerogative (6; 74–75). The *Proem* ends with a call for brotherly unity and a conviction that those who observed the customs of the *Rule* would receive the reward of eternal life. The parties of the document claim that in the meantime, however,

we shall set forth plainly in writing those customs of the Holy Rule which have been constantly and everywhere observed by the aforesaid Benedict and by his holy followers and imitators after deep consideration and examination. (8–9; 77)

The *Proem* thus delimits a site where past and present monastic practices and obligations were to be positioned and arranged on the same plane—this site, which came into being because King Edgar was "moved by the grace of the Lord," was stabilized with the help of a narrative describing spiritual as well as physical qualities of monks' and nuns' practice of monastic obedience and humility. Their labor to maintain the site was to be rewarded with eternal life. Of special interest is how the *Regularis concordia* constitutes this narrative, where, as the discussion concerning its author makes clear, the names of the scribes become secondary. On the one hand, there is the *Rule* of St. Benedict, which provides the means of securing both respect and acceptance within a monastic history. The *Rule,* we are told, has been "constantly and everywhere observed." This statement refers both to the past glorious days not only on the Continent but also in Bede's England as well as to the tenth-century monastic reform movement at the monastic houses of Cluny and Ghent. On the other hand, there is the king, whose presence secures temporal respect through his involvement in spiritual matters. The passage about the election of abbots is a good example of the merger between the spiritual and temporal history—unlike on the Continent, the election of the monastic leader was to happen both in accordance to the *Rule* and with the approval of the king.

The *Regularis concordia* opens thus with the discussion of the elements that establish its position in a temporal discourse. It writes its own history after the period of decline during which the monastic life almost disappeared and the monastic houses were "wasting away and neglected." In contrast, at the time the document was written, it was perceived to be possible, with the help of Edgar, to reestablish monasticism. But to achieve this goal, it was necessary to erase the differences and produce new meanings and practices for the representation of the physical and spiritual self, "for they were united in one faith, though not in one manner of monastic usage" (2; 70).

The preface is followed by a series of chapters describing in detail the production of new meanings and new representation of the physical and spiritual monastic self—the liturgical functions of the day and the duties of some of the monastic officials. Here the text's labor to articulate and to compose the ensemble of procedures and operations becomes visible in its relation to what is chosen to be talked about and how the practices are discussed—the following outline of chapters gives a bird's-eye view of immobilized technologies of representing the self.

Chapter 1	the regular duties to be observed by monks day and night throughout the year
Chapter 2	the order of the hymns in winter and the manner in which certain other monastic duties should be fulfilled
Chapter 3	the manner of the vigil of Christmas and of other Offices of the period from solemnity to Septuagesima
Chapter 4	the order of the regular life from Septuagesima to the end of Lent
Chapter 5	the manner in which the day and Night Office should be carried out on the feast of Easter
Chapter 6	the manner in which Saturday, the Octave of Easter, and the whole of summer time should be observed
Chapter 7	the duties of the brother who is called *Circa*
Chapter 8	the manner in which the day and Night Office should be celebrated in Whit week
Chapter 9	the manner of the Quarter Tense days
Chapter 10	the order in which the daily maundy shall be offered to the poor by the brethren and the manner in which the Abbot shall entertain strangers
Chapter 11	the order in which the brethren shall carry out the *Mundiatiae* on Saturday and certain other duties they shall perform for the good of their souls
Chapter 12	the care of a sick brother and the manner in which the death of one of the brethren will be celebrated

(10; 79)

To escape the narrative totalizations, let me articulate singular operations that are used in the *Regularis concordia* to construct a place of representation on the basis of a finite number of stable properties already mentioned in the *Proem.* Chapter 1 describes the customs observed in a monastery. Here the *Regularis concordia* fashions statements about the organization of a technology of the self that transformed the inhabitants of a monastery into monks. Not only are these customs connected with the communal religious observations, but they also refer to the private and personal behavior of the monks. Consider, for example, the following paragraph referring to the order of the day in a monk's life.

At all times when a brother arises from bed in the night hours for the work of God, he shall first of all sign himself with the sign of the Holy Cross, invoking the Holy Trinity. Next, he shall say the verse, *Domine labia mea aperies,* and then the whole of the psalm *Deus in adiutorium meum intende* with the *Gloria.* After this, having provided for the necessity of nature, if at that time he must, he shall hasten to the oratory. (11–12; 80–81)

The amalgamation of spiritual duties and everyday necessities of life is a characteristic feature both of the preceding paragraph and of the other thirteen paragraphs in this chapter on the winter *horarium.*

After "having provided for the necessity of nature," the monk was to direct his steps to the oratory.[107] On his arrival there, he was to kneel down in "his proper and accustomed place [and] pour forth in the Lord's sight prayer from the heart rather than from the lips, so that his voice, through deep compunction of the heart and recollection of his misdeeds, may efficaciously reach the ears of the merciful Lord and, by the grace of Christ, obtain pardon for all his sins" (12; 81). Once the pardon was granted, he recited the first three penitential psalms as well as the prayer for the king, queen, and benefactors. The text of the prayers was provided in the *Regularis concordia.*[108] Then the bell rang until the *schola* (a monastic school for children who were being trained to become monks in the future) entered the church and joined the *Trina oratio* in an observance of the Holy Trinity. A second bell rang when this observance was finished, and the monks and the *schola,* "ranged in order in the stalls," were then to "recite the fifteen Gradual psalms, one by one, genuflecting at a sign from the prior after each set of five psalms" (13). When the recitation of psalms ended, Nocturns (the night office) took place.[109]

After Nocturns, the monks were to say two psalms, the first especially for the King and the second for the king, queen, and benefactors, with collects for the king, the queen, and benefactors. For example, the collect for the king read:

We beseech Thee, Almighty God, that Thy servant our King, N, who has received of Thy mercy the government of his realm, may obtain also an increase of all virtues, wherewith being fittingly adorned he may be able to avoid the evils of wickedness, to overcome his enemies and to attain to Thee Who art the Way the Truth and the Life. Through our Lord. (13–14; 83)

These collects were to be repeated after Nocturns, Matins, Tierce, Sext, None, Vespers, and Compline, though not after Prime.

A short interval followed, which was said to be "laid down in the Rule" and "customary throughout the summer period" (i.e., from Easter to November). During this interval, the *schola,* with their master, left the church for "the necessity of nature" (14; 84). The others, "with the exception of those who may be under the same necessity" (14; 84), remained in prayer awaiting Matins, which was comprised of a regular body of prayer, the *Miserere,* and the two psalms for the royal house, followed by the antiphons of the Cross, of St. Mary, and of the patron saint of the church or, when the church did not have a patron saint, of the dedication of the church. After these, the monks were to go to Matins of All Saints singing an antiphon to the saint to whom the chapel they were bound was dedicated. Lauds of the Dead followed. The latter office should have ended at daybreak, when a bell would announce the celebration of Prime. If, however, Lauds of the Dead ended too quickly and before dawn, then the brethren were supposed to wait until the appointed time for Prime.

When Prime was over, two psalms were recited, one against fleshly temptation and one for dead brethren, as well as the penitential psalms with *Inclina Domine,* inserted for "the sake of devotion" (15; 84–85). The ringing of the bell announced the litany, at which all, without exception, would humbly prostrate themselves, "as was the custom" (15; 85). When finished, according to the ordinance of the *Rule,* the monks were to "give themselves to reading until the second hour" (15; 85). The sound of the bell was a sign that the brethren were to put on their day shoes, and "none but the minsters should presume to do this before the bell is heard, nor fail to do so then without permission" (16; 85). At the same time, the entire *schola,* the master of the *schola,* the abbot, and the seniors went to wash their faces "as is customary," and they were expected to be "intent on the psalms" as they did so (16; 85). The psalms meant were the seven penitential psalms or "any other spiritual prayer apt for driving away the temptation of the devil" (16; 86). After the ringing of the bell, all returned to church for Tierce (Terce), followed by the prayers for the royal house and benefactors and by Morrow Mass, about which it was stated that "on Mondays the right-hand choir shall make the offering, the left-hand choir offering at the principal Mass" (16; 86); on Tuesdays the order was reversed. After Morrow Mass, the Chapter, that is, the monastic parliament, was held. The Chapter was designed as a daily public confession of sins by the brethren. It functioned as a symbol of obedience and submission to the abbot.

Any brother who [was] conscious of having committed some fault [would] humbly ask forgiveness and indulgence. But a brother that [was] accused, no matter for what reason, by the abbot or by any of the senior officials [would] prostrate himself before speaking. . . . If he acts in any other wise he shall be deemed guilty. (17; 87)

The time after the Chapter and before Sext, that is, from about 10 A.M. to about noon, was devoted to work. After Sext and psalms for the royal house, the Principal Mass was celebrated. The *Regularis concordia* states, "When the *Pax* has been given, the brethren, except those who are conscious of the guilt or of weakness of the flesh, shall not hesitate, in their fervent practices of the exercises of the monastic state, to receive the Eucharist daily" (19; 89).

After the Mass, while the ministers partook in the *mixtum* (a drink of wine), the brethren prayed. Then, None was recited when the second bell rang and, afterward, the psalms for the royal house were said, after which the *cena* (a feasting meal) took place. The period of a few hours between the *cena* and Vespers was devoted to reading or to the Psalm, according to the ordinances of the *Rule,* or to work in the monastery. The *Regularis concordia* states that "Vespers shall be celebrated punctually" (22; 91). and that the junior monks "shall not, by God's grace, wander about after the prayer has been said but shall sit in choir, busily occupied with spiritual reading" (22; 91). After Vespers of the Day, psalms for the royal house, and anthems, followed by Vespers of All Saints, Vespers of the Dead were held.

When all these prayers had been said, the brethren retired to exchange their day shoes for night ones. On Saturdays the monks washed their feet, for which purpose each had a suitable basin; having washed their feet, those who needed to could also wash their shoes; afterward, a measure of drink was distributed and the bell was rung for the *collatio* (a fasting meal), during which the *caritas* (a special Saturday indulgence) was provided. On the remaining days, the brethren went to the *collatio,* at which the length of the reading was decided by the prior. After the reading, Compline was celebrated.

The *Regularis concordia* states, "When the bell is rung for Compline there shall be a space for prayer after which, at a sign from the prior, the brethren shall offer to one another the healing remedy of confession" (23; 93). After Compline, *Miserere mei Deus* and the psalms for the royal house were said. The *Trina oratio,* whose prayers were prescribed by the *Regularis concordia,* was part of Compline, the last canonical hour of the day. The *Regularis concordia* states: "When these prayers are finished, the brethren shall be sprinkled with blessed water by the *hebdomadarius* and shall then go to their rest with reverence and the utmost quiet. . . . Moreover, every night after Compline, when the brethren are in bed, the dormitory will be sprinkled, on account of the illusions of the evil one [*propter illusiones diabolicas*]" (24; 94).[110]

Chapter 1 is thus a collection of rules "on the observance of the monastic way of life with the reminder that every action, spiritual or temporal . . . should be begun with a blessing" (11; 80). The blessing is indispensable because "nothing can stand firm and strong which lacks the blessing of Christ" (11; 81). The regulations in this chapter refer to two different types of practices whose functions are to control every action in a monk's everyday life (all the offices and the prayers are clearly described) and to administer each of those actions (the techniques for the execution of the proper analysis of the self are presented). One technique of administration, the administrative self-examination connected with both the Chapter and the confession, merits further consideration in the discussion of the process of differentiation and accumulation of the practices that constitute the identities of the monks through the technologies of obedience, humility, and spirituality.

The Chapter and the confession are the subject of my second detour from my main narrative regarding the *Regularis concordia*. The focus of this detour is on how the *Regularis concordia* secured the rejection of everything that could be harmful to the existence and the practice of a monastic life.

Consider the following texts. The first text describes the Chapter.

After the Morrow Mass, at the sign from the prior, all shall come together for the Chapter, the prior leading. Turning to the east they shall salute the Cross and with bared heads abase themselves before one another: this act of humility is to be observed whenever the brethren are assembled together. When the brethren are seated, the Martyrology shall be read: all shall then rise and say the verse *Pretiosa in conspectu Domini* with the collect and the verse *Deus in adiutorium meum intende,* this verse being given out by the prior and said thrice, with the *Gloria* at the end, the brethren making a genuflection if the season of the year demands it. When the prior says *Et ne nos inducas* all shall rise, and, with unbowed heads, say the verse *Respice in servos,* adding the *Gloria* and bowing their heads. There follow the collect *Dirigere et sanctificare* and the *Adiutorium nostrum in nomine Domini: Qui fecit coelum et terram.* Then, all being seated again, the Rule or, on feast days, the Gospel of the day, shall be read and the prior shall explain what has been read according as the Lord shall inspire him. After this, any brother who is conscious of having committed some fault shall humbly ask forgiveness and indulgence. But a brother that is accused, no matter for what reason, by the abbot or by one of the senior officials, shall prostrate himself before speaking. And when asked by the prior the reason for this, he shall answer by admitting his fault, saying *Mea culpa domine.* Then, when bidden, let him rise. If he acts in any other wise he shall be deemed guilty. Thus whoever, when rebuked by a superior for anything done amiss in the workshops, does not immediately prostrate himself as the Rule ordains, must undergo the greater punishment. Indeed, the more the monk humbles himself and accepts blame, the more mercifully and gently shall he be dealt with by the prior. For it is meet that in our negligences, whether of thought, word or deed, we should be judged in this present life by sincere confession and humble penance lest, when this life is over, our sins declare us guilty before the judgement-seat of Christ. When this duty of spiritual purgation has been gone through, the five psalms set forth below shall be said for departed brethren. (17–18; 86–87)

The second text refers to a reversed order on Sundays throughout the year.

All that we have ordained to be carried out on week-days after Tierce shall on Sundays be arranged for before Tierce; and this in such wise that each monk shall by humble confession reveal the state of his conscience to his spiritual father or, if he be absent, to whomsoever acts in his place. (18; 88)

And the third text refers to the custom to be executed at the end of the monastic day.

Moreover, every night after Compline, when the brethren are in bed, the dormitory shall be sprinkled, on account of the illusion of the evil one. (24; 94)

These three passages allude to the practice that describes a monk's obligation of truth. It was a monk's duty to know who he was, what was taking place inside of him, and the temptations he was or could be exposed to. In Christianity in general, and in monastic life in particular, these three procedures specifically describe how a monk could manifest the truth about himself. As Michel Foucault observes, a monk was "to say these things to other people—to tell these things to other people—and hence, to bear witness against himself."[111]

This obligation of truth regarded not only the faith and the dogma, but also, or at the same time, the self, the soul, and the heart. The importance of this obligation cannot be overstated. For a monk, as the *Regularis concordia* asserts, the act of exploring the self, purification of the soul, and compunction of the heart provided the pardon for the sins, the grace of Christ, and, ultimately, the access to the divine light.[112] "Qui facit veritatem venit ad lucem," as St. Augustine observed.

This obligation of making truth was a monk's prerogative. Multiple passages in chapter 1 of the *Regularis concordia* imply that a monk was to take account of himself throughout a monastic day, through the first prayer, the Chapter, the confession to the spiritual father, the confession of faith to another brethren, and the act of sprinkling blessed water at the end of the day. These practices of spiritual and administrative self-examination were, however, modified by two elements—by obedience in the execution of a monastic lifestyle (a visual manifestation of truth about the self) and by contemplation of God through numerous prayers and physical acts of faith (an audible manifestation of truth about the self).

The act of obedience was one of the most fundamental aspects of a monastic life. The abbots and abbesses attending the Council at Winchester agreed to observe the *Rule* of St. Benedict and the *Regularis con-cordia.* As the *Proem* stipulated, the monks and nuns devoted to and joined together by the worship of Christ were to renounce their earthly possessions, to serve God, and to remain in their community for life once ordained. The head of the community governed them in an author-itarian manner, though according to the *Rule*. All monks or nuns were required to obey the abbot or the abbess unquestionably and tacitly. The rule of obedience arched over all aspects of a monastic life and a monas-tic institution. The relationship between a monk and the abbot or a senior official was clearly enunciated in the description of the Chapter. If a monk acted with humility, he might humbly ask forgiveness and indulgence. If, however, he acted in any other way, he would be deemed guilty and barred from the participation in a monastic life. This tripar-tite relationship between a monk, his superior, and the act of obedience was permanent, always in place, stable, and required, as the Chapter made clear, a conscious surrender as well as abdication of the self and the will in front of the abbot or a senior official. Only when these conditions were met, the process of the production of truth could be successfully accomplished and the pardon for the sins given. The production, rather than the examination, of truth could lead to the contemplation of God, the supreme aspect of a monastic life.

Therefore, it is not surprising that many passages in chapter 1 refer to a systematic process of self-examination and confession. Every spiritual or temporal action was never haphazard but in accord with a new or existing monastic custom and began with a blessing. When a monk arose from bed, for example, he began with the sign of the Holy Cross and a prayer. The self-examination was thus directed inward toward the thoughts rather than toward physical, external actions. A prayer was to come "from the heart rather than from the lips" (12; 81) This particular mode of operation and representation, furnished to expose and external-ize thoughts, was present in all monastic actions throughout the day. It was supposed to allow a monk to maintain the necessary purity to receive God. This self-control of his thoughts embraced all that was within and without a monk—according to Foucault, "the images which present themselves to the spirit, the thoughts which come to interfere with con-templation, the diverse suggestions which turn the attention of the spirit away from its objects, that means away from God" (10). Thus, for exam-ple, the psalm *Inclina Domine* was inserted after the penitential psalms "for the sake of devotion"; when the *schola* went to wash their faces, others, "according as God suggest[ed] to [their] heart by His divine inspiration," were to "silently and with the whole bent of [their] mind apply [themselves] to [their] duty, sanctifying [their] acts of obedience, as [they] should everything, with holy prayers, chanting the canonical hours or the seven Penitential psalms or any other spiritual prayer apt for driving away the temptation of the devil" (16; 85–86); and when they were in bed, the brethren were sprinkled with blessed water.

A monk examined all his thoughts, images, and even suggestions as well as their continuous imperceptible movements with the help of devotional practices that were designed to control their nature, quality, and substance. The self-examination was not sufficient, however. The monastic authorities needed to verify and to know if a monk's thoughts really permitted him to contemplate God. This verification was of utmost importance, as is explained by Foucault: "one must know if they [thoughts] really bear the effigy of God, that is to say, if they really permit us to contemplate him, if their surface brilliance does not hide the impurity of bad thought. What is their origin? Do they come from God, or from the workshop of demons? Finally, even if they are of good quality and origin, have they not been whittled away and rusted by evil sentiments?" (11).

The process of examining a thought in itself, rather than in its relationship to the external order of things, turned a monk into a cipher that needed to be deciphered and interpreted at all times: the *Regularis concordia* prescribes that "[e]ach monk shall by humble confession reveal the state of his conscience to his spiritual father" (18; 88) or to the congregation after the reading and the explanation of the Gospel during the Chapter. The state of a monk's conscience was verbalized openly. In the context of this particular hermeneutics of one's thoughts, one's thoughts were interpreted not by a physical act of a silent confession but in making one's faults visible and audible. During this process, the spiritual father could distinguish between truth and falsehood in the movement of thought, image, or suggestion. The urgency for a verbal verification is found in the following passage.

If, moreover, a brother urged by some temptation of soul or body, needs to confess at any other time, let him by no means delay to have recourse to the healing remedy of confession. (18; 88)

The verbal act of confession was thus the process during which thought, "a temptation of soul or body," was brought into the light of explicit discourse. The importance of this act was paramount. When not expressed verbally, these temptations inhabited the domain of darkness, that is, the domain of Satan. When, however, a defiant thought was brought into daylight, it lost its appeal. But it was not possible for a monk to simply tell his thoughts aloud to receive absolution for his temptation. The presence of a spiritual father or of a person acting in his place in his absence was necessary, because the thought had to be put under the eye of God's representative. During the Chapter, the verbalization of thoughts happened in a twofold manner: either a brother confessed in front of the congregation and asked forgiveness and indulgence, or a brother who was accused by the abbot or by the senior officials would prostrate himself until the end of their accusation, when he would be allowed to admit his fault by saying, "Mea culpa domine"—a statement of renunciation and self-sacrifice. Either manner represented a permanent, exhaustive, and sacrificial verbalization of the thoughts during the Chapter. According to Foucault, "to this permanent verbalization of the thoughts, the Greek fathers gave the name of *exagorisis*" (16).

Exagorisis implied that the mind perceived the inner reality and read books as parts of a single text. This text was the Scripture. The function of the mind was to produce truth in order to access a system of light that defined unequivocally how the text was seen and who saw it. Images and spoken words resembled one another. This may explain why a prayer was to come from the inside rather than from the lips. Therefore, images inside, or in the mind, including thoughts and suggestions, were viewed as "visible" words. The act of verbalization during the Chapter, or a spiritual confession, was the instance when this visibility was fully acknowledged. This acknowledgment was necessary for the spiritual father of the community to know that a sign designated what it signified. Foucault suggests that *exagorisis* was closely connected with the sacrifice of the self in order to discover the truth about the self. Thus, for him, truth and sacrifice are correlated—truth is a "visible" sacrifice. What is of significance in this consideration, however, is that a monk could become the subject of the manifestation of truth when the visual and audible manifestations of truth about the self erased him as a real body or as a real existence. The Chapter guaranteed that.

Whether or not this erasure "really" took place is outside and beyond this consideration. What is noteworthy is the realignment of different practices in order to secure the manifestation of truth. When coded into the narrative space of the *Regularis concordia,* these practices established a singular mode of effectivity and action without conforming to the standard assumptions about the obligation of truth.

Two elements form this system of effectivity and action. First, there is an epistemological technology of the self, which in the monastic community was a process of a continuous verbalization of the most imperceptible thought movements. Some parts of this movement were directly controlled by the prayers, some were controlled by the institutionalization of the obligation of truth, and, finally, some were controlled by bearing witness against oneself. In the act of the production of truth, there was no distinction made between the knowledge of the self and the knowledge of the monastic devotional practice. The act of Communion, that is, the reception of "the food of life, that is, the Body and Blood of Christ" (19; 89), was the moment when the binary was under a necessary erasure in order for the self to access the divine light. Second, there is a representational technology of the self: in the process of a continuous verbalization of the thought, a "gnosiologic self" (Foucault's label for a monastic self) partook, in front of a spiritual father, in the process of the annulment of the space between the thought, image, and suggestion in the mind and the words designating them. This nullification of the distance between these elements could only be achieved if the separation between the body and the thought ceased to exist. Neither the body, whose most imperceptible movements were visualized, nor the thought, whose most imperceptible movements were verbalized, differentiated between images and spoken words. It brought the images/words forth into the open and into full visibility in order for them to be correctly assessed. In this sense, as St. Augustine stated, "Qui facit veritatem venit ad lucem." The confession guaranteed that.

This obligation of verbalization of truth and self-sacrifice that provided access to light becomes a text of transmission every time a Communion is discussed in the *Regularis concordia.* For example:

When the *Pax* has been given, the brethren . . . should not hesitate . . . to receive the Eucharist daily. Let them bear in mind the words of the blessed

Augustine in his book *Of the Sayings of the Lord,* namely, that in the Lord's Prayer we ask for daily not yearly bread. There also he declares that it is as easy for a Christian never to receive the food of life, that is the Body and the Blood of Christ, as to receive it no more than once a year. *So live,* he says, *that you may be worthy to receive daily; he who is not worthy to receive daily is not worthy to receive once a year.* Nevertheless, let those who are invited to the Lord's Supper beware lest, stained with the filth of sin, they dare nigh to it unconfessed and unrepentant, and so turn the food of life into damnation unto themselves, *not,* as the blessed apostle says, *discerning the Body of the Lord.* (19; 89)

The sacrament of Communion is also mentioned in the discussion of the order of procession on Ash Wednesday (33; 103), Maundy Thursday (40; 109), Good Friday (45; 118), and Holy Saturday (48; 121) and in the description of the care for a sick monk (64; 141). Nowhere, however, is the description of the Communion so detailed as in the passage just quoted, which follows the statements about the Chapter and a revelation of the state of consciousness to a spiritual father.

The process of verbalization ended when the gnosiologic self accessed the light, that is, partook in the Eucharist. The *Regularis concordia* provides us with a sacramental vocabulary. But it does not tell us how the Sacrament fit into a hermeneutical technology of the monastic self.

The ritual of the Eucharist, which turned bread and wine into the flesh and blood of Christ, was the very center of both monastic and secular religious systems. During the Middle Ages, many claims were made in the name of the Eucharist. Some theologians, following St. Ambrose, put forth that the bread and wine were changed into the actual body and blood of Christ; others, following St. Augustine, suggested that Christ's presence in the Eucharist was only symbolic rather than physical. Throughout the centuries, the nature of the Sacrament was discussed by the best patristic and scholastic minds. As is indicated by the Eucharist controversies between Paschasius Radbertus and Ratramnus of Corbie, Berengar and Lanfranc, and St. Thomas and Ockham, for example, various preambles of faith were defined, redefined, modified, organized, and classified in the process of clarifying theology and the *logos* that calls back the body that had disappeared.[113] The controversies draw attention to the tension between the desire and the ability to produce a meaning or construct its representation, on the one hand, and, on the other, the imperatives according to which both the meaning and representation were inscribed into monastic and secular practices by the ecclesiastic authority. It is therefore not surprising to find that the reception of the Eucharist, that is, the reception by those who adhered to the idiom and by those who transgressed the adjudicated norms and the penitential systems, is constructed within a historic culture and its power relations.[114] The *Regularis concordia* articulates the most disparate experiences and local operations in the sacramental language of religion. It gives specific criteria for participation in the ritual: the Chapter, the institution of a spiritual father, the *mixtum,* the pre-Communion blessings, the gnosiologic self. This emphasis on the specific technologies of the monastic self that define and redefine the most imperceptible movements of a monk's thought may be why the *Regularis concordia* does not articulate in an equivocal manner a practice of what constitutes a central aspect of representation in the early Middle Ages—the interpretation of *Hoc est corpus meum* [This is my body]. The obligation of truth and the technologies used to access the divine light gave the discussion regarding the presence of Christ in the Eucharist a scope of a universal operation that functioned as an epistemological elucidation, rather than a technology of the self. Both labor to bring the self to the divine light, rather than describe what the light is. The *Regularis concordia,* a consuetudinary, presents us with a series of monastic codes, not with an argument that would add to the theological discussions concerning the presence of Christ in the Eucharist.

First Corinthians 11:23–26 says:

For I received from the Lord what I also delivered to you, that the Lord Jesus on the night when he was betrayed took bread, and when he had given thanks, he broke it and said, "This is my body which is for you. Do this in remembrance of me." In the same way also the cup, after supper, saying, "This cup is the new covenant in my blood. Do this, as often as you drink it in remembrance of me." For as often as you eat this bread and drink the cup, you proclaim the Lord's death until he comes.

This is the scriptural interpretation of the event that took place on the night before Jesus Christ's death. During the Mass, the actions are repeated by the celebrant. The words he says repeat the words of Christ. From the inception, the words were said, understood, and interpreted in many different ways that reflected either a ritualistic or doctrinal treatment of the Eucharist. An early discussion of the doctrinal attributes of the Eucharist was presented by Paschasius Radbertus in his *De corpore et sanguine domini* (831x833) and by Ratramnus of Corbie in his *De corpore et sanguine domini* (833x834).[115]

Paschasius Radbertus, a monk at Corbie, wrote his treatise for the Saxon monks inquiring about the liturgical changes after the Romanization of the Gallican liturgy. The Gallic liturgies emphasized a change in the species of bread and wine into the salvific presence of God; the Roman liturgy emphasized the salvific presence of Christ through the bread and the wine read as symbols.[116] These two approaches, which seemed to coexist, clashed with the introduction of the Roman liturgy into Gallic churches and with the attempt at establishing some form of uniformity. If the uniformity were to be achieved, theologians and practitioners had to resolve the eucharistic conflict embedded in these two traditions.

According to Paschasius, the body of Christ present in the Eucharist was the same body as that born of the Virgin Mary. During the Consecration, the body of Christ was present in the Eucharist—the substance of the bread and the wine was changed internally into the flesh and blood of Christ.

But since it is not proper that Christ be eaten by teeth, He wished to make truly in this mystery bread and wine into His flesh and blood by the power of the consecration of the Holy Spirit . . . so that just as real flesh was created from a virgin by the Spirit, without coition, thus from the substance of bread and wine, that same body and blood of Christ is miraculously consecrated.[117]

The divine-human existence of Christ received by the faithful observer of the Eucharist was thus united with his or her body and soul. This salvific function of the Eucharist was crucial in Paschasius's system because this unification made it possible for the believer to participate in Christ's divinity and, consequently, assure his or her own salvation.

If the Word had become flesh, and we truly consume the Word as flesh in the Lord's food, how can it not be justly judged that He dwells in us by His nature, who being God born in man, has assumed the inseparable nature of our flesh to His eternal nature in the sacrament of His flesh that was to be communicated to us.[118]

The theology of the presence of Christ, both as God and as a human being, in the Eucharist gave a physical substance and presence to the scriptural *Hoc est corpus meum.* This statement was given a different reading by Ratramnus, also a monk at Corbie. Ratramnus's *De corpore et sanguine domini* provided answers to two questions: did the faithful receive the body of Christ in mystery or in truth, and was the body and the blood in the Eucharist the same body and blood as that born of Mary? Ratramnus answered these questions by saying that Christ in the Eucharist was an image of a spiritual truth that resided elsewhere. Such an answer was possible because Ratramnus introduced a distinction between reality in truth (*in verite*), in which the nature of reality is clearly seen, and spiritual reality (*in figura*), that is, reality that signifies the existence of another hidden reality. Accordingly, the body and the blood of Christ present in the Eucharist were an example of reality *in figura,* as the bread and the wine on the altar corresponded only to the other, spiritual reality of the body and blood of Christ that could have been perceived not only by senses but also by the mind or in faith.

This is confessed most plainly by saying that in the sacrament of the body and blood of the Lord, whatever external thing is consumed is adopted to refection by the body. The mind, however, invisibly feeds on the word of God, Who is invisible bread invisibly existing in that sacrament, by the vivifying participation of faith.[119]

Thus, the answers to Ratramnus's initial two questions were that the faithful received Christ in the Eucharist in mystery and that the body of Christ, born of the Virgin Mary, was not in the Eucharist. These two statements imply that the salvific function, unlike Paschasius's salvific union of physical bodies in the Eucharist, was symbolized by a spiritual union, achieved through faith, between God-Christ and the soul of the believer. Ratramnus presented, as did St. Augustine, an understanding of physical objects in terms of how they appeared within the confines of reality in truth, even though the same objects could represent something else in spiritual reality. The Eucharist was thus a representation of the "visible" bread and wine that were quite distinct from the *res* that they signified, though they were correlated to them in a significant way through the mind and the faith of the believer. Thus, St. Augustine put forth the notion that a mystery of faith can be profitably believed but cannot be always fully examined. In this order, the truths existed rather than were examined. Accordingly, "Qui facit veritatem venit ad lucem."

In the tenth century, these two contradictory positions regarding the nature of the Eucharist coexisted. Herriger of Lobbes (ca. 940–1007) attempted to reconcile them using patristic texts.[120] Ratherius, bishop of Verona (932–68), and Remigius, master at the cathedral school at Auxerre (876/77–908), seemed to subscribe to the position described by Paschasius.[121] Atto II, bishop of Vercelli (924–61), and Aelfric, teaching at Cerne Abbas (987–1005), seemed to accept the position advanced by Ratramnus.[122] No text professes which of the two positions was favored by the monastic communities in the age of the reform movement in general and by the congregation putting together the *Regularis concordia* in particular.[123]

In the context of the discussion of the Chapter and the spiritual confession as well as the statements about the Eucharist, what is of significance is that the *Regularis concordia* provided a set of dispositions for the process of verbalization of truth—a continuous verbalization of the imperceptible movements of suggestions, images, and thoughts—that ended in a gnosiologic self accessing the light, that is, partaking in the Eucharist. The Chapter or a confession formed the technology for self-examination and self-sacrifice that produced the prerequisite conditions for the completion of the process.

The description of a daily life in a monastery in chapter 1 of the *Regularis concordia* is followed, in chapter 2, by additional information regarding the *horarium*. This information concerns the particular aspects of different offices as well as the alteration in a daily routine due to the seasonal changes of the weather.[124]

Chapters 3 through 6 deal with the proper manner in which the observances starting at the Vigil of Christmas and ending in the summer should be celebrated. Special attention is given to the most important days in the Christian religion: the Vigil of Christmas, Ash Wednesday, Palm Sunday, Maundy Thursday, Good Friday, Holy Saturday, and Easter Sunday. The offices on each of these days are described in detail. For example:

On the Vigil of Christmas, when the feast itself is announced in Chapter by the reader, the brethren shall all rise together and then genuflect, giving thanks for the unspeakable loving kindness of Our Lord Who came down to redeem the world from the snares of the devil. . . . At Vespers the psalms shall be sung with proper antiphons suitable to the fullness of time. At Nocturns on Christmas night the fourth respond shall, for extra solemnity, be sung by two cantors. After the *Te Deum laudamus* the gospel shall be read by the abbot, as is usual. . . . [T]hen all the bells shall peal and the Mass shall be celebrated. Matins shall follow, after which, if the day has not yet dawned, Lauds of All Saints shall be begun in the usual way; if, however, it is already daybreak, that office shall be said after the Morrow Mass which must itself be said in the early dawn. . . . After Prime they shall assemble for Chapter at which, when words of spiritual edification have been spoken, the brethren shall all, with lowly devotion, beg pardon of the abbot who takes place of Christ, and ask forgiveness of their many failings, saying the *Confiteor*. . . . On the Purification of St. Mary candles shall be set out ready in the church to which the brethren are to go to get their lights. . . . On entering the church, having prayed awhile, they shall say the antiphon and collect in honour of the saint to whom this same church is dedicated. Then the abbot, vested in stole and cope, shall bless the candles, sprinkling them with holy water and incensing them. (28–31; 98–99)

The consuetude not only indicates the order of the day, including the canonical hours and the description of the Chapter, but also specifies precisely the order of processions, identifies the prayers to be said, provides the texts to be sung, and describes vestments to be worn.

The mode of presentation of other observances is similar. Chapter 4, "Of the Order of the Regular Life from Septuagesima to the End of Lent," describes the observances in the following manner.

From Septuagesima until Quinquagesima *pinguedo* [fats] shall be given up, and from Quinquagesima the brethren shall observe the Lenten abstinence in the accustomed way. From Septuagesima until Maundy Thursday, when the three lessons have been read, the six psalms of the second nocturn, like those of the first, shall be most carefully sung with three antiphons taken from the psalms themselves. On Wednesdays and Fridays from the beginning of Lent until Maundy Thursday and from the Octave of Pentecost until the Calends of October processions shall be as follows: on Ash Wednesday, when None has been sung, the abbot, wearing a stole, shall bless the ashes and shall then lay the blessed ashes on the head of each brother; for to him it belongs to impose penance on his monks. Meanwhile the antiphon *Exaudi nos Domine* shall be sung with the psalm *Salvum me fac Deus*, the *Gloria, Kyrie eleison, Pater noster*, the psalm *Deus misereatur nostri, preces* and collect. They shall then proceed whithersoever they should, singing the antiphons which are in the Antiphonar. When they have reached the church to which they are bound, they shall again pray awhile and then, after the antiphon of the saint, the psalm *Ad te levavi oculos,* the *preces* and the collect, they shall there begin the Litany and return to the Mother church where the Mass shall be celebrated as usual. . . . Then the priest, deacon and subdeacon, vested in chasubles, shall fulfill their ministry. . . . Now whenever the subdeacon wears a chasuble he shall take it off when reading the epistle, and put it on again as soon as he has finished. The deacon, too, before coming forward to read the gospel, shall take off his chasuble, fold it and then adjust it crosswise about his left shoulder, making the lower end thereof fast to the girdle of his alb. When the Sacrament of Communion has been completed and before the collect is ended he shall replace the chasuble. (32–33; 102–4)

In this passage a significant stress is laid, on the one hand, on the solemnity of the Office, which was to be achieved by the proper order of prayers accompanying the symbolic events of Holy Week, and, on the other hand, on the extraliturgical details. The final lines, for example, explain the manner in which a chasuble should be worn and folded before the deacon reads the Gospel.

In addition to giving information concerning monastic celebrations, the code also regulates more mundane matters, such as indicating the time when the monks should change their shoes, shave, and have a haircut. Thus, one passage reads, "When the Chapter has been held, having taken off their shoes, they shall enter the church and as an act of obedience wash the pavement thereof while the priests and ministers of the altar wash the sacred altars with holy water" (38–39; 111). Another passage stipulates, "For the first three weeks of these days of Lent the brethren shall be unshorn; but in the middle of Lent the common duty of shaving shall be carried out and all excess of hair shall be utterly removed" (34; 105).

All these multifaceted details referring to the order of the ecclesiastical prayers, the description of liturgical paraphernalia, and the physical behavior of the monks regulate these aspects of the monastic life that are not covered in chapter 1 of the *Regularis concordia.* This unique combination of solemnity and physical elements should not be surprising if one remembers that the *Regularis concordia* aimed at institutionalizing not only monasticism but also the behavior of the monks and nuns in England at a time when laxity, simony, and secularization of offices had eroded respect for Christian worship.

This twofold purpose of this group of chapters is particularly visible in the descriptions of the *Cena Domini* (Last Supper) on Maundy Thursday and the Adoration of the Cross on Good Friday, both of which are in chapter 4 of the *Regularis concordia,* and of the candle ceremony on Holy Saturday and Nocturns on Easter Sunday, both of which are in chapter 5. The description of Nocturns is well known as it contains the *Quem quaeritis* chant. The *Quem quaeritis* passage, however, has never been discussed as part of the ceremonies described in these chapters. For this reason, it is only appropriate to present all these rulings together to direct attention to how they were to be represented within the community that was to materialize with the help of the *Regularis concordia.*

The *Cena Domini,* which follows the descriptions of the Lenten observances and offices on Palm Sunday, is presented in the following manner.

On Thursday, which is called *Cena Domini,* the night Office shall be performed according as is set down in the Antiphonar. We have also heard that, in churches of certain religious men, a practice has grown up whereby compunction of soul is aroused by means of the outward representation of that which is spiritual, namely, that when the singing of the night is over, the antiphon of the gospel finished and all the lights put out, two children should be appointed who shall stand on the right hand side of the choir and shall sing *Kyrie eleison* with clear voice; two more on the left hand side who shall answer *Christe eleison;* and, to the west of the choir, another two who shall say *Domine miserere nobis;* after which the whole choir shall respond together *Christus Dominus factus est oboediens usque ad mortem.* The children of the right-hand choir shall then repeat what they sang above exactly as before and, the choir having finished their response, they shall repeat the same thing once again in the same way. When this has been sung the third time the brethren shall say the *preces* on their knees and in silence as usual. The same order of singing shall be observed for three nights by the brethren. *This manner of arousing religious compunction was, I think, devised by Catholic men for the purpose of setting forth clearly both the terror of that darkness which, at our Lord's Passion, struck the tripartite world with unwonted fear, and the consolation of that apostolic preaching which revealed to the whole world Christ obedient to His Father even unto death for the salvation of the human race.* Therefore, it seemed good to us to insert these things so that if there be any to whose devotion they are pleasing, they may find therein the means of instructing those who are ignorant of this matter; *no one, however, shall be forced to carry out this practice against his will.* (36–37; 108–9: emphasis mine)

Consider the manner in which a new custom, a practice of certain religious men, was introduced in the *Regularis concordia* and the reasons why the custom was introduced, which are italicized in the preceding quotation. It should be remembered that this practice was used at the discretion of the community. As was the case in the description of the Vigil of Christmas, a paragraph here is an alloy of monastic details concerning the office as well as its physical execution. Thus, at least the first lines of prayers or chants are quoted, and the order of procession is specified in the part that deals with the placement of children who were to introduce an antiphonally chanted text.

The ceremony of the Adoration of the Cross took place, according to the *Regularis concordia,* after a devout veneration of the Cross by the abbot, the brethren, the town clergy, and the people. The text suggests that this ceremony was judged to be secondary in relation to the Adoration of the Cross by only the monastic community, which started at the night office with prayers, genuflection, and the reading of the lessons and the Passion; continued with the stripping from the altar of the cloth that had been under the Gospel book, done by two deacons as if they were thieves (*in modum furantis*—42; 115–16); and finally proceeded to the adoration and unveiling of the Cross. The text says that the Cross "shall straightway be set up before the altar, a space being left between it and the altar; and it shall be held by two deacons, one on either side" (42; 116). The description of the ceremony continues as follows.

Now since on that day we solemnize the burial of the Body of our Saviour, if anyone should care or think fit to follow in a becoming manner certain religious men in a practice worthy to be imitated for the strengthening of the faith of unlearned common persons and neophytes [*imitabilem ad fidem indocti uulgi ac neophytorum corroborandam*], we have decreed this only: on the part of the altar where there is space for it there shall be a representation as it were of a sepulchre [*assimilatio sepulcri*], hung about with a curtain, in which the holy Cross, when it has been venerated, shall be placed in the following manner: the deacons who carried the Cross before shall come forward and, having wrapped the Cross in a napkin there where it was venerated, they shall bear it thence, singing antiphons *In pace in idipsum, Habitabit* and *Caro mea requiescet in spe,* to the place of the sepulchre. When they have laid the cross therein, in imitation as it were of the burial of the Body of our Lord Jesus Christ [*ac si Domini Nostri Ihesu Christi corpore sepulto*] they shall sing the antiphon *Sepulto Domino, signatum est monumentum, ponentes milites qui custodirent eum.* In that same place the holy Cross shall be guarded with all reverence until the night of the Lord's Resurrection. And during the night let brethren be chosen by twos and threes, if the community be large enough, who shall keep faithful watch, chanting psalms. (44–45; 118)

Chapter 5, "Of the Manner in which the Day and Night Office Shall Be Carried Out on the Feast of Easter," focuses on Holy Saturday and Easter Sunday. It provides descriptions of the customary blessing of the new fire (None).

On Holy Saturday at the hour of None, when the abbot enters the church with the brethren, the new fire shall be brought in, as we said before, and the candle which has been placed before the altar shall be lit from that fire. Then, as is the custom, a deacon shall bless the candle saying, in the manner of reading, the prayer *Exultet iam angelica turba coelorum.* Presently, on a higher note, he shall sing *Sursum corda* and the rest. When the blessing is finished a second candle shall be lit; these two candles being held each by an acolyte, one on the right and the other on the left of the altar. After the blessing the subdeacon shall go up into the pulpit and shall read the first lesson. . . . After the prayer the sevenfold Litanies shall be begun at the entrance to the altar. Afterwards the abbot shall go down with the *schola* to bless the font. [After the collect and the threefold Litanies] all the lights of the church shall be lit, when the abbot has intoned the *Gloria in excelsis Deo,* all the bells shall peal. (47–48; 119–21)

This chapter also presents the regulations concerning other offices on that day.

On the day itself neither the Offertory, *Agnus Dei* nor Communion are sung, nor should the *Pax* be given except by those who communicate; and while Communion is being given *Alleluia* and *Laudate Dominum omnes gentes* are sung followed by the antiphon *Vespere autem sabbati* and the *Magnificat.* Thus the priest completes both the Mass and the Office of Vespers with one prayer. (48; 122–23)

Finally, on Easter Sunday, the sacrist was to take the Cross and place it in its proper place on the altar. At Nocturns (the night office) the order of the prayers was as follows: *Domine labia mea aperies, Deus in adiutorium* with *Gloria,* invitatory, three antiphons and three psalms, and three lessons with responds. The text continues:

While the third lesson is being read, four of the brethren shall vest, one of whom, wearing an alb as though for some different purpose, shall enter and go stealthily to the place of the "sepulchre" and sit there quietly, holding a palm in his hand. Then, while the third respond is being sung, the other three brethren, vested in copes and holding thuribles [censers] in their hands, shall enter in their turn and go to the place of the "sepulchre," step by step, as

dul cisone cantare· Quem queri
tis· Quodecantato fine tenus·re
spondeant hy tres uno ore Ihum·
Quibus ille· non est hic surrexit
sicut praedixerat· Ite nuntiate
quia surrexit amortuis· Cuius iussi
onis uoce uertant se illi tres adcho
rum dicentes Alta resurrexit dns
dicto hoc rursus ille residens ue
lut reuocans illos dicat antipho
nam· Venite & uidete locum;
hęc uero dicens surgat &erigat
uelũ· ostendat que eis locũ cruce
nudata· sedtantũ linteami na
posita· quibus crux inuolata erat.
Quo uiso· deponat turribula quae
gestauerant ineodem sepulchro· suma
nque linteum etextendant contra
clerũ acue luci osten dentes quod
surrexit dns &iam nonsit illo inuolu
tus· hanc canant antiphonam· sur
rexit dns desepul chro· Super po
nant quelinteum altari;
finita antiphona· prior congaudens
pro triũ pho regis nri.

British Library MS Cotton Faustina B III, f. 189: The *Quem quaeritis.*
Folio page from the *Regularis concordia* (970x973). Reprinted by permission of the British Library.

though searching for something [*pedetemptim ad similitudinem quaerentium quid*].
Now these things are done in imitation of the angel seated on the tomb [*ad imitationem angeli sedentis in monumento*] and of the women coming with perfumes to anoint the body of Jesus. When, therefore, he that is seated shall see these three draw nigh, wandering about as it were and seeking something, he shall begin to sing softly and sweetly, *Quem quaeritis*. As soon as this has been sung right through, the three shall answer together, *Ihesum Nazarenum*. Then he that is seated shall say *Non est hic. Surrexit sicut praedixerat. Ite, nuntiate quia surrexit a mortuis*. At this command the three shall turn to the choir saying *Alleluia. Resurrexit Dominus*. When this has been sung he that is seated, as though calling them back, shall say the antiphon *Venite et videte locum,* and then, rising and lifting up the veil, he shall show them the place void of the Cross and with only the linen in which the Cross had been wrapped. Seeing this the three shall lay down their thuribles in that same "sepulchre" and, taking the linen, shall hold it up before the clergy; and, as though showing that the Lord was risen and was no longer in it, they shall sing this antiphon: *Surrexit Dominus de sepulchro.* They shall then lay the linen on the altar.

When the antiphon is finished the prior, rejoicing in the triumph of our King in that He had conquered death and was risen, shall give out the hymn *Te Deum laudamus,* and thereupon all the bells shall peal. After this a priest shall say the verse *Surrexit Dominus de sepulchro* right through and shall begin Matins. (49–50; 124–27)

The text that follows the preceding passage contains the prescriptions indicating psalms for Prime, Tierce, Sext, None, Vespers, and Compline, all of which "shall be sung after the manner of Canons" (52; 131). Noteworthy is one of the changes in the arrangement prescribed by the *Regularis concordia.* The custom of the Adoration of the Holy Cross of Good Friday could be executed either in a monastic manner or by following the practice of "certain religious men." The consuetudinary does not specify who is responsible for making such a decision. It does state, however, that the latter practice can be used "if anyone should care or think fit to follow" it. A similar statement at the end of the new custom on Maundy Thursday is a good reminder that "no one . . . shall be forced to carry out this practice against his will." This being the case, how should we explain the presence of the sepulchre in this description of the night office? The sepulchre, according to the *Regularis concordia,* was legitimate only if a custom of "certain religious men" was followed on Good Friday.

The description of the celebration of the night office on Easter Sunday merits yet another detour from my main narrative regarding the *Regularis concordia,* for at least two reasons: the rubrics proceeding the *Quem quaeritis* chant have traditionally been used to justify its treatment as a liturgical ceremony in a dramatic form; and the transfer of the *Quem quaeritis* from the Introit to the Easter Mass to the Easter night office seems to have been of paramount importance for the emergence of medieval liturgical drama. Rather than following these two arguments, I will discuss the *Quem quaeritis* in the *Regularis concordia* as a singular element (or an event) that defined its individuality or whose individuality was defined by the surrounding practices to which it was assigned. By so doing, I will resingularize the *Quem quaeritis* in order for it to enunciate its position in the *Regularis concordia.*

Chapters 3 through 6 of the *Regularis concordia* narrate the manner in which the observances starting at the Vigil of Christmas and ending in the summer should be celebrated. The Vigil of Christmas and the celebrations of Holy Week are given special treatment. The offices on each of these days are recounted at length, in text that mixes liturgical and extraliturgical statements regarding the proper celebration of the Nativity, Passion, and Resurrection: the order of processions, the prayers to be said, the texts to be chanted, and the vestments to be worn are specified.

The passage referring to the night office on Easter begins with the order of parts of canonical hours to be celebrated on that day and the vestments to be worn: "While the third lesson is being read, four of the brethren shall vest, one of whom, wearing an alb as if for some other purpose, shall enter and go stealthily to the place of the sepulchre" (49; 124–25). Consider the description of the procession on Palm Sunday:

When that Mass is over the greater procession shall take place; and it shall be held, as we have said above, in the following manner: that is, the brethren, vested in albs, if this can be done and the weather permits, shall go to the church where the palms are, silently, in the order of procession and occupied with psalmody. (34–35; 105–6)

Then, the text that should be chanted during Easter Nocturns is provided. This is a characteristic feature of all of the offices—the chants and antiphons prescribed for the proper celebration of a Christian worship. Usually the titles or first lines are given because the full text would have been known by a monk or, otherwise, could have been found in either a prayer book or a *Troparium,* a collection of chants. In the celebration of the *Cena Domini,* for example, the execution of the chant is similar to that of the *Quem quaeritis;* that is, it is sung in a form of responses to a previous line. After the chant, the hymn *Te Deum laudamus* is to be sung, the bells "shall peal," and Matins will begin. We are told that the usual Office of All Saints will not be sung after the Easter Matins and during the whole week. The description of other canonical hours of the day and processions follow.

The *Quem quaeritis* passage has been assigned a significant place in theater history because it contains extraliturgical elements that could be viewed as a theatrical description of a performance. These extraliturgical elements are not, however, present only in this passage, as they can be found in the documentation of other offices, for example, in the previously quoted description of the *Cena Domini* celebrated on Maundy Thursday. Both texts describe some form of movement and make use of what is specifically labeled as "outward representation." During Nocturns on Maundy Thursday, two children stand on the right-hand side of the choir and two of them are positioned on the left-hand side of the choir. During Nocturns on Easter Day, one of the brethren is seated near a "sepulchre" and three others approach him. Both of the offices make use of the antiphonally sung chant.

Another factor frequently mentioned is the theatrical quality of the rubrics for the Easter night office. For example, "these things are done in imitation of the angel seated on the tomb and of the women coming with perfumes to anoint the body of Jesus." The word *imitation* has been a key to many interpretations of the *Quem quaeritis* passage as a documentation of early drama and theater in the Middle Ages. However, in an excerpt from one of the observances on Good Friday, the following statement can be found.

Now since on that day we solemnize the burial of the Body of our Saviour, if anyone should care or think fit to follow in a becoming manner certain religious men in a practice worthy to be imitated for the strengthening of the faith of unlearned common persons and neophytes, we have decreed this only: on the part of the altar where there is space for it there shall be a representation as it were of a sepulchre, hung about with a curtain, in which the holy Cross, when it has been venerated, shall be placed . . . where they have laid the moss therein, in imitation as it were of the burial of the Body of our Lord Jesus Christ, they shall sing the antiphon: *Sepulto Domino, signatum est monumentum, ponentes milites qui custodirent eum.* (44–45; 118–19).

Two phrases stand out in this passage: (1) "on the part of the altar where there is space for it *there shall be a representation as it were of a sepulchre [assimilatio sepulchri]*" and (2) "[w]hen they have laid the cross therein, *in imitation as it were of the burial of the Body of our Lord Jesus Christ [ac si Domini Nostri Ihesu Christi corpore sepulto]*." Both of them refer to some form of imitation and representation.

Before I proceed to a discussion of the use of representation in these chapters of the *Regularis concordia,* another aspect of the *Quem quaeritis* scholarship needs to be addressed—the explanations of the shift of the *Quem quaeritis* presented by Young (1933) and Hardison (1965) and still accepted. According to Young, a dialogue between the Marys and the angel at the sepulchre in the early morning had its only appropriate place at Matins (Nocturns), the first canonical hour of a monastic day; in this position, the dramatic potential of the *Quem quaeritis* was fully realized, and the trope "achieved a generous amount of literary freedom, and developed into an authentic Easter play."[125] Hardison, however, suggested that the shift occurred as "a result of anticipation, especially in the monastic churches that are the sources of all tenth-century manuscripts, [the *Quem quaeritis*] was detached from the Vigil Mass and moved to the only other liturgical occasion associated closely with the Resurrection—the end of matins [Nocturns] and Easter Mass."[126]

This detour from my main narrative questions not the significance of the new position of the *Quem quaeritis* for the emergence of medieval liturgical drama but how the tenth-century English monastic practice, part of which is recorded in the *Regularis concordia,* transformed the mode of existence and functioning of the *Quem quaeritis,* which, until the Winchester Synod in 970x973, was associated with the Introit to the Easter Mass. The *Quem quaeritis* redefined its individuality each time it emerged in a liturgical manuscript of any kind.

One of the ineluctable consequences of this statement is that the chant will always disrupt the totality of its history within a framework preassigned by the historian. This assumption goes against traditional recourses: (1) the historical-transcendental recourse, that is, an attempt to find an original foundation and a project of a tautological unity; (2)

the empirical recourse, that is, the process of designating the founder and describing the traditions and influences; (3) the scientific recourse, that is, the practice of the discovery of the latent order through substituting categories known to us (e.g., what theater and drama are to us) for a complex system in which the object could have functioned differently; and (4) the narrative recourse, that is, the inscription of the complex structures into the readable form of a historical investigation.

The *Regularis concordia* gives not only descriptions but also regulations concerning the Office of Holy Week. For example, on Maundy Thursday and Good Friday, the night office (about 2 A.M.) "shall be performed according as it is set in the Antiphonar" (36, 41; 108, 115). On Holy Saturday, the offices shall be celebrated according to the rules of *Ordo Romanus Primus* (47; 119). And on Easter Day,

the seven canonical hours are to be celebrated by monks in the Church of God after the manners of Canons, out of regard for the authority of the blessed Gregory, Pope of the Apostolic See, as set forth in his Antiphonar. (49, 123)

The offices of Holy Week were to be conducted either according to the rules as set by the Antiphonar[127] or by the *Ordo Romanus Primus*.[128] The employment of the secular Office in a monastery may seem contrary to the nature of the *Regularis concordia,* which attempted to draw a sharp demarcation line between the secular and monastic traditions. However, as Jude Woerdeman points out, such a substitution of the Roman (secular) for the Benedictine (monastic) Office was not an uncommon occurrence at that time.[129] It seems that monastic communities had an option regarding the celebration of Holy Week: the monks did not have to follow the elaborate Gallic order and could follow either the observances as prescribed by the Benedictine *Rule* or those specified by the Antiphonar or the *Ordo Romanus Primus* and thus use the order of processions for secular churches. Different monastic houses used either of the two traditions. For example, the Customs of Farfa (1030–48) show that Cluny followed the Roman order from Maundy Thursday to the night office on Holy Saturday and the Benedictine *Rule* for Prime, Tierce, Sext, None of the Holy Saturday, and the Office on Easter.[130] In comparison, a Lotharingian monastic code suggests that the Roman Office be used from the night office of Maundy Thursday to the end of Easter Week.

The celebrations of Holy Week as defined by the monastic and Roman codes varied considerably. The monastic Office for Easter Day as specified in the Benedictine *Rule* gave the following directions for the night office: the brethren were to rise at about 1 A.M. and go to the church where they would chant six psalms. Then four lessons with their responses would be read. Afterward, six other psalms with antiphons would be sung. Four more lessons with their responsories, three canticles, and the *Alleluia* would follow. Then another four lessons from the New Testament and responsories would be read, and when the fourth responsory was finished, *Te Deum laudamus* would be chanted. When this chant was completed, the abbot would read the Gospel. After the Gospel, the hymn *Te decet laus* would be chanted and the blessing would be given. Then Matins would begin.[131]

The Roman Office that is included in the *Ordo Romanus Primus* indicates that the secular observation of the night office was much shorter. It would begin with the hymn *Deus in auditorium,* which would be followed by the regular invitatory psalm and its alleluias. Then three other psalms with their antiphons would be sung. Afterward, only three lessons, each followed by a responsory, would be read. When the lessons were finished, *Te Deum laudamus* would be chanted. Then Matins would begin.[132] The major difference in the practice of the night office on Easter Day was that in the secular Office, instead of twelve psalms, three canticles, twelve lessons, and twelve responsories, only three psalms, three lessons, and three responsories were prescribed. Another difference was that there was no Gospel reading in the secular tradition.

Since the *Regularis concordia* followed the *Ordo Romanus Primus,* there was no Gospel reading during the Easter night office. This omission, according to Woerdeman, was of "major" consequence for theater history.

> Those [who] would try to preserve the Roman Paschal Office, would likely try to preserve as much solemnity from the monastic rite as possible. The introduction of the dramatized Easter trope [the *Quem quaeritis*] in the place of the Gospel does precisely that. It retains the sacred ministers, vestments, the incense, and provides the message of the Gospel itself. . . . The simplest motive which suggests itself as most plausible is that the ceremony compensated for the omission of the Gospel reading.[133]

Although Woerdeman offers a very attractive explanation of the shift of the *Quem quaeritis,* there are some questions to be raised. First of all, if the monks had wanted to "preserve as much of the solemnity of the monastic rite as possible," could not they have employed the Benedic-

84

tine Office for Easter Day as was the case at Cluny? Second, was the *Quem quaeritis* really a substitution for the omission of the Gospel reading? The order of the observances of the night office in the *Regularis concordia* is as follows.

[After the opening psalms] three antiphons and three psalms shall follow; and when these are finished the proper verse shall be said; and then three lessons with the appropriate responds. (49; 124)

Then, after the third response, one of the brethren "shall begin to sing softly and sweetly *Quem quaeritis*" (50; 125). When this is finished, the antiphon *Surrexit Dominus de sepulchro* and the *Te Deum laudamus* follow. Afterward, Matins begins.

As is apparent, in this section the only difference between the *Ordo Romanus Primus* and the *Regularis concordia* is that the latter prescribes two additional chants to be sung before the *Te Deum laudamus:* the *Quem quaeritis* and the *Surrexit Dominus de sepulchro.* Were they a substitute for the Gospel that the *Ordo Romanus Primus* prescribed to be read after the *Te Deum laudamus?*

To provide an answer to this question, consider, for example, the third responsory of the night office:

On Sunday, Mary Magdalene, Mary of Jacob, and Salome carried ointment, so that they might anoint Jesus. Alleluia. *Verse.* They approached the tomb with great feeling which arose in them on that Sunday morning.[134]

This responsory, which occurs after the third lesson that is based on the Gospel, prepares the monastic congregation for the chant that is to follow, that is, the *Quem quaeritis*. The *Quem quaeritis,* then, could be seen as both a part of the responsory and an introduction to the *Te Deum laudamus* rather than a substitution for the Gospel reading.[135] The musical analyses of the *Quem quaeritis* by Susan Rankin, Aselme Davril, and Andrew Hughes argue not only that it was a completely balanced structure musically but also that its musical settings, the structure, and the text were directly related to the responsory. And these analyses explain how the *Quem quaeritis* functioned within the confines of the observances on Easter Sunday.[136]

Whereas the function and the nature of the *Quem quaeritis* can be explained by the discussion of the musical, verbal, and structural components, the representational and performative practices that are linked to and made acceptable by the *Regularis concordia* require further analysis. In the celebration of Holy Week, not only does the *Regularis concordia* make use of the *Ordo Romanus Primus,* rather than the Benedictine *Rule,* but it also modifies certain parts of the offices that are not specified either in a secular consuetudinary or a monastic code. For example, the night office on Maundy Thursday should follow the rules as set down in the Antiphonar. Instead, the *Regularis concordia* introduces a new custom in the execution of the *Cena Domini,* a custom that was practiced "in churches of certain religious men." The *Regularis concordia* does not specify who these religious men were; rather, it focuses on a new manner of celebration of the Office, the *Cena Domini,* which belongs to the night office. The order of psalms, antiphons, lessons, and responsories for the night office is specified by the Antiphonar of the Roman Office. Therefore, after the last responsory, the Gospel, and the blessing, the next canonical hour should begin. However, the *Regularis concordia* institutes a new custom right after the Gospel: the *Kyrie eleison* is sung. The chant is introduced in the following manner.

We have also heard that, in churches of certain religious men, a practice has grown up whereby compunction of soul is aroused by means of the outward representation of that which is spiritual. (36; 108)

A detailed description of how two groups of boys positioned on the right- and left-hand sides of the choir should sing the *Kyrie eleison* comes next. A similar divergence from the Roman code can be seen in the Easter night office. The new custom of the *Quem quaeritis* is preceded by a detailed description of how four brethren should sing the chant.

Moreover, both chants were a part of the liturgy of the Mass proper; that is, they functioned as choral pieces in the Roman Mass—the *Kyrie eleison* was sung before the *Gloria in excelsis,* and the *Quem quaeritis* was chanted before the Introit on Easter Day. Both were "moved" to a new position. The new placement of the chants implies a shift in their mode of existence; that is, an attempt was made by the monastic authorities to elaborate on the customs that were prescribed by the Roman Office for Holy Week. Furthermore, the new position of the chants suggests a shift in their mode of functioning; that is, a step was taken in the direction of increasing the spiritual value of the night office in general and of those important feasts in the monastic tradition in particular. This shift in the mode of existence and functioning was authorized by a direct statement that they were employed for "the outward representation of that which is spiritual."

Whether or not this "outward representation" was drama depends on current taxonomies that define drama as (1) a combination of dialogue and mimetic action; (2) a combination of dialogue, setting, and impersonation; (3) a ritual performance. The seven theatrical categories used to describe the *Quem quaeritis*—that is, liturgical drama (Chambers), play (Young), play of a ritual drama (Hardison), dramatic office (Craig), liturgical music drama (Smoldon), dramatic resurrection ceremony (Bjork), and performance ceremony (Norton)—exemplify various procedures of intervention and legitimation that have been inherited from other scholarly traditions or that the scholars have established to advance their theories. However, how was representation inscribed into the practice? How was it defined? What aspects of representation were made acceptable in a monastic institution as defined in and by the *Regularis concordia*?

In the discussion of the monastic Chapter and the sacrament of the Eucharist, I indicated the process of institutionalization of the self and the formation of a close-range relationship between reality in truth and spiritual reality. Is it possible that these representational practices were correlated, dependent on each other, or transforming one another in a simultaneous interplay of their specific attributes, both visible and invisible, whose traces escaped the spatial trajectories of that which can be enunciated in the *Regularis concordia*?

For the post-Renaissance order of things, representation is connected with the problem of depth, that is, with a perspectival view of space— with the process of transforming the entire picture into a material surface on which the spatial continuum is projected. The image of the object is a cross section through a visual pyramid. The word *perspective* acquires a very specific meaning in this definition. As Dürer stated, *perspective* comes from a Latin word that means "seeing through."[137] Although *perspectiva* appeared already in Boethius's interpretation of Aristotle, the word was characterized there as a subdiscipline of geometry, rather than in terms of optics as suggested by Dürer.[138] Medieval mystics and Christian theologians advanced arguments that were closer to Plotinus's parallel projection than to Euclid's optical and geometrical formulations.[139]

For Plotinus, the image was the reflection of the subject. It needed to perform such a function in a system of reversion to source: all forms and phases of Existence flow, according to Plotinus, from the Divinity, and all strive to return to Divinity. The Divinity is a graded triad of the One, the First Existent, who transcends all knowable; the Divine Mind, the first thinker or the Divine Intellectual Principle, who connotes the highest reality knowable; and the All-Soul, the first and only principle of life or Universal Soul, who is the expression of the outgoing energy of the Divinity. The human soul is the All-Soul set in touch with the lower existence. In other words, the human soul is the All-Soul particularized for the space of the mortal life of a human being. This particularization is a necessary condition for the establishment of the modes of functioning of the All-Soul. These are the Intellectual Soul, untouched by matter, whose acts are identical with the Intellectual Principle in a human being; the Reasoning Soul, which connotes the nature of a human being, that is, will, imagination, and memory; and the Unreasoning Soul, which is equated with human emotions. In this model, salvation is possible when an individual becomes conscious of what she/he is already in her/his inmost nature, where Intellect, which is beyond the virtues, identifies itself with true being and with the idea that one forms of the self, the world, and God. This salvation is thus defined by a simultaneous movement upward from below and inside. This double movement, during which one is lifted out of the body into oneself and becomes external to all things, produces self-knowledge. Self-knowledge provides access to that which is the highest reality knowable, in this case the knowledge of God.

Consequently, all human activities should imitate spiritual things, a movement upward and inside, rather than material things. Thus, both the subject and the image are of the same nature: that is, the function of the image is not to reproduce the appearance of the subject but to allow a human being to perceive the Universal Soul, the Intellect. Only when this happens can an individual become conscious of what she/he is already in her/his inmost nature, where Intellect identifies itself with the True Being and with the idea one forms of the self, the world, and God. Plotinus's statutes of representation assert that to achieve knowledge of the Universal Soul, the observer needs to be acquainted with the physical nature of vision in general and with the reduction in size, the change in color, and the clarity of shapes of distant objects in particular. Plotinus maintained that the subject is represented in its completeness only if its representation is faithful to the true size and color of the subject. This can only be the case if the representation of the subject is very close to the eye of the observer—only such a view guarantees that all the details are assessed correctly. Consequently, distant objects are difficult to determine, and thus they are imperfect. So are their features, which are not fully seen. For the image to be a true representation of the subject, the subject needs to be shown in the foreground, in the fullness of light, in all its details, and, of course, without shadows. Accordingly, depth is to be avoided, because depth engenders shadow, ambiguity, or uncertainty.

In Plotinus's view, the eye had to become "equal and similar to the object [subject] in order to contemplate it." He maintained, "one can never see the sun without becoming similar to it, and soul can never contemplate beauty without being beautiful itself."[140] This contemplation could only be achieved with the "inner" eye rather than the physical eye of the body. Similar arguments were advanced in the *Regularis concordia*'s discussion of the Chapter and the Eucharist.

These statements found their particular setting and formation in other representational practices of the time. Consider, for example, the miniatures in the *Benedictional of St. Aethelwold* created in Winchester about 973 (or as other sources indicate, sometime between 971 and 984).[141] In his analysis of a miniature of the Nativity (fol. 15v) and of a miniature of Saint Swithun (fol. 97v), Robert Deshman observes that both these miniatures "drew a symbolic equivalency between the architectural components of the material church and the faithful who with Christ constitute the spiritual edifice of the Church." He concluded, "Though they use very different means, these two pictures basically express the same theme of the living Ecclesia."[142]

The benedictional contains twenty-eight full-page miniatures.[143] Of special interest for this study is folio 51v, which depicts the visit to the sepulchre. The miniature is within a frame, each corner of which is an ornamental flower-shaped composition of dark red/brown, yellow, blue, and green leaves embracing a gold square and a gold circle inside it. The four corners are connected by double gold bars, inside of which the leaf pattern and the color scheme are repeated. The background is green as in some other miniatures.[144] Most of the space within the frame is taken by a sepulchre, an often repeated motif of a long and narrow Byzantine-like building of the *Ecclesia*, of which one side and the facade are visible. The dark red/brown side has a dark blue opening through which a light blue linen cloth may be seen. The facade is dark red/brown. The top is a

British Library ADD 49598, f. 51v: The Visit to the Sepulchre. Folio
page from the *Benedictional of Saint Aethelwold* (ca. 973; 971x984).
Reprinted by permission of the British Library.

blue and dark red/brown gabled roof with two towers with domes on the further side. In front of the sepulchre, an angel with expanded wings is seated on a large pink-and-gold hewn stone. He is wearing a blue tunic and a gold undershirt. His wings are gold and yellow. His right hand is raised in benediction. In his left hand, he holds a gold wand or a scepter. On the right side, there are three Marys: the one in front is within the space of the miniature; the other two behind her are inside the frame. They are wearing long tunics in the shades of red, blue, and yellow. The one in front carries a censer and an unguent pot. The other one holds only an unguent pot. On the left side, behind the tomb and inside the frame, four soldiers armed with long spears and round shields are standing asleep.

Even this brief description of the pictorial components of the miniature suggests that there is no attempt made to limit the field of visibility to the scriptural narrative depicted inside the frame. This becomes even more obvious when the light, which falls on the folio page, makes the gold illuminations stand out and attract the attention of the viewer. The visit to the sepulchre and its scriptural *logos* find their equivalency not in the composition of the scene but in the objects that are trapped in gold. The choice of objects is not accidental and includes the parts of the hewn stone; the wings, the halo, and the garment of the angel; the censer; the unguent pots; the parts of the sepulchre/building; and the double gold bars of the frames. Neither is it accidental that the phrase "Benedicat uos omnipotens deus," the beginning of the benediction for Easter Sunday,[145] is also trapped in a gold frame on the opposite page (fol. 52). That frame is almost identical to the one on the left folio page of the manuscript except for the leaf ornaments in the midsection, which are a substitute for the soldiers and the Marys. The inscription within the frame consists of a gold initial "B," inside of which there are "e" and "ne," and, below it in two rows, "dicatu os / omps ds."

Unlike the miniatures with the image of a medieval city, which both identify narratives—for example, the narratives of the Annunciation, the Adoration of the Magi, Christ's entry to Jerusalem, the descent of the Holy Spirit, and the feast of St. Benedict—and place a historical subject in a collapsed space (divine and remembered location) and time (divine and historic), here there is only a homogeneous space.[146] There is no depth, no horizon, no separation between the planes.[147] There is only "smooth" space that the eye cannot transform into a recognizable spectrum of meanings and certainties; the eye cannot establish the points of reference that will allow it to order this space into a series of rational elements placing the self on the theological/historical map. There is no external visual model, like a cityscape, that can give rise to an immobile reality locating the observer. On the contrary, the homogeneity of space encourages the eye to abandon the desire to order it. Instead, the eye of the beholder is seduced by a possibility of being able to see at close range that which cannot be grasped or understood with the preestablished points of reference. The figures and the objects as well as the first part of the benediction, all of which are trapped in gold, function in this topography like orientation signs that do not reproduce a knowable landscape. They allow the self or the eye to move through different, unstriated planes to know through these objects the mystery, rather than a theological meaning, of the resurrection of Christ and the power of the *Ecclesia,* where now this image is positioned. No eye orders this image, but the visual and verbal elements provide access to the spiritual dimension. This spiritual dimension is identified with the movement upward and inside, where the knowledge of God can bestow beauty on these material objects and things.

If one abandons the post-Renaissance notion of representation, it may be suggested that all these practices, including Maundy Thursday's *Kyrie eleison* and Easter Sunday's *Quem quaeritis,* were closer to Plotinus's parallel projection, which invited the possibility that the eye could perform a nonoptical and nongeometrical function. In the visit to the sepulchre on Easter Sunday, the three Marys and the angel seated at the tomb allowed a monk to move in a direction not contained in a physical reality of the self. No human eye ordered this space: "no line separates earth from sky, which are of the same substance; there is neither horizon nor background nor perspective nor limit nor outline of form nor center."[148]

If the function of the Chapter or the spiritual confession was to produce truth that provides access to light, this light, *lux,* was the practice, the truth, and the reason for the unity in both the *Ecclesia* and a monastic house. Monks participating in the celebrations of Holy Week partook in the mystery of spiritual reality. The practices for arousing religious compunction were clearly described in unambiguous terms—they functioned as the outward representation of that which is spiritual. As the *Regularis concordia* affirms, "[t]his manner of arousing religious compunction was, I think, devised by Catholic men for the purpose of setting forth clearly both the terror of that darkness which, at our Lord's

Passion, struck the tripartite world with unwonted fear, and the consolation of that apostolic preaching which revealed to the whole world
Christ obedient to His Father even unto death for the salvation of the
human race" (37; 109).

Thus, the process of bringing truth to full light was associated not
with reproducing the appearance but, as the discussion of the Chapter,
the confession, the Communion, Plotinus's parallel projection, and the
miniatures in the *Benedictional of St. Aethelwold* suggest, with accessing
the light of spiritual reality. Recall the sections of the *Regularis concordia*
devoted to the Chapter and the confession—both fashioned the practices for the external and material representation of the most imperceptible movement of the monk's thought. Here, the events unfolding
within the hermeneutic monastic community during the Easter night
office attest to this: "Now things are done in imitation of the angel
seated on the tomb and the women coming to anoint the body of Jesus"
(50; 125). A gnosiologic self needed to lose its own consciousness to be
able to access the inner location defined by the *Regularis concordia* as the
site of a prayer (a prayer comes "from the heart rather than from the
lips"—chap. 1) and contemplate the mystery: "Quem quaeritis? . . . Ihesum Nazarenum. . . . Non est hic. Surrexit sicut praedixerat. Ite, nuntiate quia surrexit a mortuis" (50; 125). A gnosiologic self needed to lose
its own consciousness to be able to externalize, verbalize, and fully
rejoice that "He had conquered death and was risen" (50; 125). *Te Deum
laudamus* and the pealing of bells are the only appropriate manifestations
of this truth.[149]

If we can lift from the practices described here the post-Renaissance
concept of representation, defined in terms of doubling (Plato), transfer
from a real site to an imaginary site (Aristotle), or perspectival organization of monocular vision (Alberti), the observances introduced in the
Regularis concordia are examples of representational practices wrenched
away from their visual configurations and structures of recognition. Like
the Chapter and the spiritual confession, these observances were to
ensure a proper and solemn execution of the Christian dogma by a gnosiologic self. Whereas the Chapter and the spiritual confession were the
technologies for self-examination in front of the abbot or a senior
official, the *Cena Domini* and the celebration of the resurrection of Christ
were the observances externalizing and verbalizing the most important
feasts in the Christian religion. To this process, I would like to give the
name of *gnosiologic representation*.

Chapter 7 of the *Regularis concordia* describes the position of the *circa*, a monk who was appointed in accordance to the ordinance of the Benedictine *Rule* to look after the entire cloister and its inhabitants. One of his numerous duties, besides disclosing to the Chapter the names of brethren who were "given to some vanity," was to go about the choir during Nocturns and leave his lantern in front of any brother who had fallen asleep.[150]

Chapters 8 and 9 refer to the manner in which Offices of Whit Week and Tense Days should be celebrated. As in the case of the previous chapters referring to the most important observances of the Catholic church, the prayers, lessons, and canticles are prescribed by the *Regularis concordia*. This order was mandatory throughout the summer until the calends of November.

Chapter 10 deals with hospitality to strangers, guests, and the poor, with special recommendations for charity to the poor. The *Regularis concordia* specifically indicates that there should be a special place assigned for the reception of the poor, attendance on whom is treated as the common duty of all—*schola*, monks, and the abbot. Particularly, the abbot bears a special responsibility in this regard. As the code suggests, he should devote himself to the poor as often as "leisure and opportunity suggests" (61; 139). In addition, in compliance with the Benedictine *Rule*, on their arrival, the service of the Maundy was rendered to the poor. On their departure, they were to be given provisions for their journey. Moreover, each monastery would support a number of poor men from whom three would be chosen each day to receive the Maundy service and food from the monks' table.

Chapter 11 regulates the behavior of the monks who are not accustomed to their duties of the *munditiae* on Saturday and stresses the rule of obedience and modesty.[151]

The next chapter is an elaborate prescription for the ceremonies and suffrages to be followed after the death of a monk. When a brother could no longer endure his sickness, he was allowed to stay in the sick house, where he was attended by servants. The Morrow Mass was celebrated daily for his recovery. After the Mass, the whole community would visit him and sing the penitential psalms. When he felt better, the visiting was discontinued; however, when a monk was dying, it was customary to visit him until his death. The *Regularis concordia* is very specific in providing all the pertinent information of how to arrange a funeral ceremony. It indicates the garments in which a deceased should be dressed, the appropriate time for the funeral, the text of a *breve* (a death notice) to be dispatched to neighboring monasteries, and the prayers that should be said for the peace of his soul.

The *Regularis concordia* ends with a short postscript, or *Epilogus* (included in only one of the two surviving manuscripts), which frees the monasteries from paying the heriot (the customary tax) that was due the king at the death of lay owners of extensive property. Instead, on the death of an abbot or abbess, if any superabundance of goods was found, it was to be used to furnish the needs of the brethren and the poor.

The *Regularis concordia* thus gives a complete and detailed account of the duties of monastic life and the particulars of the manner of the celebration of the solemn liturgy of the church and intercession. Life in the monastic community was centered around the abbot, elected among the members of the order "according to the Rule," with the advice of the king. The abbot was the *pater spiritualis* of the whole community, and his functions in a monastery were prescribed by and defined by the *Rule* of St. Benedict. He was assisted in his work by provosts, deans (each in charge of a group of ten or more monks), and other officials, such as a sacrist; the *magister* in charge of the children of the *schola;* the cantor; and the *circa,* whose duty was to maintain order in the buildings mapping out the monastic topography.[152] The monastic life itself was organized around the prayers constituting the night office (Nocturns) and the seven day hours. The *Regularis concordia* specifies how a regular monastic day should be executed. The document recounts also a number of extra devotional practices: Offices of All Saints and of the Dead; the *Trina oratio;* psalms and prayers for the royal house; the gradual and penitential psalms; litanies; the daily Morrow Mass and Principal Mass; the Chapter; and the daily Maundy for the poor—most of which can be found in the accepted European monastic practices of the tenth century.[153]

Another addition that had only English usage were the prayers for the royal house celebrated after each of the canonical hours except Prime. The reason for this connection between the monastic and national life is explained in the *Regularis concordia* by the first words of the *Proem.* The monks and nuns recognized their king and queen as ex officio patrons of the whole monastic community. As Knowles maintains, this peculiar connection between the church and the state could not be found in any other European country at that period of time.

Moreover, he believes that

the special prayers for Edgar and his consort said after every portion of the Office save Prime, together with the offering of the Matin Mass for the same intention, are quite peculiar to England and must have given to the intercessory prayers of all the monks and nuns a strongly national sentiment.[154]

More importantly, the royal patronage contributed to the growing force of the monastic revolution. The monks needed endowments, land, and the king's protection against the lay ownership of monasteries [*saecularium prioratus*].[155] The king needed their advice in the affairs of state. The king and the monks had a common interest; that is, the monastic houses inhabited by clerics were supported by and represented the investment of local aristocrats in the church. The replacement of the clerics with the monks gave the king strong supporters for his administrative and political policies. The act of expulsion not only shifted the traditional tenurial practices, in which the owners of the estates expected to maintain their power over the ecclesiastical property often situated on the estate, but also established a new group that acquired a powerful executive voice. This may be argued especially when it is remembered that the monks came from the Anglo-Saxon upper classes, that the abbots participated in the court of the king and his magnates as well as in local shire courts, that the bishops were the heads of the local government once Edgar excluded the royal *ministri* (aldermen and the local thanes) from some of the church's estates, and, finally, that the monks' prominent status with the royal family would have also had some significance for their relatives at home.[156]

This close dependence on the royal house was also due to the fact that papal influence in England was minimal. By contrast, in Burgundy, where lay power was considerably weak, the abbots of Cluny defended their status by forging strong links with the papacy.[157] In England, as the *Proem* of the *Regularis concordia* declares, the king, rather than the pope, deposed the negligent clerks of their offices and, in their stead, placed monks in the numerous churches that became centers of monastic life in the following years. Bearing this coda in mind, it is easier to understand yet another solely English addition to the *Regularis concordia,* that is, the rule according to which the abbatial election was subject to royal approval.[158] There was also an inclusion made that when the community served a cathedral church, the monks would elect the bishop, who would conform his life to the monastic *Rule*. Then he would live in common with his clerks and would make them follow its prescriptions.

At the same time, the relationship between the king and the monks during the reform movement is complicated by a different formation that has its own structure, practices, and procedures of operation and formation. It is assumed in the *Regularis concordia* that the place of the clerks would be taken by the monks, who would entirely rebuild the structure of Christian religion in England according to the program envisioned and commanded by Dunstan, Aethelwold, and Oswald.

Because of this program, different offices received a careful and elaborate treatment in the document. Recall, for example, the Chapter, an exercise in the technology of a monastic self, which has been extensively discussed. Another office was the daily Maundy, an observance of charity, which had been stressed in the Benedictine *Rule* because in the poor "Christ is received and must be adored."[159]

All these additional offices of the *Regularis concordia* indicate its significance in relation to other European consuetudinaries in terms of the monastic life. Moreover, the document represents the labor to define the monk's everyday life inside and outside a monastery: the daily routine and human necessities; a proper time for washing, shaving, cutting hair, changing shoes, and going to toilets; the time for physical and intellectual work; the time for reading and copying manuscripts; the time for work in the kitchen and bake house; or the time for the necessary repairs in the monastic buildings.

Particularly stressed in the *Regularis concordia* are the rules concerning the behavior of monks. They were to abide by the rule of silence and reverence (20, 25, 55; 90, 95, 131). Recreational conversation both in the monastery and while on a journey was expressly forbidden. Also, the monks should not kiss and embrace; nor should they be in the company of boys without a third person present. Undoubtedly, all these regulations were put forth to strengthen the morals of the brethren the same way as the sprinkling of the holy water in a dormitory before bedtime was to be done "on account of the illusions of the evil one" (24; 94).

Yet another set of rules in the *Regularis concordia* are those that were connected with the proper celebration of the offices. Their purpose was to unify or to increase the solemnity of the main holidays in the Christian religion. We are told that the descriptions reflected either the old customs or tradition introduced by "certain religious men" (44; 118). The chapters that are concerned with the manner in which the Vigil of

Christmas, Lent, Palm Sunday, Maundy Thursday, Good Friday, Holy Saturday, and Easter Sunday should be conducted are a curious combination of religious spiritual rhetoric and descriptions of their gnosiologic representations.

All these regulations can be matched with the regulations in either the Benedictine *Rule* or other European consuetudinaries of the tenth century. The *Regularis concordia* has, however, a few provisions in which allusions are made to English practice. Thus, for example, a fire is allowed in a special room in the winter, and the monks could work in a shelter instead of a cloister when the weather was bad. On Christmas and certain other feasts, the pealing of bells was prolonged according to national tradition.[160] Moreover, processions took place not in the monastic building alone, as was the custom on the Continent, but in the streets lying between the monastic church and one of the town's parochial churches. Also, townspeople were allowed to participate in the principal Mass on Sundays and in feasts. This was an unprecedented regulation in the history of monasticism, since the Benedictine *Rule* explicitly forbade any contact with the lay population. This was also the main reason that all other celebrations took place behind the closed door of a monastery.

On the level of discursive practice, the *Regularis concordia* registered and gave visibility to the practices within its narrative space that secured their acceptance: as St. Augustine stated, "Qui facit veritatem venit ad lucem." By so doing, it institutionalized the behavior of monks and nuns by fashioning a technology of the self that enabled them to transform within a hermeneutical reality of a monastic topography. Since a self was an obscure text in need of permanent governmentality in order not to regress to the strongly wrought in pathways of a clerical life, a self's mode of functioning and existence as well as a self's relation to its own physical and mental body were continually verified in the moment of their utterance.

These practices of verification are not always clearly visible on the narrative space of the *Regularis concordia*. The consuetudinary articulates, however, the newly designed behaviors and practices: "Qui facit veritatem venit ad lucem." The obligation of making of truth provided an access to other narrative spaces attached to the space of the document. The power/knowledge relationships between 970 and 973, the Chapter, the sacrament of the Eucharist, and the observances of Holy Week left within a discursive space the remanences of representational practices. These specific practices, recorded in the *Regularis concordia*, suggest that the obligation of truth and the function of light (*lux*) modified the space of representation. Within it, a gnosiologic self (the Chapter), reality in truth and spiritual reality (the Eucharist), and gnosiologic representation (the *Quem quaeritis*) were simultaneously present and actively participating in defining and redefining their most imperceptible movements. What made them acceptable and recordable in the tenth-century consuetudinary was a brief moment when all those practices were stabilized in a place that actualized its theological space.

However, this stabilization was as ephemeral as the thought that conceived it. With the changes in a discursive formation, the discourse on representation was also transformed to produce elements that could be inscribed to the practices anew and accepted by the authority and its administrative regulations. As the *Regularis concordia* shows, representation, as it is coded into practices, is assigned a status. This status legitimizes its movement into various other networks and fields of use. Once the locus is transformed into a movement, representation can be modified or integrated into other practices. If this happens, its identity can be maintained, disseminated, or enucleated by the past and present rationalizations that established the visibility of that which keeps disappearing from view and tries to elude the technologies of power and control—thought. The *Regularis concordia* delimited the processes by which the private, imperceptible movement of thought was externalized and materialized in, for example, the open place of the Chapter, the confessor's box, and the observances of the offices, such as those on Easter Sunday. All of this was closely connected with the desire to access the divine light—"Qui facit veritatem, venit ad lucem." And the light was the truth enshrined in *Hoc est corpus meum*. Though the body is nowhere to be seen, the *Regularis concordia* presents with a labor to compose and to collate in the same place the configuration of material practices for the representation of the codified gnosiologic self always ready to access that which is neither material nor visible—the light.

CHAPTER 2

"Whom Do You Seek?":
Fides quaerens intellectum

The credibility of a discourse makes itself believable by saying: "This text has been dictated for you by Reality itself." People believe what they assume to be real, but this "reality" is assigned to be a discourse by a belief that gives it a body inscribed by the law. The law requires an accumulation of corporeal capital in advance in order to make itself believed and practiced. It is thus inscribed because of what has already been inscribed: the witnesses, martyrs, or examples that make it credible to others. It imposes itself in this way on the subject of the law: "The ancients practiced it," or "Others have believed it and done it," or "You yourself already bear my signature on your body."
—Michel de Certeau, *The Practice of Everyday Life*

In the writing of history of the emergence of liturgical drama and theater in the early Middle Ages, the *Regularis concordia,* as I suggested in chapter 1, is used to explain the different placements and to clarify the different functions of the *Quem quaeritis.* An event that took place in the second half of the eleventh century—the writing/copying of the *Regularis concordia*—prompted this inquiry.[1] Traditionally, the temporal gap between the 970x973 *Regularis concordia* and the eleventh-century *Regularis concordia* has not been taken into consideration by scholars, even though it has been duly acknowledged. Consequently, the document, seen as an unproblematic or problematic record of the past, has acquired an abstract and atemporal status of a material cipher used to establish the credibility of a discourse of the emergence of liturgical drama.

If, as Michel de Certeau proposes, the text is inscribed because of what has already been inscribed "by the law," which makes itself "believed and practiced,"[2] the tenth-century and the eleventh-century copies of the *Regularis concordia* should not be seen as the same or reduced to being a singular record of a monastic history. More importantly, I will argue that the eleventh-century *Regularis concordia* as well as three other events in the second half of the eleventh century—the Berengar-Lanfranc Eucharist controversy, Saint Anselm's prayers, and Lanfranc's *Constitutions*—disclose an epistemic break in the concept of representation, which was allowed to be conceived in a monastic place, exposing for a brief moment a space of instability in a society based, at least theoretically, on an ideological stability. By taking leave of their "authorities" (both theological/scriptural and ecclesiastical), these events not only altered the convention, which had operated until now to realign the different traditions and daily practices to control the gnosiologic self's most imperceptible movements of thought, as the tenth-century *Regularis concordia* may suggest, but also produced a space where the tension between the different positions destabilized the approved convention. By so doing, they partook in the process of proliferation of the new practices whose attributes and properties were embodied in the texts and the images produced. This momentary instability is the object of study here. I am interested in investigating the remanences of a movement within a discursive formation before this movement was classified or let itself be classified as an immobile place by an authorized representational practice and in the name of an ideological stability.

Hoc est corpus meum.
—1 Cor. 11:24

From the time of the Catholic fathers until the mid–eleventh century, there had existed the plurality of opinions regarding the nature of the Eucharist. The unresolved conflict between the different interpretations of the Eucharist came to focus, however, when Berengar of Tours questioned the accepted Paschasius's theology of the realistic mode of the presence of the body of Christ in the Sacrament and the salvific function of this sacrament. Using the *De corpore et sanguine domini* of Ratramnus of Corbie, Berengar argued that the body and the blood of Christ were not present in the Eucharist. Whereas similar controversies in the past were positioned, as I indicate in chapter 1, in a doctrinal treatment of the

Eucharist, this one, for a number of political and theological reasons, received official ecclesiastical attention and sanction.

Berengar belonged to the family of canons of Saint Martin's at Tours. At the time, Tours was a center of classical learning in France. The library possessed in its holdings the volumes by Horace, Terence, Boethius, Plato, Aristotle, Socrates, Cicero, Catilina, Caelius, Cethegus, Brutus, Cato, and Seneca.[3] A master of the liberal arts and an exponent of the Bible, Berengar opened a school where he taught church history, theory of medicine, and dialectics. Margaret Gibson notes that Berengar built a reputation as a person whose "[m]anner and matter were alike impressive." She continues:

His dignified and arresting gestures, the odd pronunciation he affected for familiar words, the involution of his rhetorical style: all this combined with real scholarly originality to attract crowds of students. He was also the count's [Geoffrey Martel] letter-writer, devising a brilliant, if untenable, justification for the treatment of bishop Gervase. . . . Berengar added lustre to count Geoffrey's court; he rose to be archdeacon and treasurer of Angers cathedral and he had every prospect of a bishopric.[4]

In the summer of 1049, however, Berengar was criticized for his ideas regarding the nature of the sacraments.[5] In a letter to Henry I of France, "Contra Brunonem et Berengarium," Theoduin of Liège claimed that according to Berengar, the Eucharist was not the body and the blood of Christ and baptism and marriage were ceremonies of no importance.[6] These views were opposed by the theologians of the monasteries of Chartres and Fécamp. The debate reached Pope Leo IX, who condemned Berengar's teachings at the Council of Rome in 1050.

The events of the council were recorded in Lanfranc's *De corpore et sanguine domini.* Apparently, Lanfranc was summoned to accompany the pope to Rome for the Lenten Council. Why he should follow the pope had not been disclosed to him until a clerk from Rheims read before the Roman Council a letter addressed by Berengar of Tours to Lanfranc, the prior of Bec. The letter addressed to Brother Lanfranc implied that Berengar heard from Ingelran of Chartres that Lanfranc had rejected the teaching of John the Scot on the real presence of Christ in the Eucharist. Indeed, because John the Scot's opinions differed from those of Paschasius, Lanfranc found them to be heretical. This being the case, suggested Berengar, Lanfranc, not yet so expert in the study of Scripture, due to accepting a monastic habit late in life only after abandoning his former profession as a lawyer, must also have rejected the writings of Ambrose, Jerome, and Augustine, all of which presented similar sacramental arguments.[7]

Having been made aware of the letter that never reached him at Bec, Lanfranc, without much difficulty, cleared himself of the suspicion before the court in Rome: "I rose; what I felt, I said; what I said, I proved; what I proved was pleasing to all, and displeasing to none."[8] This defense of the ex-lawyer of Pavia secured him a position of high visibility in the controversy, which was just about to unfold, and accelerated his promotion in the church's hierarchy.

Leo IX condemned Berengar's teachings by destroying the treatise by Ratramnus of Corbie on which his views had been based and excommunicated him. Berengar was offered a chance to defend himself and his teachings at the Council of Vercelli that was to take place later the same year. Even though Berengar agreed to attend the council, Henry I of France, for political reasons, prevented him from doing so. Using the sentence that had already been issued against Berengar in Rome, Henry I imprisoned him. The council did take place. The case was discussed, but because of Berengar's absence, there could not be an understanding reached regarding his teachings. Berengar was condemned by the pope once again. His writings, together with those of Ratramnus of Corbie and John the Scot, were burned. History adds that when one of Berengar's clerks attempted to defend Berengar, the clerk was arrested to save him from the attack of the participants of the council. Lanfranc was among those who supported the pope and his actions.[9]

The Council of Vercelli did not put an end to the debate. Berengar continued to propagate his teachings. When Duke William summoned scholars from Normandy to a court at Brionne near Bec, Berengar came with his supporters to expound his views. Even though the orthodoxy was upheld, Berengar's teachings were not rejected by his bishop, Eusebius Bruno of Angers, or by the theologians from Metz and Rome.[10] At the Council of Tours in 1054, Berengar convinced the papal legate, Hildebrand, who presided over the meeting, that he would sign a compromise creed proposed by Hildebrand that after consecration the bread and the wine on the altar became the body and the blood of Christ. Then, Berengar was supposed to go to Rome to attend a council during which the dispute would finally be settled. The death of Leo IX in April of 1054 postponed the settlement.

Berengar was summoned by Pope Nicholas II to attend the Easter Council of 1059. During a plenary session where his writings were burned, Berengar was presented with an oath drawn up by the cardinal bishop of Silva Candida, Humbert. The text was a confession of belief in physical eucharistic change. It emphasized that this change occurred in the realm of the five senses, that is, that the body of Christ, which was broken during the Mass, was not a symbol but the actuality.

I, Berengar, . . . believe that the bread and wine which are laid on the altar are after consecration not only a sacrament but also the true body and blood of our lord Jesus Christ, and they are physically taken up and broken in the hands of the priest and crushed by the teeth of the faithful, not only sacramentally but in truth.[11]

Berengar reluctantly accepted this strong statement of a physical presence. But the verbal acceptance was not enough. He was made to sign the oath acknowledging his acceptance of the change during consecration. Only now, when it was embodied in the text, did the verbal acceptance become a physical and material sign of the confession within a highly textual theological framework. A copy of the oath, incorporated into the canon collections under the opening words "Ego Berengarius," was sent by the pope to the churches in Italy, Gaul, and Germany.[12]

This statement of reality in the Sacrament was undeniably an extreme case of the identification of the eucharistic with the physical and historical presence of Christ. Its political or ideological, rather than theological, character invited diverse reinterpretations and rationalizations ever since it had been promulgated. As it is argued, Humbert's treatment of Berengar had been shaped by Humbert's involvement in the controversy with the East over the use of leavened or unleavened bread in the Eucharist.[13] This argument notwithstanding, H. Chadwick observes that "even those who thought Berengar dangerously mistaken to emphasize the non-literal, non-physical understanding of the sacrament of the altar, had deep reservations about Humbert's formula which Pope Nicholas II had blessed."[14] Berengar went almost immediately back on his oath by proving that the formula was internally self-contradictory. He asked, How can a material object represent an invisible object or a spiritual truth?

Upon his return to Tours, Berengar wrote a pamphlet in which he attacked the oath of Humbert and defended his earlier views. Around

1063, Lanfranc wrote *De corpore et sanguine domini,* in which he expressly supported the 1059 settlement against Berengar. Berengar responded and the theological controversy started anew. Finally, in 1079 Gregory VII called Berengar to Rome, where he swore an oath that was a considerably modified version of that of 1059:

> I believe . . . that the bread and wine on the altar . . . are changed substantially into the true and proper vivifying body and blood of Jesus Christ our Lord and after the consecration there are the true body of Christ which was born of the virgin . . . and the true blood of Christ which flowed from his side, not however through sign and in the power of the sacrament, but in their real nature and true substance.[15]

Richard Southern notes that the controversy and this oath were not, as it is traditionally maintained, about the real presence of the body and blood of Christ in the Eucharist but about whether the presence was real and substantial in the Aristotelian sense of substance (Lanfranc and the council) or real but *not* substantial in the Aristotelian sense of substance (Berengar).[16] In both statements, the term *substance* was critical in describing the mode of presence in the sacrament of the Eucharist. However, the very definition of *substance* was ambiguous enough to be used by the opposing parties to support their views. If Lanfranc's alternative were to be accepted, the presence of a new substance on the altar would mean the destruction of the substance of the bread, because, in this linear transfer, two substances of this kind could not occupy the same space. If Berengar's alternative were to be accepted, the material bread and wine would coexist with the spiritual body and blood, thus conveying the simultaneity of sign and *res.* Both alternatives claimed a representation of a reality in terms of objective actuality. As Southern asserts:

> The strength of the Lanfrancian position was that it made it possible to go some way towards explaining how the Eucharistic change took place: it took place by the replacement of one substance by another. The weakness of Berengar's position was that he could not explain what had happened: he could only resist the attempt to explain a revealed truth by adding explanatory words which were not (as he believed) authorized by Christ or the Fathers. He would not, he said, follow Lanfranc in adding to the true statement, *panis sacratus in altari est Corpus Christi,* the unauthorized word *substantialiter.* Lanfranc felt no scruples

about this addition. In making it, he was displaying an early symptom of the scholastic urge to use the sciences of the trivium and quadrivium to push back the frontiers of mystery and enlarge the area of intelligibility.[17]

Lanfranc was defending the formula that the body of Christ was present in the Eucharist *sensualiter* and that, as stated in Berengar's oath of 1079, "the bread and wine which are laid on the altar are after consecration not only a sacrament but also the true body and blood of our lord Jesus Christ, and they are physically taken up and broken in the hands of the priest and crushed by the teeth of the faithful, not only sacramentally but in truth." The emphasis on the physical nature of this change reflects the theological discussion stimulated by the recently discovered *Categories* by Aristotle.[18] According to Aristotle, the visible universe of individual things (*topos idios*) was juxtaposed to a substratum of invisible primary substances floating in general space (*topos koinos*) conceived as the outermost celestial sphere. The visible "accidents" or dimensions of height, width, and length of things were the sensible evidence of the primary substances.[19] Using the Aristotelian doctrine of substance, scholastics tried to clarify the meaning and the identity of physical events that accompanied spiritual or theological changes. In the light of this shift, Lanfranc's position was clear: if the body of Christ became *sensualiter* present on the altar, its substance must have replaced the substance and the earthly material of bread. That the bread was visible to the faithful was a sign of divine mercy to spare them the horror of the act, though occasionally the very flesh and blood of Jesus Christ became visible to the faithful during the Mass.[20]

This discussion of the possible interpretations of the meaning and the representation of the Eucharist introduced some logical problems that could not be resolved at that time. Using Aristotle in the discourse implied that the substantial change had an analogue in the natural order. It did so because the *Categories* presented a classification system to organize this earthly, rather than the divine, realm. There were also questions regarding the substance of bread and wine and specifically about the way in which the substance of bread and wine gave way to the substance of the body and blood of Christ: "Moreover, if after consecration the Eucharistic species are mere 'accidents,' and if it remains self-evident that accidents must be 'in' a substance, what can these accidents be said to be in? The air seemed an unpersuasive answer. One could not say that the accidents of bread are transferred to the human body of Christ if only for the obvious reason that the qualities of bread are not possessed by human bodies."[21]

Berengar appealed to the tradition of Ambrose and Augustine that emphasized the moral aspects of the ritual and figurative elements of the trinitarian theology. In *De mysteriis* and *De sacramentis,* Ambrose discusses the miraculous change of bread into the body of Christ on the altar during the Consecration. Should the question be asked about how the change occurred, Ambrose explains that, once consecrated, "the bread becomes the flesh of Christ." He continues:

It is Christ's own words that make the sacrament, the words by which all things were made: the heavens, the earth, the sea, and all living creatures. . . . If the words of Christ have such power that things which did not exist should come into being, have they not the power that things which did exist shall continue in being and be changed into something else.[22]

According to Berengar, the possibility of such a change did not indicate that the elements on the altar ceased to exist or to be what they had been before consecration. More importantly, the possibility of such a change implied that, during the Consecration, something was added to the elements. Consequently, the senses were not deceived into believing that there was a change of *essentia;* the bread was bread and the wine was wine. Berengar's argument was sound, because already Ambrose had spoken of an unbloody sacrifice (*incruenta hostia*), which excluded the possibility of bread and wine being turned into the body and blood of Christ.[23]

Trinitarian theology, in contrast, was based on the separation of the earthly and divine realms. Since Augustine, two classes of things were distinguished: *signa propria,* that is, things used to designate something else, and *res,* things that, in addition to their proper meanings, received from God the function of designating other things. They transcended human codifications. It was therefore necessary to learn how to interpret them through reason that ascended to the divine will and descended toward the thing itself. Within *res,* there existed three validating conditions: *allegoria theologica* (for an event or fact to signify another, God's will to signify is needed—stories from the Old Testament, for example, represent characters whose intentions are beyond the physical acts as they express some general truths about Christianity and the Catholic church), *allegoria historiae* (a presupposition of a progressive history), and *allegoria in factis* (real and stable similarities are necessary to validate between facts or events, as, for example, between the Last Supper and the Communion there must be homologies inscribed *in res,* in things themselves). Like Augustine's and later Ratramnus's, Berengar's theology was grounded in spiritual aspects of the Eucharist. The bread and wine remained present in the Eucharist as *sacramentum* (visible signs) of *res sacramenti* (the spiritual reality of Christ). Berengar accepted that, during the Consecration, a change took place that affected the bread and wine. This change did not, however, annihilate the substance, the underlying reality in which the accidental qualities existed.

[C]onsecration makes the species holy and effective signs of communicating the body and blood of Christ to the believer; but they are not so absolutely and totally the body and blood as to eliminate the sign. To remove the sign was to annihilate the sacrament as sacrament.[24]

The introduction of the distinction between *sacramentum* and *res sacramenti* allowed Berengar to move beyond the insistence on the physical presence of the body and blood of Christ in the Sacrament. The Sacrament was a sign and it always retained this function as distinct from the *res* it referred to. It was distinct but parallel. Actually, to insist that Christ was physically present in the Eucharist, as Lanfranc maintained, was nonsense, because it was apparent to the senses that such a change could not have taken place. Moreover, if it were true that a physical change took place, then the qualities of the objects on the altar also needed to change. Lanfranc, however, maintained that the qualities of the bread and wine remained the same after the Consecration, even though the body and blood were now present. To Berengar such a proposition was unacceptable.

Unacceptable also was the claim that the Hosts consecrated at the thousands of masses were little bits of Christ's body created by the celebrant and then "broken in the hands of the priest and crushed by the teeth of the faithful." It was unacceptable because, if it were true, this would mean that a new body of Christ came to be every day and that the little bits present at thousands of masses every day would accumulate to a total sum that was bigger than the body of Christ. For Berengar, the faithful received the whole, not a little fragment. And the whole that was received was the body of Christ in sign. Otherwise, the physical presence of the body of Christ on earth would suggest that the communicant participated not only in a kind of cannibalism but, more importantly, in an act of slicing up the incorruptible and impassible body of Christ, now seated at the right hand of his Father: "To assert a presence on earth as a sign of the presence in heaven, as Lanfranc wished, would be to split the body of Christ and to assert the existence of two Christs."[25]

Lanfranc challenged Berengar's views by forcefully reasserting the terms of Humbert's oath. Even though Lanfranc agreed with Berengar that the body of Christ could not be divided into parts in Holy Communion and that the body of Christ remained in heaven, he stated that true communion was both physical and spiritual: "The material bread feeds the body, while the spiritual and invisible body feeds the soul."[26] Also, Lanfranc concurred with Berengar that symbolic elements must be recognized in the Sacrament, just as it should be recognized that the Mass was not a repetition of the suffering and death of Christ. The breaking of the bread was not a concrete actuality of the immolation of Christ's body but a mystery acted out in ritual—his death was symbolized (*figuratur*). The symbol of the sacrifice was, however, contrasted with the truth of the presence. Consequently, if one were to follow the *Categories,* the change in terms of the distinction between primary and secondary substances was not in the accidents or qualities but in the inward essence.

It is a question whether this is a "material change" or an immaterial one. Aristotle's substance is metaphysical. The word answers the question, What is it? Therefore to speak of the "substantia" being altered is but another way of saying, in Aristotelian language (but not in a framework of Aristotelian metaphysics), that after consecration the question, What is that?, receives a different answer from that given before the consecration.[27]

Berengar agreed with Lanfranc that the answer to the question "What is that?" was different before and after consecration. However, he objected to the use of Aristotle to explain a proposition that the accidents remain after the underlying metaphysical substance had been removed. After all, Aristotle had observed in the *Categories* that if the primary substance is removed, it is impossible for the accidents to exist.[28] The argument was therefore faulty in the light of Aristotle's axiom. Neither was it acceptable in the context of the ecclesiastically authorized formulas, that is, Saint Augustine's distinction between *sacramentum* and *res sacramenti.*

In *De sacra coena,* a phrase-by-phrase reply to Lanfranc's *De corpore et sanguine domini,* Berengar appealed to the old tradition of Gregory the Great and Ratramnus of Corbie by bringing to the fore the distinction made between "enacted in image" and "received in truth." This tradition must be interpreted, preferably with the aid of reason, to illuminate the mysteries like the sacraments. Reason can be used not in a haphazard way but according to preestablished rules. Berengar reasserted his argument that bread and wine were changed by consecration into the body and blood, but he maintained that this change did not happen in the physical space of a ritual site. It took place in the mind of the faithful, rather than in the realm of the senses. Bread and wine were not therefore annihilated. On the contrary, the material bread and wine could coexist with, though they were directly opposed to, the spiritual body and blood of Christ. This argument was strengthened by Berengar's analysis of *Hoc est corpus meum, quod pro vobis traditur* [This is my body, which is given for you] (1 Cor. 11:24). According to Berengar, this sentence could only make sense if *hoc* referred to the bread and if the subject of the sentence was preserved intact until the end of the sentence. Moreover, this sentence carried an article of truth supported by the grammatical doctrine that pronouns replacing nouns signified substance. In this sentence, the subject was thus the substance of the bread, and the change of/in the substance would render the sentence meaningless. Unlike Lanfranc, who could explain how one substance was replaced by another in the Eucharist during the Mass, Berengar believed that reality existed in a manner that was only known to God and that could be perceived and affirmed by senses/grammar. The use of dialectic in discussing the articles of faith, though scorned by Lanfranc, was justified by Berengar by saying that dialectics contradicted neither God nor his wisdom. Rather, he contended, "to take refuge in dialectic is to take refuge in reason, and whoever does not take refuge in reason, loses his honourable status as a creature made according to reason in the image of God."[29]

Despite the defeat in 1079, Berengar's theology would resurface in the following centuries. The description of the sacrament of the Eucharist in terms of the visible form and invisible elements, his interpretation of Aristotle's categories of subject and accidents, and the distinction between and parallel existence of *sacramentum* and *res sacramenti* would clarify the terminology in a later period. Because of the clarity of the arguments and, as Chadwick asserts, "an enjoyment of vituperative invective, notably when speaking of some of the bishops of Rome," Berengar "appeared in [his] time and since to constitute a threat to authority in the western Church and so to the coherence of the believing community." Chadwick concludes, "The threat has been from within, not without."[30] These statements may explain (1) why, as early as 1054, Berengar was linked and associated with heretics in Liège who denied the real presence of Christ in the Eucharist; (2) the urgency with which the notion of real presence was defended; and (3) why the teachings of Lanfranc and his supporters prevailed in the second half of the eleventh century. John, abbot of Fécamp, insisted that, though the form of reception of Christ's body was spiritual, Christ was truly present, eaten, and drunk in the Eucharist. Durand, John's crossbearer and later the abbot of Troarn, defended the position that the visible species were only appearances given to the substance of the body and blood to make them more acceptable and palatable to the faithful.[31] Guitmund of Aversa, while still a monk at Bec, attacked Berengar's distinction between *signum* and *res* by saying that the Mass was a *signum* of the passion of Christ.[32] This being the case, what would be the purpose of the Eucharist, if Christ himself were not present in the Sacrament. His argument was explicit: since human beings fell by eating of real fruit, it was only fitting that they be saved by eating of the real fruit of the Cross, the body of Christ. When Berengar's views were presented, they were, as Macy indicates, quoted by the supporters of the growing number of heretical groups in the eleventh, twelfth, and thirteenth centuries: "From the evidence that remains, it appears that the teaching of Berengar was not a respectable theological option by the beginning of the twelfth century."[33]

The Berengar-Lanfranc Eucharist controversy not only is an example of institutional sanctioning of a new practice but also discloses a change in the position and the identity of a seeing or speaking subject. Within the Western theological/monastic tradition, this process of establishing the identity involved God and the self.[34] As the Supreme Being, God is the source of all that is. He exists everywhere, in all things and through all things. That he neither began to exist nor will cease to exist entails that he always was, is, and will be forever. This is what all patristic texts say. In the second half of the eleventh century, these statements are given an elaborate interpretation guided by reason—*Fides quaerens intel-*

lectum [Faith seeking reason]. Following this principle, Saint Anselm makes an argument that, in a rational manner, reveals the truth of the writings of the Catholic fathers: that is, to the extent that his Being is interpreted spatially, God exists as a whole as absolutely present in every place and in no place; to the extent that his Being is viewed temporally, God is present at all times and at no time.[35] His magnitude, as Saint Anselm later asserted in *Proslogion,* is that for which a greater cannot be thought.[36] In other words:

if our ordinary way of speaking were to permit, the [Supreme Being] would seem more suitably said to be *with* a place or *with* a time than to be *in* or *at* a time. For when something is said to be *in* something else, it is signified to be contained—more than [it is thus signified] when it is said to be *with* something else. Therefore, [the Supreme Being] is not properly said to be *in* any place or time, because [the Supreme Being] is not at all contained by anything else. And yet, in its own way, it can be said to be in every place and time, inasmuch as all other existing things are sustained by its presence in order that they not fall away into nothing. [The Supreme Being] is in every place and time because it is absent from none; and it is in no [place or time] because it has no place or time.[37]

All things, including human beings, come from nonbeing into being through something other than themselves, that is, the Supreme Being.

[S]ince whatever exists exists through the Supreme Being, and since all things other [than the Supreme Being] can exist through it only if it either [efficiently] causes them or else in the material [out of which they are made], necessarily nothing besides it exists except by its [efficient] causing. And since there neither is nor was anything except this Being and the things made by it, [this Being] was not able to make anything at all through anything else than through itself.[38]

The self was thus made not as a copy of anything that existed prior to it being begotten but as a representation defined by a similitude to divinity. All things, including the self, living in the space provided by the Creator, that is, in a homogeneous space of the divine hermeneutics, affirmed his magnitude.[39] The Supreme Being, who exists in all existing things as well as in all places, conferred on the self an identity that resided in the transmitted *logos.* The self's task was to uncover—rather than to create, order, correct, or command—the language (the Word) with which God had endowed the earth. The self's reality was not described by new words, but it was enunciated through the expression of the sacred already present in everything created, though not entirely visible. It is not entirely visible because this "Word, by which [Supreme Wisdom] speaks of creatures, is not at all likewise a word [or an image] of creatures—because this Word is not the likeness of creatures but is rather the principal Existence."[40] Even though this Word is coeternal with the Supreme Being, whereas the creation is not, when the Supreme Being/Spirit speaks of itself, it speaks of all created things: "it itself is the Supreme Wisdom and Supreme Reason, in which all created things exist. For before [created things] were made and once they have been made and after they have perished or have changed in some manner, they always exist in this Spirit. . . . And so, in this way one can, not unreasonably, maintain that when the Supreme Spirit speaks of itself, it also speaks, by one and the same Word, of whatever has been made."[41] The *imago Dei* thus turned the self into a theological self whose identity could only be fulfilled through the practice of the imitation of the structure of the divine as defined by the *logos*, perceived by a rational mind, and presented as a visible affirmation of the Supreme Truth.

The question of how to represent the Eucharist, as the Berengar-Lanfranc Eucharist controversy suggests, was no longer a matter of a patristic interpretation. Biblical and patristic writings on the Eucharist, in which the concrete stands for the abstract, the particular for the universal, were consulted but modified by an official ecclesiastical sanction applied to establish the unity of the believing community. This sanction privileged Lanfranc's view of the universe of substances made visible over Berengar's reality known only to God and made according to reason in the image of God. In other words, it is possible that medieval religious and theological practices of the second half of the eleventh century were a special instance of the *cognitio Dei* (the process of and the desire to apprehend God). This process was presented as an elaborate web of cross-references that multiplied different affirmations between divine substances and their verbal as well as visual signs embodied in, rather than recorded by, the text and, in the case of the Berengar-Lanfranc Eucharist controversy, the interpretation of *Hoc est corpus meum*.[42]

Yet the theological self needed to realize his/her presence in the homogenous space of the transcendent God. This involved the process of re-membering or recollection that happened beyond the confines of material time and space—a merger between *cogo* (to collect, bring together, assemble) and *cogito* (to know). Augustine argued that to know was to re-collect. In the act of knowing, the subject re-membered or re-collected what previously had been dispersed.[43] Recollection thus involved interiorization of "empty places" (*topoi*) into the space of memory. According to Augustine, memory was a huge storage place where images of things perceived, rather than the things themselves, as well as abstract notions and categories were brought in through a proper gate by experience to be recollected at need.[44] At the same time, the memory was the "stomach" or "belly" of the mind, that is, a place where the experiences of, for example, desire, joy, fear, and sorrow, were absorbed, associated, and distinguished without the self being disturbed when these emotions were recalled. During this process of recollection, the sequential successions of interiorization of images or unclassified and unarranged abstract notions already contained in memory were transformed into coherent propositions (*logoi*). In other words, events, objects, or ideas were fragmented and unrelated prior to recollection; recollection established links and patterns between the same elements (*topoi*), enabling the self to comprehend them through the process of gathering them together and unifying the information. Finally, words, signs, and "images of images" were referred to other verbal and nonverbal signs and images to constitute positions (*theses*) and organize a variety of propositions.

The interplay between interiorized experience and exteriorized verbal and nonverbal signs acquired a different reading in Saint Anselm's 1072 collection of prayers. Whereas earlier collections of prayers had been mainly addressed to God, an increasing number of prayers to individual saints, and especially to the Virgin Mary, Saint John the Baptist, Saint Peter, Saint Paul, Saint Andrew, Saint Stephen, and Saint Benedict, was included in prayer books. These prayers frequently focused on an incident from the life of the saint and applied to the situation in which a worshiper could have found herself or himself.

One of the forms of the prayer was meditation, which was required in monastic houses by the Benedictine *Rule.* Originally, meditation signified an act of preparation for a proper execution of the offices.[45] This act consisted of learning the lessons and chants or training the children for the choir. By the eleventh century, the time needed for preparation was becoming longer as the Office had become embellished with responses, antiphons, and hymns. The monks and nuns were to learn the words and to understand the images required for an intelligent production of meaning. By the time of Anselm, meditation was perceived as a complex exercise in the tradition of private devotion (*preces privatae*). Its purpose was to help a monk achieve an understanding of an ordered life of dedication to God through the process of interiorization and inwardization of divine truth.[46] This understanding signified the process of being able to recall the images in various ways and degrees of intensity and to relate them to the particular needs of the present situation.

For Anselm, as for Augustine, meditation was the mental activity whose function was to bridge the gap between knowledge of earthly things and knowledge of the attributes of God. That knowledge was acquired in the process of a mental movement from images to cognition (*cogitatio*), from cognition to meditation (*intellectus*), and from meditation to contemplation (*sapientia*). Thus, for Anselm, there were two ways of obtaining knowledge: first, knowledge came from the senses in the form of images (material substances) that, when stored in memory, were available for examination by the rational faculty of cognition and by meditation; second, knowledge came from the mind's introspective knowledge of itself, which, in turn, led from the intuitive self-knowledge of the mind to knowledge of immaterial substances, such as Truth, Beauty, Love, Virtue, and so on. Only through the combination of these two kinds of knowledge could the mind reach toward the knowledge of God. *Fides quaerens intellectum* expressed the belief that nothing in faith was contrary to reason.

A prayer to Saint Peter is a good example here. Even though the prayer followed the traditional Carolingian pattern of using one of the incidents from the life of the saint to reach the light of truth, Anselm strengthened the message by using the immediate images of emotional states that existed in life here and now or that were stored in and committed to the memory, the pattern that he would elaborate in his seminal *Cur Deus Homo* in a few years' time. Traditionally, the suppliant approaching Saint Peter would recall Saint Peter's denial of Christ and his role as shepherd of the sheep. Note the difference between the Carolingian and Anselmian prayers. The Carolingian prayer begins:

Most holy Peter, prince of the Apostles, my shepherd and provider, to whom power to bind and to loose has been given by your Master, loose me, I pray, from all the bonds of my iniquities, and intercede for me, that the Lord, your Master, may look on me, as he looked on you.[47]

Anselm's prayer reads:

The sheep is sickening to death: his ulcers swell, his wounds are reopened and
grow putrid. The wolves have tasted his blood. They are waiting for him to be
cast away. Faithful shepherd, turn your eyes on him: see that he is one of yours.
If he is strayed, nevertheless, he has not denied his Lord and shepherd. If,
through the filth, you cannot recognize the face of one washed white in the
fountain of Christ, at least you see that he confesses the name of Christ, who had
thrice to ask you "Lovest thou me?" before he said "Feed my sheep."[48]

The difference between these two prayers is evident. Southern suggests
that whereas in the Carolingian prayer everything is immediately clear,
as the prayer would have been a part of the Office, in Anselm's prayer,
the ideas are too subtle, too complex, and too personal to be understood
in a Romanesque monastic house and required, therefore, the seclusion
of a room.[49]

Southern's is a possible conclusion. But it could also be suggested
that this prayer describes the desire of the self (a faithful), who is
engaged in the process of re-calling verbal and nonverbal signs to erase
the distinction between earthly things and spiritual knowledge and to
present him/herself to the mediating other (an image of a saint) to affirm
the existence of God. The three states of "in the mind," "in the mind
and outside the mind," and "in the mind and necessarily outside the
mind," corresponding to the cognition/meditation/contemplation triad,
were, for Anselm, indispensable for the religious experience of the self.
This religious experience of the self existed no longer only in verbal
form, which depended on scriptural authority, but on reason alone (*sola
ratione*).[50] While the prayers retained their quality as interior reflections,
Anselm wrote them down not only to interrelate faith and reason but
also because they signified what was really taking place during the act of
meditation. In writing out the prayers, he created a model for theological investigation in which oral and written models were inseparable and
produced a new text. This text acted as an intermediary between the
words in the mind, which constituted a mental text, and the images in
and outside the mind, which gave rise to contemplation. Through his
commitment to reason without scriptural authority, Anselm succeeded
in connecting abstractions of the highest order of reality and the existence of a superior nature forming a material expression of things in the
mind either through an image of corporeal things or their conception.

Now, by "mental expression" or "rational expression" I do not mean here thinking the words which are significative of things; I mean, rather, viewing mentally, with the acute gaze of thought, the things themselves which already exist or are going to exist. . . . For example, in one way I speak of a man when I signify him by the name of "man." In another way [I speak of him] when I think this name silently. In a third way [I speak of a man] when my mind beholds him either by means of an image of a body or by means of reason—by means of an image of a body, for instance, when [my mind] beholds his perceptible shape; but by means of reason, for instance, when [my mind] thinks of his universal being, viz. rational, mortal, animal.[51]

This expression, unlike the expression of God, which does not need a model, depended on the prior existence of something else. This something else is not only the process of establishing the likeness to other things but also the reality of their being that is embodied, rather than recorded, in the text of a prayer and sustained through "the conserving presence" of the Supreme Being.[52] When a rational mind, states Anselm, conceives of itself in meditation, the thought is its own image as it is formed by impression (faith). The rational mind brings forth this image, but it cannot separate itself from it, since faith is a received text.[53] Consequently, it establishes an image that is an exploration of faith by reason. During this exploration, statements are made about reality. The prayer to Saint Peter is an example of this process, which was described in detail in *Monologion, Proslogion,* and *Cur Deus Homo,* as well as in the works of twelfth-century mystics discussed in chapter 3.[54]

The Berengar-Lanfranc Eucharist controversy and Saint Anselm's 1072 meditations are two examples of the shifts in the mode of thinking that took place in the second half of the eleventh century. The written words marked the traces of the movement of these ideas that explained the relationship between the theological/monastic self and the real essences. They did so by multiplying affirmations within the homogenous space of the mind and necessarily outside the mind.[55]

If the Berengar-Lanfranc Eucharist controversy and Saint Anselm's prayers and meditations exemplify the transformations in the spiritual and theological service to God, does the eleventh-century *Regularis concordia* partake in elucidating the epistemological and representational shift in the second half of the eleventh century? To answer this question, I will consider monastic and political activities in England in the period after the Norman Conquest.

By 1070, the Anglo-Saxon resistance to William had almost been overcome. The English bishoprics were either already occupied by foreigners or would be occupied by foreigners whose ecclesiastical appointments were secured by William himself without exciting too much hostility from the Saxons. This was achieved with the help of political diplomacy carried out by the papal legates. Thus, for example, at the Easter and Whitsuntide meetings of the Winchester and Windsor Councils, respectively, the pope was represented by three legates who conveyed to the assembly the decisions regarding new nominations that had previously been approved by William: Stigand of Canterbury and Ethelmar of Elmham were deposed of their sees on the ground of the offenses they had committed against the vows of the church.[56] At the meeting at Windsor, Thomas of Bayeux was nominated to the see of York, Walkelin to Winchester, Herfast to Elmham, the Anglo-Saxon Stigand to Sulsey, and Lanfranc to Canterbury.

Lanfranc informs us that his nomination was announced at the Council of Norman to the bishops, abbots, and barons by the papal legates Ermenfried, bishop of Sion, and Hubert, cardinal of the Holy Roman Church. It was done in such a manner because of the fear that Lanfranc might refuse to accept the nomination. As the letter to Pope Alexander II states, this precaution was justified.

I do not know to whom I may more appropriately unfold my misfortunes than to you, father, who have brought these misfortunes upon me. When William duke of the Normans had removed me from the community at Bec, where I took the religious habit, and I was in charge of the monastery at Caen, I was unequal to ruling a few monks; so I cannot conceive by what judgement of almighty God I have at your insistence been made the overseer of many and numberless. Although that duke, now king of the English, endeavoured in many different ways to bring this about, his labours were in vain. He could not win his point from me until finally your own legates came to Normandy. . . . I pleaded failing strength and personal unworthiness, but to no purpose; the excuse that the language was unknown and the native race barbarous weighed nothing with them either.[57]

At the beginning of August 1070, Lanfranc came to England hoping to persuade William to allow him to decline the promotion and return to the monastery at Caen. Having listened to Lanfranc, the king, rather than agreeing with him, emphasized Lanfranc's fitness for the work of restoration of the spiritually and politically decayed church in England. The formal induction was held on August 15 and the consecration on August 29. The activities took place at Christ Church at Canterbury. Actually, the ceremonies were celebrated in a temporary shelter not far from the ruins of the cathedral church that had burned down on December 6, 1067. Nine bishops, the monks of Christ Church and St. Augustine, and the townspeople of Canterbury were present.[58] As Lanfranc noted:

I assented, I came, I took the office. Now I endure daily so many troubles and vexations and such spiritual starvation of nearly anything that is good; I am continually hearing, seeing and experiencing so much unrest among different people, such distress and injuries, such hardness of heart, greed and dishonesty, such a decline in holy Church, that I am weary of my life and grieve exceedingly to have lived into times like this.[59]

During the first few year of his tenure, Lanfranc referred to Pope Alexander II for guidance in ecclesiastical matters.

There is a bishop in our province called Hermann who gave up his office in the time of your predecessor Pope Leo of revered memory and tried to become a monk; he is now trying to do so once more by every means he can. . . . The bishop of Lichfield, who was accused before your legates of carnal incontinence (the proof being his wife, whom he openly recognized and the children he fathered) and of other misdemeanours, refused to come to their synod; so these same legates excommunicated him, and, it is said, gave the king licence to appoint a successor in his place. The bishop came to court at the festival of Easter and did not attempt to dispute the charges in detail; but in the assembly of bishops and laity he returned his bishopric to the king, affirming voluntarily and on oath that he would have it no longer and that he would not implead or injure his successor. Then he made his way back to the monastery where he had been brought up as a monk from his childhood. Now I am a novice Englishman, virtually ignorant as yet of English affairs, except for what I learn at second hand; and I have not presumed either to consecrate the bishop in his place, or to give other bishops licence to consecrate, until instructions come from you, directing us how to proceed in a matter of such consequence.[60]

This "novice Englishman, virtually ignorant as yet of English affairs," must have had the fullest confidence of Alexander II, since the pope transferred to Lanfranc a case that had been referred to him for settlement, gave Lanfranc a free hand in the York-Canterbury controversy over ecclesiastical primacy, and allowed Lanfranc to reorganize the English church.[61]

Having settled the question of primacy, Lanfranc embarked on the reformation of the English church. By now, Canterbury had been established as the center of ecclesiastical power. The maintenance of the centralized authority was upheld by the councilor movement, a modus operandi of the reform program modeled on the Roman Council. Lanfranc called the bishops and abbots to resolve episcopal questions that had little or nothing to do with the state. The Winchester Council of 1072 resolved the question of ecclesiastical primacy in England.

The London Council of 1075, attended by all the bishops of England with the exception of the bishop of Rochester (whose see "lacked a pastor") and the bishop of Durham (who "for a canonically valid reason was unable to be present at the council"), renewed the legislations that had been in use. First, the canons of the second Council of Milevis, the second Council of Braga, and the fourth Council of Toledo were quoted to substantiate the claim that during such assemblies, the bishops "shall sit according to [their] date of ordination, except for those who have more honourable seats by ancient custom or by the privileges of their churches."[62] Second, monks were to observe a proper mode of conduct as specified by the *Rule* of St. Benedict, Gregory's *Dialogue,* and the ancient customs of monasteries: "In particular the children and the young monks shall everywhere be under supervision, suitable masters being allotted to them, and they shall carry lights at night. Monks of all ages shall eschew private property except with the permission of their supervisors. If anyone is found on his deathbed to have private property without such permission, and he fails to return it before his death, confessing his sin with penitence and grief, no bells shall be rung for him nor shall the saving Host be offered for his absolution nor shall he be buried in the monastic graveyard."[63] Third, the organization of the English church had been arranged according to a formula that considerably differed from the rest of the Western church. The council decreed that no episcopal see should be set up in a village center—a custom observed by the Continental Christianity that had organized itself around the existing structures of Roman town administration. Fourth, the council decreed that "no one shall keep a strange clerk or monk in his household or ordain him without letters of commendation."[64] Fifth, the council decreed that "with the exception of bishops and abbots no one shall speak in a council without permission from his metropolitan."[65] Sixth, decrees were passed against simony, forbidding buying and selling of holy orders, offices, and benefices. Seventh, a statute was issued according to which "no bishop or abbot nor any of the clergy shall sentence a man to be killed or mutilated; nor shall he lend support of his authority to those who are passing sentence."[66]

The Winchester Council of 1076 discussed clerical discipline as it was observed on the Continent. Clerical marriages were expressly condemned. It should be noted here that whereas cathedral clergymen were prohibited to have wives and it was decreed that, in the future, no priest or deacon was to be ordained unless he agreed to observe the rule of celibacy, parochial clergymen were allowed to stay married to whomever they had already married. Clerks and monks were not allowed to move their location without letters of recommendation from their bishops. Three other councils were recorded, the London Council of 1078, the Gloucester Council of 1081, and the Gloucester Council of 1085–86. The details of these councils are missing, however.

The decrees of the councils shed some light on the diocesan and monastic life in terms of either what it was or how it was supposed to be regulated and legitimized. Whether or not the descriptions were "reality" or "ideologically" driven, the texts of the rulings unequivocally suggest that the marriage and celibacy rules were broken, the robbery of the existing and remaining churches was frequent, tithes to the church were not paid, little respect was paid to the clergy and the monks, the clergy and the monks moved without the permission of their superior, simony was prevalent, holy orders were bought and sold, and Mass was celebrated by clerks who had not been regularly ordained.[67] A separate set of decrees was proclaimed against "heathen" behavior. An example reads: "the bones of dead animals shall not be hung anywhere as though to ward off cattle-disease; nor shall anyone cast lots, tell fortunes and prophesy the future nor practice any similar works of the devil. Holy canon law has forbidden all such things and after due sentence excommunicated those who practice them."[68]

This decline of clerical and monastic lives has been explained as a consequence of the recent military campaigns of William. Allan John MacDonald notes, however, that the diocesan organization in England could have contributed to the failure of the old Saxon system, as the boundaries were badly defined, the civil and ecclesiastical problems were frequently dealt by the alderman and other secular officers who sat in the court with the bishops, and the ecclesiastical law was not codified.[69] Consequently, before the proclamations of the councils could have been applied, there needed to be a separation between a secular and ecclesiastical jurisdiction. The London Council of 1075 did precisely this. According to the decrees, no bishop or archdeacon was to bring an ecclesiastical matter before a secular court. Henceforth, any ecclesiastical business was supposed to be tried before the bishop at the court appointed by him and according to the canon and episcopal law. Affairs of ecclesiastical policy were under the control of the Norman prelates, subject only to the prerogative of the royal supremacy.[70]

Even though the separation between a secular and ecclesiastical jurisdiction took place in 1075, the changes in ecclesiastical jurisdiction were already evident in the acts of the Winchester Councils of 1070 and 1072. For example, every diocesan was to hold one or two councils a year; only a bishop could hear confession for crimes; ordination was to take place at fixed times and only at the cathedral churches; baptism was to be administered only twice a year, at Easter and Whitsun, unless death was imminent; burials were not to be permitted within the church; and the bishops were ordered to visit the parishes.[71]

Lanfranc was often employed to resolve all kinds of problems, often of local interest. He participated in a dispute between Abbot Baldwin of St. Edmunds and a local magnate named Richard, presumably Richard fitzGilbert of Clare, in the diocese of Exeter.[72] In a letter to Herfast, bishop of Thetford, Lanfranc took a more active part bestowed on him by the ecclesiastical position. He was no longer "a novice Englishman, virtually ignorant as yet of English affairs," but a man who assumed the function of the primate of England and had a clear vision of how to strengthen the English church.[73] Other letters attest that Lanfranc was consulted in the case of a man who was found dead in the hands of his captors;[74] in the case of a monk that had been irregularly ordained, had a wife, and was not willing to send her away;[75] in the case of a person who had committed homicide, in which it was to be decided whether that person should be permitted to celebrate Mass;[76] and in the case of the proper behavior of the nuns and the handling of a dispute between the abbess and the prioress.[77] There are also indications that Lanfranc was consulted by William, abbot of St. Étienne of Caen, about the filling of the place of a prior of the monastic church and partook in Continental disputes of the time.[78] In his response to John, archbishop of Rouen, Lanfranc denies the reports that he had criticized the archbishop's insufficient control of discipline in his church.

On the contrary I have been spurred on by your example and that of other reverend fathers to prohibit by my pastoral authority any canon throughout the whole land of England, whatever his rule, from taking a wife; nor will a canon who is already installed, if he is a priest or a deacon, be permitted to have a wife from now on, if he wishes to keep his prebend.[79]

Noteworthy also is Lanfranc's letter to Reginald, abbot of St. Cyprien of Poitiers, Sewinus the monk, and Canon Henry regarding "that schismatic Berengar." In the letter, Lanfranc defended Hilary, "once bishop of your city and people," who had been accused by Berengar of holding erroneous views in discussing the divine and human nature of Christ in his *On the Divine Trinity*. Using an explanation compatible with patristic teaching, Lanfranc clearly stated that the two natures were united in one person.

In this sense it can truly be said, without endangering Christian belief, that Christ—or the body of Christ—suffered on the cross and yet did not suffer; he experienced pain and yet he did not; he died and yet did not die, and so on infinitely in this way. If on the contrary that doctor had wished it to be understood—contrary to the customary and established faith of the Church, contrary to the authority of the Gospels and contrary to the consensus of all the holy Fathers—that Christ's flesh was impassive and not subject to pain, then in the passage quoted he would never have asserted that the Son of God became a man "like us." How can the feeling be like the unfeeling or the man who feels pain be like him who does not? But he did assert it. Hence that was not the meaning he wished to convey. I entreat you to exercise all possible vigilance, for schismatics and their fellow-travellers are around you and among you. Hold them off with the shield of the fear of God and attack them with the darts of holy Scripture.[80]

Lanfranc was involved not only in the revival of diocesan life, but also in the rebuilding of monastic communities. This process was of both a physical and a spiritual nature. When Lanfranc came to Christ Church in Canterbury, he found the patrimony reduced by the mishandling of his predecessors and by the actions of Odo, bishop of Bayeux, earl of Kent, and William the Conqueror's half-brother. Whenever William was not in England, Odo was administratively responsible for the kingdom. He had seized certain lands belonging to Christ Church and distributed them and the local rights and customs to his vassals. Lanfranc appealed to the king on the matter, and all the lands and customs were regained. During the process, Lanfranc used his power to secure the confirmation of the archiepiscopal rights over the rest of the lands; over all customs relating to the lands, fields and meadows, and woods and pathways; and over the townships and villages on the property.[81]

The fire of December 6, 1067, had completely destroyed the church. The work of restoring the cathedral church was supervised by Lanfranc, who had rebuilt the abbey of Bec and watched the construction of a new house, the abbey of St. Stephen at Caen, which became the model for Christ Church. Lanfranc completely restored the church and the monastery in seven years.[82]

The spiritual rebuilding was a more complicated affair. At the time of the Norman Conquest, the English monasteries fell into disarray. The monastery buildings were destroyed by war activities, the monastic lands were distributed among the supporters of the Conqueror, and the rule of life in the monasteries was disorganized. Moreover, the treasures of the monasteries were confiscated and sent to the churches and abbeys of Normandy. Eadmer writes that Siward found only four or five brethren clothed like laymen in Rochester, Serlo found only two old monks and eight boys at Gloucester, and the monks at Christ Church had totally abandoned the discipline of the monastic life and indulged in hunting, horseback riding, playing dice, good food, and the services of their servants.[83] The reform movement started with the election of abbots to head the foundations. William of London, Gisa of Wells, Walter of Hereford, and Herman of Sherborne were foreigners who had been trained in the Continental monastic houses. Others, such as Ernest and Gundulf, bishops of Rochester, or Paul, abbot of St. Albans, were trained and promoted by Lanfranc. He concurred with the royal appointment of Vital of Fécamp, abbot of Bernay, to Westminster. These appointments illustrated the strategy employed by Lanfranc. Even though, the appointment of the abbot was in the hands of the community, the English appointments were strictly confined to the nominations by either the king or the archbishop. It seems that the monastic communities essentially agreed or accepted the choices. Lanfranc states:

In the letter which you have just sent me you made this request more urgently than the others: that when the man who is now in charge is removed I should advise you on whom to put in his place as prior of your church, and that I should send you that advice with all due speed. I put the question to the brothers who are with me here. We were all in agreement that if with God's help you can by any means bring it about you should make Dom Ernost the chief prior of your church. If he declines, or if the lord abbot should withhold his consent, let the appointment be decided by the unanimous choice of the brethren.[84]

There are records of two incidents suggesting that the monks had contested the appointment of an abbot who was not unanimously chosen by them. It is often implied, however, that the opposition was dictated by nationalistic spirit against Guido, a Norman abbot (in the community at St. Augustine's) and by Thurstan's behavior toward the community at Glastonbury. Even though, as the letter implied, some communities had the right of election, here the monks at St. Augustine's were convinced to accept the nominee, and Thurstan, after a rebuke, was elected the abbot at Glastonbury.

The introduction of the Continental (i.e., reforms based on the Benedictine *Rule* and the Cluniac model) was possible because the abbots were trained not only at Bec and Caen but at principal Norman houses—Jumièges, St. Michael, Fécamp, St. Wandrille, Cerisy, Bernay, Lire, all of which were the centers of the Benedictine revival. MacDonald, for example, observes that "thirteen of the twenty-one abbots who signed the decrees of the Council of 1075 were Englishmen, but by the time of Rufus only three of thirty abbeys which then existed were ruled over by the Englishmen."[85]

At Christ Church, Lanfranc introduced his reforms gradually without alienating the community. Lanfranc's silence about the existing practices may be interpreted as a sign that older traditions had disappeared or had fallen into complete neglect. However, a record found in Eadmer's *Miracula Sancti Dunstani* indicated that some form of the celebration of the Easter resurrection existed.

The passage describing the healing of a cripple contains a statement that he was cured when the priests, under the guise of three women, approached the sepulchre looking for the body of Christ.[86] Is this allusion to the three Marys looking for the body of Jesus Christ a reference to a monastic custom celebrated on Easter Sunday? If this is a possible scenario, this Easter ceremony belonged to a discursive formation that included the Berengar-Lanfranc Eucharist controversy, the shift in the mode of meditation as exemplified by Saint Anselm's prayers and meditations, and the *Regularis concordia* written/copied after 1066. Thus, unlike the tenth-century *Quem quaeritis,* which was an act of elaboration on the services of Holy Week that was prescribed by the secular *Ordo Romanus Primus,* this eleventh-century *Quem quaeritis* can be said to express a new mode of the functioning of physical representations accompanying spiritual changes.

Whether the *Quem quaeritis* successfully performed this function is open for discussion. The *Regularis concordia* from the second half of the eleventh century could be seen as a code that attempted to collate on the same textual plane the practices that were binding in England before the Norman Conquest. This line of reasoning would then explain why scholars have interchangeably used the tenth- and eleventh-century versions of the *Regularis concordia* to explain their theories of the emergence of liturgical drama in the early Middle Ages. However, such a practice obliterates an event that took place at that time and that may disturb the language of intelligibility that promoted current historical investigations.

Sometime between 1070 and 1075, Lanfranc compiled a collection of customs that would govern monastic life in England. He might have heard of the *Regularis concordia,* but no mention of it appears in his consuetudinary. Even though the manner of liturgical celebration was in its essentials that described by Dunstan, Aethelwold, and Oswald, the regional usage could have been altered. For example, some of the "obscure" Anglo-Saxon saints or distinctively Anglo-Saxon feasts, which had no connection with England after the Norman Conquest, were removed from the calendar; the reliquaries of the saints, who had been canonized by local acclamation, were opened, though the authenticity of the remains was never challenged.[87] More importantly, while putting together a monastic code, Lanfranc decided to depart from the existing standard and introduce a set of practices by pruning the Anglo-Saxon liturgical usage. In his statement to Prior Henry, Lanfranc noted that his *Constitutions* was "compiled from the customs of those monasteries which in our day have the greatest prestige in the monastic order." He continued: "We have added a few details and have made certain changes, particularly in the ceremonies of certain feasts, considering that they should be kept with greater solemnity in our churches."[88]

Lanfranc's *Constitutions* was primarily written for Christ Church in Canterbury. As he pointed out, "we are all free to add or to take away or to make changes if we think alteration to be an advantage, following right reason or the judgement of those better informed" (1). The changes that Lanfranc referred to were associated with the increase or decrease in the number of monks, conditions in different places, and the changes in circumstances. Consequently, no one church should imitate the practices of another church or a different congregation. Rather,

[w]hat we have to consider with the greatest care is that what is necessary for the soul's salvation should be safeguarded in every way: faith, that is, and contempt of the world, together with charity, chastity, humility, patience, obedience; penance for faults committed and a humble confession of them; frequent prayers; silence in fitting measure. (1–2)

If these practices as well as the *Rule* of St. Benedict were observed and the monastic life preserved, other things, such as the vestments worn by the cantors at Vespers or during a procession, the procedure of the execution of the Maundy, and the organization of the calendar, might vary. Discretion for the arrangement of these matters was left to the abbot, not to the bishop or archbishop, "though indeed bishops, if being in Christ's place they take a father's care of their subjects, may not improperly be called abbots, that is, fathers for the name suits the act" (2–3).

The regulations contained in the *Constitutions* refer to liturgical matters as well as to the administration and discipline of the monastic house. A brief analysis of these regulations will help explain how specific technologies of power and power relations could construct the material monastic history and will help articulate how places could be appropriated by representational practices. While reading the following discussion, recall my analysis of a daily monastic routine in chapter 1.

The *Constitutions* open with the changes that were to take place on October 1, that is, the transition between the summer and winter monastic *horaria*—the monks were to discontinue the siesta they had after dinner and before the time allotted to reading in the cloister during the summer. A description of a monastic day follows. When the bell sounded in the morning, the brethren, the children, and the young monks entered the church to say a prayer and to sing Prime, the psalms for the relatives, the seven penitential psalms, and the litany of the saints. Having finished, they were to sit in a cloister. The children read a lesson aloud and, if necessary, practiced the chant. The *Constitutions* stipulates: "No-one shall ever read or rehearse the chant in the cloister, save in silence, until the children begin to read, nor shall he go to confession. Before the bell rings for preparation for Terce no-one shall put on his day shoes save those who have been given a task to do for the monastery outside the cloister; even these should sit for a time in the cloister before they go out, and wait for the children to begin to read in their school" (3–4).

When the bell rang, the brethren were allowed to go to the dormitory to put on their day shoes and to the wash place to wash themselves. When these activities were completed, they went to the church, where they waited on their knees for the children. When the children came, five or seven psalms with prayers and, later, Terce were sung. It is stipulated that "[w]hen the psalm *Miserere* is begun those who are to celebrate the Morrow Mass shall rise, make their full bow and go to vest" (4). After the Mass, the Chapter (a monastic confession) was held separately for the monks and children. At the end of the Chapter, while the children had a light meal, the brethren were allowed to talk to each other in the cloister. The Sext followed, after which there was another opportunity for a conversation (conversation was, however, eliminated during Lent). On Wednesdays and Fridays, a procession in cloisters was held after the Sext and before the Mass: "When the sacristan perceives that the time of the procession is at hand, he shall ring one of the small bells, and when this is heard silence shall at once fall in the cloister" (5). After the Mass, the brethren, save for the weekly servers, sat in the choir and prayed or read. The office of None was said. The servers went to the refectory for their *mixtum,* a meal (a piece of bread and a drink) allowed by Saint Benedict to the kitchen staff an hour before the communal meal. When the servers returned, the None was chanted. Afterward, the dinner was served. (In the summer, a siesta followed to compensate for the loss of sleep between Matins and Prime.) After the dinner in the summer, the office of None was said. From October 1, however, the time after dinner was allotted to sitting in the cloister and reading or to manual labor and other duties. All these activities concluded when the bell rang for Vespers, Vespers of All Saints, and Vespers of the Dead. The *collatio,* a light supper, was served in the chapter house. The monastic day was closed by Compline, after which the brethren retired to the dormitory in silence.

The description of the monastic day is followed by the alterations to be incorporated into the *horarium* depending on the day of the week that November 1 fell on and by the changes in the order of psalms and hymn for the last Sunday before Advent, in the organization of Vespers for the Saturday preceding the first Sunday in Advent, and in the lessons to be read between Advent and Christmas. This section contains also information that is not connected with spiritual practices. For example, a day or two before Christmas and Easter, the brethren bathed under the surveillance of a devout and prudent senior monk whose function was to see that the monks conducted themselves in an orderly manner.

This senior shall see that all is ready, and that the right attendants are provided—mature men, neither children nor youths. If he sees anything unfitting, let him tell the chamberlain, who shall at once remedy it. Then the senior shall return to the cloister and give notice to as many of the brethren as can be accommodated. Let him take care that youths and novices go not together, but with their elders. The brethren whom he has notified shall, when saved, take their change of clothes and go to the place where the baths are prepared, and there, taking off their clothes in due order as they are wont to do in the dormitory, they shall enter the bathing place as directed, and letting down the curtain that hangs before them they shall sit in silence in the bath. If anyone needs anything let him signal for it quietly, and a servant lifting the veil shall quickly take him what he wants and return at once. (10)

When a monk finished his bath, he was not supposed to stay in the bathhouse for pleasure; having dressed, he was obliged to return to the cloister.

After this description of the bathing order, Lanfranc returns to providing directions for the celebration of the major and minor festivals of the Christian church. He specifies not only the prayers or litanies to be chanted or spoken but also what the monks should be dressed in, what they should be doing during a particular moment, and how the monastic church should be decorated. For example, on Christmas Day all the bells were rung before Prime. Four brethren wore copes at the invitatory. It is stipulated that "[i]n each nocturn at the third lesson two priests in copes shall bear two thuribles and incense first the high altar and Morrow Altar, and then the brethren seated in choir" (12). After the Gospel and the prayers, the brethren returned to the dormitory. Afterward, one of the larger bells was to be rung, and the brethren who were vested to celebrate the Mass went to "the appointed place, where there shall be a good fire prepared by the chamberlain's servants, with basins and towers and warm water for washing the hands." It is stipulated that "[o]n this occasion alone they comb their hair before washing" (13). Having accomplished these tasks, the brethren proceeded to the church for the celebration of the Mass that was sung by the officials and servants festively robed: "There shall be three converses and three cantors in choir, and in front of them two candlesticks with lighted tapers; all the children shall be in albs" (13). After the Mass, when all had unvested, Matins and Lauds were sung. After the commemoration of Saint Anastasia and the psalms for the relatives, the brethren returned to bed until dawn.

A similar mode of description was used to indicate the manner in which other feasts were celebrated. Lanfranc gives special attention to the feast of blessed Stephen, the feast of John the Apostle, the feast of Holy Innocents, Candlemas Day, Septuagesima Sunday, Ash Wednesday, Lent and its observances (including the distribution and exchange of the books), Palm Sunday, Tuesday in Holy Week, Wednesday in Holy Week, Maundy Thursday, Good Friday, Holy Saturday, Easter Sunday, the Rogation Days, Pentecost, seventeen other festivals "which are kept with solemnity, though not so solemn as the above" (59), feasts of the third rank, five principal Sundays of the year, and the feasts of the twelve lessons.

I would like to draw attention to the ceremonial character of the feasts of Holy Week, which had also received a careful treatment in the *Regularis concordia.* Lanfranc specifies that "for the Night Office of Thursday candles shall be lighted before the altar according to the number of antiphons and responsories to be sung" (27). After fifteen psalms with the usual chapters and collects and at the *Pater noster,* the brethren prostrated themselves over the desks and rose only when a *signa* was given by the abbot. During Lauds, at every antiphon and every responsory, a candle was put out. The lessons were read from the Lamentations of Jeremias, "without chant and omitting the letters of the Hebrew alphabet." Lanfranc stipulated: "in the second nocturn they shall be from the exposition of the psalm *Exaudi, Deus, orationem meam cum deprecor;* in the third, from the epistle of Saint Paul, *Conunenientibus uobis.* All the antiphons and versicles shall be without the final modulation" (27). When all the candles were out, the brethren were to "bow themselves over the desks, saying in silence *Kyrie eleison* and *Pater noster,* together with the *preces Ego dixi, Domine,* the psalm, *Miserere mei* without doxology and the collect *Respice, quaesumus, Domine.*" After the Lauds, the brethren and the children returned to bed. The high celebration did not take place until after None and was followed by Vespers. During the monastic day, the brethren and the children said the prayers, psalms, and litanies in silence. Lanfranc stipulates that during Mass "enough hosts shall be consecrated to suffice for communion for the day itself and the morrow" and that "[o]n these four days no-one shall withdraw from communion without reasonable cause" (30). After Mass, a meal of bread and water was served at the refectory. Lanfranc writes:

While this is happening, the cellarer and almoner and others concerned shall lead the poor into the cloister and cause them to sit in order side by side; before entering the cloister they shall wash their feet in warm water provided by the chamberlains. (31)

When all was prepared, the abbot and the brethren rose and stood before the poor who were allotted to them. At the sign from the abbot, the prior struck the board three times and all genuflected and adored Christ in the poor. It is stipulated that during the antiphon *Dominus Jesus,* "each one shall wash the feet of his poor man, wipe and kiss them, and touch them with his forehead" (32). Then, the hands of the poor were washed. Lanfranc continues, "when the blessing has been given they [the brethren] shall give drink to the poor, kissing their hands, and receiving back the stoups shall each give to a poor man two pence, or whatsoever the abbot orders, again kissing his hands" (32). And later in the day,

the brethren shall enter the chapter-house, where the claustral prior shall sit in the abbot's place, and the abbot and prior shall gird themselves with linen cloths: and while the claustral prior intones the antiphon *Dominus Jesus* both shall enter the chapter, the abbot to the right and the prior to the left, followed by those of the brethren who have been appointed that day in chapter to attend them, and both on their knees shall wash the feet of the brethren, dry them and kiss them. (35)

On Good Friday morning, the brethren were awakened not by the traditional sound of the bells but by the board "sounded in the cloister and at the entrance to the cellar and infirmary" (38). After the fifteen psalms were said, the candles were extinguished. Lanfranc writes, "When the board is sounded for Prime all shall go barefoot to the church and remain unshod until the office of the day is done, unless at abbot's bidding they put on their shoes owing to extreme cold" (39). No conversation was allowed in the cloister on Good Friday. Lanfranc says, "All other day hours, save Vespers, until Vespers on Saturday, shall be said as on Thursday, save that on Thursday the hymn shall be sung at a high pitch, the psalms intoned and the antiphons sung, whereas on the other two days all shall be said in a low voice and without modulation" (39). After None, the altar was covered with a single linen cloth. No candles or censers were allowed. It is stipulated that during the reading of the Passion, at the words "They have divided my garments among themselves," two ministers "in albs by the altar shall pull off towards themselves on right and left two cloths which were put on the altar before the office" but that "the linen cloth, however, shall remain under the missal" (40). When the reading of the Passion was finished, the brethren were to genuflect at the prayers "for all degrees of men, save for the Jews" (40). At Mass, two priests approached and took up a crucifix that was veiled now. When the *Sanctus* was finished, they uncovered the crucifix and began the antiphon *Ecce lignum.* All kneeled. Carpets were placed before the altar, where the abbot, the vested ministers, and the brethren, in a due order, prostrated themselves, prayed, and kissed the foot of the Crucifix. Having accomplished this, the priest and the deacon went to the place "where the Lord's body was laid on Thursday." The Host was incensed and carried back to the altar by the deacon. When the body of Christ was placed on the altar, wine and water were poured into a chalice. Lanfranc writes: "Putting the fragment of the Host in the chalice as usual, [the priest] shall give Communion to himself and all the brethren, omitting the kiss of peace" (42). After the Mass and the Vespers that followed, the brethren went to the refectory, where they had a meal consisting of bread, water, and uncooked herbs. While the meal was served, the sacristan and a few priests remained in the church to wash all the altars with water and then with wine. The day closed with the drinking of water and of *caritas* in the refectory.

On Holy Saturday, the sacristans decorated the church and all the altars—"they should place tapers everywhere, and set up the candle that is to be blessed in its place" (43). On the candle, the cantor wrote the date of the year from the Incarnation and formed a cross by pressing five grains of incense into the wax. After None, the procession proceeded to the place where the fire was consecrated and sprinkled with holy water. The thuribles were filled with coals from the new fire and carried to the kitchen, where all fires had previously been extinguished. Then, the sacristan lit the candle and carried it back to the unlit church. When the candles at the altar were relit, the litany, *Kyrie eleison,* and *Gloria in excelsis Deo* were sung at Mass.

[W]hen the last prayer has been said the cantor, and another brother of his choice, vested in copes, shall begin the litany, which shall be chanted in three parts, as follows: the cantors sing *Kyrie eleison,* the right-hand choir shall answer likewise *Kyrie eleison,* and then the left-hand choir, and so on until the end of the litany, invoking each saint thrice. Both choirs shall bow at the name of each saint, but the cantors shall not do so. (45)

Finally, the *Constitutions* prescribes the activities for Easter morning.

[B]efore the night choirs, all the bells shall be rung for Matins, then by two and two as usual. At the invitatory there shall be four in copes, and the psalms as in the Rule, that is, *Domine in virtute tua,* etc. During the lessons thuribles shall be borne around, as laid down for Christmas. All the rest of the Office shall be according to the monastic rite. There shall be a procession to the crucifix after Lauds and Vespers throughout the week. The Morrow Mass shall be said this day with a single collect, and the procession shall be in copes. At Vespers the ordinary psalms shall be said, that is *Dixit Dominus* and the others which are usually said on Sundays. The antiphons shall be those said at Lauds. (47)

Thus, the celebrations on Easter Sunday followed not a modified canonical Roman code as was suggested by the *Regularis concordia* but a far more elaborate and meditative observance as specified in the Benedictine *Rule.* The monastic Office for Easter Day described in the *Rule* gave the following directions for the night office: The brethren were to rise at about 1 A.M. and go to church, where they would chant six psalms. Then four lessons with their responses would be read. Afterward, six other psalms with antiphons would be sung. Four more lessons with their responsories, three canticles, and the *Alleluia* would follow. Then another four lessons from the New Testament and responsories would be read, and when the fourth responsory was finished, *Te Deum laudamus* would be chanted. When completed, the abbot would read the Gospel. After the Gospel, the hymn *Te decet laus* would be chanted and the blessing would be given. Then Matins would begin.[89]

The description of the observances for the monastic year is followed by the rules regarding the administration and the discipline of the house. According to Lanfranc's statutes, all the brethren had a voice and had to agree on their choice in the election of the abbot. During the first Chapter, all the keys of offices were laid before him, for the abbot to decide whether or not he intended to introduce any changes in entrusting the offices to the monks. Furthermore, the protocol of behavior was to be strictly observed at any moment during a monastic day. For example, a monk was to bow to the abbot when the abbot bowed after beginning an antiphon, when the monk was named in the list in Chapter, or when the monk did penance for a fault in psalmody (72–73). When the abbot went to read or returned from reading, the whole community was supposed to rise. These physical signs of respect should not be surprising, since the abbot was an overseer of order and discipline. Consequently, it was only fitting that in the absence of respect, penance be served, in the name of maintaining strict discipline.

[W]herever he be, either within or without the cloister, if he take the brother to task for acting or speaking contrary to good order, he who is reprimanded shall at once humbly do penance as in chapter, and stand before him until he bid him be seated. And if the brother see him in anger he shall make satisfaction, doing penance before him, until he be appeased. (73)

Significantly, this form of penance was not to take place before secular men. Lanfranc stated that whenever the abbot was seated, no one could presume to sit near him unless asked to do so, and that "[w]hen told to be seated the brother shall bow down to the abbot's knees and kiss them, and so humbly sit by him" (73). When he entered the refectory, water and a towel were brought to him. When he was in the choir, no one dared to punish the children unless instructed to do so by him. In the morning, the whole community was to be quiet as long as the abbot was in bed or asleep: "If the master of the children see that the hour is passing at which the signal is wont to be given by the prior, he should rise and rouse the children as quietly as may be, simply touching with his rod their bedclothes. This done, they shall leave the dormitory, wash and comb their hair, and after the usual prayers return to their school, sitting in silence till the abbot rises" (73–74). Other rules contained in this section described how the monks should behave when the abbot was staying outside the monastery and the protocol to be followed after the abbot's death.

The description of the office of the abbot is followed by the descriptions of the duties and the behavior of the community toward other monastic officials: the prior, who, after the abbot, was to be honored above other "servants of God's house" (75); the cloistral prior, who watched over the discipline of the cloister; the roundsman of the monastery, called also the *circa,* who, at certain times, went around the monastery "noting the carelessness and negligences of the brethren, and the breaches of regular discipline" (78); the cantor, who was responsible not only for the musical parts of the offices but also for the training of the brethren before they performed in public (80); the sacrist, whose task was to keep all the ornaments, utensils, and furnishings of the church, see that the *horarium* was preserved, and wash the chalices and prepare the Hosts (82–85); the chamberlain, whose duty was to provide the brethren with bedding, garments, and shoes, as well as with razors, scissors, and towels, and to oversee the change of straw in all the beds (85); the cellarer, whose function was to "procure all things necessary for the brethren in the way of bread and drink and all kinds of food according to the circumstances of the neighbourhood" (85); the guestmaster, who was appointed to receive guests (87); the almoner, who "either himself if occasion serve, or by means of reliable and truthful servants," took "great pains to discover where may lie those sick and weakly persons who are without means of sustenance" (89); the infirmarian, who served the sick (89); and the priest of the week, who was appointed to celebrate the High Mass (95).

The remaining part of the *Constitutions* is devoted to the maintenance of the discipline of the house. Among the topics discussed are the preparation of the Hosts, negligence concerning the sacrament of the Eucharist, how the brethren should be shaved and bled, how they should behave while being on a journey, the regular silence, the faults and their punishment, the novices, the offering of children, the daily Chapter, promotion within the community, the grant of confraternity, the treatment of the children, the treatment of the older boys, the care of the sick, the administration of the Last Sacraments, the last ceremonies of the dying, the funeral of a monk, and prayers for the dead.

The rules and regulations covered every aspect of the life in a monastery from the moment a child was offered to the community until the last rites were celebrated for a monk. The offering and the funeral marked the limits of a physical and spiritual territory that was organized around the monastic duties, the disciplinary procedures, and the status assigned to a monk. This territory was governed by the abbot, who controlled the physical and spiritual movement in it with well-designed technologies of obedience and submission. The offering to the monastery was the act of promise that, as a future monk, a novice would belong to the community and participate in its ceremonies and collective acts, both of which defined his status and standing in the house.[90]

Despite these clearly enunciated structures of belonging, there were areas of particular instability in the practice of everyday life, which made necessary a system that was authorized to safeguard the return to a striated territory. The traces of this instability can be found in Lanfranc's comments concerning the preparation of the Host and the daily Chapter. When we consider his comments as part of the narrative topography of the text, it is clear that unlike the practices presented in the *Constitutions* thus far, these practices were viewed by Lanfranc as disruptive in the otherwise smooth operation of the system. Consequently, to treat them as a part of a practice of articulating a monastic reality and its theological or liturgical aspect, the technologies of power, or the identities of its subjects would be to overlook the writing down of the procedures of verification designed for a visual representation of the structures of belonging. Consider the following practices included in the *Constitutions.*

One of the duties of the sacrist was to prepare the Host. Lanfranc provided a very detailed description of the production process. First of all, the wheat was to be picked out grain by grain and then put into a clean cloth sack prepared and used only for this purpose. The sack was carried to the mill by a monk of good character and standing in the community. He was to ensure that the corn from which the Host was to be made was free of any admixture of dirt. It is then stipulated that "[w]hen the flour is brought back the sacrist shall draw a curtain round the place and the vessel in which the flour is to be bolted, and he shall carry out this work in an alb, and with an amice over his head" (83–84). The sacrist and the monks helping him were to wash their hands and faces before making the Hosts. All of them, except for the monk holding the irons, wore albs and amices. The production process followed. While the Hosts were made and baked, the brethren recited the psalms from the office celebrated at that particular hour or, if they preferred, psalms of equal length.

Lanfranc provided not only the description of the production process of the Host but also the procedures to be employed and punishment to be administered when the Host was dropped or the wine spilled. Such an accident could not be ignored, not only because it was a sign of carelessness, but, more importantly, as the author of *De corpore et sanguine domini* and an avid opponent of Berengar's views about the Eucharist made clear, for the reasons of the real presence of Jesus Christ in the sacrament. When the Host or part of it or wine landed on the ground,

the matter was to be brought to the notice of the abbot or prior immediately, and he, taking others with him, was to go to the place where the
accident had happened. The *Constitutions* stipulates: "If the body or
blood of the Lord has fallen, or has been spilt, upon a stone or the earth
or wood or mat or carpet or anything of that kind, the surface of the
earth shall be taken up, that spot in the stone shall be scraped, and the
part affected in the wood, matting, carpet or whatever it may be shall be
cut out and thrown down the *sacrarium*. If the place where it fell cannot
be accurately determined, and yet it is certain that it fell, a like procedure shall be accomplished in and around the spot where it is thought
most likely that the particle or drops fell" (90–91).

Those responsible for the accident were humbly to beg pardon during the next Chapter. Punishment followed: "They shall be scourged on
the bare flesh, and a penance, either of fasting or abstinence or corporal
punishment or prayers or something of the kind shall be laid upon
them" (91). The punishment was not, however, limited only to those
responsible for the carelessness. All the priests present at the Chapter
would rise and offer themselves for punishment. The president of the
Chapter would choose seven of them for punishment. When the Chapter was over, all participants would prostrate themselves and say the
seven penitential psalms followed by the *Pater noster* and a series of chapters and collect for the remission of sins.

The severity of the penalty had to be matched by the gravity of the
act itself. Otherwise, how could one explain the fact that the regular
horarium was interrupted to accommodate the changes brought about by
the punishment, its execution, and additional prayers. The asking of
pardon and the process of punishment itself made clear that Humbert's
formula was in operation here—Christ was present in the Eucharist not
only sacramentally but also in truth. Scourging the bare flesh, fasting,
abstinence, corporal punishment, and prayers were ways of acting out of
an obligation to show, rather than to confess, the fault. The body of the
guilty brother was exhibited under everybody's eyes in the act of the
renunciation. The act of carelessness was perceived as the act of spiritual
poverty of a monk who had failed to recognize the significance of the
Host. The only recourse was to confess the fault. The process of reinsti-
tution involved the act of penance to be witnessed by all.

Penance is discussed in two separate places in the *Constitutions*. First,
Lanfranc describes different types of faults and punishments for them.
Second, he talks about the daily Chapter. In both cases, the acts by

which a monk was punished were to show his shame, make visible his humility, and prove that he was worthy to be readmitted to the community. The verbal confession of sins was not sufficient. The physical representation and manifestation of the penance were necessary in the act of administrative self-examination and self-revelation. Only the process of a visible expression and publication of faults could reinstate the errant monk to his previous standing in the community.

For example, when the penalty for the light fault was assigned to a brother, he ate apart from the rest of the community. A special place was assigned to him in church and in the chapter house. He was not allowed to celebrate the Mass or to read the Epistle, Gospel, or lesson. Nor was he allowed to sing or begin the antiphon. He could not carry a candle or thurible vested. He would not receive the kiss of peace. The *Constitutions* stipulates: "At the end of an office in choir, by day or by night, when *Kyrie eleison* is intoned, he shall prostrate himself before the step where the monks stand to receive blessings, and shall lie there until the words *Qui tecum vivit.* If a feast of twelve lessons occur, he shall cease from this penance until an ordinary day returns. While the brethren are eating in the refectory he shall be in the church" (99).

When a brother committed a grave fault that could not be amended by private penance, the offense was to be examined before the abbot in the Chapter. Condemned by the judgment of all, a monk underwent corporal punishment. Lanfranc writes, "When he has been scourged and has put on his clothing and girdle, he shall lay aside his knife, put up his hood and go in absolute silence to the place appointed, led by the brother who keeps the key" (100). The place of confinement was guarded by a senior monk appointed by the abbot. No one could associate with or speak to the penitent. During the time of the Office, he was brought to the church door. The *Consitutions* adds: "When the office is done he shall cover his head and prostrate himself at the feet of those who leave the church until all have passed. As they pass they shall say to him in whisper, 'God have mercy upon thee'" (101). The confinement of a brother lasted until the abbot decided that it should be over. When this happened, a brother was brought to the Chapter to confess his fault once again. He was stripped and underwent corporal punishment once again. After this, the abbot would say:

I have been moved by the prayers of our brethren, and by your patience and humility and promise of amendment, and I grant you pardon, that henceforth you may be with the brethren; you shall eat in the refectory, sitting in the place allotted to you; and you should receive no further corporal punishment for your fault. (102)

The *Constitutions* specifies that if the renunciation of one's fault did not follow the administrative pattern established by Lanfranc (i.e., if a monk persisted in his obstinacy), "a certain number of the brethren shall be told to rise and lay violent hands upon him, and drag or carry him into the prison appointed for rebels such as he" (102). Of course, when a brother did not show promise of amendment or the prayers of the whole community did not bring about the change, the abbot had to decide whether to keep him further in confinement or to expel him from the community.

The penance of a monk at fault spoke in the name of the accepted lifestyle by the community. It was made visible to produce the convention allowing for the self-revelation of a monk. But it was also necessary to produce the place where one could see amendment and where one could visibly make a promise of amendment. The Chapter performed this representational function.

When the bell rang for the Chapter, all brethren were to cease all the activities they were engaged in. At the beginning of the Chapter, the reader, upon a sign given by the superior, read the customary lessons and notices, followed by the sermon. Afterward, the superior opened the floor for matters pertaining to the religious life or to discipline among the community members. The brother who was accused of a punishable act would prostrate. Then he would be questioned and was allowed only to answer, "Mea culpa," when interrogated. The type of punishment was at the discretion of the abbot: "He who is to undergo punishment shall be scourged either with a single stout rod while he lies in his shift on the ground, or with a bundle of finer rods while he sits with his back bare" (112). During the execution of punishment, all brethren were to bow down and feel compassion for the monk being scourged. Except for the seniors, who could make intercession for him, none of the brethren were allowed to speak to or look at him. The discipline was administered by a monk selected by the abbot, never by children, young boys, or novices.

Lanfranc never specified the kinds of faults to be punished, except for making a distinction between light faults and grave faults. A judicial principle involved here adjusted the punishment not as much to the kind of faults as to the physical, rather than verbal, enunciation of the structures of belonging. For an errant monk to be readmitted to the community, a confession of sins, verbal examination of the inner movement of thought, and a private penance were insufficient. A physical and visual representation and expression of fault was necessary. This type of penance placed a strong emphasis on the obligation of truth defined in terms of bearing oneself and showing the body that had committed the sins. The monks attending the Chapter and participating in the administrative process of executing the penance watched the penitent, who was excluded from the ceremonies by standing at the church door, but who did not cease to be a Christian, since the brethren constantly prayed for his reintegration into the community. The status of the penitent was clearly defined by Lanfranc. He was a monk who was excluded by being unable to participate in the daily duties together with other brethren until a promise of amend was made and the abbot released him from the penance. The moment was marked by a double shift: it marked a promise of a spiritual amendment as well as an amendment in truth in being readmitted physically to the community. The recognition of the fault happened thus on two representational levels that described the modes of monastic cognition rather than, since the types of faults were irrelevant to Lanfranc, an object of cognition. The modes of cognition as well as modes of penitent operation were addressed in the *Constitutions* to prevent any disruptive spiritual or true intervention in the operation of a monastic system.

To use a metaphor, Lanfranc, like Berengar and Anselm, was a foreigner in a foreign land. The "land" was different for each man. In Berengar's case, it was the ecclesiastical framework. In Anselm's case, it was the private devotion (*preces privatae*). In Lanfranc's case, it was monasticism in England. The three of them constructed and brought new representational practices into a place that had already been designed by and for someone else. These practices were not homogeneous, however. On the contrary, each one of them—the Berengar-Lanfranc Eucharist controversy, Anselm's meditation practices, and the *Constitutions*—destabilized the authorized or accepted practice. This moment of instability is when the play of heterogeneity of representational practices became visible before its traces were washed away by different mechanisms of a classificatory grid; or, to paraphrase de Certeau, in the place of the traces, there appeared facts that were recorded and are today assumed to be historically valid and that are shaped from conflicting imaginations, at once past and present.[91]

If we were to circumvent this process and its reality effect (Barthes), it could be argued that the eleventh-century copy of the *Regularis concordia* functioned in a place that produced and was produced by the representational practices positioned in the dynamic landscape of ecclesiastical conflicts, *preces privatae,* and new monastic regulations. The physical layout of the manuscript expressed this complex new mode of functioning of representational practices. Although in medieval Latin, the text, and especially the descriptive parts and prayers added to the standard monastic or liturgical observances, was to be deciphered with the help of the Anglo-Saxon glosses running above it, to perform functions that had been designed for it a century earlier.

Whether or not the *Regularis concordia* functioned in this way is not entirely clear. It is possible to suggest, however, that Lanfranc's collection of monastic customs, which showed little resemblance to the customs in the tenth-century consuetudinary, altered the earlier practices. They either were superseded by or coexisted with other practices, as indicated in *Miracula Sancti Dunstani.* It is impossible to indicate with any certainty which monastic houses used the *Regularis concordia,* with or without the description of the *Quem quaeritis.*[92] Moreover, since Lanfranc did not have the authority to impose his *Constitutions* on every monastic house, which guarded carefully its privilege of being an autonomous institution, their acceptance was due to the initiative of the abbot of a community. Often, the *Constitutions* was introduced in a community because of its or its abbot's relation to the community of Bec or Lanfranc.[93]

This being the case, the tenth-century *Regularis concordia,* which was copied in eleventh-century post–Norman Conquest England, performed functions that were foreign to its initial design. On the one hand, the *Regularis concordia* was used to express the strength of the Anglo-Saxon tradition that had been established by Dunstan, Aethelwold, and Oswald and that was now eradicated by Norman abbots in various ways, including the removal of the feast of St. Dunstan, the Anglo-Saxon monastic reformer, from the calendar. On the other hand, the celebrations described in the tenth-century consuetudinary accommodated the theological changes that redefined not only the Eucharist but also the function of a written text in the eleventh century.

Is it possible that the *Quem quaeritis* from the eleventh-century *Regularis concordia,* executed by the monks during the night office on Easter Day, was no longer a practice of verification of a gnosiologic representation that defined and redefined the most imperceptible movements of thought? When used at all, the post–Norman Conquest *Quem quaeritis* functioned alongside other narratives within the historiographic field. Like the Eucharist when viewed in terms of Lanfranc's real and substantial presence, the three Marys and the angel, when allowed to appear, could not perform the function initially designed for them—to express the obligation of truth contained in the statement "Qui facit veritatem venit ad lucem"—and were now used to embody, clarify, and affirm the theological *logos:*

> Quem quaeritis?
> Ihesum Nazarenum.
> Non est hic. Surrexit sicut praedixerat.

The interplay between the verbal and the visual signs and bodies within the homogeneous space affirmed the Christian dogma. Positioned within an enclosed monastic discourse and territory (a place), the *Quem quaeritis* was defined by the monastic experience of the self, be it meditation or the Chapter, which was executed "in the mind," "in the mind and outside the mind," and "in the mind and necessarily outside the mind"—*Fides quaerens intellectum.*

The real and visual representation of the Eucharist, the real and visual representation of prayers, the real and visual representation of monk's faults, and the real and visual representation of the resurrection of Christ were used to redefine and stabilize a terrain occupied by the authorities of the ecclesiastical power in the second half of the eleventh century. The Berengar-Lanfranc Eucharist controversy, Saint Anselm's prayers, Lanfranc's *Constitutions,* and the *Regularis concordia* appeared in a place that was foreign to them. The singular interpretation of *Hoc est corpus meum* that the Berengar-Lanfranc Eucharist controversy sanctioned camouflaged the political practice that had determined it, and it defended the notion of real presence in the Eucharist. Defenders of this notion used Aristotle's *Categories,* rather than the writings of the Catholic fathers, as a guiding force in the argument, to affirm the real presence of Christ. Saint Anselm altered the mode of operation of prayers along the trajectory of cognition, meditation, and contempla-

British Library MS Cotton Tiberius A III, f. 21v: The *Quem quaeritis*. Folio page from the *Regularis concordia* (second half of the eleventh century). Reprinted by permission of the British Library.

tion. Now, meditation, rather than being an unrestrained process, was embodied in the text. The text was a guide through the landscape of oral and written traditions of Christian imagery. Its function was to affirm the *logos* through finding the connection between thoughts and words. Lanfranc designed the monastic praxis in England while "virtually ignorant as yet of English practices." His constitutions established not only new monastic practices in England but also a grid of control in order not to diminish the real presence of Christ. Whereas the tenth-century *Regularis concordia* presented a labor to compose practices that would reveal the most imperceptible movements of monks' thoughts, the *Constitutions* embodied the relationship between faith and reason. Its function was to affirm the monastic practices of the most prestigious monastic orders of the time. The *Regularis concordia* described practices that were seen as intrusive in the monastic space produced and circumscribed by Lanfranc's *Constitutions*.

These discourses, which emerged in post–Norman Conquest England, draw attention to the areas of instability within physical and spiritual territory. The lack of information about how some of these practices were used indicates that only their mode of operation can be taken into account. Consequently, they can only be situated within a field of innumerable historiographic practices, none of which was given the power to authorize and stabilize the appearance of the real. Bereft of their "authorities," these practices produced a space where representation was described in terms of heterogeneous moments before they were rendered invisible through the establishment of the structures of belonging.

The lack of "authority" brings us back to *Hoc est corpus meum*. "This is my body," said Christ during the Last Supper. The words were assigned spiritual value by the apostles. This central *logos* to Christian worship calls back the memory of the one that has disappeared. It constitutes the point of departure for incarnating discourse by giving it a place and a practice where it can manifest itself and become effectual. In the eleventh-century monastic practices, the ephemeral body of Christ was embodied as *substantialiter* in the real presence, in the interconnections between thoughts, written words, and things, in the theological coherence, and in the material representation of the scriptural *logos*—in the Berengar-Lanfranc Eucharist controversy, Saint Anselm's prayers, Lanfranc's *Constitutions,* and the eleventh-century *Quem quaeritis.*

CHAPTER 3

Hoc est corpus meum:
The Ternary Mode of Presence

But the Other is neither an object in the field of my perception nor a subject who perceives me: the Other is initially a structure of the perceptual field, without which the entire field could not function as it does. . . . It is the structure which conditions the entire field.
                                              —Gilles Deleuze, "The Theory of the Other"

In medieval studies, the twelfth century is referred to as the time of proto-Renaissance that was marked by a new understanding of humanity. Such a perception is justified when one takes into consideration the shifts and transformations that took place in a variety of fields ranging from secular to monastic intellectual practices and traditions—in scholasticism, mysticism, theology, Platonic and Aristotelian logic, grammar and rhetoric, mathematics and music, natural sciences, cosmology, the quadrivium, and the trivium. These changes, to paraphrase Boethius, were employed for the integral comprehension of the truth of the "things that are" (*integra comprehensio veritatis eorum que sunt*).

This integral comprehension of the truth of the "things that are" led to the proliferation of discourses in the realm of patristic interpretations of the Catholic dogma in general and to representational practices generated by *Hoc est corpus meum* in particular. As the tenth-century *Regularis concordia* or the Berengar-Lanfranc Eucharist controversy indicate, the processes of clarifying the *logos,* which calls back the body that had disappeared, and of establishing the practices, which secured the presence of Christ, were not stable but were defined and redefined within a monastic culture and its spiritual and physical power relations. The *Reg-*

ularis concordia speaks about the procedures that guaranteed an outward representation of the most intimate movements of thought in the process of producing truth. The Berengar-Lanfranc Eucharist controversy gave rise to the practices that realigned the body of Christ in heaven, his body and blood present on the altar after the Consecration, and the sensed reality of bread and wine.

The discussion about the body of Christ and the reception of the Eucharist was continued in the twelfth century. Even though the theology of the Eucharist that had been developed in the earlier periods was carried over, the writers who discussed it in the twelfth century made use of different approaches. In that century, a corporeal, spiritual, and ecclesiological discourse on the Eucharist—a ternary mode of thinking—can be seen as an unprecedented epistemological moment of the proliferation and dissemination of different views that, on the one hand, were grounded in either Paschasian or Berengar's theology and, on the other hand, were modified by what was possible within the changing conditions of the monastic as well as secular discursive formation. This epistemological moment gave *Hoc est corpus meum* a space, which was delimited by a ternary mode of seeing the body of Christ, and a structure, which conditioned the entire perceptual field within it.

To substantiate this statement, in this chapter I will discuss representational practices exemplified and supported by a corporeal, spiritual, and ecclesiological discourse on the Eucharist in the twelfth century. I will draw attention to how the ternary discourse on the presence of Christ in the Eucharist relates to other medieval practices that are considered to be theatrical or dramatic by contemporary medieval scholarship, as exhibited in a twelfth-century version of the *Quem quaeritis,* Hildegard of Bingen's *Ordo Virtutum,* and the Anglo-Norman *Jeu d'Adam.* Using these three texts, rather than exploring the reception or perception of a gendered body of Christ, I will focus on its mode of presence in the practices that were used to secure the execution of the dogma as well as on how this mode conditioned the representational practices that made the body of Christ materialize.

One of the advocates of the corporeal understanding of the Eucharist was Honorius Augustodunensis (Honorius of Autun). Three of his works, *Elucidarium, Gemma animae,* and *Eucharisticon,* discuss the Eucharist.[1] He was one of the supporters of the Paschasian understanding of the Eucharist—Christ became a human being, so that through the reception of his flesh in the sacrament of the Eucharist, the faithful might be naturally joined to him and, through him, to God. The salvific union of our body with that of Christ was accomplished by sacramental reception that was essential for salvation. The redemption of the body of the faithful was associated with reception of Christ's body, and the expiation of the sins of the soul was associated with reception of Christ's blood.[2] The power of this union was such that, though the unworthy could receive the sacrament of the Eucharist, they would never receive Christ's living body. Thus, Honorius upheld the indivisibility and incorruptibility of Christ in the Sacrament.

The corporeal understanding of *Hoc est corpus meum* articulates as well as constructs a place where the absent body can speak and become visible. To observe the manner in which this was accomplished, consider the following passage, Honorius Augustodunensis's "De tragoediis," often quoted in books on theater history to justify the treatment of liturgical celebrations as dramatic activities

It is known that those who recited tragedies in the theatres represented to the people, by their gestures, the actions of conflicting forces. Even so, our tragedian represents to the Christian people in the theatre of the church, by his gestures, the struggle of Christ, and impresses upon them the victory of his redemption. So, when the priest says *Pray,* he expresses Christ placed for us in agony, when he admonished the apostles to pray. By the liturgical silence, he signifies Christ as a lamb without voice being led to the sacrifice. By the extension of his hands, he delineates the stretching out of Christ on the cross. By the singing of the preface, he expresses the cry of Christ hanging on the cross. . . . By the "peace" and the imparting of it, he depicts the peace given after Christ's resurrection and the imparting of joyful tidings. When the sacrament is brought to completion, peace and communion are given by the priest to the people, because, when our accuser has been overthrown by our champion in the conflict, peace is announced by the judge to the people, and they are invited to the feast.[3]

Bearing this text and its opening analogy in mind, it becomes apparent that the Paschasian understanding of the Eucharist infiltrated not only Honorius's statements regarding the Sacrament but also his treatment of the religious practices associated with it. Noteworthy is, for example, the tripartite relationship established between the language used by the priest during the Mass, the images employed by Honorius to illuminate the *logos,* and the theological allegory exemplifying the divine truth: "when the priest says *Pray,* he expresses Christ placed for us in agony, when he admonished the apostles to pray. By the liturgical silence, he signifies Christ as lamb without voice led to the sacrifice. By the extension of his hands, he delineates the stretching of Christ on the cross. By the singing of the preface, he expresses the cry of Christ hanging on the cross."

As evidenced by these textual examples, a corporeal understanding of a eucharistic practice necessitated that Christ be really, naturally, and substantially present during the Mass. Since the act of sacramental reception signified the process of reception of "Christ's" flesh and of being naturally joined with Christ, it needed to be administered by Christ's representative on earth, a priest. The priest was to mediate the presence of Jesus Christ to the believer so that the believer could be united with the Lord and, consequently, saved. This presence of Christ is physical; but this physical—that is, biological or substantial—presence should not be viewed as the only component of the corporeal understanding of the Eucharist. As noted by Honorius, the two requisite unions for the worthy reception of the Sacrament were the *corporeal union* between the body of the faithful and the humanity of Christ and the *spiritual union* between the faithful and the divinity of Christ. The unworthy could receive the true body and blood, but, because of being corrupted, they could never partake in the second and salvific function of the Sacrament, that is, a spiritual union.[4] Accordingly, even though the levels and subtleties of material being and allegorical meaning were of theological significance, they were secondary to the procedures and methods of how the knowledge of the true presence of Christ in the Eucharist should be transmitted to the faithful and how it organized other related practices in which they partook.

The passage from "De tragoediis" is an example par excellence of the appearance of the real in the sacrament of the Eucharist, which structured the whole system of representations. It did so by describing the authority (the priest), the site of delimitation (the church), and the position of the faithful within it. More importantly, without the presence of the real in the sacrament of the Eucharist, the entire field of ecclesiastic practices could not function as it was envisioned by Honorius or other theologians, such as Rupert of Deutz and Harvaeus of Bourg-Dieu, all of whom supported the Paschasian understanding of the Eucharist.

Honorius organized and brought forth a particular reception and visibility of the Eucharist: if the daily food, which the faithful eat, becomes part of them, then so too does the Eucharist when they receive it administered by the priest. The act is placed under the warrant of the real and defines the expression of the relationship between the "real" act of eating and the "real" act of receiving the Eucharist. With the help of this reality index, the priest speaks in the name of the real—"Hoc est corpus meum"; that is, once the words are spoken and the Eucharist is administered, Christ, now part of the faithful, gives *Hoc est corpus meum* the body. In this process, the language used of "De tragoediis" gave *Hoc est corpus meum* a narrative structure that, in the universe of material codification, becomes both the intelligible sign of a Paschasian understanding of the Eucharist and a proof of both reality and the real.[5]

The second component of the ternary discourse, the mystical approach toward the Eucharist, received its clear enunciation at the cathedral school of Laon. Anselm, the chancellor, deacon (ca. 1109–14), and archdeacon (1115–17) of Laon, and his students, Abelard, William of Champeaux, William of St. Thierry, and Gilbert of La Porrée, emphasized the spiritual union, in faith and love, between Christ and the believer. The focal point of Anselm's teaching was that the true work of God was faith working through love. When applied to the Eucharist, this meant that the true reception was the unity of spirit achieved in the Sacrament. For Anselm, the body of Christ received in the Eucharist was the same body on which the Angels fed in heaven through contemplation. However, because human beings were incapable of this kind of spiritual reception, the Word necessarily needed to become flesh to provide the faithful with food that would revert to its "original" form once they reached heaven. Anselm considered sacramental reception as the union of wills between Christ and the faithful.

The theology of the school of Laon produced a precise terminology to specify the relationship between the different realities signified by the Eucharist. The *res* of the Eucharist was believed to be the true body of Christ and the *panis celestis* (heavenly bread) on which the angels fed. The true body of Christ was a sign of the heavenly bread. During the Communion, the worthy received thus the true body of Christ, a physical presence, that symbolized the *panis celestis,* the spiritual body of Christ, by which they were united with Christ in faith and love.[6] Consequently, there existed three kinds of reception of the Eucharist: sacramental, sacramental and real, and real reception. Sacramental reception referred to reception by the unworthy, who received the true body of Christ but did not receive it in faith or in love. Sacramental and real reception referred to both the unworthy, who received the true body of Christ, and the worthy, who received the true body of Christ and the *panis celestis,* the union in faith and love. Real reception referred to those who received the *panis celestis* and were joined to Christ in faith and love, even if they did not receive the true body and blood of the Sacrament. Thus, in the mystical interpretation of the Eucharist, the union in faith and love, which did not necessarily involve sacramental reception, organized the salvific function of the Sacrament.

One of the most interesting interpretations of the mystical approach to the Eucharist was offered by Guibert, abbot of Nogent-sous-Coucy, near Laon, in his texts written before 1119–20. He argued that there were three bodies of Christ: (1) the body of Christ who died and suffered on earth, (2) that which is present on the altar, and (3) that which ascended to heaven. Consequently, the body on the altar contains the attributes of the body that suffered and died as well as those of the body in heaven.[7] Thus, even though the true body was present on the altar during the Mass, the function of the Sacrament was to direct attention away from the physical presence and toward the mystical presence in heaven and in the hearts of the worthy until that time when they joined God in heaven. The mystical approach to the Sacrament expressed the belief that the faithful could communicate with Christ as present in the Eucharist and, as Baldwin of Canterbury (1120–90) asserted, that the spiritual reception of the Eucharist consisted of living a life of faith and love and imitating the sufferings of Christ.[8]

The spiritual understanding of the Eucharist coexisted with other practices that structured the discourse on a mystical body. The devotion to the Eucharist was the devotion to the human Christ present on earth out of love for the faithful. In the devotional practices surrounding the Eucharist, the soul of the faithful, according to Peter the Venerable (1092–1156), was moved to love the presence of Christ until united with him in heaven.

[The human soul] is moved more by presence than by absence, is moved more by having seen Christ than by having heard Him; is moved to admiration, is moved to love. . . . The Sacrament of the Body and Blood of Christ . . . is not superfluous, because not only through that which is God, but even through that which is human, He is with us until the consumption of the world. The sacrament is not superfluous, because He Who redeemed us through his body, renews us through the same Body, in order that redeemed through His Body and renewed by His Body, we are nourished and fed by His humanity until that time when we will be filled with his deity and glory.[9]

One of the devotional practices surrounding the Eucharist was meditation. The faithful was required not only to learn the words but to understand the images required for an intelligent production of meaning. As I mentioned in chapter 2, by the time of Saint Anselm of Canterbury, meditation was perceived as a complex exercise whose function was to achieve understanding through the process of interiorization and inwardization. This understanding signified the process of being able to recall images in various ways and degrees of intensity.

Meditation was thus the mental activity whose function was to bridge the gap between knowledge of earthly things and knowledge of the being and the attributes of God. That knowledge was acquired through the process of a mental movement from images to cognition (*cogitatio*), from cognition to meditation (*intellectus*), and from meditation to contemplation (*sapientia*). Prayers, for example, described the desire of the self (a faithful), who is engaged in the process of re-calling verbal and nonverbal signs to erase the distinction between earthly things and spiritual knowledge in order to affirm the transcendent God. Three states, "in the mind," "in the mind and outside the mind," and "in the mind and necessarily outside the mind," were, according to Anselm, indispensable for the religious experience of the self. Anselm's statements in *Monologion* or *Proslogion,* as well as the work of the twelfth-century mystic, Aelred of Rievaulx, substantiate this claim.

The phrases "I long to be dissolved, to be with Christ" and "the sweetness of inward contemplation, just as it is deep, by knowledge of celestial things, so it is short and rare because of the heaviness of the spirit, chained still by the bonds of the flesh" describe how to enter the practices that are inaccessible.[10] As Aelred observed, through inward contemplation, the faithful, though chained to the corruptible flesh, yearn for union with Christ. This union is granted only to the worthy; more importantly, though the contemplative life is begun on earth, its complete fulfillment will be attained in heaven. The language used by Aelred comes close to the language of the mystical discourse on the Eucharist. In his *The Mirror of Love* (ca. 1141), Aelred treats a soul— "my soul, an arid soul, a sterile and fruitless soul" that thirsts for "that heavenly bread which feeds the angels"—as the site where the inward contemplation occurs.

May Your voice sound in my ears, dear Jesus, and teach me how the bowels of my soul should love You. May my inmost heart of hearts enclose You, my one and only treasure, my sweet and lovely joy.[11]

This union can be achieved through love.

For he who loves You knows what You are: and as he knows You, so he loves You, for You are earthly love, You are divine love. These are the riches of Your house, with which your lovers are made drunk, losing knowledge of themselves that they may come to You. (106)

The process of coming to Christ has nothing to do with a physical movement of the body but is associated with the invisible movement in the mind, "into which its Creator has put three powers of nature, which make it able to partake of God's eternity, to share in His wisdom, to taste His sweetness." Aelred explains:

These three I call memory, knowledge and love, or will. Memory can comprehend eternity, knowledge can comprehend wisdom, and love can comprehend sweetness. Man was made with these three powers in the likeness of the Trinity, of God Whom his memory keeps without forgetting, his knowledge knows without deceit, his love embraces without desire of anything else. (108)

The image of God in a human being was, however, corrupted by sin. God the Father was appeased by the death of Jesus Christ on the Cross.

[B]y the proofs of Holy Scripture our memory was restored, our understanding by the pact of the Faith, our love by the daily increase of His love. Now there could be a perfect reforming in man of God's image, if it were not for the memory's failure through forgetfulness, knowledge's darkening through error, love's impending through cupidity. (108)

Aelred showed that a human being's ignorance of God could be dispelled by wisdom and that he or she could be reformed to the image of God by divine love. What follows in Aelred's text are the chapters discussing the interior conflict between divine love and cupidity or between good and evil. These conflicts could be resolved by grace of free will, even though free will is not alone sufficient to achieve a will for good. At the same time, as the biblical story proved, nothing of perfection lacked in divine love. Aelred's conversion closes the mystical text.

Who chooses You cannot go astray, for there is nothing better than You: his hope cannot fail, for nothing is loved more blessedly than You: he need not fear excess, for no limit is set to loving You: he need not dread death, that severer of the bonds of the earthly love, for you give eternal life which cannot die. He need not fear estrangement, for nothing estranges You from him except the cooling of his love: no suspicion will come between You, for you judge him by the witness of his conscience. Here is the joy which shuts out fear: here the peace which stills anger: here the safety which despises the world. And so little by little You began to taste sweet upon my tongue, sick though I was, and I said: If only I might be cured, and might be taken to you. (120–21)

The union Aelred desired could only be accomplished when the worldly habits were abandoned and when "other delights," which Aelred describes as "those which my spirit saw by the power of reason" (121), allowed for the spiritual union between the *panis celestis* symbolized by the true body of Jesus Christ and the faithful.

The third component of the ternary discourse on the Eucharist in the first half of the twelfth century was the ecclesiological approach toward the Sacrament. Whereas the corporeal and spiritual treatments of the Eucharist referred to a private perception of the body of Christ, the ecclesiological discourse focused on the invention of the strategies of the visible that would reestablish a link between the authoritative code and individual practices. Gilbert of La Porrée and his school, Gerhoh of Reichersberg, and Peter Abelard and his school (to mention a few names) altered the mode of presence of Christ and the mode of his existence in the Eucharist.

Gilbert of La Porrée was a student of Anselm of Laon, which explains his treatment of the Eucharist as the *panis celestis* that became bread so the worthy could partake of it. He did not, however, describe the *res sacramenti* as the spiritual union, in faith and love, between Christ and the believer; rather, he described it as a bond of all the saved that comprise the Church. Consequently, the forms of reception of the Sacrament—sacramental, spiritual, sacramental and spiritual, and neither sacramental nor spiritual—rested on the traditional Judeo-Christian notion of the community as the chosen people represented by the church. Thus, to receive the body of Christ spiritually was to remain in the unity of the Church. This form of reception was sufficient for the salvific function to be fulfilled, if one was prevented from receiving sacramentally. The emphasis here on the ecclesiastical mode of the Sacrament defined as the union of Christ and his church had far-reaching consequences. The Host became a visible sign of the unity. The *res* of the Eucharist and the true reception bound by faith and love delineated the structure of belonging of the faithful.

Other theologians were particularly concerned to explain the body of Christ that was the Church. Peter of Vienna indicated that it was not the reception of the body of Christ that was salvific but the spiritual union of faith and love that was the community of the Church. The unity of the church was the reality signified by the Eucharist. This unity itself would be salvific even if one refrained from sacramental reception out of reverence for the Sacrament. The sacramental reception was, however, significant for two reasons: first, it was a visible sign of the unity of and salvific membership in the church; second, it was a visible sign of a believer's good canonical standing and continuing membership in the church. Gerhoh of Reichersberg distinguished two forms of effect found in the Sacrament: *effectus passivus*, that is, that by which the Sacrament is effected whenever the rite is observed; and *effectus activus*, that is, that which the Sacrament effects within the church. Consequently, *effectus passivus* was possible outside the church, but *effectus activus* never was. It could not happen, because the *res sacra*, which the Sacrament effects, was the unity of the Church. The sacrament of unity could not be performed outside the unity it represented. The Eucharist outside the church was therefore ineffective, because the *res* of the Sacrament was not the true body of Christ but the Body of Christ that was the Church.[12] Peter Abelard gave a similar treatment of the Eucharist by advocating that the *res sacramenti* was the union of head and members of the church. Those who belonged to the church could be saved even without sacramental reception. Sacramental reception itself indicated that true substantial change could take place on the altar, but the form of the species could not reside in Christ. The form existed in the air, and the change on the altar was nothing more than an illusion for the good of the faithful.[13]

The ecclesiological tradition institutionalized thus the ritual that had always been the symbol of the unity of the Christian community. Through the sacrament of the Eucharist, ecclesiastical authority was strengthened. The union achieved in the Eucharist, that is, the identification of the church with Christ, rather than the salvific identification of the individual with Christ, turned the *Ecclesia,* the *corpus verum,* into the *corpus mysticum* that needed to be venerated and was the sign of juridical standing in the community. Therefore, it is not surprising that membership in the community of the saved was becoming more and more defined by canon law procedures and statutes. The reception of the Eucharist was a formal social occasion. The common practice was that the faithful would receive the Eucharist on the feasts of Christmas, Easter, and Pentecost. It is noteworthy that later in the twelfth century in France, the custom was to receive the Communion only for Easter, and that in 1215, the Fourth Lateran Council ruled that the Easter Communion would be the minimum requirement for adult Christians. The reception of the Eucharist on the high feasts was also the time when the faithful paid their tithes and made offerings to the church. Often, these fees were considered indispensable for the reception of the Sacrament. The financial aspect of eucharistic reception was accompanied by a ritual of preparation. The faithful were supposed to fast, refrain from conjugal relations, and confess sins before approaching the altar.[14]

The elevated Host, the sacramental body, became the focal point of different gazes. The visible sign of ecclesiological belonging reestablished a link between a private experience of the Eucharist and the church. Corporeal and spiritual understanding of the Eucharist were individualized practices that could easily separate themselves from the institution of the church. The desire to control the proliferation of private practices led to returning the representation of the most ephemeral sacrament to the field of a visible institution. The ecclesiological approach to the Eucharist reinforced the church representation by diminishing the invisible, the private, and the mystical. It did so by increasing a performance of meaning in order to establish the Church's spiritual supremacy. The *Ecclesia* was the *corpus mysticum.* By displaying the sacramental body, the visibility of consolidated clerical power was produced and disseminated. Whereas in the corporeal and mystical approaches, the body of Christ was silent, now the silent body was to speak the language of theological pedagogy that delimited the space of representation by consolidating the structures of belonging. At the same time, the language of theological pedagogy and the structures of belonging were institutionalized for the faithful. Both of them secured the practice of the dogma.

In considering the phrase *Hoc est corpus meum,* we must ask how a body can be made from the Word. This question raises another question that is connected with the initial privation of the body: where is the body? In the ternary discourse on the body, the ecclesiological approach occupied a very strong position in terms of Anselmian *Fides quaerens intellectum.* Nothing in faith is contrary to reason. This statement distributed the practices of representation by levels of meaning and of physical representation. The ecclesiological approach stood in opposition to mystical knowledge, as a visible to an invisible. It showed a different time and space for the salvific function of the Eucharist that could be rendered in a physical way through a good standing in the community. It established a point of reference, a visible sign of the body, that gave a privileged status to the question of where the body was. By so doing, it modified the corporeal and spiritual discourses on representation and their representational practices and modes of operation.

These three approaches toward the Eucharist firmly established that the outward (i.e., visible) sign of the Sacrament was necessary in order for the faithful to be saved. They might have differed in their particular statements regarding how the sign was linked onto the actual presence of Christ in the Sacrament, but they supported the belief that a faithful person could communicate with Christ as present in the Eucharist. The process of communication either was mediated by the priest (corporeal), was a part of the meditative practice of leading one's mind to the love of God (mystical), or was a bond that linked all faithful of good standing in the church (ecclesiological). The discussions concerning the Eucharist were not limited only to the realm of academic theology. These discussions had their popular equivalent that complemented what was written by the theologians. The mode of this complementarity provided a specific language that grounded the presence of Christ in the universe inhabited by the faithful.

As many scholars demonstrated, in the early twelfth century a new phenomenon appeared in the history of the Western church between the death of Berengar and the opening of the Fourth Lateran Council (November 11, 1215)—a devotion to Christ in the Sacrament. It manifested itself in the proliferation of miracles, visions, and miracle stories. As the research of Peter Browe and Édouard Dumoutet demonstrates, these stories exhibit a change in the attitude toward the Eucharist.[15] Unlike similar stories from the past, these new accounts tell about present events as well as manifest a desire to see and to communicate with

Christ present in the Sacrament. For the sake of clarity, let me draw attention to the comparison made by the scholars who have done the most research in this area. In his *De corporis et sanguinis Christi veritate in eucharistia*, Guitmund of Aversa writes that Lanfranc, the archbishop of Canterbury, witnessed a miraculous change of appearance of bread and wine on the altar into the flesh and blood of Christ. When consulted, Lanfranc ordered that the miraculous objects should be placed in the middle of the altar as relics.[16] Almost a century later, in 1171, the community of Fécamp removed such a relic in order to display it to the faithful.[17] Thus, what had been concealed in the eleventh century was revealed in the latter part of the twelfth century.

This reversal in the treatment of the relic was not an isolated event. The miracles recounted by Browe indicate that the devotion to the Eucharist was somehow connected with the desire to see the substantial presence of Christ in the Sacrament. A miracle Host was no longer a relic to be removed from sight but an object to be seen and venerated by the great masses of the faithful. New practices were established to increase adoration of Christ as present in the Eucharist: the practice of burning a perpetual light, the prayer before the reversed species, and the introduction of the elevation of the Host were the three liturgical customs that emerged in the twelfth century.[18]

The devotion to the Eucharist as well as the desire to see and to communicate with Christ have been explained by scholars in a variety of ways. One theory puts forth the possibility that the introduction of the new eucharistic devotional practices was a deliberate action on the part of the church to counter the teachings of Berengar as well as to combat heresy of Waldensians and Cathars—the miracle stories were told to assert and reassert the real presence of Christ.[19] Another theory, advanced by Albert Mirgeler, suggests that the reverence for the Eucharist was the result of a refinement of relic worship popularized by the new Cistercian order—a worship that had been limited to relics was now extended to embrace the central sacrament of the church.[20] In this version, the Host was not hidden; it was exhibited in glass reliquaries or, after the Consecration, held aloft to be seen by the people. A third theory presents a hypothesis that the desire to see Christ was connected with the dissemination of the legend of Holy Grail by the poets and troubadours.[21] Finally, a fourth theory implies that the desire to see Christ physically present in the Eucharist was similar to the appearance of other devotional practices, such as, for example, a personal devotion to the Blessed Virgin or to the Passion. What moved the faithful and their desire for some form of contact with him was the devotion to Christ, who is present here and now out of love for humankind, rather than the words of the human Christ.

The real presence, the human Christ, and the desire for contact are often quoted as the elements contributing to a new understanding of humanity that characterized the twelfth century. However, it is possible that these three elements marked a shifting status of *Hoc est corpus meum* by giving a physical shape to the invisible. During this process, (1) the miracles gave rise to the invisible, (2) a personal devotional experience was returned to the field of a visible institution, and (3) Christ was given visibility outside the textual theology. With this increased performance of meaning, the real manifested itself in a particular manner as well as redefined the strategies for establishing visibility through representational practices. I contend that all these practices were necessary in order for the church to lead the minds of the faithful to the love of God, be it personal experience or institutionalized belonging to the *Ecclesia,* through the outward signs that functioned as the substitutes for the body. The production of the body of Christ, as manifested by the corporeal, spiritual, and ecclesiological approaches toward the Eucharist, was not heterogeneous. Three different strategies corresponded to three different ways of seeing that, though they differed in theological detail, organized the practices of showing what can be seen. This drive toward transparency (the desire to reveal that which was hidden from view) established a map where the physical images reorganized the vision around the text. The text gave rise to a spectrum of practices. The practices collated on the same plane the elements to be distributed in accord with the order of the structures of belonging.

The twelfth-century drive toward transparency manifested itself not only in the theological discussions about the presence of Christ in the Eucharist but also in the changes in the *interpretatio Christiana* and, in particular, in the discussions about Christ's life on earth. Until the end of the eleventh century, Christian liturgy and representational practices, including iconography, primarily focused on celebrating the divine nature of Christ or in promulgating the image of triumphant divinity.

Christ was most often represented as an abstracted and symbolic image or icon illustrating and emphasizing the nonhuman nature of God's son. Paintings and drawings whose subject matter was crucifixion presented Christ as a divine savior who died on the Cross to atone for original sin.[22] Other images of Christ were Christ the Shepherd or Christ in Majesty, both of which are derived from the biblical description of the position and function of Christ.

Saint Anselm was one of the theologians who was instrumental in initiating the shift in Christian dogma from the divine to the divine-human nature of Christ. The central problem governing *Cur Deus Homo* (ca. 1099) is twofold: on the one hand, Anselm tries to give a reasoned explanation of the theology of atonement or redemption; on the other hand, he focuses on the question, Why did God become man and redeem human beings by his death, although he could have accomplished this by other means?[23]

One of the achievements of Anselm was the challenging of the Christian doctrine of redemption, which had been referred to, from the times of Origen (185–ca. 254), as the "ransom theory" or "the rights of the devil theory." This doctrine can be summarized in the following manner: the sin of Adam involved all members of the human race and its consequences; that is, by the act of sinning, we became slaves of Satan. God promised a Redeemer. The Redeemer "redeemed" the human race by abrogating the contract with the devil. By so doing, the Redeemer, the God-Man, restored a human being's right to heaven. Anselm objected to this explanation by saying that both a human being and the devil are under God's domination and that it would be demeaning to God to make a payment to or plead a cause with his own creation. In its stead, Anselm offered an explanation that was grounded in the definition of sin as the refusal to render to God what is due to him. What is due to God is honor given by subjection of one's will to God's will. A human being who refuses God his due detracts from his honor and insults him. Here arises an obligation to restore the honor and to undo the insult.

Anselm: "To sin," then, is nothing else than not to render to God His due.
Boso: What is the debt we owe God?
Anselm: The will of every rational creature must be subject to the will of God.
... This is the debt which angel and man owe to God, so that no one sins if

he pays it and anyone who does not pay it, sins. This is justice or rectitude of will, which makes persons upright or *right in heart,* that is, in will. This is the only and the total honor which we owe to God and which God exacts of us. . . . A person who does not render God His honor due Him, takes from God what is His and dishonors God, and this is to commit sin. . . . Similarly, for one who violates the honor of some person, it does not suffice to render honor, if he does not make restitution of something pleasing to the person dishonored, in proportion to the injury of dishonor that has been inflicted. . . . Thus, therefore, everyone who sins must pay God the honor he has taken away, and this is satisfaction, which every sinner must make to God.[24]

Satisfaction thus will restore human beings to the state of grace and save them from everlasting punishment. Neither a human being nor an angel, but only the God-Man, can give this satisfaction.

Anselm's argument is as follows: a human being is unable to make satisfaction, because satisfaction must be made in accordance with the measure of the sin and the gravity of the sin was immense. Moreover, a human being, having given in to the devil, is weak and mortal by his own doing and cannot overcome the devil "as long as, due to the wound of the first sin, he is conceived and born in sin."[25] Consequently:

It is absolutely wrong and even impossible for man to receive from God what God intended to give him; if he does not render back to God all that he took from Him; so that as God has lost through him, so He was to regain it through him. This cannot occur in any other way than that, as through him who has vanquished, the whole human nature was corrupted and, as it were, leavened, by sin—and God takes no one afflicted by sin to complete that heavenly city— so by his triumph, as many men were justified as were required to total that number which man was created to complete. But it is absolutely impossible for sinful man to do this, because a sinner cannot justify a sinner.[26]

As Anselm further explains, as long as human beings did not render to God what they ought, they could not be happy. Hence, the incarnation and the death of the God-Man were necessary for human redemption. Only the God-Man, by his divinity, was able to render God the satisfaction due to him and, by his humanity, to represent a human being, "who has a rational nature [and was] created in the state of justice precisely for the purpose of being happy in the enjoyment of God."[27] The God-Man, perfect God and perfect man (two complete natures retained and joined in one), can accomplish what God will not accomplish because it is not his obligation, and human beings will not accomplish it because they do not have the ability.[28] This is why God assumed human nature from the race of Adam and from a virgin.

[I]t is extremely fitting that, as the sin of man and the cause of our condemnation took their origin from a woman, so the cure for sin and the cause of our salvation must be born of a woman. And so that women may not despair of attaining to the lot of the blessed, because such great evil has issued from a woman, it was fitting that such a great good should issue from a woman, to revitalize their hope. . . . If it was a virgin who was the cause of all evil to human race, it is far more fitting that it be a virgin who will be the cause of all good. . . . If the woman whom God made from a man without a woman was made from a virgin, it is extremely fitting that the man who will originate from a woman without a man be born of a virgin.[29]

The implications of this dual nature of Christ, as described by Anselm, were momentous—although Christ had superhuman qualities, he acquired a human body, suffering weariness, thirst, hunger, and blows to save people. The act of Christ's suffering and death on the cross was to inspire human beings never to abandon justice they owe to God, no matter what disadvantages they could experience. Christ gave his life without being compelled; neither was he obliged to by reason of debt. According to Anselm, Christ's death brought about human salvation because his sacrifice deserved a reward, though no reward was worthy of him. Therefore, it was necessary that the reward be given to others for whom he willed it, that is, human beings. Human beings are thus the beneficiaries of what is due Christ for his act of satisfaction to God. God will not reject anyone who comes to him in the name of Christ or by imitating the actions of Christ. Anselm presents his argument in the form of a question.

To whom will it be more appropriate for Him to transfer the fruit and recompense of His death than to those for whose salvation, as we have heard from reliable arguments, He made himself man and to whom, as we said, He gave by his death an example of dying for the sake of justice?[30]

The notions of satisfaction and justice given to God are crucial in providing the final answer to why God became man: God had no need to do so; however, the unalterable truth required it, because God required human beings to conquer the devil and give him due satisfaction for sin. This, as Anselm confirms, was achieved through the birth, life, and death of the God-Man, Jesus Christ. Nothing divine nor human was foreign to this vision. Consider, for example, Anselm's "Prayer to Christ," in which he provides us with the images shaped by both the divine and human attributes of the God-Man.

> I am like an orphan deprived of the presence
>   of a very kind father,
> who, weeping and wailing, does not cease to cling to
>   the dear face with his whole heart.
> So, as much as I can, though not as much as I ought,
>   I am mindful of your passion.
> your buffeting, your scourging, your cross, your wounds,
>   how you were slain for me,
>   how prepared for burial and buried.[31]

Anselm puts himself in the position of the Virgin Mary watching the body of Christ being taken down from the Cross.

> My most merciful Lady
> what can I say about the fountains
>   that flowed from your most pure eyes
> when you saw your only Son before you,
>   bound, beaten and hurt?
> What do I know of the flood
>   that drenched your matchless face,
> when you beheld your Son, your Lord, and your God,
>   stretched on the cross without guilt,
> when the flesh of your flesh
>   was cruelly butchered by wicked men?[32]

The attempt to think about Christ as a human being who was like an ordinary human being but without sin gave rise to further theological speculations in the following decades. Studies by Bernard of Clairvaux, Abelard, Bruno of Segni, Odo of Cambrai, and Peter Lombard in the twelfth century show a new concern for a better understanding of Christ's humanity and a need to discuss the details of his life as a human being.[33]

The twelfth-century devotion to the human Christ manifested itself either in the devotion to the Eucharist or in the fascination with Christ's life on earth, which would lead the faithful to the love of God through the outward signs. It led to the appearance of the real that organized the system of representation. An initial privation of the body went on producing institutions and systems of representation that were the effects of and the substitutes for that absence. The effects of that absence were coded into versions of the *Quem quaeritis,* which, I argue, performed different functions at different times in the Christian theology. Accordingly, its mode of functioning depended on the discursive formation where it emerged as well as the systems of representation that existed within it. "Quem quaeritis?" sings/asks the angel, to which the Marys reply "Ihesum Nazarenum." How can a body be made from the Word? In the twelfth century, an answer to this question was structured around the discourse on the visible as it was delimited by the corporeal, spiritual, and ecclesiological understanding of the body of Christ.

Numerous versions of the *Quem quaeritis* from the twelfth century not only register an exchange between the Marys and the angel but also include additional dialogue between the Marys, the meeting on the road to Emmaus, and the race between Peter and John.[34] A text from Ripoll (ca. 1100), presented during the Easter vigil in the church, contains an element that cannot be found in the earlier versions of the chant, that is, a description of Mary Magdalene's grief over Christ's missing body and her mistaking of Christ for the gardener. "Her words," notes Richard Axton, "are of the bride of the *Song of Songs* lamenting for her princely lover who has vanished in the night, 'descended' into his garden-grave."[35] Before the Marys approach the sepulchre, an exchange between a merchant and one of the Marys takes place. The merchant says:

> Women, listen to me.
> This ointment, if you wish to buy it,
> has a marvelous potency,
> whereby, if you anoint a body with it,
> the body will be unable to decay further,
> nor can worms eat it.[36]

The mystery of the Easter liturgy is revealed not in the words spoken by the angel but in those spoken by the holy women: "It is proper, sisters, to weep; and weeping to seek Christ; and seeking to anoint the body; and anointing, to gratify. . . . We are, O sisters, believing in our hearts and eager that our eyes see Christ, the power of the ages Who can move the great stone of the tomb or the malice of people? The power of the heavenly banquet. So great a vision, sisters, of splendor and ceremony, should not amaze you; to you be exaltation. Death and the life of death die. Arise, our Resurrection." Upon the women's arrival at the tomb, the exchange between the angel and the Marys takes place. The exchange in the Ripoll text is similar to the exchanges in other *Quem quaeritis* versions.

Where is Christ, my Lord and the son of the Most High? Let us go to see the tomb.
The Angel should reply: Whom do you seek in the sepulchre, O followers of Christ?
The Marys should reply: Jesus of Nazareth, crucified, O Heaven-Dweller.
The Angel should reply: He is not here, he has arisen as he foretold; go, announce that he has arisen, saying:
The Marys should reply: Alleluia, the angel at the sepulchre says Christ has arisen. We praise thee, O Lord.

What follows is the scene between Christ, mistaken for a gardener, and Mary Magdalene. Mary Magdalene approaches the sepulchre with the watchman, to anoint the body of Christ with perfumes and spices.

Mary: The King had taken himself to rest
and my fragrant nard had perfumed the air;
in the garden I came, where he had been,
but he had already left.
Through the night therefore I seek him;
going here and there I cannot find him
Angels: Woman, why do you lament?
Mary: There must be vigils with burning zeal;
When these are done, I will find my spouse.
Gardener: Woman, why do you lament?
Mary: They have taken away my Lord, and I do not know where they have placed him. If you have removed him, tell me, and I will take him.
Gardener: Mary, Mary, Mary!
Let Mary reply: Raboni, Raboni, Raboni!

Though it draws on two gospel accounts, this Easter *Quem quaeritis,* which introduces Mary's lament, adds the episode with perfumes and spices and, with the image from the Song of Songs of a bride lamenting over the departure of her "princely lover," alters the terms of sacramental theology. Although the divine nature of God, who is beyond time and space, is still celebrated, the emphasis on the sacred-human history of Christ draws attention to the change, characteristic for a human being who is mutable because of Adam's sin and its consequences, rather than to the abstract moment of stillness extolling the unchanging nature of God. The conversation between Mary and the gardener is bereft of the universal aspect of sacred history and adopts sequences that can be found in human history or storytelling: the suffering in Mary's lament and the episode with perfumes and spices. The final moments of the Ripoll version of the *Quem quaeritis,* that is, the meeting on the road to Emmaus, adds to the proclamation of the truth of the resurrection of "Jesus of Nazareth, who was a prophet, powerful in deed and word before God and all the people, alleluia."

The added elements to the *Quem quaeritis* increased the performance of meaning associated with the real presence of Christ within the Catholic church. There is no question that, unlike its tenth-century or eleventh-century equivalents, the Ripoll version—and, I suggest, other twelfth-century *Quem quaeritis* forms—enunciated a shift in the practice of representing. Unlike, for example, the *Quem quaeritis* from the *Regularis concordia,* whose function in a monastic house was to reveal the movement of thought (gnosiologic representation), the Ripoll version is marked by giving a physical or material shape to that which had thus far been invisible or missing—the body of Christ, which until now had been only referred to but never seen, was given visibility outside the theological text. This Easter chant celebrated the divine-human nature of Christ as well as his real presence in the Catholic church. As was the case in the corporeal understanding of the Eucharist, the participants in this *Quem quaeritis* were to mediate the presence of Jesus Christ to the believer so that the believer could be united to the Lord and thus saved. The Ripoll version of the *Quem quaeritis* brought into focus the practice of manifesting what can be seen. The real presence of Christ combined with the desire to see him, rather than chanting the words announcing his resurrection, emphasized the union of Christ and the faithful and established their belonging to the community.

This performance of meaning and the practice of showing what can be seen coexisted with other practices that were associated with the ternary mode of thinking about the nature of the Eucharist. Consider, for example, the spiritual discourse and the texts that were produced within its boundaries. The mystical text, colonized by theology, not only authenticated the presence by transcending the ambivalent physicality of the body of Christ but also disclosed an invisible inner life by realigning the relationship between the visible and the invisible. At the same time, the mystical text determined the course of action necessary to make such an utterance possible. It created a place where one can hear, where one can experience, and where one can see that which has vanished or has never been visible. Michel de Certeau may be right when he observes:

> Mystics are engaged in a politics of utterance—they are comparable to lawyers who make the most complete list possible of the situations and addresses apt to lead a proceeding to a "felicitous" conclusion. This kind of "politics," like contemporary rhetoric, sets forth operational rules determining the rational usage of a language that has become uncertain of the real.[37]

Consequently, politics of utterance and visibility can only be designated by a field, observable phenomena, a fixed theological doctrine, and a definition of a mystical experience itself.

Hildegard of Bingen's account of her visionary experiences is a case in point. It presents us with a mystical experience par excellence that "sets forth operational rules determining the rational usage of a language that has become uncertain of the real." When this happens, a mystical experience will always escape the objectifying procedures of the rational usage of a language. In a 1075 letter to Guibert of Gembloux, she describes her revelations in the following manner. Her soul "ascends . . . to the heights of the firmament, . . . and spreads itself out among various peoples, very distant from me, in far away regions." She perceives this topography not with any of her physical senses "but rather in [her] soul, with [her] external eyes open." Her external faculties are not affected, and she can hear and see everything that is going on in the physical world. The light that she experiences, "far brighter than a cloud that bears the sun on it," she calls "the shadow of the living light," in which "the scripture, the virtues, and certain works of men" are reflected, or mirrored, "as the sun, the moon, and the stars appear on the waters." The words that she hears "are not like the words that resound from the mouth of a man, but shine out like flames, and like clouds moving in the pure air." She does not comprehend the form of this light any more than she does the light coming directly from the sun. Finally, she notes that she has, though rarely, been able to see, within the shadow, the living light itself, and that when this happens her sadness and anxiety disappear, so do her exhaustion and pain, and her soul feels refreshed.[38]

This account has been analyzed in terms of linguistic features and poetic imagery that are particularly Hildegardian. Scholars draw attention to the fact that because Hildegard's faculties were not affected, she was able to keep secret the fact of her visions and to only reveal it when, as she notes in *Scivias* (1141), she was "pressed down by the scourge of God."[39] This is in striking contrast to the experience of other mystics, for example, Elizabeth of Schönau, who entirely lost her senses during the ecstasies. Another characteristic feature of Hildegard's account is the level of the immediate generalization of Hildegard's vision: she is interested not in her experience of the revelation but in the truths that were granted to her through contact with many souls close around her and far away from her.

Such a treatment of a mystical experience is dangerously close to conflating a mystical experience and the discourse about the experience into one and the same object of inquiry. Moreover, the analysis of a mode of cognition as if it were an object of cognition, rather than an open and changing territory, defines a mystical experience as a singular and recognizable practice. This practice can be used to constitute the identity of the subject (or a person), "Hildegard of Bingen," who will provide the historian with the "real" that will be placed in his or her narrative.[40] In other words, Hildegard's mystical experience and the way of describing this experience should not be viewed as one. Neither should there be an equation mark placed between the mode of cognition as experienced by Hildegard and what we are to learn from this mystical experience. According to de Certeau, "The question at hand concerns modes of operation or schemata of action, and not directly the subjects (or persons) who are their authors or vehicles."[41]

If such a formulation is tangible, the text of Hildegard's letter to Guibert reveals how Hildegard both produces and guards the place from which she speaks: "My soul ascends . . . to the heights of the firmament, . . . and spreads itself out among various peoples, very distant from me, in far away regions." It may be suggested that Hildegard "forms with [her] body and [her] text, a frontier that divides the space and transforms [her] reader into an inhabitant of the country far from nowhere where [she] houses the essential."[42]

After receiving the divine command "O weak person, both ashes of ashes, and decaying of the decaying, speak and write what you see and hear," Hildegard undertook the work of writing *Scivias,* which begins:

Because you are timid about speaking and simple about explaining and unskilled about writing those things, speak and write those things not according to the mouth of a person nor according to the perception of human inventiveness nor according to the wishes of human arrangement. But according to the extent that you see and hear those things in the heavens above in the marvelousness of God, bring to light those things by way of explanation . . . and write those things not according to yourself but according to the will of the one knowing, see and arrange all things in the secrets of the divinity's own mysteries. (1)

Hildegard was made to create a means of articulating the unsayable (*apophasis*). The shift from the unsayable (*apophasis*) to the sayable (*kataphasis*) was to occur within the space of the *logos,* that is, in the topography of the text dictated to and written down by Volmar and Richardis von Stade. Not Hildegard herself but Volmar and Richardis von Stade constructed a physical site for and a legible record of the articulation of her visions. We can thus only experience the articulation of Hildegard's vision. The mystical was experienced elsewhere, where Hildegard housed the essential that was only accessible to her. Therefore, her words describing "those things not according to [herself] but according to the will of the one knowing" were heard or written outside of the mystic's body but were indecipherable in themselves. For these words to be deciphered, a theological discourse and an institution had to determine precise words and transparent images. Volmar and Richardis von Stade expressed what the institutional language of intelligibility allowed them to express.

Hildegard, however, spoke about something that could not be expressed according to the known or recognized language, according to human perception or logical arrangement. She could only use language to show what it did not or could not say. Therefore, it is not surprising that before the unsayable (*apophasis*) was articulated, it was preceded by a visual description that allowed us to perceive and acknowledge the distance between the image of the mystical experience and the way it was constructed by the words of a theological discourse. What passed for presence in the topography of the text—that is, the words and the images—articulated the foreignness of our place and justified a mystic's desire to travel through the landscape of the unsayable (*apophasis*). Hildegard's contemporary Richard of Saint Victor, in his commentary on the *Apocalypse,* described revelations as

perceived with the help of the Holy Spirit by the eyes of the heart, whereby the human spirit is led through the likeness of visible things or figures and signs to knowledge of invisible ones.[43]

Interestingly, unlike in hagiography, where the virtues and the miracles of male and female saints organized the visible experience of Christian truth (*vera sapientia christianorum*), now a mystic body (*corpus mysticum*) was to perform this function. In order for this truth to be transparent of meaning, it was articulated in socially recognizable terms that were legible to the eyes or pleasing to the ears of believers and unbelievers. A mystical experience and the discourse in search of words and images to express it were conflated. When the visions were written down, the historicity of the moment camouflaged the very conditions of production and the mystical experience itself. The mode of historicity constructed the "real mystical experience," which found its locus in a particular and physical location: in the placement of the discourse (Disibodenberg, Rupertsberg), the administrative function and position of Hildegard in 1141 (abbess or *magistra*), her social status (the tenth child born to a family of upper nobility, Mechtild and the knight Hildebert of Bermersheim), her group identity (Catholic abbess), her modes of operation (her lecture tours, prophesies, and written works: *Scivias, Liber vitae meritorum, Liber divinorum operum, Liber simplicis medicinae, Causae et curae, Lingua ignota, Symphonia harmoniae caelestium revelationum*), and her power relations (her relationships with Eugene III, Bernard of Clairvaux, Thomas Becket, Henry VI of Germany, the emperors Conrad III and Frederic Barbarossa), all of which are the focus of the current Hildegard of Bingen scholarship desiring to systematize her speech and delineate the institutions of meaning.[44] However, we are not well served by a lan-

171

guage of intelligibility propelling a historical and historiographic investigation to obtain the representation of the event and glossing over the conflated discourses. As de Certeau writes,

whatever this new understanding of the past holds to be irrelevant—shards created by the selection of materials, remainders left aside by an explanation—comes back, despite everything, on the edges of discourse or in its rifts and crannies: "resistances," "survivals," or delays discreetly perturb the pretty order of a line of "progress" or a system of interpretation.[45]

At the edges of discourse, the unsayable (*apophasis*) becomes the sayable (*kataphasis*) through the language of allegory—a mode of representational practice.

The structure of *Scivias* is tripartite: the first section is divided into six visions, in which God and the creation are depicted; the second into seven, in which Christ's work of salvation and the continuation of his work through the church and the sacraments are recounted; and the third into thirteen (that is, the sum up of part 1 and part 2), in which the power of the Holy Ghost, the third member of the Trinity, is presented. Each vision is followed by Hildegard's commentary. The collection opens with a view of the Creator on a throne on a mountaintop, bathed in a blinding glorious light, and portrays his encounter with humanity. It includes revelations about the Fall (Adam and the cloud of light that emanates from his side, which symbolizes Eve, allow themselves to be tempted by the snake); the ur-form of the world egg (the six zones of the world egg: the shining fire = God, the dark fire = the zeal of God, the pure ether = belief, the humid zone = baptism, the white zone = Christ, the earth = humanity); the three stages of life; the female figure of the Synagogue, who was given the command to prepare humanity for the Savior; and nine choirs of angels arranged according to the heavenly hierarchy, playing various kinds of music reflecting a perfect harmony. Part 2 opens with the fall of Adam, symbolized by the darkness covering the universe, and the promise of redemption, symbolized by the twinkling stars in the darkened universe and a bright figure who pours his light against the darkness. The remainder of that part is devoted to Christ's work of salvation and the visions of Mother Church, depicted with a net spread over her lap, into which she catches people and strengthens them with the sacraments. Part 3 focuses on the circle of light where the light of the Holy Ghost shines. Inside this circle, on the rock of the fear of God, there begins a construction of the Church of God, which is the object of the visions.

The following is the opening vision in *Scivias,* which was related by Hildegard and transcribed by Volmar or Richardis von Stade.

I saw a great mountain which was iron colored, and a certain person of very great brightness was sitting upon it. The person's brightness was so great that I could not look upon the person, but a soft shadow—actually a wing of extraordinary width and length—was stretched out from each side of the person. Before the person there was a kind of image which was filled with eyes, and this image was standing at the foot of the mountain, but I could discover no human form in this image of very many eyes. And before this image, there was a young girl standing. She was clothed in a pale tunic with white cloth covering her feet. There was such a great brightness descending from the one sitting upon the mountain down to her head that I was not able to see her face. Indeed many sparkling rays shone from the one sitting upon the mountain, and these rays surrounded these other two images very pleasantly. I also saw a lot of stars upon the mountain, and pale and white heads of people appeared among the stars. (7)

As this texts implies, Hildegard was able to perceive the images while she was removed from the source of the images, and as the successive parts of the first vision make clear, she was able to provide an explanation of what she saw. Her ternary mode of seeing corresponded to the three practices described by the Latin noun *visio,* which signified the ability to have visions, the experience of the ability to have visions, and the images of the experience of the ability to have visions.

On yet another level, Hildegard's visions fall into the category of *signa naturalia* that escape the human codification of meaning—they were organized according to the "will of the one knowing." Thus, they were the province of a divine hermeneutics and its *allegoria theologica,* expressing a mode of thought capable of seeing things from the spaceless and timeless point of view of God, who uses the world as his discourse; of *allegoria historiae,* expressing the temporalization of the Christian exegesis, a progressive history that has eternal salvation at the end of its linear trajectory; and of *allegoria in factis,* expressing the spatialization of the historical symbolism between the theological doctrine and facts, events, or known qualities existing here and now. Whereas *allegoria theologica* and *allegoria historiae* depended in their entirety on the divine *potentia absoluta* that shaped the mystical experience and the discourse about the experience, *allegoria in factis* depended on a metaphysics of "qualities" attached to it and an epistemology that could define these qualities. As Hugh of Saint Victor noted, real and stable similarities were necessary to validate an agreement between historical symbolism and facts or events.[46] In *Scivias,* for example, such an agreement exists between the Synagogue, the Virgin Mary, the Mother of the Incarnation, and the woman. Each of them exhibits certain similar qualities necessary to form the basis of comparisons between them. Had this not been the case, the *allegoria in factis* would have degenerated into an endless proliferation of random allegories that signified nothing.

The thirteenth vision of part 3 of *Scivias* and the *Ordo Virtutum,* based on that vision, exemplify this process of realigning the qualities of the unsayable (*apophasis*) with the sayable (*kataphasis*). In the thirteenth vision, Hildegard describes the following experience.

Thereupon the sky got very bright, and I heard all the previously mentioned virtues sing in a wondrous manner to the various types of music. They persisted strongly in the way of truth as they sang the praises of the city of celestial joy. . . . And they persisted in exhorting and encouraging themselves so that they might fight back the snares of the devil and help people gain salvation. But these virtues do overcome the snares of the devil, so that the faithful may pass over at last from sin to celestial reward through repentance. (375)

What follows are the songs of the virtues, "singing a musical performance with harmony in praise of the celestial orders" (375). They sang about the Holy Mother ("O most brilliant gem and serene glory of the sun"), the nine orders of heavenly spirits ("O most glorious light"), the patriarchs and prophets ("O remarkable teachers who pass through the eyes of the spirit"), the apostles ("O cohort of the military"), the martyrs ("O most victorious triumphant ones"), the confessors ("O successors of the strongest lion"), the virgins ("O beautiful faces beholding God and building in the dawn"), and those called back to the same orders ("O bewailing voice, this is of the greatest sorrow"). And then that sound of the voice of the multitude sang aloud harmoniously an exhortation of the virtues—the helpers of people—and a contradiction of the opposing skills of the devil, with the virtues overcoming the faults and with people at length coming back by divine inspiration to repentance (382).

The voices of the multitude included the souls placed in the body, the faithful soul, the virtues, the burdened soul, the soul repenting in the body, and Humility. At the end of this section, that is, once the virtues overcome the faults and the "old serpent has been bound," Hildegard observes:

These voices were the voices of a multitude lifting its voice on high. The sound of these voices passed through me, and I did not have any slowness or difficulty in understanding them. And again I heard the voice from the bright sky speak to me. (389)

The remaining part of the vision is devoted to a description of the voice of "a multitude singing a musical performance with harmony in praise of the celestial orders," in which "[t]he words of the musical perfor- mance stand for the body, and the musical performance itself stands for the spirit" (390).

A description of the experience tells of a manifestation that does not receive its verification or rationale from the outside world.

Thereupon, you see, o people, the sky got very bright. This stands for the joy of the heavenly city. And I heard all the previously mentioned virtues sing in a wondrous manner to the various types of music. . . . This musical performance exists in the heavenly city and perseveres in God in pleasant devotion. It also exists in the complaints of those whom the old serpent has tried to destroy, but whom divine virtue nevertheless has led through to the company of blessed joy. The blessed joy contains those mysteries which the human mind cannot know while on earth. (389–90)

Under the sign of a song and a musical performance, the self no longer writes according to "the will of the one knowing" but, in a single moment, initiates a mode of cognition that diffused *allegoria theologica* ("This musical performance exists in the heavenly city and perseveres in God with pleasant devotion") and *allegoria historiae* ("It also exists in the complaints of those whom the old serpent has tried to destroy, but whom divine virtue nevertheless has led through to the company of blessed joy") into *allegoria in factis*.

Listen, as well, to the sound coming from the sharpness of the living lights shining in the heavenly city, to the sound coming from the profound sermons of the prophets, to the sound spreading out from the wonderful words of the apostles, to the sound coming from the pouring of the blood of those who are offering themselves faithfully, to the sound coming from the secrets of the priestly office, and to the sound coming from the highest greenness of those flowering on virginity. (391)

The mode of cognition was no longer the province of a divine hermeneutics. Having reorganized vision around the text of *allegoria in factis,* it became visible under the guise of a distinct representational practice that gave rise and presence to an invisible.

As Hildegard observes in the thirteenth vision, "the soul of people can be aroused from sluggishness to watchfulness by a musical performance," and "a musical performance also softens hard hearts, leads in the humor of reconciliation, and summons the Holy Spirit" (391). The *Ordo Virtutum* does precisely that. In it, the virtues and the devil fight for the possession of a soul. It opens with a dialogue chant between the patriarchs and prophets and the virtues.

Patriarchs and Prophets: Who are these who look like a cloud?
Virtues: O holy ancients, what makes you wonder at us? The Word of God becomes clear in the form of man, and therefore we shine with Him, edifying the members of His glorious body.[47]

After this introduction of the virtues to the patriarchs and prophets, the souls imprisoned in bodies, a fortunate soul, virtues, and a troubled soul have an exchange that is reminiscent of the discourse presented in Aelred's *The Mirror of Love:* the souls imprisoned in bodies, who should be the daughters of the king but are imprisoned in bodies because of the original sin, complain of a heavy weight of the garment of this life: "I cannot wear the garment wherewith I have been clothed. I wish I could shed it." Discouraged by the slow process of weaving her immortal dress, the troubled soul succumbs to the devil's call: "Serve the world, and it will embrace thee with great honor." Corrupted by nature and its carnality, the troubled soul goes out into the world. As she departs, the virtues lament the weakness of her soul: "O unhappy conscience, o wretched soul, why do you hide your face in the presence of your creator" (51; see also *Scivias,* 383–84). The chorus of virtues, who reveal their nature and their relation to the human and the divine, follows.

O bewailing loudly is the voice of great sorrow. Alas! Alas! a wonderful victory has arisen in the marvelous desire of God, in which the delight of the flesh concealed itself secretly. Alas! Alas! where the will knew no fault, and where the desire of man fled lust. Lament, lament then in these things, O innocence, thou who didst not give up the selfishness in good shame, and thou who didst not eat up the old serpent's greed of the throat there. (53)

This section, not present in *Scivias,* brings forth the relationship between the virtues and charity, fear of God, obedience, faith, hope, innocence, contempt of the world, heavenly love, discipline, modesty, mercy, victory, discretion, and patience. All of these qualities, as Richard of Saint Victor observed, are real and stable, so they could be attached to the epistemology or theology that defined these qualities. The relationship between the virtues and these qualities was clearly defined through the words and the divine *logos* that prevented it from degenerating. The absence of the *logos,* as the troubled soul experienced, would only lead to an endless proliferation of false allegories inhabiting the dark domain of Satan.

The troubled soul returns, however, to the territory of the light and *allegoria in factis:* "O you so regal virtues, how beautiful and how shining you are in the highest sun, and how sweet is your dwelling" (61). She calls for help clothed in the armor of light, and Humility responds to her cry: "Most miserable daughter, I wish to embrace thee, because the great physician has suffered painful and bitter wounds on account of thee" (63). Humility gathers the virtues and descends to battle Satan for the troubled soul.

O living fountain, how great is thy sweetness, thou didst not turn thy face away from these, but foresawest keenly, how thou mightest drag them away from the fall of the angels. . . . Wherefore rejoice, daughter of Sion, because God restored many things to thee which the serpent wished to take away from thee, which now shine in greater light, than they did in the beginning. (63)

The devil is overthrown and Chastity places her heel on Satan's head. The devil is chained but not defeated. The virtues celebrate the meaning of redemption specified here as the incorporation of all souls into the divine body of Jesus Christ.

O god, who art thou, thou who within thy own person heldest this great consultation, which destroyed the infernal poison among the publicans and sinners, who now shine in the celestial goodness! . . . O omnipotent father, from these the fountain flows in fiery love; lead thy sons into the wind favorable for the sail of the waters, so that we also may lead them so into the celestial Jerusalem. (67)

The final section of the *Ordo Virtutum* begins with an invocation of the beginning of time.

[A]ll creatures grew and flourished, in the middle flowers bloomed; afterwards the bloom of the green grew brown. And this man, a jouster, saw and said: This I know, but the golden number is not yet full. Therefore, mirror of the Father, behold, in my body I sustain a weariness, also my little ones fall off. Now be mindful, because the fullness which was made in the beginning, ought not to run dry, and then thou hadst in thyself, that thy eye should never yield, until thou mightest see my body full of the buds. For it wearies me, because all my members become a mockery. Father see, I show my wounds to thee. Therefore now, all men, bend your knees to your Father, so that he can stretch out his hand to you.

Who are these who look like a cloud?
We, however, are all [*Nos autem omnes*]. (69)

The concluding passage evokes Christ's reaching to his people in love and reminding them of the virtues who "shine with Him, edifying the members of His glorious body." These images are reminiscent of the visions in part 3 of *Scivias* that are devoted to the building of the Church of God, whose individual walls and towers are raised by the virtues, which symbolize the manifold powers of grace.[48] Whereas the closing part of the *Ordo Virtutum* refers to the mystical body of Christ, the focus is on the God-Man and his wounds. The last line, "Nos autem omnes," returns the reader/viewer to the biblical promise of the end of time, when everything that is mortal will cease to exist—or will shed the garment it was clothed with, to use a metaphor from the *Ordo Virtutum*—and will begin to exist in marvelous harmony.

The *Ordo Virtutum* is a spectacular manifestation of that which remained unsayable, invisible, and exceptional. It is a manifestation that organized vision around a mystical phenomenon. It did so with the excess of a presence that could never be possessed. It is true that the phenomenal was made visible when the virtues appeared: "the soul of people can be aroused from sluggishness to watchfulness by a musical performance." This will often be practiced in later texts, such as *Everyman* and *The Castle of Perseverance*. But while the phenomenal was made visible, the mystical remained secret and invisible. The representational practice was a projection not of the human eye engaged in the process of doubling but of the inner eye. In the description of her visions, Hildegard often stresses that she hears with the inner ear of the soul and sees with the inner eye of the spirit. The body, in the expression of mystical phenomena, does not have a physical or corporeal presence that we can recognize with current taxonomies: "The sound of these voices passed through me, and I did not have any slowness or difficulty in understanding them." The body, not yet colonized by medicine, mechanics, psychoanalysis, gender studies, or virtual technology, formed a frontier that divided space into a guarded place where the mystical was housed and a territory that could be accessed by those listening and watching. The place was where the movement of the sound and music dissolved the rational discourse by erasing the horizon—there was no longer a separation between the elements: "The sound of these voices passed through me . . ." The territory, a field epistemologically foreign to those listening and watching, was a background on which local, transitory, and ephemeral traces of the reality of the unsayable (*apophasis*) and the spiritual domain of the inner light were projected. It made visible what lies within and what could temporarily be possessed through the words of Volmar and Richardis von Stade or the theologically correct images of *Scivias* and the *Ordo Virtutum*.

By realigning the unsayable (*apophasis*) with the sayable (*kataphasis*) or the invisible with the visible, the *Ordo Virtutum* returned *the* mystical experience to the field of theology and the visible institution. They defined it as *a* mystical experience and gendered this type of practice so it could constitute the identity or identities of the subject. It did so by linking mystic knowledge and its representational practices of that which moves as sound within *apophasis* to the practices of representing transparent meaning that can no longer be separated from the hierarchical organization of knowledge and the validity of visions in a secure theological articulation of the "real": "Hoc est corpus meum."

Whether presented for the dedication of the new convent at Rupertsberg (Potter), as the *ordo* for the consecration of virgins (Sheingorn), or as psychotherapy for Hildegard (Holloway), the *Ordo Virtutum* determined the course of a representational practice that was designated by a site, observable movements, heard words, and a fixed theological doctrine.[49] The revelations and the musical performance, however, were theatrical or dramatic representations not only of the traces of the affects that produced them in the process of doubling but of the codes that determined the possibilities of comprehension and the mode of operation (that is, articulation, circulation, dissemination, and appropriation) of the *corpus mysticum* within the field of a visible institution and its *allegoriae in factis*.

Whereas the *Ordo Virtutum* exemplifies the practice of realigning the unsayable with the sayable to bring the mystical experience into full view, the *Jeu d'Adam* presents us with a different practice within a heterogeneous discourse on representation in the twelfth century. The *Jeu d'Adam*, an Anglo-Norman text, was written sometime between 1125 and 1175.[50] The incomplete manuscript refers to three episodes that convey the traditional doctrine of the Catholic church—the original sin, the recurrence of sin, and the promise of redemption: that is, the story of Adam and Eve, the killing of Abel, and the Procession of the Prophets. The work of such scholars as E. K. Chambers, Hardin Craig, O. B. Hardison, Grace Frank, Kenneth Urwin, William Calin, Wendy Morgan, and Stephen Justice, to mention just a few names of people working in the area, contributed immensely to our understanding of and knowledge about the *Jeu d'Adam*.[51] Their scholarship describes the text's function; mode of presentation; place in the history of medieval drama and theater; linguistic, stylistic, and thematic patterns; and historical, cultural, and social relevance. The *Jeu d'Adam*, we are told, abounds in information and terminology that suggests that it was staged outside a church; that, because of its vernacular dialogue, it can be viewed as an example of secularization of church drama; that it had a unified composition; that it conveyed a religious message; that it can be seen as an assertion of feudal or clerical authority; and that its author must have been acutely aware of the dissonance between the twelfth-century system of social relationships as encapsulated in the feudal, courtly, and ecclesiastical institutional codes and the credal code inherited from scripture, liturgy, and doctrine.

One of the most recent works on this text, Steven Justice's "The Authority of Ritual in the *Jeu d'Adam*," aspires to move beyond marking the dramatic/linguistic patterns or institutional power relations by proposing:

the significance of the Adam's dramaturgic novelty can be traced to particular ideological disturbances created by particular developments in ecclesiastical life. The play appropriates the liturgy of public penance to reassert traditional authoritative forms at the time when the disposition of spiritual authority was being reimagined, both in formal theological discussions and in the concrete act of sacramental absolution. . . . [T]he innovations express in a new way the old idea that submission to the ecclesiastical hierarchy is a healthy way to live. In placing the action before the church doors the author made the church building not merely the context of the play (as it was in the indoor liturgical drama), but also its subject.[52]

Justice goes on to say that "the rites of public penance and absolution determine the form and scope of the play, at a time when those rites were themselves the focus of a crucial change in institutional spirituality."[53] Two elements are worth noting in this particular approach to the *Jeu d'Adam:* first, the possibility that the church building is the subject of the play, rather than merely the site of action; second, the significance that is attributed to public penance in the process of reforming institutional spirituality. These elements, according to Justice, "determine both specific dramatic gesture and the narrative trajectory of the play; the dramatic action redefines the history of salvation around the ritually defined pattern of penance and reconciliation, around the numinous presence of the church building, the authority found there, and the desire to enter it."[54] Justice implies that the play does so due to its historical situation. To be more precise, the play registers the shift in a theological interpretation of the world: an earlier tradition of identifying sacred theology with sacred places—monasteries and church—is now being modified by the idea of apostolic mission and vernacular preaching. The traces of this shift can be found in the play. The text can be said to express the changing relationship between penitent and priest by emphasizing the manner of the administration of sacramental penance and absolution that privileges a penance that stresses answerability to the ecclesiastical hierarchy rather than the private adjudication of penance. This is the reason why Justice locates the play in a season during Lent and thus at the time when the faithful were to contemplate the original sin and their share in its recurrence, before they were allowed to participate in the Easter Sunday ceremonies.

I quote Justice's argument at length here because it introduces many interesting possibilities for investigating the *Jeu d'Adam.* Even though I fully agree with the author's intricate train of thought, I suggest an alternative course of action in the treatment of the *Jeu d'Adam.* Rather than arguing that "the rites of public penance and absolution determine the form and scope of the play" and that "the dramatic action redefines the history of salvation around . . . the numinous presence of the church building," I would like to discuss the *Jeu d'Adam* not as a feudal metaphor or in terms of penance and reconciliation but as a representational practice within the twelfth-century theological discourse on *Hoc est corpus meum* and the extent to which it constructed a practice of what can be seen within the ternary mode of perception of the body of Christ. Even though the *Jeu d'Adam*, like the *Ordo Virtutum*, is not directly Christocentric, it provides us with a possibility of grasping the degree to which the ternary mode of understanding the Eucharist regulated and determined representational practices within the entire theological field and the institutions it created in order to administer its interpretation of the world.

Beyond and above its dramatic and theatrical qualities, the *Jeu d'Adam*, both as a text and as a physical manifestation, can be seen as a practical application of ecclesiological theology. Viewed as such, it partakes in the process of establishing that which was put forth by ecclesiological theology—the desire to realign a private experience of the Eucharist with the church; the treatment of the *Ecclesia*, rather than the body of Christ, as the *corpus mysticum;* the consolidation of the structures of belonging and unity by advocating the need for good juridical standing in the Catholic community. These were accomplished with the help of such liturgical practices as the elevated Host effecting what happens within the church during the Mass in general and the sacrament of the Eucharist in particular. The reception of the Eucharist was a formal occasion that, at the time of the growing devotion to Christ in the Sacrament, was infrequent for the general population and always connected with the high feasts in the Christian calendar and, specifically, with the feast of Easter. In order for the people to be able to participate in the celebration of the unity of the Christian community, they needed to prepare themselves before approaching the altar. The ecclesiastical authority prescribed different ways of how this could be accomplished, many of which referred to private practices controlled by a priest. Consider, for example, a confession, paying of tithes, or offerings to the church, all of which were used to establish the transparency of the bodies gathered inside the church. If a person was admitted to receive the Eucharist, it meant that he or she was "purified"; so was the person standing next to him or her, and together they were marked as the chosen people represented by the church.

However, the production of visibility (the elevated Host) and the drive toward transparency (confession) were not the only practices institutionalizing the structures of belonging. A popular movement of devotion to Christ in the Sacrament and the *Jeu d'Adam* were other practices within the complex topography of the ecclesiological approach toward the Eucharist that were used to achieve the same goal.

The *Jeu d'Adam* was to be presented outside the church.[55] Its opening statement reads:

Let paradise be constructed in a prominently high place [*constituatus paradisus loco eminentori*]; let curtain and silken hangings be placed around it at such a height that those persons who will be in paradise can be seen from the shoulders upwards; let sweet-smelling flowers and foliage be planted; within let there be various trees, and fruits hanging on them, so that the place may seem as delightful as possible [*ut amoenissimus locus videatur*].[56]

Thus, paradise is to be exhibited in a prominently high place, possibly at the top of the stairs leading to the west portal of the church. This is where God (*Figura*), wearing a bishop's stole, will talk to Adam, clothed in a red tunic, and to Eve, clothed in a woman's white garment.

The first sequence is the story of Adam and Eve and the events leading to their expulsion from paradise. It begins with the biblical account of the creation of heaven and earth ("In principio creavit Deus celum et terram"), which is followed by the choir's responsory, "And the Lord God formed [man]" [*Formavit igitur Dominus*]. Both the account and the responsory are in Latin. The text then continues:

Quo finito dicat Figura
Adam! Who must answer: Sire?
Figura: Fourme te ai de limo terre.
Adam: Ben le sai.
[let the Figure say
Adam! Who must answer: Sire?
Figure: I have formed you of loam of the earth
Adam: I know it well.]

(81; 43–45)

Unlike the lesson and the responsory, the exchanges between the Figura and Adam as well as those between other participants in the story unfolding in front of the church are in vernacular. The Figura informs Adam that he was formed in God's likeness and that he must never make war against God. Adam agrees to obey his creator.

These opening lines establish the duty of obedience. The language used in the exchange introduces terminology and expressions that allow us to define this duty of obedience either in terms of the feudal systematization of loyalty within a feudal code or in terms of institutional pedagogy. According to Morgan:

The first departure from the biblical account occurs in line 5 ["Ne moi devez ja mais mover guere," which translates, "You must never make war against me"]. The particularity of its prohibition is extraordinary. . . . The reason that the notion of taking up arms against one's lord can sum up any betrayal is presumably because it was the threat to peace—and to survival—which a medieval audience could most easily comprehend. . . . There is nothing in the prelapsarian situation which calls for so specific a warning as this, but in a context which emphasizes that Adam is literally God's "creature," his "homme" (in feudal terminology the vassal), there is surely an echo of the oath of fealty which accompanied the act of homage or self-surrender.[57]

According to Justice:

In his first sentence God quotes, in Latin, a line from a responsory that the audience has just heard ("De limo terre"). Then he translates, "A ma imagene t'ai feit de terre." God's claim to authority derives from his act of creation, but his proof of that authority lies in his Latinity. He enacts a familiar institutional pedagogy, translating and explaining an authoritative text for an unlettered parishioner. That pedagogical authority entails another authority as well. . . . [T]he Latin that signals the authority to teach signals also the authority to discipline.[58]

Both of these possibilities are illuminating, and there is no question, as the articles by Morgan and Justice unequivocally contend, that the use of vernacular opened up the biblical account to accommodate both of them at the same time. However, when viewed in terms of a representational practice engendered by ecclesiological theology, this opening sequence indicates that the presence of Latin and the vernacular was a conscious choice made to close the gap between the church apparatus and a lived Christianity. It seems that the emphasis on the ecclesiastical mode of the sacrament of the Eucharist defined as the union of Christ and his church infiltrated other surrounding practices. To speak Latin meant that a majority of the Christian population was marginalized and that only the elite class (monastic communities and priests) could fully participate in an apostolic discourse. The rest could engage in different forms of private experiences. These individualized, private experiences could easily separate themselves from the institution and degenerate into the proliferation of thoughts and practices that went against the doctrinal teachings. And they did—the condemnation of the translation of the Bible presented by the followers of Peter Waldes and the excommunication of the Cathars during the three sessions of the Third Lateran Council in March, 1179, seem to have been directed toward strengthening the unity of the church.[59] Here, however, a link was established between the ecclesiastical authority and a vernacular Christianity. This link delimited what should be seen and heard by the people standing at the bottom of the stairs and watching the events, which absorbed different gazes, presented in a prominently high place in front of the church.

The story continues: the Figura gives Adam a worthy companion.

> wife, Eve by name . . .
> Born of you. . . .
> Govern her by reason.
> Let no dissention come between you,
> But great love and mutual obedience:
> Such is the law of marriage.
>
> (81–82; 45)

Then, the Figura turns to Eve and establishes her duty of obedience—to love and honor God as her creator and acknowledge him as her lord (*Seignor*)—as well as her duty as wife according to the law and the sacrament of marriage. If she performs these duties, she will be placed with Adam in glory. Eve's answer can be read in terms of an enactment of a feudal code, an institutional pedagogy, or a lived Christianity.

> Sire, I will do according to your pleasure;
> I do not wish to stray from it.
> I will acknowledge you as sovereign [*seignor*]

185

Him as my partner and stronger than I.
I will always be faithful to him;
From me he will have good counsel.
Your pleasure, your service
I will perform, Sire, in every way.

(82; 47)

This promise, spoken in vernacular, gives a space where the act takes place, a truth; a truth which thus far only existed in Latin in the oath of fealty or the sacrament of marriage.

Once the truth is established, the Figura points out paradise to Adam and charges him to guard it. The nature of the Garden of Eden is revealed in the following passage:

You will find [there] no lack of any delight.
There is no earthly good a creature might desire
That each cannot find to his own pleasure.
Here woman will receive from man no anger,
Nor man from woman have shame or fear.
Man is no sinner for begetting children,
Nor does woman experience pain in bearing them.
You will live forever, thus you will have a wonderful
   existence here;
Your age can never alter.
Death you will never fear, nor can it ever harm you.
I do not wish you to leave; here you must make your dwelling.

(84; 53)

The beauty of paradise is thus established not only by describing its sweet-smelling flowers, foliage, and trees with fruit hanging on them but also by contrasting it with what those watching the figures on the church steps would recognize as their own ills and toils of everyday life. Of particular interest are statements concerning the relationship between a woman and a man, sex, bearing of children, the lack of aging, and the absence of death. The division between the biblical world of the Church and the practices of everyday life, and thus between the life that could have been and the life that is, is clearly pronounced here in a manner that strengthens the consequences of the original sin that has not yet been committed. The space of representation collapses past time and future time into a present time in which both Adam and Eve and the people watching are marked by the loss. They are reminded that there was once a world in which they would not have felt pain or anger, aged, or died. Now this world is beyond their reach—it is up there in a prominently high place, whereas they are at the bottom of the stairs leading to it. Their eyes go up. The vision is delimited by the walls of the church. They are not up there. The following sequence will remind them why this is the case.

Having warned Adam that to eat the fruit from one of the trees is forbidden, the Figura goes to the church. In the meantime, the devils appear and the temptation of Adam and Eve ensues. The devil promised Adam knowledge and power but fails to succeed with him. The devil then approaches Eve and seduces her, an inferior creature, with the possibility of obtaining knowledge from which she has been excluded. This transgression can be seen either as the desire to throw off feudal subjection—for Adam would have equal power to God's and Eve would become more than Adam's equal by knowing the secrets he now would be excluded from (Morgan)—or as a tropological exegesis of the Fall (Justice), in that this particular sequence does not follow the biblical emphasis on the knowledge of good and evil.

The temptation of Adam and Eve is a transgression against the structures of belonging described by the Figura in his speech about the nature of paradise and Adam's position in it. The devil promises the establishment of the self; however, the self cannot be an autonomous being in this environment but is a part of the community created by the Figura and, in collapsed time, by the authority of the church. Adam and, by extension, those watching are reminded about this by the Figura, who emerges out of the church.

> I created you in my likeness;
> Why have you transgressed my commandment?
> I shaped you after my own image;
> Why have you done me this outrage?
> You paid no attention to my prohibition;
> Deliberately you transgressed it.
> You ate the fruit which I told you
> I had forbidden you.
> Did you think by this to be my equal?
>
> (99; 93)

The description of Adam and Eve's life, reminiscent of the description of what paradise is not, follows. When Adam and Eve fall, they fall from a prominently high place down the stairs leading to the church: "On earth you will have your dwelling" (101; 99), says the Figura. The life on earth is full of misery and suffering, which are the consequence of the lack of obedience to the Creator. Adam and Eve's lament discloses eloquently both the emotional condition and the theological didacticism of their life in sin, which will be perpetuated by their progeny until the time of the full reconciliation for the sin.

> God will tend me his grace and his favor;
> He will rescue us from hell by his might.
>   (105; 107)

Past and future are present. Adam and Eve's life is the life of the people in the space where Adam and Eve found themselves after the expulsion. Because of sin and the recurrence of sin, they are barred from entering the biblical paradise, which here and now is the church. Those watching are reminded about this by Jeremiah, who explicitly says in the closing section of the *Jeu d'Adam:*

Hear the word of the Lord, all you men of Judea, that enter at these gates to worship the Lord. *And with his hand he will point to the doors of the church.* Thus says the Lord of hosts, the God of Israel: Make your ways and your doings good, and I will dwell with you in this place. (118; 139)

Before this closing takes place, however, the story of Cain and Abel is presented. The second part of the *Jeu d'Adam* focuses on this postlapsarian event that takes place on earth. Cain, dressed in red garments, and Abel, dressed in white, cultivate the fields. From the very beginning, their existence is marked by the notion of the collapsed, present time. This is achieved through the use of the vernacular as well as through the statements that establish their and the audience's relationship to Adam and Eve. The comments made by Abel describe also, in a paradigmatic way, the manner in which the people surrounding them should view their position and duties in respect to both God and the church. Consider, for example, the following passage.

> Brother Cain, we are two kinsmen
> And sons of the first of men:

That was Adam, our mother was named Eve.
In serving God let us not be churlish.
Let us be at all times obedient to the Creator;
Let us so serve that we will win back his love,
Which our parents lost by their folly. . . .
So let us serve God that it will please him always;
Pay him his due, let nothing be held back.
If with willing heart we will obey him
Our souls will have nothing to fear.
Let us pay his tithes and all that is justly his due.

(106; 109–11)

In no uncertain terms, this passage is a reminder of the duty of obedience as well as a straightforward explanation of the reasons why the tithes should be justly paid to God and, by extension, to the church. Cain's response is a refusal to listen to advice that could impoverish him. He retorts: "This giving of tithes has never suited me" (106; 111). Thus, the duty of obedience is here reduced to the focus on tithes rather than on the acceptability of a religious teaching. Morgan explains this shift in focus by suggesting that it sheds some light on the attitude of the church toward those who were profiting under the agricultural, economic, and monetary revival in the twelfth century. It is possible to suggest that the church feared that the accumulation of wealth in private hands might lead to the church's loss of the exclusive social and political control.[60] Cain's response is thus a response of a person who refuses to live according to the traditional feudal code. More importantly, he defies the kinsmanship by claiming his own autonomy to be able to follow his own inclinations. This establishes a double threat—the desire to break a feudal bond as well as the desire to liberate oneself from the religious moral and institutional code.

Abel attempts to convince his brother to make an offering to God to please him, arguing that in turn God will "give us his love and defend us from evil, night and day" (107; 113). Cain agrees to do so, though the tone of his agreement, as the Latin text suggests, carries with it an element of ambiguity: "Then Cain will answer as if Abel's counsel has pleased him" [*Tunc respondebit Chaym, quasi placuerit ei consilium Abel*] (107; 113).

The linguistic duplicity, expressed in the vernacular and suggested in Latin, marks the exclusion of the vernacular from the established system of truth and transparency—that is, from the system of both theological and feudal law written in Latin—and posits the possibility of conflict. This conflict is articulated within the topography of the represented biblical story, which in turn is supported by the practices of a unified and functioning *corpus mysticum,* that is, the Church. Thus, the only way to avoid this conflict is to expose this duplicity. This can be done not by treating the vernacular as the "other" that is outside the language (Latin) where God and his truths reside but by postulating and determining how the vernacular should move and function within the biblical topography. To achieve this, the vernacular needs to be realigned with the body of doctrines so that it corresponds precisely to the divine truth. Once this happens, the vernacular will be able to absorb specific procedures and practices. They will, in turn, mold it into the language that will express the accounts of truth *of* and *in* a lived Christianity.

Before this happens however, a visual representation of this duplicity is staged—Abel's sacrifice of a lamb and incense and Cain's sacrifice of a handful of his harvest are presented.

The Figure will bless Abel's gift but disdain that of Cain. Wherefore, after the oblation, Cain will make a savage face against Abel; and, when their oblations have been completed, they will go to their own places. Then Cain will come to Abel, seeking cunningly to lead him forth in order to kill him. (109; 117)

Cain accuses Abel of treachery and disloyalty. He feels excluded from Abel's relationship with God as well as rejected by God because of this relationship. Abel asks for mercy, then kneels facing east. "Turning 'toward the east' in a production executed at the west door," says Justice, "Abel turns toward the lost paradise, toward the Church."[61] Cain kills Abel.

When Abel is dead, the choir sings a responsory: "Ubi est Abel, frater tuus?" [Where is Abel, your brother?] (112; 124) The Figura appears from the church and, when the choir has finished the responsory, says to Cain, "Chaim, u est ton frere Abel?" [Cain, where is your brother Abel?] (112; 125). The responsory in Latin and the Figura's repetition of its first line in the vernacular stops a further degeneration of the vernacular into duplicity. Now they are realigned, and both can express the truth articulated by the Figura. Unlike in the first section of the *Jeu d'Adam,* the Figura makes the last speech in the Cain and Abel section. Having descended from the church, he pronounces the judgment against Cain: he will endure his life in sorrow, and because his brother died in God's faith, Cain's penance will be grave (113; 127). The Figura returns to the church. The devils come and lead Cain to hell, beating him. The text says, "They will lead Abel away more gently" (113; 127).

The desire for the return to paradise is not fulfilled. Adam and Eve, despite their remorse, and Abel, a person leading his life according to the rules, are returned to hell. So will be the prophets who are called by name to announce their prophecies "clearly and distinctly" in the closing section of the *Jeu d'Adam*.

All of the prophets in this section of the text speak to the same topic, the coming of the Redeemer. They first declare their prophecies in Latin and then present an expanded version in the vernacular. After reading a lesson, the choir cries out, "You, I say, I do summon before a tribunal, O Jews" [*Vos, inquam, convenio, O Judei*]. Abraham, an old man with a long beard and dressed in ample garments, emphasizes the need to stay faithful to God and to trust him. Moses, bearing a rod in his right hand and the tablets in his left, announces, "from our own brethren, from our law, God will raise up a man" (114; 131). Aaron, in bishop's attire and holding a rod in his hand with flowers and fruit, says: "such a rod will come from [his] lineage who will be Satan's nemesis. . . . This is the fruit of salvation, Who will release Adam from prison" (115; 131). After him, David, with royal insignia, comes forward to say: "Out of the earth truth shall arise, And justice, from divine majesty" (115; 131). Solomon, wearing the same attire as David, observes that though the Jews did not judge Christ with justice or reason and crucified him, Christ will deliver them from sin. Balaam, an old man sitting on an ass, asserts that Christ will rise out of Israel and says: "he will be that shining star. All things will be illuminated by him. His faithful one he will safely lead, His enemies he will all confound" (116; 135). Daniel, a youth wearing an old man's garment, says his prophecy while stretching out his hand toward/against those to whom he is speaking ("manum extendens contra eos ad quos loquitur"):

> To you, O Jews, I deliver my sermon,
> You who are excessively wicked toward God.
> When the greatest of all the saints appears . . .
> Then your anointing will cease.

> By the greatest of saints, I mean Christ,
> He who wishes his people gain eternal life through him.
> For them he will come to earth.
>
> (117; 134)

After Daniel speaks, Habakkuk, an old man, lifts his hand toward the church ("eriget manus contra ecclesiam") and amplifies his prophesy in Latin by saying in the vernacular:

> I have heard strange tidings concerning God: . . .
> Between two beasts he will be recognized;
> By all the world he will be feared.
> He of whom I have such great wonder
> Will be pointed out by a star;
> Shepherds will find him in a crib . . .
> Then, he will reveal himself to kings;
> The star will lead the kings there;
> All three will bear offerings.
>
> (117; 136)

Jeremiah, with a scroll in his hand and pointing to the portals of the church, stresses that those who are of God's doctrine will be able to enter his household if their hearts are pure and free of wickedness.

> If you do thus, God will come . . .
> The son of God, the glorious ones,
> Will come down to earth for your sake . . .
> He will be among you as mortal man . . .
> He will release Adam from prison,
> Giving his own body as ransom.
>
> (118; 139)

Finally, Isaiah, with a book in his hand and wearing a cloak, delivers his prophesy concerning the spirit of God who shall rest on a rod out of the root of Jesse.

When Isaiah finishes, a person, a Jew, appears from the synagogue (*de synagoga*) to dispute the prophesies with him. This section is incomplete; it ends abruptly with Nebuchadnezzar, though, as scholars suggest, the theme follows the concern of medieval Christianity with the conversion of the Jews.[62]

Quoting Jeremiah's prophesy, Justice argues: "the focus of expectation is not Christ, but the return through the gates of paradise, gates now explicitly defined as 'portas ecclesiae.' This moment appropriates the desire to reenter paradise as the desire to enter the church."[63] This desire, according to Justice, could be encouraged and even enforced by the practice of the excommunications that were imposed on Ash Wednesday and lasted until Maundy Thursday: "The ceremony clearly provides the model for the staging and action of the *Jeu d'Adam*."[64] In the view of the ceremony, and as the *Jeu d'Adam* implies, sin signifies alienation from an ecclesiastical paradise and the desire to recover it. This argument is further strengthened by the fact that the *Jeu d'Adam* was presented in front of the church and used its topography to visualize the traditional biblical story that is now modified by the vernacular. Therefore, Justice proposes that the *Jeu d'Adam* was presented in the time around Ash Wednesday: "The only satisfying ending to the story—the reapproach to the church—is not available within the story; the audience must seek it outside the story by recapitulating the penitential submission of Adam and Eve, in order to receive the restoration promised by Jeremiah."[65]

If, indeed, the *Jeu d'Adam* was associated with Ash Wednesday and the liturgy of absolution, its sections—the story of Adam and Eve, that of Cain and Abel, and the Procession of the Prophets—functioned to give visibility to that which had existed as the biblical text presented in sacred places in Latin. The prophesies of the prophets, for example, are the theme of the fourth vision of the third part in Hildegard's *Scivias*.[66] With the focus on the power of the Holy Ghost, Hildegard describes what she has seen and interprets it by the "divine voice." Here, she saw a three-sided column.

The side which faced the east had branches coming out of it. These branches started at the root and continued right up to the top. I saw Abraham sitting on the first branch near the root. Moses was sitting on the second branch, Joshua on the third, and the rest of the patriarchs and prophets were sitting on separate branches, starting at the bottom and working upwards.[67]

In her commentary, Hildegard explains that even though the prophets were joined together, they were "not yet fastened to and lifted up by the perfect work of the Word of God." Rather, she claims, "They were still prophesying with the outward sounds of their own words."[68]

In the *Jeu d'Adam,* the prophets, "prophesying with the outward sounds of their own words," do not join God (i.e., enter the church) but are taken to hell. This experience, however, is not a private, mystical exploration of the vision generated within the confines of a sacred place and its theology but is presented with the church, the *corpus mysticum* of the ecclesiological theology, in full view. So are the section on Adam and Eve and that on Cain and Abel. By giving visibility outside the textual theology, these sections return the experience of the dogma to the field of the visible institution. They clearly enunciate what should be seen and how it should be seen. The places where the biblical story (past time) unfold are clearly described. At the same time, the text in the vernacular (future time) establishes the structures of belonging in the collapsed, present time. This collapsed, present time reestablishes the link between the biblical story and the ecclesiastical apparatus. With the church assuming the function of the *corpus mysticum,* and with the unity of the Christian community established through the identification of the church with Christ, the placement of the *Jeu d'Adam* in front of the church building a few days before the Easter Mass and its sacrament of the Eucharist was to inspire belief and unity. In this sense, the *Jeu d'Adam* was a representational practice that partook in the production of the visible through the process of an increased performance of the biblical meaning. If the faithful wanted to be saved—and he or she could be because of Christ's sacrifice as predicted by the prophets—the only way to achieve this was to go through the portals of the church. This procession would take place a few days after the presentation of the *Jeu d'Adam,* during the Easter Mass, when the whole community would join the priest in the celebration of *Hoc est corpus meum.* The raised Host would then be the focal point of all the gazes now gathered inside the church. The unity would be achieved; the desire to enter paradise would be fulfilled.

In "The Theory of the Other," Deleuze observes that the Other is initially a structure of the perceptual field that conditions the entire field and without which the field could not function. This statement, which challenges the authority of the perspectival, linear relationship between a subject and an object, is especially useful in the considerations of this chapter. The ternary discourse on the Eucharist conditioned the entire field within which the interpretation of *Hoc est corpus meum* emerged. The corporeal, spiritual, and ecclesiological approaches described in detail the mode of presence of Christ and how it molded in turn the desire to materialize his body. Taking a cue from Deleuze, I argue that this mode of presence was a structure that conditioned how the body was made visible both in the Eucharist and in other practices associated with the execution of the dogma. They were never homogeneous. On the contrary, they draw our attention to the possibility that, in the twelfth century, representation was a complex discursive formation engendered by and engendering *Hoc est corpus meum* and attempting to reveal the integral comprehension of the things that are in the perceptual field. The Ripoll version of the *Quem quaeritis,* Hildegard of Bingen's *Ordo Virtutum,* and the *Jeu d'Adam* reveal a tension among the visible and invisible space, body, and *logos* before it faded and was washed away by the ever shifting relationship between theological, historical, and metaphysical formulations that defined the conditions of existence of the ternary discourse on the Eucharist in the twelfth century.

CHAPTER 4

Ecclesia universalis: "This Is My Body"

The problem is . . . to determine what occurs in a field which is delimited by a name and within which the work is being done in obedience
to a relevant set of rules.

—Michel de Certeau, *The Mystic Fable*

The Fourth Lateran Council, which was held on November 11, 20, and
30, 1215, is remembered for its constitutions regarding confession and
Communion that have been observed in the Catholic church since that
time. Chapter 21 of the constitutions unequivocally states: "All the
faithful of either sex, after they have reached the age of discernment,
should individually confess all their sins in a faithful manner to their
own priest at least once a year. . . . Let them reverently receive the sacrament of the Eucharist at least at Easter."[1] These statements regarding
the sacrament of the Eucharist exist alongside other constitutions that
were of great significance at the time. Among those are the definition of
the dogma of transubstantiation, comments regarding the position of
Jews within Christendom, and a general call for the crusade of 1217.[2]

    In the annals of the history of the Catholic church, this particular
council holds a prominent position. Its place was secured not only by its
regulations, which are binding even today, or by its statements concerning the holy war, which altered the course of medieval history, but
also by the function assigned to it by Pope Innocent III—that is, "to
eradicate vices and to plant virtues, to correct faults and to reform
morals, to remove heresies and to strengthen faith, to settle discords and
to establish peace, to get rid of oppression and to foster liberty, to
induce princes and christian people to come to the aid and succour of the
holy Land" (227).[3] The seventy constitutions, divided into fourteen sub-

categories, and the announcement of the expedition for the recovery of the Holy Land were to be a material representation of his plan.[4]

Whereas the constitutions of the Fourth Lateran Council are a record of an ecumenical meeting of 404 bishops and abbots of the church as well as priors and chapters of churches and of religious orders, the council represents a space, which will articulate a very specific ensemble of movements and operations within it, and an apparatus, which will safeguard the configuration of the new operations, the order in accord with which the elements are distributed, and the identity of the practices.[5]

Consider this chapter's epigraph, from Michel de Certeau.[6] By shifting the focus from the ecumenical value and historical function of the council toward the process of determining the practices within a field whose boundaries were logocentrically established, it can be argued that the constitutions of the Fourth Lateran Council mark an epistemological shift in making visible what emerges in a field. In other words, the constitutions of the Fourth Lateran Council disclose a moment of producing the notion of representation and how it was defined, rationalized, and institutionalized in the early thirteenth century. With the emphasis on the presence of the church itself rather than the mode of presence, this epistemological shift manifested itself and was made apparent in, for example, the process of reducing the ternary mode of thinking about *Hoc est corpus meum,* which marked the twelfth century, to the binary, or oppositional, discourse regarding the sacrament of the Eucharist and, after 1215, separating those who accepted the idiom from those who transgressed the adjudicated norm. As a consequence of developing the new procedures, the biological, spiritual, or ecclesiological experience of the body of Christ was no longer viewed as one of the coexistent discursive formations differentiated by its individual practices of what can be seen. Rather, the experience of the body of Christ was determined by the production of a body that would make a "spirit" visible. In this process of producing and disseminating the visibility of the sacramental body, the debates regarding the body of Christ centered on the mode of seeing, as opposed to the domain of touch and hearing that dominated, for example, Hildegard of Bingen's visions.

The mode of seeing manifested itself in a variety of ways in the constitutions of the council. Its traces can be found in the statements about the catholic faith, the liturgical practices of displaying the sacramental body, the pronouncements against the Cathars, and the doctrine of the universal Church, the *ecclesia universalis,* outside of which there was no possibility of salvation. What is therefore essential in the constitutions of the Fourth Lateran Council is not what was established through the various regulations or whether or not they were implemented but the formation of practical actions that were to be disseminated through the apparatus. The reinterpretation of the twelfth-century tradition of the ternary mode of the body of Christ in the Eucharist by an ensemble of statements that redefined the ternary as the binary, or either/or, proposition was not just a shift in theological knowledge or the popular devotional practices of the scriptural corpus. It presented us with a new configuration of statements regarding the production of the body and created the standard for what should be seen, who should see it, and how it should be seen to encourage the identification of a community—the *ecclesia universalis*.

These multiple traits of the debate about seeing as registered in the constitutions of the Fourth Lateran Council make us realize that what was discussed in 1215 would reemerge in Western civilization in some two hundred years and assume the form of the laws of perspective. In the process of constructing the "new" standard for seeing by arching over the medieval tradition to reach the constructs of Euclidean geometry, the discourse on the laws of perspective camouflaged the standards institutionalized by the Fourth Lateran Council as nothing more than a code of ecclesiastical rulings. The constitutions that will be discussed here suffice to single out this event as a threshold in Western epistemology and phenomenology that was buried under the debris of the secular fascination with seeing and shaping the phantasmagoric image of the body. They show us that representation is not only the process of doubling or transfer by a historic subject that is or is not aware of its own historicity but also a practice of establishing the visibility, the ownership, and the structures of belonging of what can be shown within the limits of a particular culture, ideology, politics, history—thus, a space of representation in which public access to the sign of identity and its collective deciphering are secured.

Among the constitutions of the Fourth Lateran Council, chapter 1, "On the Catholic Faith," is a profession of faith that confirms the binding belief in "one true God, eternal and immeasurable, almighty, unchangeable, incomprehensible and ineffable, Father, Son and holy Spirit, three persons but one absolutely simple essence, substance or nature" (230). It emphasizes the consubstantial, coequal, co-omnipotent, and coeternal nature of the Holy Trinity as well as the divine and human nature of Christ: "although he is immortal and unable to suffer according to his divinity, he was made capable of suffering and dying according to his humanity" (230). It then restates the promise of the salvation of the human race by Christ, who "will come at the end of time to judge the living and the dead" (230).

The profession of faith ends with a decree that has come to be regarded as the dogma of transubstantiation.

There is indeed one universal church of the faithful [*una vero est fidelium universalis ecclesia*], outside of which nobody at all is saved, in which Jesus Christ is both priest and sacrifice. His body and blood are truly contained in the sacrament of the altar under the forms of bread and wine, the bread and wine having been changed in substance, by God's power into his blood and body, so that in order to achieve this mystery of unity we receive from God what he received from us. Nobody can effect this sacrament except a priest who has been properly ordained according to the church's keys, which Jesus Christ himself gave to the apostles and their successors. (230)

These statements, whether or not enunciated before, acquired a new currency in 1215. Not only did they confirm the Catholic creed, but the very particular procedure that they disclosed for defining and constructing a body made an incomprehensible and ineffable mystery visible by producing a focal point identified with a dogmatic meaning—Christ's body and blood were truly contained in the sacrament of the altar. Anyone opposed to this article of faith was to be condemned.

More specifically, chapter 2, "On the Error of Abbot Joachim," reviews and rejects Joachim of Fiore's concept that the unity of the Father, the Son, and the Holy Spirit "is not true and proper but collective and analogous, in the way that many persons are said to be one people and many faithful one church." Joachim's view is further explained: "Christ's faithful are one in the sense of a single reality which is common to all. They are one only in this sense, that they form one church through the unity of the catholic faith, and finally one kingdom through a union of indissoluble charity." (231) Instead of adopting Joachim's concept, the council confesses with Peter Lombard that there exists a certain supreme reality that truly is the Father, the Son, and the Holy Spirit, "the three persons together and each one of them separately" and that "[t]his reality neither begets nor is begotten nor proceeds" (232). Chapter 3, "On Heretics," condemns all heretics, "what-

ever names they may go under" (233), and suggests that those condemned be handed over to the secular authorities present, or to their
bailiffs, for due punishment. The text declares, "Catholics who take the
cross and gird themselves up for the expulsion of heretics shall enjoy the
same indulgence, and be strengthened by the same holy privilege, as is
granted to those who go to the aid of the holy Land" (234).

Even though this configuration of how to understand the nature of
the sacrament and how to secure its acceptance signified the desire "to
remove heresies and to strengthen faith," the pronouncements of the
first three chapters as well as the urgency to implement them stand in
sharp opposition to the practices that existed in the previous centuries.
Consequently, Gary Macy may be right when he suggests: "the creed of
Lateran IV was neither the culmination of twelfth-century eucharistic
theology nor a prohibition against further speculation about the mode
of Christ's presence in the sacrament. . . . It was not the mode of presence which Innocent III wished to affirm, but the presence itself; it was
not theological discussion which he wished to curtail, but the spread of
the heresy of the Cathars."[7]

Macy's last statement merits further investigation. The theological
discussions and the sacramental practices in the twelfth century positioned the ternary discourse on the Eucharist in a field dominated by the
explorations of the mode of presence. This mode of presence was an open
space in which the biological, mystical, and ecclesiological bodies of
Christ coexisted and gave rise to both private and institutionalized
experiences of the mystery of *Hoc est corpus meum*. The remanences of this
dynamic exchange can be found in Honorius's statements in which he
uses a metaphor of "those who recited tragedies in theatre" to explain
the relationship between the practice of a priest and a historical/dog-
matic event from the life of Christ, in Aelred of Rievaulx's *The Mirror of
Love* and his desire to establish the soul as the site where the absent body
of Christ could be produced and venerated, and in Hildegard of Bingen's visions in which she stressed that she heard with the inner ear of
the soul and saw with the inner eye of the spirit.[8]

In an important sense, the doctrine of the real presence of Christ was
not an article of faith but a matter of theological debate. In a text written in 1201/2, Peter of Capua asserted three possible explanations for
the real presence of Christ in the Eucharist—consubstantiation, annihi-
lation, and transubstantiation. Any one of these could be used to illus-

trate how the presence of Christ came about in the Sacrament. Even though he favored transubstantiation, other alternatives were not, in his judgment, heretical.[9]

The creed of faith of the Fourth Lateran Council delimited the field by privileging an ecclesiological approach toward the Eucharist and established the parameters within this field by describing the presence itself in obedience to a relevant set of theological regulations. By so doing, it not only excluded Joachim of Fiore and Amalric of Bène, or the Cathars, but created a singular standard that curtailed the ongoing debates around the mode of perception of the Eucharist. Whereas the twelfth-century mystics, Hildegard of Bingen or Aelred of Rievaulx, constructed the language that manifested that which remained unsayable, invisible, and exceptional and which formed the frontier that divided space into a private space where the mystical was housed and a place that could be accessed by those listening to the words obedient to theology, the ecclesiological approach and the standard of the Fourth Lateran Council shifted the ternary mode toward the binary discourse centering around the body of Christ in the Eucharist (and to be more precise, around reverence for the Host/divine in the material or for the material Host/divine), or toward the either/or debate around "seeing."[10]

There are several consequences of this shift. First, there is a technology of returning the mystical practice into the field of a visible institution. The sacramental body became the focal point of different gazes that needed to see the same body. This could happen during the Mass. In order for different gazes to be able to access the divine light, the Fourth Lateran Council stipulated that all the faithful should confess their sins and partake in the Eucharist at least once a year, at Easter. The Easter Communion was a sign of one's belonging to the Catholic church and a confirmation of its codes of operation. One's belonging was now institutionalized through the gesture of exclusion of those who offered a different reading of the presence of Christ. The visible sign and the real presence of Christ in the Eucharist reestablished a link between a private experience of the Eucharist and the apparatus. It was no longer possible to separate oneself from the institution of the church, because other or individualized practices were either condemned (the Cathars) or made invisible (the corporeal and spiritual approaches to the Eucharist). By displaying the sacramental body, the visibility of consolidated clerical power was produced and disseminated. By displaying the sacramental body with respect to the codes, other elements were marginalized. By displaying the sacramental body, the mystical and the incomprehensible was turned into the real that opened up the possibilities for its representation. When the debates about the Eucharist centered around seeing, the production of the body was essential. The real presence of Christ in the Eucharist increased the performance and the staging of the body not only inside but also outside the church. The council declared in its constitutions that at the Mass, Jesus Christ's "body and blood [was] truly contained in the sacrament of the altar under the forms of bread and wine, the bread and wine having been changed in substance, by God's power into his blood and body" (230).

The council stipulated that outside the church, the truth of the dogma had to stage itself differently for the lack of "a priest who has been properly ordained according to the church's keys, which Jesus Christ gave to the apostles and their successors" (230). It was not a coincidence that the feast of the Eucharist, Corpus Christi, was established after the Fourth Lateran Council.

The institution of Corpus Christi is attributed to the efforts of St. Juliana (ca. 1193–1258), a saintly woman who worked at the leprosarium attached to the Praemonstratensian house of Mont Cornillon in Liége.[11] She belonged to a group of women who were greatly influenced by a Flemish laywoman, Marie of Oignies. Marie of Oignies renounced her marriage, retired to live beside an Augustinian community, and dedicated her life to the care of lepers. She was also the central figure of the new devotion to the sacrament of the Eucharist. Miracles and visions of Marie of Oignies and her followers exemplified the desire to see and to acknowledge the presence of Christ on earth.[12] In 1208/9, St. Juliana had a dream in which the moon was partially eclipsed by a blemish. The dream kept recurring for about twenty years until its meaning was revealed to her by Christ in a vision: the moon represented the church and the missing part signified the lack of a feast in the church to celebrate the Eucharist.[13] Even though it was celebrated during the Mass daily, Juliana felt that the observance of the mystery of the Host needed a day of its own.

In 1246, Robert of Thourette (Turotte), bishop of Liége, under the pressure of the women living in the Beguine communities in the diocese of Liége and at Juliana's request, established the feast of the Eucharist in his diocese.[14] His pastoral letter *Inter alia mira* specified that the celebration was movable and could take place between May 21 and June 24 (the Thursday following Trinity Sunday).[15] In 1261, a former archdeacon of the diocese of Liége and a subordinate of Robert of Thourette, Jacques Pantaleon, was elected pope and assumed the name of Urban IV. He tried to institute the feast for the whole church in his bull *Transiturus* (1264). However, he died shortly after its writing, and his decree was only ratified by Pope Clement V at the Council of Vienne in 1311–12. The death of Clement V prevented the publication of the decrees of the council. They were published by Pope John XXII in 1317 under the name of *Clementines.* The feast of Corpus Christi spread throughout Western Christendom through the papal letter *Si dominum* that was incorporated into the canon law of *Clementines* under the title "On Relics and the Veneration of Saints" (*De reliquiis et veneratione sanctorum*).[16]

The sacrament of the Eucharist not only had been included in the liturgical celebrations during a daily Mass but also had received a solemn observation on Palm Sunday and Maundy Thursday. In a letter dated August 11, 1264, however, Urban IV noted,

For the day of the Supper of Our Lord, the day on which Christ himself instituted the sacrament, the entire church, fully occupied as she is with the reconciliation of penitents, the ritual administration of the holy oil, the fulfilling of the commandment concerning the washing of feet, and other matters, does not have adequate time for the celebration of this greatest sacrament.[17]

Having a separate day for the celebration of the sacrament of the Eucharist would allow the faithful and the clergy join one another in the observance of the day when the Sacrament was instituted by Christ.

The Office and Mass for the feast of Corpus Christi were composed. Though the evidence remains uncertain, it has been suggested that one of the compilers was St. Thomas.[18] The feast was an occasion for the sermons that narrated the miraculous stories of the real presence of Christ in the Eucharistic wafer as well as the power of the Eucharist in the conversion of a doubter. By 1275, the celebration of the feast of Corpus Christi was not limited only to the church building but moved to the streets of the town. The elevated Host, the real body of Christ, became a focal point of all the gazes when it was carried in a procession through the streets of Cologne, stopping at certain sites for worship, until it arrived at the parish church or the cathedral, where a solemn Mass would be celebrated.

Historians of drama and theater are familiar with the ceremonial character of Corpus Christi and the theories of the emergence of the cycle plays in the following centuries. The consequences of the establishment of the feast of Corpus Christi are realized in the work of such scholars as E. K. Chambers, Hardin Craig, O. B. Hardison, V. A. Kolve, Martin Stevens, Margaret Dorrell, Stanley Kahrl, Peter Travis, Mervyn James, Miri Rubin, Theresa Coletti, Alexandra Johnston, Ruth Evans, and Sarah Beckwith, who contributed immensely to our knowledge about processional theater in the fourteenth and fifteenth centuries.[19] Here, however, the emphasis is not on the dynamic relationship between the civic government, the guilds, and the church; social, political, and administrative preoccupations of diverse institutions; the social, economic, and political power of the participating groups; the order and the hierarchy; the conceptualization of the ritual in terms of the body—the body that provided the society with a mythology that helped to affirm both social wholeness and social differentiation; the relationship between a religious practice and cultural production; the feminist approaches to reading the body of Christ in the Corpus Christi cycles in terms of sexed and gendered corporeal inscription; or the concept of ritualization, that is, a process of construction of a series of tensions, rather than a set of monolithic beliefs, used to articulate the body (both symbolic and ritual) in a simultaneous process of production and communication rendered possible by the performance of the cycles. Rather, the emphasis is on the technology of returning the mystical practice into the field of a visible institution in the post-IV Lateran Council. Thus, the focus is on the representational practices that made the body visible as well as on securing the procedures for seeing the same body outside the church.

The language of the dogma of transubstantiation clearly specified that Christ's body and blood were "truly contained in the sacrament of the altar under the forms of bread and wine, the bread and wine having been changed in substance, by God's power into his blood and body" (230). The Host, which was elevated after the priest had announced, "Hoc est corpus meum," was a symbol of the unity and identity of the "universal church of the faithful, outside of which nobody at all is saved" (230). The *ecclesia universalis* was a place of the articulation of new practices of evoking a sense of identity through the process of exclusion of those who did not accept the dogma. The *ecclesia universalis* was a place of a representation that institutionalized the structures of belonging through the process of displaying the sacramental body. By so doing, it institutionalized not the representation of the self but the representation of the self within a particular community. By displaying the sacramental body, the *ecclesia universalis* provided public access to the sign of identity and a language for its collective deciphering. The ternary mode of seeing the body of Christ was no longer possible—corporeal and spiritual understanding of the body of Christ could easily separate themselves from the institution, for they were grounded in individualized practices of the experience of the Eucharist.

The feast of Corpus Christi led to the convergence between the dogma and the increased performance of meaning of *Hoc est corpus meum.* Outside the church, it made use of the processional mode not only to make the participants and the spectators feel the sense of identity and belonging but also to express those aspects of identity experienced most publicly and collectively. The processional mode employed ordered the processing bodies hierarchically around the Eucharist, which was in a monstrance—the clergy were followed by the guilds (from the highest to the lowest in importance) and then the laity. The order surrounding the Host could be translated into a diagram and a map of ecclesiastical and political power. The spatial quality defined as well as delimited the desire to see the Eucharist, the real body of Christ. The scopic drive immobilized the body; at the same time, the body totalized the eyes. The Host projected optical knowledge that erased the contradictions of the past or the ternary mode of presence and established the certainty of the present moment. It produced its own space outside the church, where its location was always the same, with the help of a processional movement that, at least on the day of Corpus Christi, tried to repress all the physical, social, and political elements that could compromise it. Finally, it created a universal and anonymous subject, the city itself, whose contours were "delimited by a name and within which the work [was] being done in obedience to a relevant set of rules," that is, the doctrine of the *ecclesia universalis* as well as the dogma of transubstantiation and the practice of exclusion. Maybe such a reading of the feast of Corpus Christi will explain why, in later periods, it was contested by the Lollards and challenged by Luther.[20] In the thirteenth century, however, the day of Corpus Christi reinforced the church's representation by diminishing the invisible in *Hoc est corpus meum* and increasing a sense of identity with the *ecclesia universalis* among the participants who were moving along the streets of a universal and anonymous subject.

Another consequence of the shift from the ternary mode of the celebration of the body of Christ in the Eucharist to the binary debate around "seeing" was the need to establish a representational practice of what is to be seen and what is to be rendered invisible—in other words, to determine how to represent an object in a space designed for it. The discussion of the creed in chapter 1 of the constitutions makes clear that representation was defined as a practice of staging a visibility of the real presence of Christ in the Eucharist in the Catholic church. It was a practice of establishing the structures that would solidify one's belonging to the institution. In this sense, representation in the post-IV Lateran Council was a practice of the production and the dissemination of a certain mode of governmentality, that is, of how to govern souls and lives. It is noteworthy that, in the representation of the body or in the process of making the mystical visible through the dogma of transubstantiation, the church authorities were concerned not only with securing the acceptance of the dogma and the obedience to divine law but also with the moral and organizational practices in other domains. For example, chapters 14 to 21 of the constitutions refer to the behavior of the clerics. Chapter 14 announces, "in order that the morals and conduct of clerics may be reformed for the better, let all of them strive to live in a continent and chase way, especially those in holy orders" (242). Special emphasis is laid on the need to punish clerical incontinence on account of lust and marriage. Chapter 15 makes it clear that clerics should abstain from gluttony and drunkenness—"Let no one be urged to drink, since drunkenness obscures the intellect and stirs up lust" (242). Chapter 16 forbids clerks to attend theatrical entertainment.

They should not watch mimes, entertainers and actors. Let them avoid taverns altogether, unless by chance they are obliged by necessity of a journey. They should not play at games of chance or of dice, nor be present at such games. (243)

Their outer garments should be closed and neither too long nor too short. They should avoid green and red colors, pointed toes, ornamentation, and embroidery. Chapter 17 commands that the Divine Office be celebrated with zeal and devotion. Chapter 18 decrees that clerics should not be involved in dueling. Chapter 19 forbids the deposition of profane objects in churches. Chapter 20 tells us that "the chrism and the eucharist are to be kept locked away in a safe place in all churches, so that no audacious hand can reach them to do anything horrible or impious" (244). Chapter 21 describes the punishment for a priest revealing the secrets of the confession. Chapter 22 stipulates that physicians should urge their patients first of all to summon a priest, as the well-being of the soul is of more value than the health of the body.

If any physician transgresses this our constitution, after it has been published by the local prelates, he shall be barred from entering a church until he has made suitable satisfaction for a transgression of this kind. Moreover, since the soul is much more precious than the body, we forbid any physician, under pain of anathema, to prescribe anything for the bodily health of a sick person that may endanger his soul. (246)

This mode of governmentality was closely associated with the practice of a production of the presence itself, the establishment of the authorities that would execute the dogma, the site where it was executed, and the language that defined a standard of what should be seen, how it should be seen, and where it should be seen. As noted before, the dissemination of the presence itself was not limited to the church itself—the feast of Corpus Christi was another site. The *Quem quaeritis* celebrated at Easter was yet another site of the production of the body that would be finally visible.

Since its emergence in the tenth century, the chant that describes a visit of three Marys to the sepulchre on Easter morning was concerned with trying to find an answer to the question, Where is the body? Well known are the texts in which the angel asks, "Quem quaeritis?" and the Marys answer, "Ihesum Nazarenum," to which the angel responds: "Non est hic. Surrexit sicut praedixerat. Ite nuntiate quia surrexit a mortuis." The Marys' statement "Alleluia, resurrexit dominus" ends the exchange. Christ has risen, though his body is nowhere to be seen. Not until the thirteenth century do versions of the *Quem quaeritis* (e.g., those from Rouen, Rheinan, Fleury, Prague, and Nuremberg) go beyond this formula and introduce the exchange between Mary and Jesus.[21] The thirteenth-century Prague version reads:

Having looked into the tomb, Mary turns towards Jesus and says the antiphon:
Tvlerunt Dominum meum, et nescio ubi posuerunt eum.
Jesus responds:

Woman, why are you crying? Whom do you seek?
Mary sings the antiphon:
Domine, si tu sustulisti eum, dicito michi ubi posuisti eum, et ego eum tollam.
Jesus says:
Maria
With her head lowered, she responds:
Raboni
Withdrawing, Jesus sings the antiphon:
Noli me tangere Maria; vade autem ad fratres meos et dic eis Ascendo ad
   Patrem meum, et Patrem uestrum
While Mary is leaving, the chorus sings the antiphon:
Venit Maria annuncians discipulis Quia uidi Dominum.[22]

Unlike versions from the tenth, eleventh, and twelfth centuries, the thirteenth-century Prague version of the *Quem quaeritis* affirmed the visibility of *Hoc est corpus meum*. This mode of seeing, which until now had always been in flux and crossed by different modes of perception, was stabilized by the constitutions of the Fourth Lateran Council. The document registered the labor to compose a space where the representational practices acquired an identity that would become a standard for centuries to come. The traces of the heterogeneous representation practices of the past centuries were camouflaged by a homogeneous definition of the presence of the body of Christ. With the help of ecclesiastical hierarchy, the orders, which were incorporeal and belonged to the domain of conceptual or mystical, materialized as perceptible symbols supporting the authority of the church. As such, they were to lift the faithful upward until they were brought into the unity with the divine and to establish their unity with the *Ecclesia*. The sacrament of the Eucharist, the Corpus Christi, and the Prague version of the *Quem quaeritis* are a select few examples of how representation was defined, disseminated, and circulated in the post-IV Lateran Council mode of governmentality.

From this point of view, it is not surprising that, in the thirteenth century, Dionysius the Areopagite was to become a reference.[23] Even though his *Celestial Hierarchy* was already known through Hugh of St. Victor's translation and commentary (1125–37), though his ideas and terminology circulated among the Cistercians in the twelfth century, and though his comments about uplifting and luminous beauty were known to Suger, abbot of Saint-Denis from 1122 to 1151, Dionysius the Areopagite was given a new and academic consideration with a translation of his work and commentary by Robert Grosseteste made available between 1240 and 1243. In the thirteenth century, or in the post-IV Lateran Council space of representation, Dionysius's vision of all reality as hierarchic and triadic (the divine, the angelic, and the human, each subdivided into three orders) served to conceive the possibility of a homology between the invisible and the visible.

The Celestial Hierarchy proposes an overall framework and terminology for understanding the angelic beings and arranging them into three triads of angelic beings, as they are presented in the scriptures. On a more general level, it describes a method for interpreting religious symbols—especially those that stand for angels and God—as well as the actions of the liturgy. The first three chapters are of special interest in these considerations. Chapter 1 clarifies the Dionysian concept of procession and return, which is understood here as the way God's revelation reaches and uplifts us.

"Every good endowment and every perfect gift is from above, coming down from the Father of lights." But there is something more. Inspired by the Father, each procession of the Light spreads itself generously toward us, and, in its power to unify, it stirs us up by lifting us up. It returns us back to the oneness and deifying simplicity of the Father who gathers us in. For, as the sacred Word says, "from him and to him are all things."[24]

The procession and return of "the Light" can only be comprehended through Jesus Christ, "the true light enlightening every man coming into the world, through whom we have obtained access to the Father" (145), and through sacred scripture, which reveals to us this truth in symbolic and uplifting fashion. However, a human being needs to raise up from this outpouring of illumination to be able to be returned to the divine ray. The spatial imagery is further elaborated on in the next paragraph of Dionysius's text, which encapsulates the Dionysian view of God's self-revelation and its impact on the people.

Of course this ray never abandons its own proper nature, or its own interior unity. Even though it works itself outward to multiplicity and proceeds outside of itself as befits its generosity, doing so to lift upward and to unify those beings for which it has a providential responsibility, nevertheless it remains inherently stable and it is forever one with its own unchanging identity. And it grants to creatures the power to raise up, so far as they may, toward itself and it unifies them by way of its own simplified unity. However, this divine ray can enlighten us only by being upliftingly concealed in a variety of sacred veils which the Providence of the Father adapts to our nature as human beings. (146)

These sacred veils are the "material means capable of guiding us" (146), such as signs of an invisible loveliness, odors, material lights, the contemplative capacity of the mind, order and rank, and the reception of the Eucharist. Thus, the sacred veils are revealed to us by God in the scriptures and the liturgy. He does so to "lift us in spirit up through the perceptible to the conceptual, from sacred shapes and symbols to the simple peaks of the hierarchies of heaven" (147).

Chapter 2 of *The Celestial Hierarchy* is concerned with those symbols that may seem incongruous and even insulting to the angles. Dionysius observes that we should not "profanely visualize these heavenly and god-like creatures as actually having numerous feet and faces" (147) or as oxens or lions or eagles. He argues:

The Word of God makes use of poetic imagery when discussing these formless intelligences, but . . . it does so not for the sake of art, but as a concession to the nature of our mind. It uses scriptural passages in an uplifting fashion as a way . . . to uplift our mind in a manner suitable to our own nature. (148)

According to Dionysius, the Bible uses poetic imagery for two reasons: first, giving shape to what is actually without shape is necessary because "we lack the ability to be raised up to conceptual contemplations"; second, it is most fitting that "the sacred and hidden truth about the celestial intelligences be concealed through the inexpressible and the sacred and be inaccessible to the *hoi polloi*," because "[n]ot everyone is sacred, and, as scripture says, knowledge is not for everyone" (149).

Chapter 3 of *The Celestial Hierarchy* introduces a triad of divine actions—purification, illumination, and perfection—that constitute a sacred order. The sacred order is defined as a state of understanding and an activity approximating as closely as possible the divine that "reaches out to grant every being, according to merit, a share of light and then through a divine sacrament, in harmony and in peace, . . . bestows on each of these being perfected in its own form" (154).

The first three chapters of *The Celestial Hierarchy* not only provide us with terms and conditions for understanding the Dionysian fundamental allegory of timeless spiritual truths, with the help of a spatial metaphor of anagogical movement from the perceptible to the conceptual, but also introduce concepts that form the foundation of *The Ecclesiastical Hierarchy*—procession and return, a way to interpret material symbols, and the triad of purification, illumination, and perfection.

The Ecclesiastical Hierarchy makes use of a triple triad that can be represented in the following manner: sacraments (baptism; *synaxis,* or the sacrament of the Eucharist; the sacrament of *the myron* or the sacrament of ointment/confirmation), clergy (hierarchs, priests, deacons), and laity (monks, communicants, those being purified). The overall format, which focuses on an ecclesiastic liturgy and institution, clarifies the Dionysian belief that in the quest for uplifting and divinization, the Fathers "put material on what was immaterial," that "[i]n their written and unwritten initiations, they brought the transcendent down to our level." More importantly, they did this for us, because "our own hierarchy is itself symbolical and adapted to what we are" and "[i]n a divine fashion it needs perceptible things to lift us up into the domain of conceptions."[25]

Thus, within this created world of space and time, in which human beings are dependent on their sense of perception, the divine message is clothed in perceptible symbols so human beings can start with them in order to ascend to higher things. Consequently, the awareness of space and time are the material starting points for the process of anagogy available only to those who are initiated (baptized) and who will gradually learn the truth with the help of the hierarch who is charged with revealing and sharing these truths with them.

Accordingly, perceptible symbols materially represent the divine realities they are unable to contain: "We see our human hierarchy . . . , as our nature allows, pluralized in a great variety of perceptible symbols lifting us up upward hierarchically until we are brought as far as we can be into the unity of divinization. The heavenly beings, because of their intelligence, have their own permitted conceptions of God. For us, on the other hand, it is by way of perceptible images that we are uplifted as far as we can to the contemplation of what is divine. . . . Let no one who is uninitiated approach this spectacle" (197, 201). For this act of similitude to happen, a "hierarch," someone who not only understands all sacred knowledge but also admits that he is "the one to undertake a sacred task far beyond him," conducts the execution of the precise images of the divine reality and, thus, divinization "in accordance with the rules laid down by God himself" (221).

One of these images is the rite of the Communion (*synaxis*). Dionysius explains: "Every sacredly initiating operation draws our fragmented lives together into a one-like divinization. It forges a divine unity out of the divisions within us" (209). He specifies that during the ritual of Communion, "the hierarch speaks in praise of the sacred works of God, sets about the performance of the most divine acts, and lifts into view the things praised through the sacredly displayed symbols" (211).

A description of the rite of the *synaxis* and of the explanation of its mystery is followed by a section entitled "Contemplation." Here Dionysius considers the nature of the Psalms and the scripture readings. For example:

The sacred chanting of the scriptures and the readings teach the rules of virtuous living. Above all, it teaches the need for the total purification of the self from destructive evil. (212)

The Psalms unite and harmonize the worshipers and prepare them to hear the readings from the Old and New Testament, "of which the source is the spirit of the Deity" (214). Dionysius describes the function of the Psalms and the readings in the following manner.

When these sacred hymns, with their summaries of holy truth, have prepared our spirits to be at one with what we shall shortly celebrate, when they have attuned us to the divine harmony and have brought us into accord not only with divine realities but with our individual selves and with others in such a way that we make up one homogeneous choir of sacred men, then whatever resumé and whatever opaque outline is offered by the sacred chanting of the psalmody is expanded by the more numerous, more understandable images and proclamations in the sacred readings of the holy texts. (214)

Dionysius then offers a description of the Communion. The covered bread and cup are brought forward, the kiss of peace is exchanged, the names of the dead are read, and the clergymen wash their hands. The hierarch sings the praises of the sacred works of God and proceeds to the symbolic sacred act, "in accordance with the rules laid by God himself, which is the reason why . . . he apologizes . . . for being the one to undertake a sacred task so far beyond him." Having reverently said, "It is you who said 'Do this in remembrance of me,'" (221) the hierarch lifts into view the things "praised through sacredly clothed symbols" (222). The bread is divided into many parts. The cup is shared with all. The act of uncovering and dividing of the bread and wine is explained in terms of the Incarnation: "For the simple, hidden oneness of Jesus . . . has become a reality that is composite and visible" (222). Dionysius repeats and expands this point in a passage that follows.

By resorting to the perceptible, to imagery, [the hierarch] makes clear that which gives life to our minds. He offers Jesus Christ to our view. He shows how out of love for humanity Christ emerged from the hiddenness of his divinity to take on human shape, to be utterly incarnate among us while yet remaining unmixed. (222)

Once he receives Communion, the hierarch distributes it according to the order and the arrangement appropriate to the divine realities. The Communion concludes with the hierarch's sacred thanksgiving.

The Dionysian interpretation of the eucharistic liturgy was in itself an attempt to expand the boundaries of the commentaries regarding the Sacrament. It is difficult to suggest whether or not Dionysius supported those patristic texts that advanced the notion of Christ's real presence in the sacrament of the Eucharist. Was the *synaxis* only a set of symbols? The answer to this question will not be found either in *The Celestial Hierarchy* or in *The Ecclesiastical Hierarchy*. Instead, we are presented with a complex system for understanding the notion of hierarchy and order as well as interpreting religious symbols. It is worth repeating here that according to Dionysius, perceptible symbols, which materially represented the divine realities, would allow the faithful to leave the realm of the perceptible and ascend to the realm of the conceptual order of higher truths. Anagogy and homology defined this created world of space and time and the faithful's awareness of extension in space in movement in time as the starting points of his or her knowledge of the divine truths.

These notions emerged at different times and in different places in medieval Western and Byzantine theories of symbols in Christian liturgical practices and buildings. Well known are the studies about the twelfth-century Abbot Suger of Saint-Denis credited with employing the anagogical power of stones and stained-glass windows in the construction of the abbey of Saint-Denis.[26] Current scholarship investigates the relationship between light and architecture in Byzantine art and, in particular, the relationship between the symbolic articulation and disposition of space in sacral buildings, on the one hand, and, on the other, the depiction of symbolic space in paintings and mosaics.[27]

When they appeared and were given a new academic consideration in the post-IV Lateran Council space of representation, the texts of Dionysius exemplified what could be thought about reality and what could acquire a meaning within reality's framework of representation. Thus, the interest here is not in how these works in Grosseteste's translation supported the Christian typology but in the extent to which they could emerge in a field "which is delimited by a name and within which the work is being done in obedience to a relevant set of rules."

Dionysius' texts provided a very particular reading of what it meant to represent the body of Christ (through doubling) within practices of Communion that were well defined (in the dogma of transubstantiation), rationalized (in the seventy constitutions), and institutionalized (in the Catholic church) after the Fourth Lateran Council. It should be remembered that, though still tolerated for some time after the Fourth Lateran Council, consubstantiation was vigorously criticized and attacked by William of Auxerre (1220–22), Hugh of St. Cher (ca. 1232), Alexander of Hales (1323–27), William of Militona (1245–49), and Albert the Great (1246–48).[28] Finally, St. Thomas and Scotus labeled consubstantiation heretical, because it would "involve the local motion of the body of Christ to many different places simultaneously" (St. Thomas), or because it worked against the confession of faith of the Fourth Lateran Council and the authority of the postapostolic church (Scotus).[29]

Consequently, Dionysius's texts, the feast of Corpus Christi, and the thirteenth-century versions of the *Quem quaeritis* composed the place of representation where the ternary discourse of the twelfth century was reduced into a binary of exclusion (of what should be seen and who can see it) and entered Western epistemology as such.[30] With *Hoc est corpus meum,* a material symbol is lifted into view. All those who are gathered inside the church, the *ecclesia universalis,* are united in their veneration of the Host, Jesus Christ offered to their view. The Host is carried through the streets of the city, which becomes an anonymous extension of the church. The Host, Jesus Christ, is offered to the view of those participating in the procession and to those standing on the side. A sense of identity, experienced most publicly and collectively, is evoked in spectators. Finally, Jesus Christ talks to Mary on Easter morning, providing an answer to the question that had haunted Christianity until this moment.

The labor of these representational practices to compose a body within a field, which is delimited here by the name of the Fourth Lateran Council, could only be successful if the work was being done in obedience to a relevant set of rules—the dogma of transubstantiation, which provided the singular standard for the interpretation of the presence of Christ in the Eucharist. *Hoc est corpus meum* was to be given a secular and ideological viewing in 1435 with Alberti's rules of perspective and their resemblance-oriented concepts of power, culture, ideology, and society.[31] They reversed the hierarchy from its vertical to its horizontal axis: "This is my body," said an actor on stage, and all the gazes on the other side focused their attention on it.

Afterword

This book ends with the event that established a singular standard for seeing the body of Christ in the Eucharist. This standard was coded into the religious and nonreligious discursive formations and manifested itself, under different guises, in various other networks and fields. The history of drama and theater adds that in the following centuries, there emerged other forms that altered how we see, think about, and represent a body on stage. This diversity is a testimony to the power of representational practices as well as to the conditions under which they were produced, circulated, and disseminated.

As I tried to show on the preceding pages, the notion of representation in the early Middle Ages (970–1215) was never homogeneous. It was always in flux and modified by different modes of seeing and materiality. Thus, the famous Easter morning exchange of the *Quem quaeritis* could only ask:

Quem quaeritis?

The answer to this question, though invariably the same, was always already modified by a representational practice that, at that moment, shaped the mode of seeing and materiality of

Ihesum Nazarenum.

The four epistemological fragments discussed in this book disclose the spaces where the idea of what it meant to represent was carefully reviewed in the process of ordering thoughts, affirming the existence of

God, establishing the structures of belonging, and defining the real presence of Christ.

Non est hic. Surrexit sicut praedixerat.

The desire to give visibility to the body, which had disappeared, propelled and gave representational form to a complex theological thought. It also created a place where this body could emerge and become a focal point of all the gazes that were brought into unity with the divine, the *Ecclesia,* and the city.

Ite nuntiate quia surrexit a mortuis.

Notes

Introduction

1. *Medievalism and the Modernist Temper,* ed. R. Howard Bloch and Stephen G. Nichols (Baltimore, MD: Johns Hopkins University Press, 1996), p. 1.

2. Hayden White, *Tropics of Discourse* (Baltimore, MD: Johns Hopkins University Press, 1978). White observes that historiography emerged as a distinct scholarly discipline in the West in the nineteenth century as a direct consequence of a profound hostility to all forms of myth: "Both the political Right and the political Left blamed mythic thinking for the excesses and failures of the Revolution. False readings of history, misconceptions of the nature of the historical process, unrealistic expectations about the ways that historical societies could be transformed—all these had led to the outbreak of the Revolution in the first place, the strange course that Revolutionary developments followed, and the effects of the Revolutionary activities over the long run" (124).

3. See Stephen G. Nichols, "The New Medievalism: Tradition and Discontinuity in Medieval Culture," *The New Medievalism,* ed. Kevin Brownlee, Marina Brownlee, and Stephen G. Nichols (Baltimore, MD: Johns Hopkins University Press, 1991), pp. 1–28.

4. Ibid., p. 4.

5. See, for example, *Approaches to Teaching Medieval English Drama,* ed. Richard Emmerson (New York: The Modern Language Association of America, 1990); Norman F. Cantor, *Inventing the Middle Ages* (New York: William Morrow and Co., 1991); Anne Middleton, "Medieval Studies," *Redrawing the Boundaries: The Transformation of English and American Literary Studies,* ed. Stephen Greenblatt and Giles Gunn (New York: The Modern Language Association of America, 1992), pp. 12–40; *Feminist Approaches to the Body in Medieval Literature,* ed. Linda Lomperis and Sarah Stanbury (Philadelphia, PA: University of Pennsylvania Press, 1993).

6. *The Theatre of Medieval Europe,* ed. Eckehard Simon (Cambridge: Cambridge University Press, 1991), p. xi.

7. Although the list of publications that could fall into this category is rather substantial, the publications that come immediately to mind are those by Marius Sepet, Alessandro D'Ancona, E. K. Chambers, Gustave Cohen, and Karl Young. See, for example, Marius Sepet, *Les prophet es du Christ: Etude sur les origines du théâtre au moyen âge* (Paris: Didier, 1878) or *Le drame religieux au moyen âge* (Paris: Blaud, 1890); Alessandro D'Ancona, *Origini del teatro italiano,* 2 vols. (Turin: Ermanno Loerscher, 1891); E. K. Chambers, *The Mediaeval Stage,* 2 vols. (Oxford: Clarendon Press, 1903); Gustave Cohen, *La théâtre en France au moyen âge* (Paris: Reider, 1931); Karl Young, *The Drama of the Medieval Church,* 2 vols. (Oxford: Clarendon Press, 1933).

8. *The Theatre of Medieval Europe,* pp. 86–87. See also O. B. Hardison, Jr., *Christian Rite and Christian Drama in the Middle Ages: Essays in the Origin and Early History of Modern Drama* (Baltimore, MD: Johns Hopkins University Press, 1965); Glynne Wickham, *Early English Stages: 1300 to 1660,* 2 vols. (London: Routledge and Kegan Paul, 1963); and V. A. Kolve, *The Play Called Corpus Christi* (Stanford, CA: Stanford University Press, 1966).

9. For a discussion of the concept of the differend see Jean-François Lyotard, *The Differend: Phrases in Dispute,* trans. Georges van deu Abbecle (Minneapolis, MN: University of Minnesota Press, 1990).

10. See Hardison, pp. 1–34. This essay will be discussed later in this chapter.

11. *The Theatre of Medieval Europe,* p. 1.

12. Among the scholars who wrote the essays are David Bevington, C. Clifford Flanigan, Andrew Hughes, Alexandra Johnston, Stanley J. Kahrl, Alan E. Knight, Hansjürgen Linke, David Mills, Eckehard Simon, David Staines, Sandro Sticca, Elsa Strietman, Ronald E. Surtz, and Glynne Wickham. It should be noted that, as the editor explains, the coverage of scholarship is limited to what is Western Europe today; thus, it does not include Slavic drama, Portuguese and Aragonese theater, or Czech drama of Bohemia, either because the information was not available or because there is agreement among the scholars that drama in the area did not constitute a major tradition or was heavily influenced by other major traditions.

13. It should be noted, however, that when the external history of the discipline is discussed in *The Theatre of Medieval Europe,* it refers primarily to the changes that had been felt in literary studies. For the shifts in the external history of the discipline see, for example, C. Clifford Flanigan, "Medieval Latin Music-Drama," *The Theatre of Medieval Europe,* pp. 21–41; Lee Patterson, *Negotiating the Past: The Historical Understanding of Medieval Literature* (Madison, WI: University of Wisconsin Press, 1987); David Aers, "Rewriting the Middle Ages: Some Suggestions," *Journal of Medieval and Renaissance Studies* 18 (1988): 221–40; Lee Patterson, "On the Margin: Postmodernism, Ironic History, and

Medieval Studies," *Speculum* 65.1 (January 1990): 87–108; *Approaches to Teaching Medieval English Drama*.

14. See, for example, Peter Novick, *That Noble Dream: "The Objectivity Question" and the American Historical Profession* (Cambridge: Cambridge University Press, 1988).

15. Alexandra F. Johnston, "'All the World Was a Stage': Records of Early English Drama," *The Theatre of Medieval Europe*, p. 117.

16. *The Theatre of Medieval Europe*, p. 119. It should be noted that Johnston's information regarding the Beverley miracle is not entirely correct—the account of the miracle is appended to Folcard's twelfth-century vita of St. John of Beverley and described as a resurrection, attributed to God, who did not want the church dedicated to his confessor, tainted with human slaughter. See also Patricia Badir, "Representations of the Resurrection at Beverley Minster circa 1208: Chronicle, Play, Miracle," *Theatre Survey* 38.1 (May 1997): 9–41.

17. See, for example, *Records of Early English Drama* for Chester (1979); York (1979); Coventry (1981); Newcastle-Upon-Tyne (1982); Norwich (1984); Cumberland, Westmorland, and Gloucestershire (1986); Devon (1987); and Cambridge (1989)—all published by Toronto University Press.

18. See Glynne Wickham, *The Medieval Theatre* (New York: St. Martin's Press, 1974).

19. See Eleanor Prosser, *Drama and Religion in the English Mystery Plays: A Re-Evaluation* (Stanford, CA: Stanford University Press, 1961); volumes of *Records of Early English Drama*; and David Staines, "The English Mystery Cycle," *The Theatre of Medieval Europe*, pp. 80–96.

20. "Attempts to reconstruct the Doomsday pageant wagon have tried to solve the technical problems in different ways, but of course can give only a general notion of the actual appearance of the pageant stage. The Toronto reconstruction of Alexandra Johnston seems to be convincing in many respects, though the small puppet angels should most likely circle clockwise around Christ instead of being placed above in a row facing to his left. The technology of the apparatus for lowering Christ has been treated by Peter Meredith, whose detailed drawing nevertheless possibly errs with regard to the placement of the hell mouth, which probably should be at the left of Christ—the conventional location of the place of eternal punishment" (Clifford Davidson, *Illustrations of the Stage and Acting in England to 1580* [Kalamazoo, MI: Medieval Institute Publications, 1991], p. 22).

21. See, for example, Mervyn James, "Ritual, Drama, and Social Body in the Late Medieval English Town," *Past and Present* 98 (February 1983): 3–29; Theresa Coletti, "A Feminist Approach to the Corpus Christi Cycles," *Approaches to Teaching Medieval English Drama*, pp. 78–89; Ruth Evans, "Body Politics: Engendering Medieval Cycle Drama," *Feminist Readings in Middle English Literature: The Wife of Bath and All Her Sect*, ed. Ruth Evans and Lesley Johnson (London and New York: Routledge, 1994), pp. 112–39; Sarah Beckwith, *Christ's Body: Identity, Culture, and Society in Late Medieval Writings* (Lon-

don and New York: Routledge, 1993); Caroline Walker Bynum, *The Resurrection of the Body in Western Christianity, 200–1336* (New York: Columbia University Press, 1995).

22. See Michel de Certeau, *The Writing of History,* trans. Tom Conley (New York: Columbia University Press, 1988); Michel Foucault, *The Archaeology of Knowledge and the Discourse on Language,* trans. A. M. Sheridan Smith (New York: Random House, 1972); Stanley Aronowitz, *Science as Power* (Minneapolis, MN: University of Minnesota Press, 1988); Pierre Bourdieu, *Distinction: A Social Critique of the Judgement of Taste,* trans. Richard Nice (Cambridge, MA: Harvard University Press, 1984); Joseph R. Roach, "Slave Spectacles and Tragic Octoroons: A Cultural Genealogy of Antebellum Performance," *Theatre Survey* 33.2 (November 1992): 167–87.

23. For a critical appraisal of the theories see the review articles by C. Clifford Flanigan: "The Liturgical Drama and Its Tradition: A Review of Scholarship, 1965–75," *Research Opportunities in Renaissance Drama* 18 (1975): 81–102; 19 (1976): 109–36; "Comparative Literature and the Study of Medieval Drama: Review of Scholarship," *Yearbook of Comparative and General Literature* 35 (1986): 56–104; and "Medieval Latin-Music Drama," *The Theatre of Medieval Europe,* pp. 21–41.

24. Hardison, p. 33.

25. See, for example, David A. Bjork, "On the Dissemination of *Quem quaeritis* and the *Visitatio Sepulchri* and the Chronology of Their Early Sources," *Comparative Drama* 14 (spring 1980): 46–69; Rainer Friedrich, "Drama and Ritual," *Themes in Drama: Drama and Religion,* ed. James Redmond (Cambridge: Cambridge University Press, 1983), pp. 159–223.

26. Roland Barthes, "The Discourse of History," *The Rustle of Language,* trans. Richard Howard (New York: Hill and Wang, 1986), p. 127. The narratological model of historiography is also discussed by Gianni Vattimo; see Gianni Vattimo, *Transparent Society,* trans. David Webb (Baltimore, MD: Johns Hopkins University Press, 1992), chaps. 1 and 2.

27. Barthes, p. 139.

28. Jacques Rancière, *The Names of History: On the Poetics of Knowledge,* trans. Hassan Melehy (Minneapolis, MN: University of Minnesota Press, 1994), p. 2.

29. Rancière, p. 9.

30. Chambers, 1:vi. Subsequent references will appear as volume and page numbers in parentheses in text.

31. According to Chambers (1:3–7), farce and pantomime were the most popular forms of entertainment in Rome during the times of the "corrupt" emperors—Tiberius (14–37), Caligula (37–41), Claudius (41–54), and Nero (54–68). The emergence and development of Christianity is perceived by him as the immediate factor that led to the banning of mime performances. To prove the validity of his observation, Chambers quotes numerous legislations against theater or its actors—canons of Hippolitus; councils of Elvira (306),

Arles (314), Carthage (397–98); code of Theodosius (435). He concludes that the history of minstrelsy can only be traced by analyzing the written attacks of the ever more powerful ecclesiastics and ecclesiastical groups best summed up by Tertullian's three condemnations, that is, scriptural evidence against spectacles, their idolatrous nature, and the fact that theater encourages a loss of self-control (1:38).

32. Rather than uproot what Chambers calls the "mimetic instinct," the church decided to purify the old sites to serve the new God. Chambers writes: "Two letters of Gregory the Great, written at the time of the mission of St. Augustine [ca. 601–3], are the key to the methods adopted by the apostles of the West. . . . Before Mellitus could reach England, he received a letter instructing him to expound to Augustine a new policy. 'Do not, after all,' wrote Gregory, 'pull down the fanes. Destroy the idols; purify the buildings with holy water; set relics there; and let them become temples of the true God. So the people will have no need to change their places of concourse, and where of old they were wont to sacrifice cattle to demons, thither let them continue to resort on the day of the saint to whom the church is dedicated, and slay their beasts no longer as a sacrifice, but for a social meal in honour of Him whom they now worship'" (1:95–96). Consequently, the old sites became part of the parochial organization and, as such, were administered by the parochial machinery. Chambers provides extensive examples of festivals that entered the Catholic calendar of annual celebrations after having been "christened"—agricultural customs (May games), winter festivals (the mummer's play), domestic customs (celebrations for the dead ancestors), and New Year's customs. He thus concludes that the church did not succeed in suppressing the mimetic tradition; on the contrary, the mimetic instinct was preserved in pre-Christian charms, rites, and games whose symbolic meanings he equates with the dramatic element existing in man's subconscious instinct for imitation.

33. The first chapters of Chambers's work detail the history "by which the Church itself, through the introduction of dramatic elements into its liturgy, came to make its own appeal to this same mimetic instinct" (1:vi). Chambers is primarily interested in the sociological implications of the compromise between the church and the folk tradition as well as in the forces that influenced the merger of the two traditions. In books 1 and 2, he shows that the church was unable to suppress the histrionic sensibility of the *ludi* performers and, therefore, adopted certain village festivals for the purpose of converting pagans into Christians. Thus, the church recognized the necessity to admit the elements of heathen rituals into a spiritual service in order to appeal to the majority of the churchgoers.

34. The Roman Mass consists of five parts: (1) the Preparation, (2) the Oblation, (3) the Consecration, (4) the Communion, and (5) the Dismissal. The Introit is the first part of the Preparation. It is a chant sung by the chorus after the celebrant has reached the altar.

35. This text appears in Latin in Chambers, 2:309. The translation of the

passage is quoted after Hardison, pp. 193–94. Note that the layout of the text is Chambers's, not Hardison's.

36. Young, 1:vii. Subsequent references will appear as page numbers in parentheses in text.

37. The oldest extant text of the *Quem quaeritis* trope is found in St. Martial at Limoges (923–34). However, according to Young (1:204–5), this text cannot be treated as the trope in its simplest version.

38. See Young, 1:231. Matins is the first and earliest canonical hour, celebrated in monasteries at about 3 A.M. in winter and at about 2 A.M. in summer. Throughout this study I will refer to this service as either the night office or Nocturns, which was a tenth-century equivalent of Matins. The only exception is this chapter, in which, to avoid confusion, both terms are provided. See tables 1 and 2 in chapter 1.

39. Hardison, p. 43. Subsequent references will appear as page numbers in parentheses in text.

40. Hardison's belief that the Mass is drama is directly opposed to Young's perception of the service. To support his assumptions, Hardison refers to *Liber officialis* (833) by Amalarius, bishop of Metz, and *Gemma animae* (ca. 1100) by Honorius Augustoduneusis (Honorius of Autun) and suggests that the Mass was a sacred drama in which the idea of commemoration merged with the doctrine of Incarnation, that is, the Real Presence of Christ. This doctrine can be explained by the statement that if the bread and the wine are changed at the moment of consecration into the flesh and blood of Christ, then Christ must be present at every Mass. Although he cites Amalarius, Hardison develops his argument along the same lines as Chambers, for whom the dramatic character of the Mass was in the actual repetition of Christ's suffering, not in its symbolic act. At the same time, Hardison's interpretation of the Mass differs from Chambers's historical analysis as Hardison emphasizes the similarities and the links between the Mass and other dramatic rituals of the so-called primitive societies.

41. Gilbert Murray distinguishes six ritual forms in Greek drama: (1) an *agon* (a struggle or contest), (2) a *pathos* (involving suffering and death), (3) a messenger who announces the death, (4) a *threnos* (lamentation), (5) an *anagnorisis* (discovery and recognition), (6) a *theophany* (a period of joy occasioned by rebirth). For a detailed discussion of these forms see Gilbert Murray's "Excursus on the Ritual Forms Preserved in Greek Tragedy" in Jane Ellen Harrison, *Themis: A Study of the Social Origins of Greek Religion* (Cambridge: Cambridge University Press, 1912), pp. 341–69.

42. The three publications by Chambers, Young, and Hardison discussed in text—which established the origins of medieval drama and theater through a process of a slow upbuilding from simple to complex forms, a literary analysis of the tropes, and a theory of Christian rite—generated a lot of criticism. Throughout the years, a series of publications emerged that tackled the question of the origins of medieval drama and theater in terms of a link between classical theater or "pagan" traditions and the theater of the Middle Ages, the

monastic reforms in the ninth century, Gallican recitations of saints' lives, Marxist theory, the relationship between an Easter Matins responsory and early drama, and, most recently, the relationship between rhetoric and drama.

For example, Benjamin Hunningher suggests that religious drama came into being through the dramatic tradition represented by the mimes. The mimes were employed by the clergy in the presentation of tropes and actually performed them. Hunningher rejects the possibility that drama developed in isolation inside the monastery. His assumption is based on the contradiction, best reflected in the many interdictions hurled at the theater by the church, between the spirit of Christian faith, the nature of the church, and the spirit of theater. Hunningher proves his argument by presenting numerous instances in which "lays" (secular ballads) intruded into the divine service, by quoting various warnings of the councils against *clerici vagantes,* and by drawing attention to the fallibility of the laws formulated first by Gustave Cohen—that every religion spontaneously produces drama, that every religious service shows by its nature dramatic and theatrical aspects. See Benjamin Hunningher, *The Origin of the Theatre* (New York: Hill and Wang, 1961. Hunningher's argument was criticized by Helena Gamer in her "Mimes, Musicians, and the Origin of the Medieval Religious Play," *Deutsche Beitrage zur geistigen Überlieferung* 5 (1965): 9–28.

A publication that questioned commonly accepted theories is Axton's *European Drama of the Early Middle Ages* (London: Hutchinson, 1974). As did Hunningher, Axton stresses the importance of the activities that took place outside the church. He rejects the argument that *mimi* could have had any influence on the activities within its walls. The diversity of the earliest drama in medieval Europe makes him believe that its different forms evolved independently and enriched each other only when fully grown. Having analyzed some thirteen plays in Latin and plays in the vernacular that, he maintains, represented distinctively different traditions, Axton claims that a balanced critical view of medieval drama can only be achieved by investigating the clerical perspective, by examining scattered and fragmentary sources, and by a comparative study of plays in different languages. Only such an extensive analysis might bring out the elements of the common traditions on which drama depends.

An investigation of the scholarship of the last two decades indicates yet another shift in the treatment of the question of the origin of theater and drama in the Middle Ages. New methodologies and schools of thought have been employed to revise the traditional history and its arrangement of the record. The historical scholarship of the last two decades aimed at decentering the privileged theories by bringing to the fore those aspects of historical records that had thus far been neglected or dismissed as irrelevant.

Even though Johann Drumbl's *Quem quaeritis: Teatro sacro dell'alto medioevo* (Roma: Bulzoni, 1981) returns us to the quest for the literary origins of medieval drama and theater, this publication differs from the critical studies by Chambers, Young, and Hardison, in that in it the origins of the *Quem quaeritis* are discussed in the context of monastic history and in liturgiological scholarship. Drumbl does not study the *Quem quaeritis* for its dramatic quality but perceives it as a liturgical ceremony associated with monasticism, and, in particular, with the Benedictine house at Fleury. Therefore, the questions he poses are not questions concerning the theatrical elements but questions about the place, the reason for the appearance of the *Quem quaeritis,* and the liturgical significance the "author" intended for the ceremony.

To answer his questions, Drumbl recapitulates that during the first half of the tenth century, the *Quem quaeritis* ceremony could be found in three different liturgical positions, that is, in the procession before the Easter Mass, in the Introit to the Easter Mass, and at the end of the night office, before the hymn *Te Deum.* Such documents as the *Regularis concordia* provide an explicit description of the manner in which this ceremony should been executed. This is why, according to Drumbl, such ecclesiastical or monastic sources as the *Regularis concordia* are insufficient evidence for the liturgical origins of medieval drama— because they treated the *Quem quaeritis* as nothing more than a liturgical enrichment.

Drumbl is interested in finding where this particular ceremony would be normally inserted but not in justifying or explaining its position. An answer to the question about the location of the ceremony can be provided by the textual study of various forms of the *Quem quaeritis*—a study whose solid foundations were established by de Boor's *Textgeschichte.* Drumbl, however, rejects de Boor's theory of the Italian origin of the *Quem quaeritis* and suggests that it emerged in Fleury in about 930. The *Quem quaeritis* was a new liturgical ceremony that was composed to accommodate the changes in the Easter procession that had been introduced in the ninth century in France. Because of the reform, says Drumbl, the Easter procession was limited to the interior of the church, whereas previously it had moved around the entire monastic complex. He substantiates his argument by analyzing the order of the procession at Fleury. The procession of Easter Day would take place inside the monastic church after the Matins Mass. It would stop at two stations. The second station was where the *Quem quaeritis* ceremony would take place. Drumbl suggests that it was created by Odo of Cluny, who at that time came to Fleury to reform this monastic house. Thus, the *Quem quaeritis* was born as an autonomous liturgical ceremony in the form of poetry (Young) rather than as a ritual practice (Hardison). For critiques of Drumbl's theory see Anselme Davril, "Johann Drumbl and the Origin of the *Quem quaeritis:* A Review Article," *Comparative Drama* 20 (spring 1986): 65–75; Flanigan in *Theatre in Medieval Europe,* pp. 28–30.

43. E. Catherine Dunn, "The Saint's Legend as *Mimesis:* Gallican Liturgy and Mediterranean Culture," *Medieval and Renaissance Drama in England: An Annual Gathering of Research, Criticism, and Reviews,* ed. J. Leeds Barrol, III (New York: AMS Press, 1984), p. 13. See also E. Catherine Dunn, *The Gallican Saint's Life and the Late Roman Dramatic Tradition* (Washington, DC: Catholic University of America Press, 1989).

44. *Medieval and Renaissance Drama in England,* p. 14. Subsequent references will appear as page numbers in parentheses in text.

45. This hypothesis has not been fully worked out. Therefore, it is difficult to assert whether Dunn perceives the recitation of saints' legends as the origin of medieval drama and theater or as a continuation of the classical heritage that manifested itself in the saints' legends or whether she thinks that the saints' legends contained dramatic elements that later were absorbed into liturgical dramas.

46. Jody Enders, *Rhetoric and the Origins of Medieval Drama* (Ithaca, NY: Cornell University Press, 1992).

47. Ibid., pp. 3–5. Subsequent references will appear as page numbers in parentheses in text.

48. Having constructed a possible site of the origins of medieval drama and theater, Enders provides examples of how that drama developed. She discusses the theater of Basoche and a select few French plays from the fifteenth century where the aforementioned theatrical elements can be found. She demonstrates the influence the structure of a legal discourse exerted on both thematic and structural elements of the medieval plays. Enders's argument is thus that rhetoric, with its forensic oratory and theological debate, and medieval drama, including the Mass as Hardison suggested, is best understood by seeing all these forms on a relatively fluid continuum of interlinked performances rather than by indicating that the staging of the passion plays, comedies, and farces took place in a social, political, ideological, cultural reality. For a different reading of the relationship between rhetoric and drama see William Arrowsmith, "The Criticism of Greek Tragedy," *Tulane Drama Review* 3 (March 1959): 31–57. Arrowsmith suggests that Greek drama and theater could have been shaped by rhetoric and the law court rather than by antiphonal dialogue and ritual. See also Gerald Else, *Aristotle's Poetics: The Argument* (Cambridge, MA: Harvard University Press, 1957) for an insightful discussion of Aristotle's *Poetics* and for Else's critique of ritual origins of drama.

49. Leonard Goldstein, "On the Origin of Medieval Drama," *Zeitschrift für Anglistik und Amerikanistik* 29 (1981): 101–15.

50. The complex argument starts with Harrison's statement that "the drama arises at that point when ritual breaks down and loses its social function and becomes emptied of its social content, only to become refilled with a new content, becoming a *drama,* a thing done, like dromenon, but a thing done by someone else whose action you now passively observe as spectator not as participant" (102–3). Goldstein provides a critique of this definition to indicate that Emile Durkheim's sociology, on which Harrison based her theory, is problematic for at least two reasons. First, it does not explain the mechanism by which social relations are alienated. Second, it does locate the process of alienation within the context of historical change. Referring to Marx, Goldstein shows "the dialectic relation that functions between social relations and consciousness as such and consciousness in its various historical forms" (106). In particular,

the essential points are that the alienation of labor is what makes consciousness possible, that the content of this consciousness is the social relation abstracted as thought, and, finally, that the history of thought is the history of production. Referring George Thomson, Goldstein maintains that the origin of tragedy can be understood in the context of democratic revolution in Greece in the sixth century. He uses dialectical materialism and political history to explain not only the genesis of tragedy in Greece but also the emergence of medieval drama.

51. For a critique of Marxist scholarship see *Ideology and Power in the Age of Lenin in Ruins,* ed. Arthur Kroker and Marilouise Kroker (New York: St. Martin's Press, 1991). To readers interested in the perception of medieval drama as social practice, I recommend Jean-Charles Payen, "Théâtre medieval et culture urbane," *Revue d'historie du théâtre* 35 (1983): 233–50, and Henri Rey-Flaud, *Le cercle magique* (Paris: Gallimard, 1973) and *Pour une dramaturgie du moyen âge* (Paris: Presses Universitaires de France, 1980). Payen suggests that medieval drama was almost exclusively an urban production articulating quasi-bourgeois practices. Using Lacanian theory, Rey-Flaud implies that medieval drama gave a visual expression to the conflicts that existed within a society, to create the unity of the society of viewers by pointing to social differences.

52. Jean-François Lyotard, *Postmodern Fables,* trans. Georges van den Abbeele (Minneapolis, MN: University of Minnesota Press, 1997), p. 168.

53. Michel Foucault, *The Order of Things: An Archaeology of Human Sciences* (New York: Random House, 1973), p. 330.

54. Foucault, *The Archaeology of Knowledge,* pp. 7–8.

55. De Certeau, *The Writing of History,* p. 4.

56. Kojève is quoted in Michael S. Roth, *Knowing and History: Appropriations of Hegel in Twentieth-Century France* (Ithaca, NY: Cornell University Press, 1988), p. 98.

57. See Chambers, 2:15; Young, 1:249.

58. Wolfgang Michael, "Tradition and Originality in the Medieval Drama in Germany," *The Medieval Drama,* ed. Sandro Sticca (Albany, NY: State University of New York Press, 1972), p. 24.

59. Harain Craig, *English Religious Drama* (London: Oxford University Press, 1955), p. 33.

60. William L. Smoldon, "Melodies of the Medieval Church Drama and Their Significance," *Medieval English Drama,* ed. Jerome Taylor and Alan H. Nelson (Chicago: University of Chicago Press, 1972), p. 77.

61. William Tydeman, *The Theatre in the Middle Ages* (Cambridge: Cambridge University Press, 1978), p. 35.

62. *The Medieval Theatre,* p. 39.

63. See Mary Desiree Anderson, *Drama and Imagery in English Medieval Churches* (Cambridge: Cambridge University Press, 1963), p. 26; Sandro Sticca, *The Latin Passion Play: Its Origin and Development* (Albany, NY: State University of New York Press, 1970), p. 23; Axton, p. 65.

64. Hardison, p. 216.
65. Ibid., p. 194.
66. *The Archaeology of Knowledge*, p. 7.
67. Jean-François Lyotard, *The Postmodern Condition: A Report on Knowledge*, trans. Geoff Bennington and Brian Massumi, with a foreword by Frederic Jameson (Minneapolis, MN: University of Minnesota Press, 1988), p. 57.
68. *The Writing of History*, p. xv.
69. *The Archaeology of Knowledge*, pp. 9–10.
70. Young, 1:178.
71. Hardison, p. 162.
72. De Boor's *Die Textgeschichte der lateinischen Osterfeiern* (Tübingen: Niemeyer, 1967) is an analysis of the versions of the *Quem quaeritis* and their variants. Rather than being a chronological study, his is a study that emphasizes regional differences. De Boor refers to his analysis as a *Textgeschichte*, that is, a textual history that can be reconstructed by setting categories for the analysis of the *Quem quaeritis* as a verbal text. To make a distinction between the forms and the position of the *Quem quaeritis* and the *Visitatio Sepulchri*, de Boor reintroduces two functional categories, a *Feier* and a *Spiel*, which had been used in German scholarship of the nineteenth century. Unlike Young's ritual imitation and dramatic impersonation or Hardison's ritual and drama, de Boor's *Feier* and *Spiel* decisively break with the tradition of the centrality of impersonation for the emergence of drama. Instead, he claims that it is possible to talk about the *Quem quaeritis* as a text, rather than a liturgical ceremony or ritual, because it occupies a position—which gives it freedom of movement—between liturgy and art. This is why the *Quem quaeritis* could either "grow," "maintain its shape," or "shrink" to accommodate different occasions. De Boor's *Quem quaeritis* is thus open to change, and this is what makes possible the discussion of the biblical sources for the trope (*Die biblische Grundlage des Ostertropus*), the "characters" (*Das Personal*) used, and the biblical sources for specific lines (*Die Textworte*). Having provided the literary paradigm, de Boor proceeds to a sentence-by-sentence analysis of the text of Easter tropes. The tropes are categorized through a precise analysis of the variations in the question posed by the angel ("Quem quaeritis [christocolae]?"), the answer given by the Marys ("Ihesum Nazarenum"), the subsequent statement by the angel ("Non est hic. Surrexit sicut praedixerat"), and so forth. The next step in his *Textgeschichte* is the analysis of tropes as self-contained units and the establishment of geographical types. De Boor creates five major groups of tropes: Italian, French, Spanish, Lotharingian, and St. Gallen, whose elements would be found in the *Quem quaeritis-Feier*. De Boor's *Textgeschichte* is the study of the literary qualities of the *Quem quaeritis* compositions in order to indicate patterns, traditions, and similarities between the types, which order and systematize various forms of the *Quem quaeritis-Feier* or the *Quem quaeritis-Spiel* according to their literary value, overlooking, for example, the secular or monastic context where these forms appeared. Despite its totalizing paradigms, the *Textgeschichte* has exerted a con-

siderable impact on medieval scholarship in Germany. Rolf Steinbach's *Die deutschen Oster- und Passionsspiele des Mittelalters* (Cologne: Bohlau, 1970), Hans-Jürgen Diller's *Redeformen des englischen Misterienspiels* (Munich: Fink, 1973), and Theo Stemmler's *Liturgische Feiern und geistliche Spiele* (Tübingen: Niemeyer, 1970) are just a few examples of studies based on de Boor's distinction between a *Feier* and a *Spiel* and on textual histories.

73. For bibliographies and general overviews of scholarship concerning the musical nature of the *Quem quaeritis* and tropes in general see, for example, Paul Evans, "Reflections on the Origin of the Trope" *American Musicological Society Journal* 14 (summer 1961): 119–30; Timothy McGee, "The Liturgical Placement of the *Quem quaeritis* Dialogue," *Journal of the American Musicological Society* 29 (1976): 1–29; Alejandro E. Planchart, *The Repertory of Tropes at Winchester,* 2 vols. (Princeton, NJ: Princeton University Press, 1977); Susan Rankin, "The Music of the Medieval Liturgical Drama in France and England" (Ph.D. dissertation, University of Cambridge, 1981); Andrew Hughes, "Liturgical Drama: Falling between the Disciplines," *The Theatre of Medieval Europe,* pp. 42–62; William Smoldon, "The Origin of the *Quem quaeritis* and the Easter Sepulchre Music-Drama as Demonstrated by Their Musical Settings," in *The Medieval Drama,* pp. 121–54; C. Clifford Flanigan, "The Liturgical Context of the *Quem quaeritis* Trope," *Comparative Drama* 8 (spring 1974): 45–62.

As early as 1860, the famous musicologist and literary scholar Edouard de Coussemaker had voiced his concern about the treatment of the trope as merely a literary creation as was proposed by the numerous scholars of his time. Coussemaker's concerns have also been voiced by Smoldon. In his analysis of tropes, Smoldon emphasizes that music was their essential aspect. This point was either not adequately treated or entirely ignored by Chambers, Young, and Hardison, who viewed the trope as either a literary ornamentation or as a part of preexisting church ceremonies. Smoldon redefines the tropes as additions to various parts of the Christian liturgy that originated in the ninth century or earlier. Three categories of tropes can be distinguished:

1. musical tropes, which feature vocal embellishment, or *melisma*—a term used with reference to passages in plainsong or in other songs in which one syllable is extended into a passage of several notes;

2. textual tropes, which feature the addition of a new text that is fitted to the notes of an already existing *melisma;*

3. musical-textual tropes, which feature the addition of both new text and new music.

The third type was most frequently employed for troping Introits and some other chants of the Mass. Moreover, the troping could be in the form of phrases that were inserted between the original liturgical phrases or in the form of some relevant motif inserted into the beginning of the Introit. The *Quem quaeritis* thus belongs to the third category of tropes, since, as the records indicate, it was placed as the introduction to the Introit of the Easter Mass. Furthermore, its concomitant music, which was written above the syllables, indicates that the text was chanted. Having established the nature of the *Quem quaeritis,* Smoldon turns to an analysis of the *Quem quaeritis* dialogue in the *Regularis concordia.* He claims that the dialogue in this consuetudinary is a "shorthand version"; that is, it was only a verbal text that, when celebrated, was expanded into the form containing the text and the music. The music that was its inherent part was contained in the collection of tropes. Consequently, Smoldon argues that the *Visitatio Sepulchri,* whose core was the trope, cannot be considered simply as literary drama but has to be viewed as music-drama.

Taking a different approach, Flanigan's study, "The Liturgical Context of the *Quem quaeritis* Trope," combines the musicologists' stance with the ritualistic-liturgical studies of Mircea Eliade and Dom Odo Casel, the founder of the *Mysterientheologieschule.* After discussing the works of Young and Hardison, Flanigan suggests that even though it has been accepted that the *Quem quaeritis* trope was the nucleus of Latin medieval drama, little is known about the way the trope functioned within the context of the liturgy of the Mass. The purpose of his study is to concentrate on the nature and function of the liturgy. Flanigan defines the trope as an addition of text and music to the beginning of a liturgical chant. Such an understanding of tropes finds its support in the studies of another musicologist, Paul Evans, who has pointed out:

tropes as we know them from even the earliest of Western manuscripts appear to have been conceived, not as extensions of a line of plainchant but rather as introduction to it. . . . The introductory nature of the trope lines is made clear by the frequent use of such connective expressions as "saying," "singing," and "proclaiming," a particle like "and," or the subject of the verb which occurs in the subsequent line of chant. Furthermore the final line of a chant is never followed by a line of trope. . . . Tropes originally functioned primarily as introductions to liturgical actions. (128–29)

Evans's final statement, which asserts that tropes provided commentary on liturgical texts and actions, is Flanigan's hypothesis. He proves it by analyzing the *Quem quaeritis* in the text of the Introit to the Easter Mass and by looking at the *Quem quaeritis* dialogue in the *Regularis concordia.* His findings lead him to the conclusion that this trope, which can be perceived as a commemoration of the life and passion of Christ, was nothing more than a commentary on the significance of the Easter liturgy. It served, therefore, the same ritual function whether it appeared as an Introit trope, as a processional ceremony, or as a quasi-independent *Visitatio Sepulchri.* Even though the execution of the text of the *Quem quaeritis* might have varied—that is, words or actions could have been employed to achieve its purpose—these means were only secondary to the message. And the message of the trope was clear—it was a liturgical commemoration of the resurrection of Jesus Christ. Accordingly, Flanigan observes that to consider the *Quem quaeritis* as the nucleus of the medieval drama is unjustified; such a view only reflects a lack of understanding about the true function of the Christian liturgy.

74. This particular approach and the location study of the various forms of the *Quem quaeritis* enable Bjork to discover that its versions that are associated with the Introit to the Easter Mass were mainly confined to Italy, the south of France, and Catalonia; those that are connected with Matins (Nocturns) were used in the north of France, England, Lotharingia, and Germany. See David A. Bjork, "On the Dissemination of *Quem quaeritis* and the *Visitatio Sepulchri* and the Chronology of Their Early Sources," *Comparative Drama* 14 (spring 1980): 46–69.

75. See Michael L. Norton, "Of 'Stages' and 'Types' in *Visitatione Sepulchri*," *Comparative Drama* 21 (spring and summer 1987): 34–61, 127–41. Having reviewed major arrangements of texts by Gustav Milchsack (1880), Carl Lange (1887), E. K. Chambers (1903), Karl Young (1933), O. B. Hardison (1965), and Helmut de Boor (1967), Norton proposes his theory of periodization based on the concept of the discrete elements.

Clearly if we wish to understand connections that unite—or separate—the sources of a repertory, any repertory, we must begin with the discrete elements that compose those sources. In the case of the *Visitatio Sepulchri* we must begin not with whatever levels of textual or dramatic complexity or variations in poetic structure may be evident, but with the individual textual/musical settings themselves. These are the discrete elements. Although classifications built along other matrices are possible, even desirable, such classifications must always be derivative in nature, in that their base is either abstracted from the discrete textual/musical elements or related to the contexts in which these settings are found (classifications, for example, based on liturgical placement or geographical distribution). (133)

Two types of the *Quem quaeritis* emerge in this search for the common denominator: type 1, composed in the ninth and tenth centuries and sung within a variety of liturgical positions, that is, before the Mass, at the end of Matins [Nocturns], or even before the Office; and type 2, composed around the eleventh century as an amplified revision of type 1 with an emphasis on the dialogue between the Marys. Such a division allows Norton to see the *Visitatio Sepulchri* as a whole as two largely independent, although clearly contiguous, traditions of performance.

76. See Hughes in *The Theatre of Medieval Europe*, pp. 42–66. Hughes is particularly interested in the musical analysis of the *Quem quaeritis*. Basing his comments on the conclusions reached independently by Susan Rankin and Anselme Davril that "the musical shape of the five lines, within each phrase and, more importantly, in the overall structure, 'forms a coherent and balance structure,'" Hughes suggests an explanation of what the *Quem quaeritis* was (56;

see also Susan Rankin, "Musical and Ritual Aspects of *Quem quaeritis,*" *Münchener Beitrage zur Mediavistik und Renaissanceforschung* 36 (1985): 181–92; Davril, 68–69). He does so, first, by analyzing the position and variants (marked with "and") of the musical units (identified by capital letters) and texts (identified by small letters) in a typical medieval responsory and verse and, second, by collating this information, now coded into symbols, with an Easter responsory and the *Quem quaeritis.* Hughes uses the following diagram to explain his argument (57).

Responsory			Drama	Responsory	Drama
R.	A	A	Quem quaeritis . . .	solo	(Angel)
	B	B	Jesum Nazarenum . . .	chorus	(three Marys)
V.	C	C	Non est hic . . .	solo	(Angel)
	B'	B'	ite nunciate . . .		
R.	A	D	Alleluia resurrexit . . .	chorus	(three Marys)
	B'	B'	resurrexit leo . . .		
	x	E	Deo gratias . . .		

Hughes writes: "Substituting D in the drama where A repeats in the responsory can be explained by the need to repeat the joy of 'Non est hic' at 'Alleluia,' so that sentence D takes the high melody characteristic of C in the drama" (57).

77. Undoubtedly, such investigations, as Andrew Hughes shows in his essay, can yield interesting information about variability of test and methods of transmission. (See Hughes in *The Theatre in Medieval Europe,* pp. 42–66, especially his discussion of the "o" in the vocative "o christocolae.") However, as various editions of the medieval liturgical drama suggest, these catalogues of troping practices often overlook historical or cultural conditions at the time when the tropes were created. See, for example, Walther Lipphardt, *Lateinische Osterfeiern und Osterspiele,* 6 vols. (Berlin and New York: Walter de Gruyter, 1975–81); de Boor; Diane Dolan, *Le Drame liturgique de Paques en Normandie et en Anglettere au moyen âge* (Paris: Presses Universitaires de France, 1975); Collins Fletcher, *The Production of Medieval Church Music-Drama: A Repertory of Complete Plays* (Charlottesville, VA: University Press of Virginia, 1972), Norton.

78. De Certeau, *The Writing of History,* p. xi.

79. Michel de Certeau, *Heterologies: Discourse on the Other,* trans. Brian Massumi, with a foreword by Wlad Godzich (Minneapolis, MN: University of Minnesota Press, 1986), 205.

80. Bourdieu, p. 467.

81. I am using here de Certeau's definition of a strategy. In *The Practice of Everyday Life,* de Certeau defines a strategy as "the calculation (or manipulation) of power relationships that becomes possible as soon as a subject with will and power (a business, an army, a city, a scientific institution) can be isolated." He continues: "It postulates a *place* that can be determined as its *own* and serve as the base from which relations with an *exteriority* composed of targets and threats

(customers or competitors, enemies, the country surrounding the city, objectives and objects of research, etc.) can be managed" (36). For further information see, Michel de Certeau, *The Practice of Everyday Life,* trans. Steven Rendall (Berkeley, CA: University of California Press, 1984), pp. 34–42.

82. Barthes, pp. 127–48.

83. *The Writing of History,* 4.

84. See Elizabeth Grosz, *Space, Time, and Perversion: Essays on the Politics of Bodies* (London and New York: Routledge, 1995), chap. 8.

85. De Certeau, *Heterologies,* p. 194.

86. *The Archaeology of Knowledge,* p. 5.

87. Gilles Deleuze, "Nomad Art: Space," *The Deleuze Reader,* edited with an introduction by Constantin V. Boundas (New York: Columbia University Press, 1993), p. 167.

88. See the works by Bynum, Coletti, Evans, and Beckwith cited in n. 21.

Chapter 1

1. For discussion of the changes happening in the field of medieval studies see Lawrence Stone, "History and Postmodernism," *Past and Present* 131 (May 1991): 217–18; Patrick Joyce's and Catriona Kelly's response to "History and Postmodernism," *Past and Present* 133 (November 1991): 204–13; Anne Middleton, "Medieval Studies," *Redrawing the Boundaries: The Transformation of English and American Literary Studies,* ed. Stephen Greenblatt and Giles Gunn (New York: Modern Language Association of America, 1992), pp. 12–40; *Medievalism and the Modernist Temper,* ed. R. Howard Bloch and Stephen G. Nichols (Baltimore, MD: Johns Hopkins University Press, 1996). For discussion of a general belief concerning the emergence of the liturgical ceremonies in dramatic form see, for example, Glynne Wickham, "The Romanesque Style in Medieval Drama," *Tenth-Century Studies: Essays in Commemoration of the Millennium of the Council of Winchester and Regularis concordia,* ed. David Parsons (London: Phillimore, 1975), pp. 115–22; Jack Watson, *A Cultural History of Theatre* (London: Longman, 1993), p. 71. These two publications are a summary par excellence of what is currently presented to students in classrooms.

2. Michel de Certeau, *The Writing of History,* trans. Tom Conley (New York: Columbia University Press, 1988), p. 1.

3. Ibid., p. 2.

4. Ibid., p. 2.

5. Michel de Certeau, *Heterologies: Discourse on the Other,* trans. Brian Massumi, with a foreword by Wlad Godzich (Minneapolis, MN: University of Minnesota Press, 1986), p. 67.

6. De Certeau, *Heterologies,* p. 91.

7. *The Writing of History,* p. xv.

8. Ibid., p. 4.

9. For an insightful analysis of place and space see "Spatial Stories" in Michel de Certeau, *The Practice of Everyday Life,* trans. Steven Rendall (Berkeley, CA: University of California Press, 1984), pp. 115–30. In *The Practice of Everyday Life,* de Certeau introduces the following distinction between space and place:

[a] place (*lieu*) is the order (of whatever kind) in accord with which elements are distributed in relationships of coexistence. It thus excludes the possibility of two things being in the same location (*place*). The law of the "proper" rules in the place: the elements taken into consideration are *beside* one another, each situated in its own "proper" and distinct location, a location it defines. A place is thus an instantaneous configuration of positions. It implies an indication of stability. A *space* exists when one takes into consideration vectors of direction, velocities, and time variables. Thus space is composed of intersections of mobile elements. It is in a sense actuated by the ensemble of movements deployed within it. Space occurs as the effect produced by the operations that orient it, situate it, temporalize it, and make it function in a polyvalent unity of conflictual programs or contractual proximities. . . . In contradiction to the place, it has thus none of the univocity or stability of a "proper." (117)

This distinction between place and space suggests that space is a practiced place: "Thus the street geometrically defined by urban planning is transformed into a space by walkers. In the same way, an act of reading is the space produced by the practice of a particular place: a written text, that is, a place constituted by a system of signs" (117). Consequently, the doer of the action is constantly transforming places into spaces or spaces into places. By so doing, she or he engages in a continuous play of changing relationships between places and spaces. This play of changing relationships can acquire different shapes that are positioned somewhere between places of immobile and striated order and spaces multiplied by the movement of actions. Since they are immobile, places can be identified. Since they are multiplied, spaces can be actualized. This identification and actualization happens in "an open field of specifiable and describable relationships" where the doer of action and her or his representational practices occupy diverse positions defined by orientations, references, and linkages that are in a continuous variation.

10. "The one who makes truth has access to the light."

11. We do not have the exact date for the Council in Winchester. The dates that are currently given are 970x973. Dom Thomas Symons suggests that the date for the council could be moved from 970 to 973:

Thus whereas in 970 there would have been an attendance, besides the three leaders [Dunstan, Aethelwold, Oswald], of four other monk-bishops, Eadnoth (Dorchester 964–75), the two Aelfstans (Rochester 964–95; Ramsbury 970–81), Sidemann (Credition 970–77), and the abbots and abbesses of the houses listed above under that year as certain or likely; in 973, on the other hand, there would have been two more monk-bishops, Athulf (Hereford from 973) and Aelfheah (Lichfield, from 973), the abbots already mentioned under 970 together with the Abbots of Ramsey, Winchcombe, Pershore—a most important reinforcement from Oswald's group—Westminster and Thorney . . . and, possibly the Abbess of Ramsey. . . . The coronation of King Edgar at Bath on Whit Sunday, 973, would not have been incompatible with the holding of the Council at Winchester later in the same year; on the contrary, no more suitable time could have been chosen for the carrying through of a project designed to secure and to safeguard the unity and the solidarity of the monastic movement on which Edgar, now the 'anointed of the Lord,' had for long set his heart" (Dom Thomas Symons, *"Regularis concordia:* History and Derivation," *Tenth-Century Studies,* ed. David Parsons, pp. 41–42).

12. The difference between a town church and a monastery has frequently been overlooked by theater historians. It should be pointed out here that, especially in the tenth century, the town churches were filled with secular clerks who were accused by the monastic leaders of all possible abominations. Through his disciplines, Dunstan was trying to reestablish in monastic churches the strict order that had been suggested by St. Benedict. While describing the *Rule* of St. Benedict, David Knowles wrote: "Although some details of the Rule have given rise to controversies among both monks and scholars, it is not difficult to grasp the broad lines of the monastic life for which it was written, and which, therefore, it always tended of itself to reproduce. The monastery which it describes is a unit, completely self-contained and self-sufficient, both economically and constitutionally. A community, ruled by an abbot elected by the monks for life, is supported by the produce of its fields and garden and has within the wall of its enclosure all that is necessary to convert the produce into food and to make and repair clothing and other articles of common use. It has no function in the life of the Church save to provide an ordered way of life based on the teaching of the gospel, according to which its inmates may serve God and sanctify their souls apart from the life of the world. No work done within it, whether manual, intellectual or charitable, is directed to an end outside its walls. It is the home of a spiritual family whose life and work begins and ends in the family circle; like other families it may on occasion support dependents, give hospitality and relieve the spiritual and bodily necessities of those who dwell in its neighbourhood or who seek from it such relief, but its primary concern is with itself, not with others, and the evils of corporate selfishness are excluded by its *raison d'être,* which is the service of God in simplicity of life and without contact with the world" (David Knowles, *The Monastic Order in England* [Cambridge: Cambridge University Press, 1950], pp. 3–4).

13. ". . . the assembly as one man made a solemn vow to our Lord Jesus Christ, confirming their oath with a spiritual act, that, living all their life under the yoke of the Rule, they would carry out these self same monastic cus-

toms openly and with one uniform observance" (*The Monastic Agreement of the Monks and Nuns of the English Nation,* translated with an introduction and notes by Dom Thomas Symons (London: Thomas Nelson and Sons, 1953), p. 4. See also *Consuetudinum saeculi X/XI/XII monumenta non-Cluniacensia,* ed. Kassius Hallinger, Corpus Consuetudinum Monasticarum t. 7, pars. 3 (Siegburg: Franz Schmitt, 1984), p. 73. All citations will refer to page numbers in these two volumes.

14. Symons maintains that the *Regularis concordia* is probably the oldest of the codes and gives the most complete account of the duties and organization of monastic life in England at that time (*The Monastic Agreement,* p. xxix).

15. Monasteries were established in England with the arrival of Augustine and his companions in 596, the year when Christianity was reintroduced into the country (see Peter Hunter Blair, *An Introduction to Anglo-Saxon England* [Cambridge: Cambridge University Press, 1962], p. 117). In his *Historia ecclesiastica,* Bede Venerabilis documents the next 350 years of English monasticism. Unfortunately, his ecclesiastical history ends in 731. Although it may be a pure historical coincidence, this date also marks the period when all other extant records are so limited that it is difficult to know exactly what happened during the next two hundred years. These records suggest, however, that from the time of Bede, many of the monasteries disappeared because of the process of secularization in the eighth, ninth, and tenth centuries. In the *Regularis concordia,* Aethelwold states that monasticism in England had been destroyed in the past by *saecularium prioratus* (secular domination). The local magnates and their families, who owned ecclesiastical property, used their power to be in control of the endowments as well as of the people who headed them. It was expected that the estates and the buildings on them, including monasteries, would stay in the family. Consequently, monasteries became hereditary; and so did the abbatal office itself (*The Monastic Agreement,* p. 1; *Consuetudinum,* p. 69). See also Eric John, "The King and the Monks in the Tenth-Century Reformation," *Bulletin of the John Rylands Library* 42.1 (September 1959): 61–87. Also, Blair notes: "canons passed by a synod held at Clofeshoh in 747 referred to priests prating in church like secular bards, to monks and nuns dressing themselves in gorgeous apparel, to monasteries becoming retreats for versifiers, harpers and buffoons, and to nunneries becoming secret meeting-places for evil talk, drunkenness and luxury. At about the same time Boniface wrote to the archbishop of Canterbury inveighing strongly against the evils of drunkenness and fine clothing. Not only did bishops get drunk, he had been told, but they forced others to drunkenness as well by offering them overlarge cups. The English Church was also being brought into disrepute abroad by nuns who went on pilgrimage and succumbed to temptation by the way, so that English harlots were to be found in most towns of Gaul and Lombardy. Later in the century Alcuin wrote frequently from abroad exhorting monks to observe their vows, to avoid luxury in dress and listen in the refectory to holy Scripture rather than to heathen songs" (*Anglo-Saxon England,* pp. 161–62). This laxity among clergy and

monks can also explain why, as David Knowles notes, many of the *monasteriola,* for example, "were so only in name, being actually the family strongholds of those who hoped to attain immunity from taxation and public service by the nominal consecration of an estate to God." "[O]thers," continues Knowles, "in origin genuine monasteries, fell down the scale, as did so many all over Europe in periods of decay, and became first houses of clerics and then the residence of one or two priests, of which the owner and titular *abbot* was often a lay landowner or magnate" (David Knowles, *The Religious Houses of Medieval England* [London: Sheed and Ward, 1940], p. 14). Even though this general trend toward the secularization of ecclesiastical life was the major factor that contributed to the fall and disappearance of organized observances of the Benedictine *Rule* in England, the Viking attacks and the settlements, which followed them, could also be seen as the force that might have contributed to the destruction of monastic life throughout the eastern part of England from the Thames in the south to Coldingham in the north. The bishoprics of Dunwich, Elmham, and Lindsay were completely destroyed. The see of York was reduced to a state of obscure poverty, and the sees of Hexham and Whithorn ceased to exist. The cathedral of Lindisfarne was abandoned, and its bishop and some of the younger clerks tried to preserve the relics of Saint Cuthbert traveling from one place to another for seven years until a new church was built for them at Chester-le-Street (see Frank Merry Stenton, *Anglo-Saxon England* [Oxford: Clarendon Press, 1943], p. 427).

This destruction of the orders also meant the disappearance of the libraries and, thus, any records that could have provided information about of the monastic movement at the time. This is why the history of East Anglia and the eastern Midlands is very scanty. The charters that survived, however, note some activity in the establishment of ecclesiastical, if not monastic, institutions (see *Anglo-Saxon Charters,* ed. Agnes Jane Robertson [Cambridge: Cambridge University Press, 1939], p. 15).

The history of the south and west of England is known to us only from the writings of King Alfred and Asser. Evidence provided by them implies that, because of either warfare or decay in the monasteries themselves, regular life according to the *Rule* of St. Benedict had ceased to exist in the south and west with the possible exception of Canterbury (*The Monastic Agreement,* p. x). Asser, in his *Life of King Alfred,* refers to this situation when he writes about Alfred's attempt to build two monasteries.

At first he [Alfred] had no one of his own nation, noble and free by birth, who was willing to enter the monastic life, except children, who as yet could neither choose good nor reject evil by reason of their tender years. This was the case because for many years previous the love of a monastic life had utterly decayed in that as well as many other nations; for though many monasteries still remain in that country, yet no one kept the rule of that kind of life in an orderly way, whether because of the invasions of foreigners, which took place so frequently both by sea and land, or because that people abounded in riches of every kind, and so looked with contempt on the monastic life. (Asser, *Life of King Alfred,* trans. Albert S. Cook [London: Ginn, 1906], p. 55; see also Asser, *Alfred the Great,* ed. and trans. Simon Keynes and Michael Lapidge [Harmondsworth, Middlesex: Penguin Classics, 1983])

In 895, King Alfred complained about illiterate clergy and secular clerks in the preface to his translation of the *Pastoral Care* of Gregory the Great—he did not know of a single clerk south of the Thames who was able to conduct the Mass in Latin or translate a letter from that language into English (Knowles, *Religious Houses,* p. 32). Consequently, he stated that to re-create the ideals of the Christian faith, the education of the younger generation should be the prime necessity. He gathered around himself a group of teachers, of which Asser and two foreigners, Grimald and John, were monks.

First he [King Alfred] placed there [Athelney] John the priest and monk, an Old Saxon by birth, making him abbot; and then certain priests and deacons from beyond the sea. Finding that he had not so large a number of these as he wished, he procured as many as possible of the same Gallic race; some of whom, being children, he ordered to be taught in the same monastery, and at a later period to be admitted to the monastic habit. (Asser, *Life of King Alfred,* p. 55).

King Alfred did not attempt to reform any of the old monasteries, since Asser claimed none of them kept the monastic rule properly, but the king established new foundations in Athelney and Shaftesbury.

Concerning his desire and intent of excellent meditation, which, in the midst both of prosperity and adversity, he [King Alfred] never in any way neglected, I cannot in this place with advantage forbear to speak. For when he was reflecting, according to his wont, upon the need of his soul, he ordered, among the other good deeds to which his thoughts were by night and day especially turned, that two monasteries should be built, one of them being for monks at Athelney. This is a place surrounded by impassable fens and waters on every hand, where no one can enter but by boats, or by a bridge laboriously constructed between two fortresses, at the western end of which bridge was erected a strong citadel, of beautiful work, by command of the aforesaid king. In this monastery he collected monks of all kinds from every quarter, and there settled them. (Asser, *Life of King Alfred,* p. 54).

The lack of native monks, however, did not bring the hoped-for revival that was to take place during the reign of Athelstan. The year 924 marks only the time of the monastic revival and the spreading of new reforms throughout the Continent and England. The foreign policy of Athelstan made ecclesiastical contacts easier, but the extent of the changes that might have resulted from these contacts is difficult to ascertain. If we were to believe unquestionably in the text of the *Regularis concordia*, then we would know that at that time, monastic life ceased nearly to exist: "When therefore he [King Edgar] learned that the holy monasteries in all quarters of his kingdom, brought low, and almost wholly lacking in the service of our Lord Jesus Christ, were wasting away and neglected, moved by the grace of the Lord he most gladly set himself to restore them everywhere to their former good estate" (*The Monastic Agreement,* pp. 1–2; *Consuetudinum,* pp. 69–70).

16. *The Monastic Agreement,* p. xi.

17. The following rudimentary discussion of monasticism should be treated as an introduction for those readers who are not acquainted with the subject. By no means should this discussion or suggested bibliography be treated as complete.

Monasticism (the term derived from the Greek word *monachos,* meaning "solitary") began in Egypt in the fourth century C.E. In the first formative period, early monks and nuns were often simple peasants who had little education. Their eremitical form of life soon made them popular with the common people, who were well acquainted with the splendor of the lives of the urbanized episcopate and clergy. When, in 393 C.E., Theodosius had made Christianity the official Roman religion, monasteries and solitaries were established closer to the cities, where they started to exert a strong influence on the urban population. Bishops objected to this new movement, therefore Theodosius forbade monks to come into cities or to live within their boundaries and gave them his permission to inhabit only deserted places. After his death, his sons issued a rule stipulating that when a bishop had a vacancy among his clergy, he should appoint someone who was a monk. In 451, the Council of Chalcedon finally recognized the monastic movement.

The sixth century was a significant period for the movement because monastic lifestyles were clearly defined and the difference between monastic and ecclesiastical orders was established by St. Benedict (ca. 480–550), St. Columban (543–615), and St. Gregory (Gregory the Great, 540–603). St. Benedict founded a cenobite monastery in Monte Cassino, for which he designed a code explaining the basic principles of monasticism. This *Rule* is a relatively short piece of writing that consists of four parts dealing with the formation and nature of the monastery (detailed liturgical and penal provisions), its administration (legislation covering every department of the life of the monastery), its renovation (rules for receiving brethren, pilgrims, etc.), and the behavior of all the members and officials of a monastic family. Benedict's idea of a monastery can be described as a self-contained, self-sufficient, and self-supporting community of monks who were devoted to and joined together by the worship of Christ. Its members were to renounce their earthly possessions, to serve God, and to remain in their community for life. The head of the community was the abbot, who was elected by the monks for life and governed them autocratically but according to the rule. All the monks were required to obey him implicitly.

Moreover, they were supposed to participate in communal praise of God in the sevenfold daily Office, in manual labor in the fields, and in *lectio divina*—the study of Scripture. St. Columban, an Irish missionary, represents an exceedingly severe kind of monasticism. It enjoined the monks to fast, pray, read, and work every day. It demanded absolute humility, patience, and silence. This ascetic life, which had been introduced in Ireland, spread and was accepted in Gaul (France) and Italy. Columban's *Rule* was gradually modified, however, by its contact with the Benedictine *Rule,* which, in the time of Charlemagne, became the standard for monastic centers in Europe. St. Gregory's writings and especially his *Dialogues* indicate that he was a promoter of the monastic tradition as defined by St. Benedict. He introduced a clear distinction between the two religious traditions. Since the time of his papacy, the monastic and clerical vocations were treated as separate entities. This separation had a direct source in his conviction that no one should be considered fit to perform both ecclesiastical and monastic duties.

The history of monasticism between the death of Pope Gregory (604) and the foundation of the abbey of Cluny (910) is the history of numerous houses that appeared and disappeared. As was the case with the institution of the church, the religious orders were susceptible to the pressing problems of the period. The Councils of Trullo (692) and Nicea (778), specifically referring to monks guilty of fornication or marriage, forbade them to go to the baths when women were present, prohibited them from attending plays performed at weddings, and called for rules against double monasteries. Moreover, the gradual dissolution of the Carolingian system brought disorder and corruption to many centers of monastic life. Yet one should not assume that monasticism lost its ascetic spirit. The *Rule* of St. Benedict gradually achieved universal acceptance thanks to Benedict of Aniane (751–821), who, on behalf of Louis the Pious, was authorized to impose it on all the monasteries of the king's territory to revive the idea of a strict and regular monastic life. Benedict of Aniane modified the code. First, agricultural work was perceived by him as extraordinary for monks who should only concentrate on the necessary work of the house. Second, since Charlemagne had issued legislation specifying that the education of the laity was a duty of the clergy, teaching by monks of anyone except oblates was forbidden. And third, a considerable addition was made to the daily liturgical prayers of the *Rule.* The addition was a consequence of the two former orders and aimed at filling up the free time of monks who no longer had to be involved in manual labor or teaching. All these characteristic features of a monastery and monastic life were altered at the beginning of the tenth century, during the period of the church's spiritual disintegration caused by feudal control of ecclesiastical properties by lay magnates, the involvement of the papacy in the struggle for power in the world of politics, and the invasions that took place in the last decades of the ninth century. At the same time, Odo and his friend Adhegrin attempted to reestablish Benedictine monasticism in a monastery that was founded at Cluny in 910.

In the early autumn of 910, William of Aquitaine, marquis of Gothia and count of Auvergne, Velay, and Bourges, signed the charter that was to give the abbey of Cluny its independence from lay and episcopal supervision in terms of both administration and jurisdiction. Berno (910–26), Odo (926–42), Maieul (943–94), Odilo (994–1049), and Hugh (1049–1109) strengthened the spirit of Benedictine monasticism by a strict observance of the *Rule* and its modified version, the *Capitula* of Aachen. The *Rule* set up the principal framework regarding the formation and nature of the monastery. Monks were not allowed to have personal property. They all slept in a dormitory and dined together at times that were specified by tradition and the seasons of the year. Privacy as such did not exist. All the matters connected with life in a monastery, that is, regarding its administration as well as the behavior of monks, was discussed during the Chapter meeting, which was usually held after the morning Mass. Moreover, the brethren were obliged to abide by the rules of keeping silence, of humility, and of uncontested obedience to the abbot. The primary precept of the house was that the life of monks was completely and entirely devoted to the service of God. The balance between spiritual and manual labor, as stipulated in the *Rule,* was changed. Psalm singing and prayer became the labor of monks, while the cultivation of their lands was left to lay brethren, serfs, and servants. Cluny became a model institution for other orders that aimed at reviving the old tradition. Its abbots were consulted regularly and asked for help to reform and found other monasteries. Consequently, an affiliation was created between these houses, which were subjected to a single common superior, the abbot of Cluny. Among the houses so reformed was the ancient monastery at Fleury (ca. 930), which would play a crucial role in the development of English monasticism in the years to come.

Simultaneously with the rise of Cluny, two other revivals in Upper and Lower Lorraine occurred. The monasticism of Upper Lorraine, which was much more physically severe than Cluny, spread throughout the districts of Cologne, Metz, Verdun, and Toul. The rule of Lower Lorraine was accepted in Flanders and especially in St. Omer and Ghent. Ghent was another center that would supply a model for the monastic revival in England.

For further information see Judith Herrin, *The Formation of Christendom* (Princeton, NJ: Princeton University Press, 1987); Philip Schaff, *History of the Christian Church,* 8 vols. (New York: Charles Scribner's Sons, 1910); David Knowles, *The Christian Centuries,* 2 vols. (New York: McGraw-Hill Book Co., 1968); Williston Walker, *A History of the Christian Church* (New York: Charles Scribner's Sons, 1985); H. G. Koenigsberger and Asa Brigs, *Medieval Europe, 400–1500* (London: Longman, 1987); Charles A. Frazee, "The Origins of Clerical Celibacy in the Western Church," *Church History* 41.2 (June 1972): 149–67; *Documents of the Christian Church,* ed. Henry Bettenson (London: Oxford University Press, 1963); Charles A. Frazee, "Late Roman and Byzantine Legislation on the Monastic Life from the Fourth to the Eighth Centuries," *Church History* 51.3 (September 1982): 263–79; David Parry, *Households of God:*

The Rule of St. Benedict with Explanations for Monks and Lay-people Today (London: Darton, Longman, and Todd, 1980); Knowles, *The Monastic Order in England;* Joan Evans, *Monastic Life at Cluny, 910–1157* (London: Oxford University Press, 1931); Giles Constable, "Monastic Legislation at Cluny in the Eleventh and Twelfth Centuries," *Cluniac Studies* (London: Variorum Reprints, 1980), pp. 151–61; Eric John, *Orbis Britanniae and Other Studies* (Leicester: Leicester University Press, 1966); Margaret Deanesly, *The Pre-Conquest Church in England* (London: A. and C. Black, 1963); John Godfrey, *The Church in Anglo-Saxon England* (Cambridge: Cambridge University Press, 1962).

18. Dunstan's paternal uncle Aethelhelm was the first bishop of the see of Wells from 909 until he was transferred to Canterbury in 923. Two of his other relatives, Aelfheah and Cynesige, became bishops, and another one, Lady Aethelflaeda, was the niece of King Athelstan. See Barbara Yorke, "Aethelwold and the Politics of the Tenth Century," *Bishop Aethelwold: His Career and Influence,* ed. Barbara Yorke (Woodbridge, Suffolk: Boydell Press, 1988), pp. 66–67.

19. Information regarding Dunstan's life can be found in five biographies written by Auctore B, Adelard (Auctore Adelardi), William of Malmesbury (Auctore Willelmo Malmesberiensi), Eadmer (Auctore Eadmero), and Osbern (Auctore Osberno) and printed in *Memorials of Saint Dunstan, Archbishop of Canterbury,* ed. William Stubbs, *Rerum Britannicarum medii aevi scriptores, or Chronicles and Memorials of Great Britain and Ireland during the Middle Ages,* 99 vols. (London: Longman, 1874), vol. 63. See also J. Armitage Robinson, *The Times of Saint Dunstan* (Oxford: Clarendon Press, 1923).

20. *Memorials of Saint Dunstan,* p. 55.

21. Auctore B tells us that Dunstan, having been expelled from court, was pulled about by his enemies and half smothered in a muddy pond. Half-dead, he managed to escape from his oppressors. See *Memorials of Saint Dunstan,* p. 12.

22. *Memorials of Saint Dunstan,* pp. 13–14.

23. As Barbara Yorke indicates, Dunstan's promotion to Glastonbury was not unintentional. While the decision was made, the king must have taken into consideration family connections: "[t]he main land holdings of Dunstan's kin seem to have lain in Somerset, and Dunstan is reputed to have been born in Baltonsborough, some four miles from Glastonbury. Dunstan studied at Glastonbury as a boy, and other family members, including Aethelhelm and Aelfheah, may have been members of the community. Aethelflaeda . . . possessed a house in Glastonbury, where Athelstan visited her, and she may have left this and other estates to Dunstan after her death" (*Bishop Aethelwold,* p. 67).

24. The status of Glastonbury previous to Dunstan's appointment and the first years of Dunstan's rule there as abbot are discussed by Knowles in *The Monastic Order in England,* pp. 695–96. See also D. H. Farmer, "The Progress of the Monastic Revival," *Tenth-Century Studies,* pp. 10–19. We may assume that the *Rule* was followed. Symons states: "the want of detailed and ceremonious observance affords no indication that the early reform at Glastonbury differed

essentially from those of twenty or thirty years later when Continental ideas were exercising a direct influence in this country. Particular devotional practices, ritual splendour and the like have always been dependent on the fashion of the day, and our early authorities for this period lend no support to the view that any essential change in the character of its monasticism took place at some further stage of the movement" (*The Monastic Agreement,* p. xvi).

25. *Chronicon Monasterii de Abington,* ed. Joseph Stevenson, *Rerum Britannicarum medii aevi scriptores, or Chronicles and Memorials of Great Britain and Ireland during the Middle Ages,* 99 vols. (London: Longman, 1858), 2:255–66. See also *Three Lives of English Saints,* ed. Michael Winterbottom (Toronto: Published for the Centre for Medieval Studies by the Pontifical Institute of Medieval Studies, 1972).

26. Wulfstan of Winchester, *Life of Saint Aethelwold,* ed. Michael Lapidge and Michael Winterbottom (Oxford: Clarendon Press, 1991), chaps. 2, 7.

27. Ibid., chap. 9.

28. Ibid., chap. 10. According to Yorke, the decision to leave Glastonbury can suggest that Aethelwold was dissatisfied with Dunstan's reforms at the monastery. From the written sources, we can infer that this move happened with Dunstan's permission. In the style of diplomatic writing, Aethelwold says in his account of King Edgar's establishment of monasteries that Glastonbury had been the only true monastic house before Abingdon was founded. Obviously, this statement is a tribute to Dunstan and his role in the monastic revival in England. See "King Edgar's Establishment of Monasteries," *Councils and Synods with Other Documents Relating to the English Church,* ed. Dorothy Whitelock, Martin Brett, and Christopher Brooke, 2 vols. (Oxford: Clarendon Press, 1981), 1:148–49.

29. Among others, C. E. Hohler and Alan Thacker question this strict observance of the *Rule* in Abingdon that we are led to believe in by Aethelwold's biographers. For example, Hohler states: "It will be recalled how the Abingdon chronicler in the twelfth century, writing for private circulation only, explains with gratitude how St. Aethelwold, by moderating the rigours of St. Benedictine's stern Rule, made it possible for gentlemen to live in monasteries" (C. E. Hohler, "Some Service-Books of the Later Saxon Church," *Tenth-Century Studies,* p. 71). Hohler refers here to three passages in the *Chronicon Monasterii de Abington.* The first two refer to refreshments served in the monastery and especially to three gallons of beer a day that were customary (*Tenth-Century Studies,* p. 71; *Chronicon Monasterii de Abington,* 1:346). The third one refers to the fur bedcovers for monks (*Tenth-Century Studies,* p. 71; *Chronicon Monasterii de Abington,* 1:346). Thacker adds to this relaxation of the rule that Aethelwold allowed his monks, besides the usual vegetables and pulses, cheese, fried food, and some meat. Also, on feast day, the monks were allowed, besides beer, mead. See Alan Thacker, "Aethelwold and Abingdon," *Bishop Aethelwold,* p. 56. See Wulfstan, chap. 11, for the narrative about the establish-

ment of the monastery and the names of monks and canons who followed Aethelwold to Abingdon.

30. *Chronicon Monasterii de Abington,* 1:129.

31. Ibid., 1:129; Wulfstan, chap. 14. Alan Thacker suggests that the dominating influence in reforming Abingdon had been Fleury. By analyzing the content of an early eleventh-century manuscript, he comes to the conclusion that an annotated calendar, a version of Usuardus's *Martyrologium,* and Smaragdus's *Diadema Monachorum* could have been obtained from Fleury. Moreover, it was believed in Abingdon that the *Rule* of St. Benedict came from the French house. Thacker writes: "But interestingly the text in the Abingdon manuscript seems to derive from two different exemplars: one Carolingian, based upon St Benedict's original, the other English, dependent of the eight-century Worcester manuscript which is the earliest surviving text of the Rule" (in *Bishop Aethelwold,* p. 55).

32. Wulfstan, chap. 11.

33. Wulfstan describes how Aelfstan's obedience was tested by Aethelwold, who ordered Aelfstan to put his hand into a boiling cauldron to fetch Aethelwold some food from the bottom. The monk followed the order without hesitation: "He plunged his hand to the bottom of the pot and took out a hot morsel, without feeling the heat of boiling water" (Ibid., chap. 14).

34. We are told by Auctore B that on his coronation day, Eadwig left the hall where the bishops and nobles were celebrating and spent his time with two women, mother and daughter, who, in fact, were related to him. (Later, Eadwig married the daughter, Aelfgifu. He was obliged to renounce the marriage in 958 because of their kinship.) Archbishop Oda sent Dunstan and Bishop Cynesige to bring the young king back: "When in accordance with their superiors' orders, they had entered, they found the royal crown, which was bound with wondrous metal, gold and silver and gems, and shone with many-coloured lustre, carelessly thrown down on the floor, far from his head, and he himself repeatedly wallowing between the two of them in evil fashion, as if in a vile sty" (*Memorials of Saint Dunstan,* pp. 32–34). The sudden appearance of the abbot and the bishop and their action of making the king attend the banquet angered Eadwig. As a result of this incident, Dunstan was exiled. As Yorke suggests, "Cynesige witnessed very few of Eadwig's charters" (*Bishop Aethelwold,* p. 75).

35. The pope expressed his gratitude to Edgar I for restoring to the bishops and the monasteries all the property that had been taken away from them and for revoking Eadwig's decrees hostile to the church ("Letter from Pope John XII Granting Permission for the Ejection of the Secular Canons from Winchester Cathedral," *Councils and Synods,* pp. 111–13).

36. It is interesting to note after Auctore B that the English land was divided into two parts by the river Thames (*Memorials of Saint Dunstan,* p. 36). As C. R. Hart observes, the bishops and aldermen whose offices and lands were located south of the Thames attested Eadwig's charters, and those north of the

river attested Edgar's (C. R. Hart, *The Early Chapters of Northern England and the North Midlands,* Studies in Early English History 6 [Leicester: Leicester University Press, 1975], pp. 322–23).

37. The following are the names and the dates of reign of the rulers of England during the period discussed here: Alfred (871–99), Edward the Elder (899–924), Althelstan (924–39), Edmund (939–46), Eadred (946–55), Eadwig (955–59), Edgar (960–75).

38. These sees were vacant because Archbishop of Canterbury Oda died in 958. His successor, Bishop Aelfsiege of Winchester, died of cold in the Alps while traveling to Rome to receive his pallium.

39. In 960x962, Edgar issued a code divided into an ecclesiastical and a secular section. The following ordinances were made "for the glory of God, and his own royal dignity, and the good of all his people."

[1] First, namely, that God's churches are to be entitled every right.

[1.1] And all payment of tithe is to be made to the old minister, to which the perish belongs; and it is to be rendered both from the thegn's demesne land and the land of his tenants, according as it is brought under the plough.

[2] If, however, there is any thegn who has on his bookland a church with which there is a graveyard, he is to pay the third part of his own tithe into his church. . . .

[3] And the tithe of all young stock is to be rendered by Pentecost, and of the fruits of the earth by the Equinox, and all churchscot is to be rendered by Martinmas, under pain of the full fine which the lawbook prescribes. . . .

[5] And every Sunday shall be observed as a festival from Saturday noon until dawn on Monday, under pain of the punishment which the lawbook prescribes, and every other festival as it is enjoined.

[5.1] And every appointed fast is to be observed with all diligence.

See *Councils and Synods,* pp. 97–102; *The Laws of the Kings of England from Edmund to Henry I,* ed. Agnes Jane Robertson (Cambridge: Cambridge University Press, 1925), pp. 21–23).

40. The *Promiso Regis* reads:

This document has been copied, letter by letter, from that which Archbishop Dunstan gave to our Lord at Kingston, on the day when he was consecrated as king, forbidding him to give any pledge except this one on which he laid upon Christ's altar, as the bishop directed him:

I. In the name of Holy Trinity, I promise three things to the Christian people who are under my authority:
   1. Firstly, that true peace shall be assured to the church of God and all Christian people in my dominions.

2. Secondly, I forbid robbery and all unrighteous deeds by all classes of society.

3. Thirdly, I promise and enjoin justice and mercy in the decision of all cases, in order that God, who liveth and reigneth, may in his grace and mercy be brought thereby to grant us all his eternal compassion.

See *Laws of the Kings of England,* p. 43.

41. *Memorials of Saint Dunstan,* pp. 110–13.

42. "For at that time there had been no monks in England except at Glastonbury and Abingdon" ("Vita S. Aethelwoldi," *Chronicon Monasterii de Abington,* 2:261).

43. For an interesting discussion of marriage in Anglo-Saxon England see Margaret Clunies Ross, "Concubinage in Anglo-Saxon England," *Past and Present* 108 (August 1985): 3–34.

44. Henry Charles Lea, *History of Sacerdotal Celibacy in the Christian Church* (New York: University Books, 1966), p. 134.

45. *The Monastic Agreement,* p. xx.

46. It is difficult to ascertain what was Aethelwold's position in England during Dunstan's exile years. In his own description of the establishment of the monastic life in the country, written sometime between 970 and 984, Aethelwold criticized Eadwig for dividing the kingdom and distributing "the lands of holy churches to rapacious strangers" (*Councils and Synods,* p. 146). The biographers, however, do not provide any information that could indicate whether or not Aethelwold and his community suffered directly from Eadwig. The statements made in the *Chronicon Monasterii de Abington,* for example, indicate that Eadwig granted Abingdon a large number of charters and was described as a benefactor (1:168). Even though, as Yorke cautions us, this grant of privileges is probably a forgery, there are other charters that seem to be legitimate. During the years between the death of Eadred and Edgar's coronation in 959, Aethelwold seems to have managed to maintain a beneficial political relationship not only with Eadwig and Aelfgifu, whose marriage was not recognized by Dunstan and Oda, but also with the royal kinsmen advanced by Eadwig. Yorke observes: "[Aethelwold] appears to have recognised the marriage of Aelfgifu and Eadwig as legitimate. The only document of Eadwig's reign in which Aelfgifu is acknowledged as Eadwig's wife is an Old English memorandum from Abingdon. . . . The will of Aelfgifu also suggests an alliance between Aelfgifu and Aethelwold. Aethelwold and his foundations are major beneficiaries. Old Minster, New Minster and Abingdon each received an estate under the will, and the Old Minster, where Aelfgifu intended to be buried, had the reversion of two estates. . . . Bishop Byrhthelm, the royal kinsman was a patron of Abingdon; he gave the estate of Stowe to the monastery. Aelfhere and his brothers were also patrons of the house, and Aethelwold's appearance as a witness in royal charters, towards the end of Eadwig's reign, seems to have coincided with

the appointment of Aelfheah as ealdorman of Wessex" (*Bishop Aethelwold,* pp. 80–81).

The Old Minster was dedicated to Saints Peter and Paul in 648. The church had a cruciform structure, with north and south porticoes opening off the nave, and with an eastern arm that was possibly apsidal. For further information regarding the architecture of the Old Minster see *Winchester in the Early Middle Ages,* ed. Martin Biddle (Oxford: Clarendon Press, 1976).

47. Wulfstan, p. 31.

48. We do have a record from Winchester that indicates that marriage among clergy was not uncommon. The 955x956 will of Aelfsige I, bishop of Winchester, indicates that the estates be granted to his "young kinsman" (probably the Goodwine of Worthy, his son) and his "kinswoman" (probably Goodwine's mother): "And I grant to my young kinsman the estate at Ann for his lifetime, and after his death to the New Minster; and the estate at the two Worthys to my kinswoman as long as her life lasts, and then to my sister and my young kinsman" (*Councils and Synods,* p. 85).

49. The pertinent letter states that Pope John XII grants King Edgar's request conveyed to the apostolic see by Dunstan concerning the monastery in Winchester, built in honor of the Holy Trinity and "the most blessed apostles Peter and Paul, that is, the Old Minster. The canons therein, who have become hateful to open turpitude of their faults, shall be ejected by Bishop Aethelwold, and the bishop shall establish regular monks in their stead." See Arthur Worthington Goodman, *Chartulary of Winchester Cathedral* (Winchester: Warren and Son, 1927), pp. 12–13; *Councils and Synods,* pp. 111–13.

50. Wulfstan, pp. 31–33.

51. Ibid., p. 33. Eadsige's decision to be converted and accept the monastic habit was seen as an event of great importance. After the expulsion, Eadsige, Aethelwold's kinsman, went to live near Winchcombe. In 969, St. Swithun appeared in a dream to a smith, who was supposed to report it to Eadsige, who in turn was supposed to report the revelation to Aethelwold, which he did. The translation of St. Swithun's remains in 971 was also the moment of reconciliation between Aethelwold and Eadsige. Eadsige stayed at the Old Minster, where he was appointed the sacrist of St. Swithun's tomb. On Aethelwold's relic cults see Thacker in *Bishop Aethelwold,* pp. 61–63.

52. "Later, after the brethren had begun to observe the rule of regular life in the Old Minster, and many flocked there to serve God, old men who had been professed, novices, and child oblates, the envy of the clerics caused the bishop to be given poison to drink when he was dining in his own hall and showing them every kindness. The clerics intended, upon his death, to drive away the servants of God and regroup to form a new assembly, free to indulge their former shameful practices. It was Aethelwold's custom, after eating three or four morsels, at once to drink a little. On this occasion he drank, quite unawares, all the poison brought to him in a goblet. . . . The poison crept through all his limbs, threatening immediate death. But he eventually took

thought and began to reproach himself, saying to his heart: 'Now where is your faith? Where is your understanding? Is not Christ's promise in the gospel true and trustworthy: "And if believers drink any deadly thing, it shall not hurt them."' . . . The pain caused by the raging of the poison was banished. . . . So, by God's miraculous power, the evil plan of the clerics was brought to nought; they saw their wickedness had no effect, and they were scattered through the different provinces of England until the end of their lives" (Wulfstan, p. 35).

53. *English Historical Documents,* vol. 1: *500–1042,* ed. Dorothy White-lock (London: Eyre and Spottiswoode, 1955), 849.

54. *Councils and Synods,* pp. 103–4.

55. Ibid., pp. 107–9.

56. Even though the concept of the monastic cathedral may seem unusual when evaluated in terms of both Continental and English traditions, it becomes better understood when viewed in terms of English history. In "An Account of King Edgar's Establishment of Monasteries" (970x984), Aethelwold con-structed a narrative arch binding together the time of the establishment of the first monasteries by Pope Gregory (the account based on Bede's *Historia ecclesi-astica*) and the reign of Edgar. Aethelwold says that Edgar "availed himself con-tinually of the counsel of his archbishop, Dunstan," that "through his admoni-tion he constantly inquired about the salvation of his soul, and not that alone, but likewise all the religion and welfare of his dominion" (*Councils and Synods,* pp. 149–50). Having collapsed the past and his present, Aethelwold erased the passage of time between the historical moments and, thus, established the Old Minster as the ever present monastic house. This being the case, the presence of secular canons was out of the question and was not open for negotiation in a place that was to become a seat of a monastic community.

57. According to the regulations from the *Regularis concordia,* on great liturgical occasions, such as Palm Sunday, for example, a solemn procession would take place. It would start at the Old Minster and proceed to one of the parochial churches—St. James, St. Martin in the Ditch, St. Mary in Tanner Street, St. Pancras, or St. Peter in Colebrook Street—before it would return for the celebration of the Mass to the Old Minster (*The Monastic Agreement,* pp. 34–35; *Consuetudinum,* pp. 105–7). The dates of earliest mentioning of these parish churches are as follows: St. James, ca. 970; St. Martin in the Ditch, ca. 934–39; St. Mary in Tanner Street, tenth century or earlier; St. Pancras, tenth century or earlier; St. Peter in Colebrook Street, tenth century. See Derek Keene, *Survey of Medieval Winchester,* 2 vols. (Oxford: Clarendon Press, 1985), 1:134–36. Except for St. James and St. Martin in the Ditch, the churches stood in close proximity to the Old Minster.

58. Robin Fleming, "Rural Elites and Urban Communities in Late Anglo-Saxon England," *Past and Present* 141 (November 1993): 26–29.

59. The Old Minster was founded by Cenwalth of Wessex in or about 648. It has been described as follows: "A cruciform structure with north and south porticus opening off the nave, and an eastern arm, perhaps apsidal, it was

built just south of the Roman forum, astride an east-west street of the Roman town, and on a site which lies today immediately north of the nave of the present cathedral. . . . It was the scene of royal ceremonies and of a long sequence of royal burials. . . . 971x980, Old Minster extended eastward, and the eastern part of the original structure was entirely remodelled to form the principal crossing and high altar of the new church" (*Winchester in the Early Middle Ages,* pp. 306–7). For detailed information about Winchester see *Object and Economy in Medieval Winchester,* ed. Martin Biddle, 2 vols. (Oxford: Clarendon Press, 1990).

60. Wulfstan, p. 45.

61. P. H. Sawyer, "Charters of the Reform Movement: The Worcester Archive," *Tenth-Century Studies,* pp. 84–93. This argument will be further developed when Oswald's reforms are discussed.

62. At the same time, it should be remembered that the rules concerning daily existence were relaxed—consider, for example, the references to the fur bedcovers, customary three gallons of beer a day, and dietary requirements in Abingdon, all of which made it possible for a person to live in a monastery. See Hohler in *Tenth-Century Studies,* pp. 60–83.

63. The "Renewal of the Freedom of Taunton by King Edgar" yields information not only about the Old Minster but also about Winchester itself. The king was the owner of the soil of the city, that is, of the land that was not occupied by buildings. There is no evidence that Winchester was a royal manor; there is, however, evidence that the king received market dues, tolls levied at the gates, and dues payments for stalls on the street or that he could allocate them to a monastic community. The "Renewal of the Freedom of Taunton" states: "Here it is declared in this document how King Edgar, with the advice of his councillors, renewed freedom of Taunton for the episcopal see of the Holy Trinity and St Peter and St Paul at Winchester, exactly as King Edward had freed it, and granted that both noblemen and commoners on the manor of God should be entitled to the same dues as his own men are on his own royal manors. And all [the proceeds of] lawsuits and all dues shall be given for the benefit of the church in the same proportion as they are exacted on his own behalf, and the trading dues of the town and the receipt of the market dues shall go to the holy foundation, as they used to do in the days of my ancestors and as was allowed to Bishop Aelfheah and each of those who enjoyed the estate" (*Anglo-Saxon Charters,* pp. 92–95). See also *Bishop Aethelwold,* pp. 81–82.

64. "Then Bishop Aethelwold gave to his royal lord 200 mancuses of gold and a silver cup worth five pounds in return for the renewal of freedom, and to Aelfthryth, his wife, 50 mancuses of gold, in return for her help in his just mission" (*Anglo-Saxon Charters,* p. 95). "And he saw to it wisely that the Queen, Aelfthrith, should be the protectress and fearless guardian of the communities of nuns" (*The Monastic Agreement,* p. 2; *Consuetudinum,* p. 70).

The list of witnesses for the New Minster Charter, written probably by Aethelwold in 966, shows that a clear distinction was made between Edmund, the first son of Aelfthryth and Edgar, and Edward, presumably the son of a nun of Wilton and Edgar. Both were Edgar's sons; however, the difference in their legal status is marked distinctly. Even though Edward was older than Edmund, Edmund's name and the phrase "clito legitimus prefati regi filius" stand above Edward's name, which is accompanied by the phrase "eodem regem clito procreatus" (see *Councils and Synods,* p. 131). After Edgar's death in 975, Aethelred and Edward were both pretenders to the crown. Aethelwold supported Aethelred, and Dunstan supported Edward. As Yorke observes, Aelfhere of Mercia, another supporter of Aethelred, "seems to have reacted violently to the accession of Edward and to have attacked monastic houses which were associated with Dunstan and Aethelwine" (*Bishop Aethelwold,* p. 85).

65. Little is known about the foundation of the New Minster in ca. 901. It was positioned on the north side of the Old Minster. The precinct was defined to the west, north, and east and partly to the south by streets that were later absorbed into the precinct. Because of its size (790 square meters), it could accommodate a congregation of considerable size. It had several chapels: St. George, St. Gregory, St. Thomas, St. Maurice, and St. Pantaleon. While the Old Minster was the bishop's see, the New Minster was to be the burh church. In the first half of the tenth century, the New Minster was closely associated with the royal house. The bodies of Alfred, Ealhswith, Edward the Elder and his two sons, and Eadwig were buried there. In 979/80x988, a tower of twenty meters in height was added. The precinct contained two cemeteries. See *Winchester in the Early Middle Ages,* pp. 313–20.

66. "Thereupon Bishop Aethelwold, the eagle of Christ, spread his golden wings, and with the permission of King Edgar drove the canons away from the New Minster, introducing there monks living according to the Rule and ordaining as their abbot his pupil Aethelgar, who later became bishop of the province of the South Saxons and then, after Dunstan's translation to the kingdom of heaven, archbishop of Canterbury" (Wulfstan, p. 37).

67. The "New Minster Charter," written in gold letters, consists of chapters on the Fall of the Angels, the Creation, the Fall of Man, and the Redemption that constitute a preface to the section defending the replacement of secular canons by monks, three anathemas, dispositive clauses, the statement of the king's motives, the immunity clause, the passage acknowledging free election of an abbot, and a list of witnesses (see British Library, MS Cotton Vespasian A VIII, fols. 2v–33v; *Councils and Synods,* pp. 119–33). The following is reported in *Winchester in the Early Middle Ages,* pp. 283–84: "King Edgar is credited with having introduced a fine stream of water into New Minster in the 970s. New Minster had a mill which stood on ground to Old Minster. A watercourse with at least two mills on it flowed through the ground between New Minster and Nunminster. There was also a watercourse adjacent to the land which Aethel-

wold enclosed with a wall extending from the Minster to the old town wall. In addition, Aethelwold caused a stream of fresh running water to be brought through the monastery building for sanitary purposes."

68. Wulfstan, pp. 37–39. The Nunminster was to the south of High Street, east of the New Minster. In 964x970, its boundaries were extended over adjacent land from which secular dwellings had been removed. See *Winchester in the Early Middle Ages*, p. 321.

69. The New Minster, founded by King Alfred at the persuasion of Grimbald, whom he had brought from Flanders for reasons that are not fully understood, was originally built against the southern boundary of the land that was acquired from the bishop of the community of Old Minster as well as private landowners, immediately adjacent to the north side of the Old Minster. There were about four meters between the buildings of the New Minster and the Old Minster. The New Minster was a large church, 790 square meters in size as compared to the 354 square meters of the Old Minster.

70. The "New Minster Charter" provides us with the following details of the agreement of the land exchange between the Old Minster and the Nunminster: "Here it is declared in this document how King Edgar caused the monasteries in Winchester to have their privacy secured for them by means of space, after he had made them adopt the monastic life, by the grace of God, and ordered to be devised so that none of the monasteries involved should have any quarrel with any other, because of the spacing, but if the property of one monastery lay within the space assigned to another, then the superior of the monastery which took possession of the space should acquire the property of the other monastery by such exchange as might be agreeable to the community which owned the property. For this reason, therefore, Bishop Aethelwold, with the cognisance of the king and of the community attached to his episcopal see, has granted two plots of ground outside the south gate to the New Minster, in exchange for the mill belonging to that minster which stood in the space which the king ordered to be assigned to the Old Minster, and Abbot Aethelgar, with advice of our royal lord and of Bishop Aethelwold and of the community, has granted the aforesaid mill, which the bishop gave him, and another which they already possessed within the town to the Nunnery, for the sake of peace and concord, and has assigned it to the Abbess Eadgifu, the king's daughter, in exchange for the watercourse which he has diverted to the New Minster with the king's leave, and which formerly belonged to the community of nuns—and the diverting [of the water] destroyed a mill of his—and he has given the king 120 mancuses of red gold in acknowledgment, before the Lady Aelfthryth and Bishop Aethelwold, in return for the land through which the water runs, extending lengthwise from the north wall to the south wall of monastery, and 2 rods in breadth where the water first flows in, and where the land is narrowest it must be 18 feet in breadth" (*Anglo-Saxon Charters*, pp. 103–5).

71. *Winchester in the Early Middle Ages*, p. 289.

72. See, for example, the 970 charter in which Edgar renews to the monks

of the Old Minster their hereditary liberty of Chiltecumbe and "adds the injunction that none of his successors shall introduce clerks into the monastery, but that regular monks shall always praise God there, since he expelled the clerks for their foul living"; and see the 975 charter in which Edgar gives the Old Minster "5 manses in Bledone with 15 hides, and 15 ploughs, with 18 serfs, and 16 villeins, and 10 bordars, with 60 a. of meadow, and pasture 1.5 leagues in length and 0.5 a. in breadth, to dispose thereof at their pleasure and to have therein a free market every Monday" (Goodman, pp. 13, 233).

73. Wulfstan, p. 43.

74. *Bishop Aethelwold,* p. 71.

75. The political aspect of "An Account of King Edgar's Establishment of Monasteries" has already been mentioned (see n. 56). In his study of the *Benedictional of St. Aethelwold,* Robert Deshman draws attention to the propagandistic aspect of the representation of the coronation of the Virgin Mary that could be viewed in terms of Aelfthryth's special position as protectress of the nunneries. See Robert Deshman, *"Christus rex et magi reges:* Kingship and Christology in Ottonian and Anglo-Saxon Art," *Frühmittelalterliche Studien* 10 (1976): 367–405.

76. *Chronicon Monasterii de Abington,* 1:47–49.

77. *Councils and Synods,* pp. 116–18.

78. See Daniel J. Sheerin, "The Dedication of the Old Minster in 980," *Revue Bénédictine* 88.3 (1978): 261–73.

79. British Library, MS ADD 49598, fol. 97v. See also Robert Deshman, "The Imagery of the Living Ecclesia and the English Monastic Reform," *Sources of Anglo-Saxon Culture,* ed. Paul E. Szarmach (Kalamazoo, MI: Medieval Institute Publication, Western Michigan University, 1986), pp. 261–82.

80. Wulfstan, pp. 39–43.

81. J. Armitage Robinson, *The Times of Saint Dunstan* (Oxford: Clarendon Press, 1923), p. 128.

82. "Whence now the monastery, which the aforesaid Bishop Oswald has endowed in the episcopal see of Worcester in honour of Mary, the Holy Mother of God, and has granted to religious monks serving God—the debased, degraded, lascivious clerks having been eliminated, with my consent and favour. I confirm [the monastery] to these religious monks by my royal authority. With the counsel and agreement of my ealdormen and my magnates, I grant and confirm [the monastery] so that in the future the clerks shall have no right or title for reclaiming anything there, at least those who prefer to stick to their wives, to the detriment of their order and the loss of their prebends rather than serve God chastely and canonically. Therefore everything belonging to that church that the clerks formerly possessed with the church, either spiritual or secular, movable or immovable, I hand over to these servants of God, the monks, by my royal munificence, to hold from this day forward for ever" (quoted in Eric John, *Orbis Britanniae,* p. 238). For the Latin text see the *Altitonantis* (1135 charter) in *Cartularium Saxonicum: A Collection of Charters Relat-*

ing to Anglo-Saxon History, ed. Walter de Gray Birch, 3 vols. (London: Charles J. Clark, 1893), 3:377.

83. There are different dates for the monastic reforms in Worcester. According to *Altitonantis,* the change happened abruptly in 964. In her analysis of British Library, Cotton Tiberius A XIII, fol. 77b, Agnes Jane Robertson states that "in 969 Oswald expelled from the community all those who refused to become monks, but if this is true they must have been allowed to return later (probably after the death of Edgar in 975) as his grants from 977 onwards are invariably witnessed by a number of *clerici,* the majority of whom are found before 969." J. Armitage Robinson (129) suggests that the monks must have been brought to Worcester by 977. See also *Tenth-Century Studies,* p. 88; *Anglo-Saxon Charter* p. 360.

84. *Tenth-Century Studies,* p. 93.

85. The documents show that the land was leased under the following conditions: the estate was "free from everything except church dues," "free from every burden except military service and the construction of walls and bridges and carrying service for the church," and "free from every duty of a secular nature except the repair of bridges and fortifications and military service against enemies." See, for example, *Anglo-Saxon Charters,* pp. 62–63, 86–87, 96–97, 114–15, 116–17, 118–19, 120–21, 126–27, 132–33, 134–35, 138–39.

86. *Historians of the Church of York and Its Archbishops,* ed. James Raine, *Rerum Britannicarum medii aevi scriptores, or Chronicles and Memorials of Great Britain and Ireland during the Middle Ages,* 99 vols. (London: Longman, 1879), vol. 71, part 2, pp. 492–93.

87. *Tenth-Century Studies,* p. 138; *Winchester in the Early Middle Ages,* p. 301.

88. *Bishop Aethelwold,* p. 72; Fleming, pp. 26–28.

89. *Tenth-Century Studies,* pp. 127–28; *Winchester in the Early Middle Ages,* p. 321.

90. The following is a list of the monastic houses that existed at that time: Abingdon, Athelney, Bath, Canterbury, Chertsey, Chester, Glastonbury, Leominster, Malmesbury, Milton, Muchelney, Pershore, Peterborough, Ramsey, St. Albans, Thorney, Westbury, Westminster, Winchcombe, Winchester Old Minster, New Minster, Nunminster, Worcester. See Alison Binns, *Dedication of Monastic Houses in England* (Woodbridge, Suffolk: Boydell Press, 1989), pp. 61–92.

91. British Library, MS Cotton Faustina B III, fols. 159–98; Tiberius A III, fols. 177–77v, 3–27v. The tenth-century manuscript (Faustina B III) does not have a title and begins with the first words of the *Proem,* "Gloriosum etenim Eadgar" [Edgar the glorious]. The *Proem* is followed by twelve chapters (it breaks in the course of chapter 12 with the words "quibus fuerit unitus"; the end of this chapter can be found in Tiberius A III, fols. 177 and 177v). This manuscript does not have an epilogue. The titles of all the chapters are written

in red ink; the text is in black ink. Illuminated letters are the only other ornamentation in the text. The tenth-century *Regularis concordia* is written in
medieval Latin. This manuscript was probably written for use in Christ Church
in Canterbury. The manuscript from the second half of the eleventh century
(Tiberius A III) has a title, a full-page illustration, a list of chapters, the *Proem,*
twelve chapters, and the *Epilogue.* Anglo-Saxon glosses are placed above the
Latin text. The illustration depicts three figures seated under the canopy of
three arcades. In the middle, there is the king; on the right, there is an archbishop with pallium; on the left, there is a bishop. The three figures are holding a long scroll. Below them, there is an image of a monk with a scroll. He is
looking toward the figures. The text is written in black ink, and the titles of the
chapters are in red. There is no information available about where the manuscript was written or what its destination was. The text was in a book that was
mentioned in the Christ Church Canterbury Catalogue from the fourteenth
century.

92. The attestation in the New Minster charter reads: "I Aethelwold,
bishop of the Church of Winchester, blessed the generosity of the glorious king
[Edgar] with the sign of the cross, commending to him the abbot [Aethelgar]
raised by my humble self, as well as the pupils whom I trained" (quoted in
Bishop Aethelwold, p. 96).

93. The passages from the *Regularis concordia* are hereafter cited by page
numbers in *The Monastic Agreement* and *Consuetudinum,* respectively.

94. *The Monastic Agreement,* p. 1; *Consuetudinum,* p. 69.

95. *Bishop Aethelwold,* p. 98.

96. *Consuetudinum,* p. 155.

97. *The Monastic Agreement,* pp. li–lii.

98. The contacts with these monasteries were established in different
ways. As has already been mentioned, Dunstan was forced to leave England in
955 and take refuge at the monastery of St. Peter of Ghent in Flanders. Aethelwold sent one of his monks, Osgar, to study the observances of Fleury. The
abbot of the St. Peter monastery in Ghent, Womar, spent some time at the Old
Minster with Aethelwold's community. It is difficult, however, to state precisely what customs were copied down from these two branches of the tenth-
century reform monasticism, because we do not have early consuetudinaries
from either Ghent or Fleury. See *The Monastic Agreement,* pp. xlvii–xlviii. See
also Eric John, "Some Latin Charters of the Tenth Century Reformation in
England," *Revue Bénédictine* 70.2 (1960): 333–59.

99. "Straightway, then, they [the monks] obeyed his [Edgar's] commands
with the utmost gladness; and calling to mind the letters in which our holy
patron Gregory instructed the blessed Augustine that, for the advancement of
the rude English Church, he should establish therein the seemly customs of the
Gallic Churches as well as those of Rome, they summoned monks from St.
Benedict's monastery at Fleury [the abbey of Fleury-sur-Loire, reformed in 930
by St. Odo of Cluny] and from that eminent monastery which is known by the

renowned name of Ghent [the abbey of St. Peter (Blandinium) at Ghent, reformed by Gerard of Brogne about 937], gathered from their praiseworthy customs much that was good and thus, even as honey is gathered by bees from all manner of wild flowers and collected into one hive, so also the said monastic customs, tempered by great and subtle judgement of reason were, by the grace of Christ the Saviour of the world, embodied in this small book" (*The Monastic Agreement,* p. 3; *Consuetudinum,* pp. 71–73).

100. See, for example, 7; 74 (arrangement for saying the Office when journeying on horseback) and 27; 96–97 (drink after None). It also should be remembered that, sometime between 964 and 975, Aethelwold translated the *Rule* of St. Benedict into English, for which King Edgar and Queen Aelfhryth granted him an estate at Sudbourne. It is believed that Aethelwold knew and used a text from Fleury as well as a ninth-century commentary, *Expositio in Regulam S. Benedicti,* by Smaragdus of Saint-Mihiel. See Mechthild Gretsch, "Aethelwold's Translation of the Regula Sancti Benedicti and Its Latin Exemplar," *Anglo-Saxon England,* ed. Peter Clemoes (Cambridge: Cambridge University Press, 1974), pp. 125–51.

101. 28; 98 (customs on Christmas Eve), 39; 112 (blessing of the New Fire on Maundy Thursday). Also, the discovery of a customary by a Theodoric or Thierry, who was a monk at Fleury, and its close correspondence to parts of the *Regularis concordia* indicate that Aethelwold was acquainted with and used the customs of Fleury. See *Consuetudinum,* pp. 331–93.

102. 8; 76–77 (the relations between master and boys), 20; 90 (silence on feast days), 39; 112 (blessing of the New Fire), 49–50; 123–29 (Easter celebrations).

103. 20–21; 90–91 (the psalmody during the manual work), 29; 99 (confession on Christmas Eve), 67; 142 (the recording of the name of a dead brother). Symons suggests that the observances in the *Regularis concordia* show "a higher proportion of agreement with the Lotharingian customeries of *Einsiedeln, Trèves* and *Verdun* than with those of *Cluny, Farfa,* and *Fleury*" (*Tenth-Century Studies,* p. 59).

104. Symons notes, "To the first group belong practices such as the Drink after None (30, 3), the observance of claustral enclosure (64, 7), the psalmody accompanying the manual labour (25, 9), arrangements for saying the Office when journeying on horseback (11, 4f.), and, notably, the observance taken bodily from the tract known as *Ordo Qualiter,* the only document which we can affirm have been extensively used in the Concordia (Ch. I *passim*)" (*The Monastic Agreement,* p. xlviii).

105. Symons notes that the *Regularis concordia* makes use of "one short citation (8, 10) from Amalar's *Rule of Canons,* drawn up in 816 at the first of the two Aix assemblies, and two (11, 21–23; 63, 12–13) from the famous *Capitula* put forward by Benedict of Aniane at the second assembly in 817." He continues, "As there is nothing to show that early ninth century Saxon monasticism had been influenced by the Anianian reform we may assume that the English

obtained their knowledge of that movement and of its writings through direct contact with Continental monasteries in the tenth century" (*The Monastic Agreement,* p. xlix).

106. Symons writes: "As regards liturgical customs, it looks very much as though in some instances the English must have drawn on liturgical books newly obtained from abroad, some of them, indeed, from some monastery of the Lotharingian reform. Thus the principal services of Holy Week and Easter are based on, and some half dozen rubrical directions are cited verbally from, *Ordo Romanus Primus,* or some form of that document; of two special Holy Week rites, one (37, 6f.) is almost certainly indirectly dependent on *Verdun;* the famous Easter 'play' (51) has points of contact with a large number of versions of a custom then widespread on the Continent. . . . Of a large number of the monastic observances of this group little can be said. Most of them appear in both Cluniac and Lotharingian consuetudinaries" (*The Monastic Agreement,* pp. xlix–l). This subject has been a topic of recent Anglo-Saxon scholarship—see, for example, Antonia Gransden, "Traditionalism and Continuity during the Last Century of Anglo-Saxon Monasticism," *Journal of Ecclesiastical History* 40.2 (April 1989): 159–207.

107. Even though the *Regularis concordia* provides meticulous details regarding monks' daily activities, little is said directly in it about the buildings of a monastic community. The document does, however, contain a considerable amount of information about what buildings were needed by an English monastery at the time. For an illuminating study of this aspect of the *Regularis concordia* see Mark Spurrell, "The Architectural Interest of the *Regularis concordia," Anglo-Saxon England,* ed. Michael Lapidge et al., vol. 21 (Cambridge: Cambridge University Press, 1992), 161–76.

108. "O God Who hast poured forth the gifts of love into the hearts of thy faithful through the grace of the Holy Ghost, grant to Thy servants, for whom we beseech Thy clemency, health of mind and body that they may love Thee with all their strength, and with all their love to those things which are pleasing to Thee. Through our Lord" (12–13; 81–82).

109. Monastic life revolved around the celebration of the night office, Nocturns (Matins, according to modern terminology), and the seven day hours: Matins (Lauds, according to modern terminology), Prime, Tierce (Terce), Sext, None (Nones), Vespers, and Compline. The monks also observed daily Morrow Mass (celebrated after Tierce and before the Chapter in winter and after Prime and before the Chapter in summer) and Principal Mass.

110. Tables 1 and 2 show the monk's daily duties in the period from November 1 to Lent (winter *horarium*) and from Easter to the end of September (summer *horarium*), as presented in chapter 1 of the *Regularis concordia.* The hours listed are approximate because the monk's day was regulated by the rising and setting of the sun. Therefore, the hours in the winter were shorter than the hours in the summer—thus, there was a difference between the hours for the winter and the summer *horaria.* For example, during the summer months,

the monks would rise at about 1:30 A.M. and go to bed at about 8:15 P.M.; during the winter months, they would rise at about 2:30 A.M. and go to bed at about 6:30 P.M. Since the hours of the day would be longer in the summer than in the winter, there would be a short interval between Nocturns and Matins in the summer, because the office of Matins was to be celebrated at dawn. Also, according to the *Regularis concordia* (25; 94–95), due to the fact that the length of the day was regulated by the rising and the setting of the sun, longer hymns were sung in the summer and shorter ones in the winter. Only with the invention of the mechanical clock in the fourteenth century could time be divided into equal hours, allowing the length of the working day to be fixed in both winter and summer. For an account of the changes caused by the imposition of clocked time see Gerhard Dohrn-van Rossum, *History of the Hour,* trans. Thomas Dunlap (Chicago: University of Chicago Press, 1996), pp. 29–43.

TABLE 1.   Winter *Horarium*

about 2:30 A.M.	Rise	
	Trina oratio	
	Gradual psalms	
3:00 A.M.	NOCTURNS	(night office)
	Psalms, etc., for the royal house	
	Vigil of the Dead	
	Matins of the Dead	
	Matins of All Saints	
5:00 A.M.	Lectio	
6:00 A.M.	MATINS of the day	(first hour)
	Miserere	
	Psalms, etc., for the royal house	
	Anthems	
6:45 A.M.	PRIME	(second hour)
	Four psalms, penitential psalms, litany	
7:30 A.M.	*lectio*	
8:00 A.M.	Interval (change shoes, wash)	
	Trina oratio	
	TIERCE	(third hour)
	Psalms, etc., for the royal house	
	Morrow Mass	
	Chapter	
	Five psalms (for the Dead)	

about 9:45 A.M.	Work	
2:00 Noon	SEXT	(fourth hour)
	Psalms, etc., for the royal house	
	PRINCIPAL MASS	
about 1:30 P.M.	NONE	(fifth hour)
	Psalms, etc., for the royal house	
about 2:00 P.M.	*Cena*	
about 2:45 P.M.	*Lectio* or work	
	VESPERS of the day	(sixth hour)
	Psalms, etc., for the royal house	
	Anthems	
	Vespers of All Saints	
	Vespers of All the Dead	
	Change to night shoes	
	Drink	
6:00 P.M.	*Collatio*	
6:15 P.M.	COMPLINE	(seventh hour)
	Miserere	
	Psalms, etc., for the royal house	
	Trina oratio	
6:30 P.M.	Retire	

Both the winter and summer *horaria* in tables 1 and 2 are based on Symons's tables (*The Monastic Agreement,* pp. xliii–xliv). These two tables might explain the confusion concerning the time of celebrating Nocturns. According to the *horarium,* Nocturns was celebrated at about 3 A.M. in winter and about 2 A.M. in summer. Thus Easter Nocturns, which contained the *Quem quaeritis,* was celebrated at about 3–3:30 A.M. in the morning according to the summer *horarium.*

111. This part of this chapter is based on Michel Foucault's unpublished essay "Christianity and Confession" that was delivered as a lecture at Dartmouth College, New Hampshire, on November 24, 1980. I am grateful to Professor James Bernauer of Boston College for sharing with me the transcript of Foucault's presentation. All page numbers in the text refer to page numbers in the transcript. The quotation in the text here is from page 2.

112. "Then, kneeling down in his proper and accustomed place, he shall pour forth in the Lord's sight prayer from the heart rather than from the lips, so that his voice, through deep compunction of heart and recollection of his misdeeds, may efficaciously reach the ears of the merciful Lord and, by the grace of Christ, obtain the pardon of all his sins" (12; 81).

TABLE 2.   Summer *Horarium*

about 1:30 A.M.	Rise		
		Trina oratio	
		Gradual psalms	
2:00 A.M.		NOCTURNS	(night office)
		Psalms, etc., for the royal house	
		Short interval	
3:30 or		MATINS of the day	(first hour)
4:00 A.M.		*Miserere*	
		Psalms, etc., for the royal house	
		Anthems (of the Cross, B.V.M., and patron of the house)	
		Matins of All Saints	
		Matins of the Dead	
	Interval (if day: change shoes, wash, etc.; if dark: sleep for those who wish, change shoes, wash, etc.)		
about 5:00 A.M.		*Trina oratio*	
		Lectio	
6:00 A.M.		PRIME	(second hour)
		Four psalms, penitential psalms, litany	
		Morrow Mass	
		Chapter	
		Five Psalms (for the Dead)	
7:30 A.M.	Work		
8:00 A.M.		TIERCE	(third hour)
		Psalms, etc., for the royal house	
		PRINCIPAL MASS	
9:30 A.M.		*Lectio*	
11:30 A.M.		SEXT	(fourth hour)
		Psalms, etc., for the royal house	
12 Noon		*Prandium*	
about 1:30 P.M.	Siesta		
2:30 P.M.		NONE	(fifth hour)
		Psalms, etc., for the royal house	
	Drink		
about 3:30 P.M.	Work		

	VESPERS of the day	(sixth hour)
	Miserere	
	Psalms, etc., for the royal house	
	Anthems (as after MATINS)	
	Vespers of All Saints	
	Vespers of the Dead	
	Cena	
	Vigils of the Dead	
7:30 P.M.	Change into night shoes	
	Collatio	
8:00 P.M.	COMPLINE	(seventh hour)
	Miserere	
	Psalms, etc., for the royal house	
about 8:15 P.M.	*Trina oratio*	
	Retire	

113. The literature on the subject is quite substantive. However, for the general discussion, see, for example, Miri Rubin, *Corpus Christi: The Eucharist in Late Medieval Culture* (Cambridge: Cambridge University Press, 1991); Gary Macy, *The Theologies of the Eucharist in the Early Scholastic Period: A Study of the Salvific Function of the Sacrament according to the Theologians c. 1080–c. 1220* (Oxford: Clarendon Press, 1984); Edith Dudley Sylla, "Autonomous and Handmaiden Science: St. Thomas Aquinas and William of Ockham on the Physics of the Eucharist," *The Cultural Context of Medieval Learning,* ed. John Emery Murdoch and Edith Dudley Sylla (Dordrecht: D. Reidel Publishing Co., 1975), pp. 349–96. The Berengar-Lanfranc controversy will be discussed in chapter 2.

114. See, for example, Mervyn James, "Ritual, Drama, and Social Body in the Late Medieval English Town," *Past and Present* 98 (February 1983): 3–29; John Bossy, "The Mass as a Social Institution," *Past and Present* 100 (August 1983): 29–61; Charles Zika, "Hosts, Processions, and Pilgrimages in Fifteenth-Century Germany," *Past and Present* 118 (February 1988): 25–64.

115. Paschasius Radbertus, *De corpore et sanguine domini, Patrologiae Cursus Completus, Series Latina,* ed. Jacque Paul Migne, 221 vols. (Paris: Garnier Fratres, 1884), 120:1255–1350; Ratramnus, *De corpore et sanguine domini,* in *Patrologiae,* 121:103–70.

116. Macy, p. 24.

117. Paschasius, *De corpore et sanguine domini,* chap. 7, *Patrologiae,* 120:1285. See also Paschasius, *De corpore et sanguine domini,* ed. Beda Paulus, Corpus Christianorum: Continuatio mediaevalis 16 (Turnhout: Brepols Editores Pontificii, 1969), 38–39.

118. Quoted in Macy, p. 27. For the Latin text see Paschasius, *De corpore et sanguine domini, Patrologiae,* 120:1296; in the edition by Beda Paulus, see p. 56.

119. Quoted in Macy, p. 29. For the Latin text see Ratramnus, *De corpore et sanguine domini,* chap. 44, *Patrologiae,* 121:146.

120. Charles R. Shrader, "The False Attribution of an Eucharist Tract to Gerbert of Aurillac," *Medieval Studies* 35 (1973): 181–83; Macy, p. 31; Rubin, *Corpus Christi,* p. 16.

121. Macy, p. 31.

122. Allan John MacDonald, *Berengar and the Reform Sacramental Doctrine* (London: Longman, 1930), pp. 245, 247–49.

123. Henry Chadwick, "Ego Berengarius," *Journal of Theological Studies,* n.s., 40.2 (October 1989): 436. There are, however, two records that may shed some light on Aethelwold's knowledge of the eucharistic disputes at the time. The first record is the document entitled "The Gifts of Bishop Aethelwold to Peterborough." Among the many things presented to the monastery there are twenty-one books that presumably belonged to Aethelwold. One of them was *De Eucharistia* (see *Anglo-Saxon Charters,* p. 73, for a complete list of objects and books presented to the Peterborough monastery). Michael Lapidge suggests that *De Eucharistia* was "probably Ratramnus of Corbie's *De corpore et sanguine domini*" (*Bishop Aethelwold,* p. 103; see also *Learning and Literature in Anglo-Saxon England,* ed. Michael Lapidge, Helmut Gneuss, and Peter Clemoes [Cambridge: Cambridge University Press, 1985], pp. 52–55). The second record is less direct. It is "An Account of King Edgar's Establishment of Monasteries" (970x984), almost certainly the work of Aethelwold, which was probably written as a prologue to his translation of the *Rule* of St. Benedict (*Councils and Synods,* p. 142). Following the passage describing Edgar's command for the *Rule* to be translated into the English language is the comment "keen-witted scholars who understand clearly the two-fold wisdom—that is, the wisdom of things actual and spiritual—and each of those again admittedly consists of three divisions—do not require this English translation" (*Councils and Synods,* p. 151). The phrases used here are reminiscent of Augustine's and Ratramnus's view of the Eucharist as "visible" words distinct from, though correlated to, the *res,* or a distinction between reality in truth and spiritual reality.

124. Thus, for example, the *Regularis concordia* tells us: "[f]rom the Calends of November until the beginning of Lent one general rule for the distribution of the hymns shall be followed, namely, that on short days shorter hymns shall be sung and on long days longer ones. Thus at the first Vespers of Sunday *O lux beata* shall be sung, at Compline *Christe qui lux es,* at Nocturns *Primo dierum* and at Matins *Aeterne rerum Conditor;* but at Nocturns, Matins and Vespers throughout the year, Sundays and saints' days excepted, the usual ferial hymns shall be said. On very great and festival solemnities proper hymn shall be sung according to custom" (25; 94–95). During the winter months, starting in November, the brethren were allowed to have a fire in a suitable room assigned especially

for this purpose, where they could gather in silence to fulfill their monastic duties (25–26; 95). However, the *Regularis concordia* stipulates: "[a]nd when it is necessary for them to leave the cloister and to enter the special room of which we have spoken, there let them keep in all the things the observance which is kept in the cloister. Nor shall anyone, at any time whatsoever, dare to leave the cloister and go to the aforesaid building in order to dwell therein, nor leave that building without the permission of the prior" (26; 96).

125. Karl Young, *The Drama of the Medieval Church,* 2 vols. (Oxford: Clarendon Press, 1933), 1:231.

126. O. B. Hardison, Jr., *Christian Rite and Christian Drama in the Middle Ages: Essays in the Origin and Early History of Modern Drama* (Baltimore, MD: Johns Hopkins University Press, 1965), p. 199.

127. The reference is made here to a mass book that was put forth by Gregory the Great. In the sixth century, Gregory the Great revised *Gelasianum,* that is, a sacramentary or mass book of the Pope Gelasius I, which had been used until that time. Gregory's sacramentary was to be a new mass book that would reflect his understanding of the Christian community: "in the Church, because united in one faith, diversity of usages does not harm." This statement makes clear that Gregory the Great acknowledged the legitimacy of the existing customs at the time when there was great regional variety in the celebration of the liturgy. Note that, in the sixth century, the church was not centralized. Diversity in unity was one of his pastoral principles—Gregory conceived each individual community under its own bishop as a church in its own right. Consequently, the multiplicity of churches made the church, according to Gregory, a "concordant diversity of members." Gregory wrote: "Safeguarding the unity of the sacrament, the Church gathers together the faithful peoples according to the manifold variety of their customs and languages. The purpose of organisation and hierarchy in the Church was to foster diversity within unity." See R. A. Markus, *Gregory the Great and His World* (Cambridge: Cambridge University Press, 1997), p. 73. See also Carole Straw, *Gregory the Great: Perfection in Imperfection* (Berkeley, CA: University of California Press, 1988), chap. 4.

128. The *Ordo Romanus Primus* is a consuetudinary of the Roman Office for the secular churches. Thompson suggests that its oldest form can be dated as early as the seventh century. Thompson writes: "It included a careful description of the papal stational service as it was performed in the era of Gregory the Great. Besides the Mass, which was celebrated on Sundays and feast days in the churches of Rome, there arose a civic service, which was conducted by the pope in a church designated as the *statio* of the day, and which was attended by people from all parts and parishes of the Eternal City. Here we see the Mass in a moment of stability, when all of its parts had found their place in a fixed arrangement, and before the liturgical initiative passed from Rome to the Carolingian empire. And here is revealed the transcendence of the Roman 'soberness and sense' in a pattern of magnificent detail and solemn splendor" (Bard

Thompson, *Liturgies of the Western Church* [Cleveland, OH: Meridian Books, 1961], p. 37). Also see *Ordo Romanus Primus,* with introduction and notes by George Cuthbert (London: Alexander Morning, 1905).

129. Jude Woerdeman, "The Source of the Easter Play," *Orate Fratres* 20 (April 1946): 266–67.

130. Dom Thomas Symons, "Sources of the *Regularis concordia,*" *Downside Review* 59 (January 1941): 18.

131. Saint Benedict, *The Rule of Saint Benedict,* trans. Dom Justin McCann (England: Stanbrook Abbey Press, 1937), pp. 31–34.

132. Woerdeman, p. 264.

133. Ibid., p. 267.

134. Ibid., p. 269.

135. By analyzing the *Quem quaeritis* in the context of the Introit to the Easter Mass and by looking at the *Quem quaeritis* in the *Regularis concordia,* Clifford Flanigan concludes that this trope was nothing more than a commentary on the significance of the Easter liturgy. It served, therefore, the same ritual function whether it appeared as an Introit trope, as a processional ceremony, or as a quasi-independent *Visitatio Sepulchri.* Even though the position of the *Quem quaeritis* might have varied, the message of the trope was clear—it was a liturgical commemoration of the resurrection of Jesus Christ. See C. Clifford Flanigan, "The Liturgical Context of the *Quem quaeritis* Trope," *Comparative Drama* 8 (spring 1974): 45–62.

136. See my critique of the studies by Michael Norton, Susan Rankin, Davril Anselme, and Andrew Hughes in the introduction.

137. Dürer quoted in Erwin Panofsky, *Perspective as Symbolic Form* (New York: Zone Books, 1991), p. 27.

138. Marie Dominique Chenu, *Nature, Man, and Society in the Twelfth Century* (Chicago: University of Chicago Press, 1968), pp. 72–79.

139. Euclid's theory of vision explained the mechanism of seeing by implying that visual rays are sent by an eye to form a visual pyramid. This theory gained full acceptance in the fourteenth century, when optics was freed from metaphysical readings of theory of seeing.

140. Plotinus, *The Enneads,* trans. Stephen MacKena (London: Faber and Faber, n.d.), ennead 1, chap. 6, p. 64. See also Massimo Scolari, "Elements for a History of Axonometry," *Architectural Design* 55.5/6 (1985): 77; Eyjólfur Kjalar Emilsson, *Plotinus on Sense Perception* (Cambridge: Cambridge University Press, 1988); Henri Oosthout, *Modes of Knowledge and the Transcendental* (Amsterdam: B. R. Grüner, 1991).

141. For discussion of the text of the benedictional see Andrew Prescott, "The Text of the Benedictional of St. Aethelwold," *Bishop Aethelwold,* pp. 119–47. For discussion of some of the illuminations see Deshman in *Sources of Anglo-Saxon Culture,* pp. 261–82. For dating and sources see J. J. G. Alexander, "The Benedictional of St. Aethelwold and Anglo-Saxon Illumination of the Reform Period," *Tenth-Century Studies,* pp. 169–83.

142. *Sources of Anglo-Saxon Culture,* pp. 272–73.

143. British Library MS ADD 49598. For the analysis of the text and the iconography of the *Benedictional of St. Aethelwold,* see, for example, *The Benedictional of Saint Aethelwold,* ed. George Frederic Warner and Henry Austin Wilson (Oxford: Privately printed for presentation to the members of the Rorburghe Club, 1910) (a black-and-white facsimile, including a color frontispiece of the visit to the sepulchre); Prescott in *Bishop Aethelwold,* pp. 119–47; Alexander in *Tenth-Century Studies,* pp. 169–83; Francis Wormald, *The Benedictional of St. Aethelwold* (London: Faber and Faber, 1959) (contains eight color plates); Deshman, *"Christus rex et magi reges";* Richard Deshman, "The Iconography of the Full-Page Miniatures of the Benedictional of Aethelwold" (Ph.D. dissertation, Princeton University, 1970; Ann Arbor, MI: University Microfilms, 1976).

144. See, for example, miniatures on fols. 3v, 4, 5v, 15v, 19v, 22v, 24v, 34v, 45v, 64v, 92v, 95v, and 102v in the benedictional.

145. For the full text of the benediction see British Library, MS ADD 49598, fols. 52–52v.

146. See, for example, miniatures on fols. 2v, 3, 5v, 24v, 45v, 67v, 99v, and 118v in the benedictional.

147. For the discussion of the space of close-range vision see Gilles Deleuze, "Nomad Art: Space," *The Deleuze Reader,* edited with an introduction by Constantin V. Boundas (New York: Columbia University Press, 1993), pp. 165–72.

148. Ibid., p. 167.

149. These statements may explain the position of the *Quem quaeritis* as well as why the Gospel reading was omitted in the night office on Easter Day, even though there was one on Maundy Thursday. The *Regularis concordia* presents us with a unique English practice concerning the Sunday Mass, that is, laypeople were admitted to the monastery to assist at the chief Mass on Sundays and feasts: "Now on feast days . . . while the Morrow Mass is being said the ministers of the following Mass shall vest and then, Tierce being said, the bells shall ring to call the faithful people together and the Mass shall begin" (19; 88). Since the *Regularis concordia* does not mention the celebration of the Mass on Easter Day, we can assume that it followed the Roman Office. The Gospel reading is a part of the service, so the Gospel of Saint Mark, which is designed for this occasion, would be read during the celebration on Easter Day in the presence of both the monks and the lay congregation. Because the Gospel was read in Latin, it would have been appropriate to include the *Quem quaeritis,* as it was presented during the night office, at the Mass. In this position it would have served its educational purpose, as Hardison suggested (204). However, it seems that the *Quem quaeritis* never performed this function and that "the outward representation of that which was spiritual" was never included in the chief Mass on Easter Day. Therefore, the placement of the *Quem quaeritis* at the night office was not motivated by the literary potential of the *Quem quaeritis,* nor was it an

act of anticipation, nor was it a substitution for the Gospel reading. Its position may only be explained by the fact that the *Regularis concordia,* which followed a secular Office for the monastic celebration of Holy Week, attempted to provide means with the help of which the English monastic community would codify the function and the practice of one of the most significant dogmas in sacramental theology, the resurrection of Christ.

150. ". . . and when the lessons are read at Nocturns . . . and if he finds a brother drowsy with sleep he shall put the lantern before him and return to his place. Whereupon this brother, shaking off sleep, shall do penance on his knees and, taking up the lantern, shall himself go round the choir, and if he finds another overcome by sleep, he shall do to him as was done to himself and so return to his own place" (56; 132–33). It is quite possible that the duties of the monastic *circator* were described to Aethelwold by his Fleury informants, who presented to him customs that were later recorded by Theodoric in *Consuetudines,* a tenth-century Fleury observance. See Wulfstan, p. lx.

151. "On Saturday, according to the ordinance of the Rule, let the brethren carry out the Maundy and the *munditiae* with loving care; and let those who are as ignorant of these duties study carefully how they should be performed and so, in the accustomed way, fulfill them conscientiously. Let no one presume to do anything whatsoever, however small, of his own, and as it were personal choice; neither let him leave the church during the celebration of the appointed hours nor the cloister, as the Rule enjoins, nor puffed up by overweening pride, let him dare to do the least thing without the permission of the prior. Let no one scorn to grease shoes or to wash garments or to minister water. . . . Let each one according to his strength and with thanksgiving fulfill the duties of the kitchen and bakehouse as the Rule commands" (63; 140).

152. We have little information about plans of English monasteries in the tenth century. Symons points out, however: "we know from the *Concordia* that there would have been the *oratorium* or church, in which all assembled at stated times for the daily round of prayer and praise; the refectory where all fed together; the dormitory where all slept together; the cloister in which the monks read and studied together; a room set apart for the daily Chapter of meeting of the community; 'a suitable place' with a fire where all could carry out the full claustral observance in the cold of winter; the *coquina* (kitchen) and *pistrinum* (bakehouse); the guesthouse, infirmary and *auditorium*" (*The Monastic Agreement,* p. xxxi). See also Biddle, *Winchester in the Early Middle Ages;* Keene.

153. Some of the observances, however, have no exact parallel in medieval monastic history. These are an Office of the Dead that consisted of Nocturns, Matins, and Vespers and another Office of the Dead, which consisted of Matins and Vespers. Their position in the monastic day varied and depended on the season when they were celebrated. According to Symons: "In the Summer period (Lent to November 1) Matins Of All Saints and Of the Dead were placed after Nocturns and Matins of the day, Vespers Of All Saints and Of the Dead after Vespers of the Day with Vigils of the Dead after the second meal (*cena*) or,

when there was no second meal, immediately after the three Vespers Offices. In the Winter period (November 1 to Lent) on ferial days Vigils and Matins Of the Dead together with Matins Of All Saints were said in the interval between Nocturns and Matins of the day, and Vespers Of All Saints and Of the Dead after Vespers of the day. On Sundays and feasts of twelve lessons the same order was kept except that Vigils were after the second meal (*cena*). From Maundy Thursday to Saturday in Easter week both Offices, and thence to the Octave of Pentecost that Of the Dead only, were omitted" (*The Monastic Agreement,* p. xxxii).

154. Knowles, *The Monastic Order in England,* p. 45.

155. For specific information concerning land endowments see the charters in *Anglo-Saxon Charters* and the legal documents in *Councils and Synods.* For information about the use of the land, management of estates, and economic system see, for example, Michael Moissey Postan, *The Medieval Economy and Society* (London: Weidenfeld and Nicolson, 1972); Jan Zbigniew Titow, *Winchester Yields: A Study in Medieval Agricultural Productivity* (Cambridge: Cambridge University Press, 1972); Georges Duby, *The Early Growth of European Economy* (London: Weidenfeld and Nicolson, 1974); Edward Miller and John Hatcher, *Medieval England: Rural Society and Economic Change, 1086–1348* (London: Longman, 1978); Keene; Rodney Hilton, *Class Conflict and the Crisis of Feudalism* (London: Hambledon Press, 1985); John Day, *Medieval Market Economy* (Oxford: Basil Blackwell, 1987); Mark Bailey, *A Marginal Economy* (Cambridge: Cambridge University Press, 1989); Kathleen Biddick, *The Other Economy* (Berkeley, CA: University of California Press, 1989).

156. Eric John suggests: "Every monastery in the country which obeyed the command of the *Concordia,* with its constant round of prayers for the king, was a *foyer* of royalist propaganda. . . . Abbots were counted among the king's *witan;* they appear regularly and in quantity at *witenagemotan:* we may guess that they were equally prominent in the local shire courts. . . . The new monks, like the old clerks, tended to be well-born, and any heightening of their respect for the West Saxon royal house is likely to have communicated itself to their relatives at home. In other words the monasteries offered an atmosphere permeated with devotion to the royal family: on the great occasions and in the shire meetings, with their monastic connections of whatever kind and degree, the English upper classes were forced to breathe that atmosphere" (*Orbis Britanniae,* p. 179). This view is opposed by Patrick Wormald who argues against the approach that focuses on the common interest of king and monks in reform. Wormald suggests that "the ideology of reform in Aethelwold's favored abbeys was powered by a bright vision of England's religious history" (Patrick Wormald, "Aethelwold and His Continental Counterparts: Contact, Comparison, Contrast," *Bishop Aethelwold,* p. 40). It seems to me that both positions are viable especially in terms of history, which considers events within a complex network of relationships positioned in a dynamic space of historiographic topography.

157. Farmer in *Tenth-Century Studies,* p. 17.

158. The royal patronage over English monastic life was a mixed blessing. Farmer states: "Goscelin's life of Wulfhilda [a nun who refused to accept King Edgar's love in the early 960s], besides giving evidence for hereditary owner-ship of monasteries, also tells us of the manoeuvres through which discontented nuns at Barking, by intriguing with Queen Aelfthryth their 'protector,' could exile their abbess of distant Horton for twenty years" (*Tenth-Century Studies,* p. 17).

159. Benedictine *Rule* cited in *The Monastic Agreement,* p. xxxvii. Further-more, Symons states: "no doubt the poor were equally well cared for by the monks of other lands: certainly the daily washing of the feet of three or more poor men was, and had long been, of common observance. But the picture drawn by the *Concordia* of the love and reverent care lavished on the poor has not its like in any contemporary consuetudinary; and if perhaps the daily Maundy was itself taken from Continental monasticism there is no reason to doubt that the general admonitions of the *Concordia* on this point, above all the advice given to the abbot, reflect the personal sanctity, the unworldliness, of one or other or all of the three leaders of the English movement" (*The Monastic Agreement,* p. xxxvii).

160. Knowles, *The Monastic Order in England,* p. 44.

Chapter 2

1. Like its tenth-century equivalent, the *Regularis concordia* from the sec-ond half of the eleventh century—British Library, MS Cotton Tiberius A III, fol. 3–27v—was associated with Christ Church in Canterbury. The manuscript is written in medieval Latin. Unlike its tenth-century counterpart, it has Anglo-Saxon glosses above the descriptive texts or the prayers that were added to the monastic or liturgical observances, such as the prayers for the king and the benefactors. The names and prayers that constitute a legitimate part of the Christian worship are in Latin only, however. This manuscript contains a full-page illustration that depicts three figures seated under a canopy with three arches. In the center is the image of King Edgar. Under the arch on the right is an archbishop with pallium, possibly Dunstan; and under the left arch is a bishop, possibly Aethelwold. The three figures hold a long scroll. Below the scroll is a monk looking upward, apparently in the act of genuflecting. The manuscript begins with the *Proem,* which is followed by a list of chapters and then by the twelve chapters themselves. There is also an epilogue that ends in the middle of fol. 27v. The remaining portion of this folio page is filled by a new text written in red ink, which does not belong to the body of the *Regularis concordia.* Unlike its tenth-century equivalent, the eleventh-century *Regularis concordia* comes from the time when William the Conqueror attempted to reor-ganize the English church with the help of Norman monks who brought with them a form of monasticism influenced by the Cluniac model. They were

appointed to a number of vacant abbacies. As a corollary of this action, two separate traditions began to coexist in England: English monasticism shaped by modified versions of the tenth-century *Regularis concordia,* the *Rule* of Saint Benedict, or the individual customs of monastic houses; and Norman monasticism shaped by Cluniac consuetudinaries. For discussion of the Old English gloss—its purpose, quality, and transmission—as well as glossing techniques see Lucia Kornexl, "The *Regularis concordia* and Its Old English Gloss," *Anglo-Saxon England,* ed. Michael Lapidge et al., vol. 24 (Cambridge: Cambridge University Press, 1995), 95–130. For discussion of the changes in English monasticism and the controversies connected with the appointment of foreign monks to the English monastic houses see *English Historical Documents,* vol. 2: *1042–1189,* ed. David C. Douglas (London: Eyre and Spottiswoode, 1953), 631–65.

2. Michel de Certeau, *The Practice of Everyday Life,* trans. Steven Rendall (Berkeley, CA: University of California Press, 1984), pp. 148–49.

3. Allan John MacDonald, *Berengar and the Reform of Sacramental Doctrine* (London: Longmans, 1930), pp. 28–29.

4. Margaret Gibson, *Lanfranc of Bec* (Oxford: Clarendon Press, 1978), p. 55. Also see Gibson for discussion of the conflict between Geoffrey Martel, count of Anjou, and Gervase, bishop of Le Mans.

5. Margaret Gibson (64–65) suggests that the criticism of Berengar's teaching is connected with the weakening of the political position of Geoffrey Martel after the 1048 Council of Rheims where he was excommunicated until he released Gervase from prison.

6. Theoduin of Liège [Deoduinus], "Contra Brunonem et Berengarium," *Patrologiae Cursus Completus, Series Latina,* ed. Jacques Paul Migne, 221 vols. (Paris: Garnier Fratres, 1884), 146:1439 B.

7. *Patrologiae,* 150:63 CD.

8. Lanfranc, *De corpore et sanguine domini, Patrologiae,* 150:413 B.

9. *Patrologiae,* 150:413 A–414 C.

10. See, for example, Eusebius Bruno, *Ad Berengarium Magistrum, de sacramento Eucharistiae, Patrologiae,* 147:1201 D–1204 C.

11. Lanfranc, *De corpore et sanguine domini, Patrologiae,* 150:410 D–411 A. See also Margaret Gibson, p. 81; Gary Macy, *The Theologies of the Eucharist in the Early Scholastic Period: A Study of the Salvific Function of the Sacrament according to the Theologians c. 1080–1220* (Oxford: Clarendon Press, 1984), p. 36; Henry Chadwick, "Ego Berengarius," *Journal of Theological Studies,* n.s., 40.2 (October 1989): 414–45.

12. See *Patrologiae,* 150:411 BC for the text of the oath that is a slightly modified version of the already quoted statement regarding physical presence in the Eucharist; see *Patrologiae,* 150:411 D–412 A for the description of the actions undertook by of Pope Nicholas II.

13. Macy (38) argues: "The Greeks defended their use of unleavened bread by claiming that it symbolized the Trinity, the Spirit represented by the

leaven, while the unleavened bread of the West would be a *corpus imperfectum et inanimatum*. In reply, Humbert and others insisted that only the salvific body and blood of Christ were present here. . . . Further to speak of the bread *symbolizing* anything would be a deep error. Firstly, because after the consecration, there would be no true bread present and, secondly, somehow to think that there would be a presence of the Lord in the bread different from that of the incarnate, risen Lord, would split the unity of Christ."

14. Chadwick, p. 416.

15. Macy, p. 37.

16. Richard William Southern, *Saint Anselm* (Cambridge: Cambridge University Press, 1990), p. 44.

17. Ibid., 45.

18. See John Marenbon, *Early Medieval Philosophy* (London: Routledge and Kegan Paul, 1983), chap. 8.

19. Aristotle, *Categories,* chap. 5 of *The Complete Works of Aristotle,* ed. Jonathan Barnes (Princeton, NJ: Princeton University Press, 1984).

20. In *De corporis et sanguinis Christi veritate in eucharistia,* Guitmund of Aversa says that his master Lanfranc, when still a boy in Italy, was present at a mass where a priest had found real flesh and blood on the altar after the Consecration. The priest informed his bishop about the incident. At the ad hoc meeting of the bishops, it was decided that the visibly converted elements should be sealed as relics within the altar. See *Patrologiae,* 149:1449 D–1450 A.

21. Chadwick, p. 418.

22. Ambrose, *De sacramentis, Patrologiae,* 16:458 C–460 A; see also Margaret Gibson, p. 72.

23. The phrase *incruenta hostia* is used by Ambrose in *De sacramentis,* bk. 4, chap. 6, *Patrologiae,* 16:464 B. The notion of "an unbloody sacrifice" is also discussed by Ambrose in *De sacramentis,* bk. 6, chap. 1, *Patrologiae,* 16:474 C.

24. Chadwick, p. 425.

25. Macy, p. 40.

26. Chadwick, p. 425.

27. Ibid., p. 426.

28. Aristotle, *Categories,* chaps. 7–8.

29. Quoted in Marenbon, p. 91.

30. Chadwick, p. 415.

31. Durand, *De corpore et sanguine domini, Patrologiae,* 149:1375–1424 B.

32. *De corporis et sanguinis Christi veritate in eucharistia, Patrologiae,* 149:1427 A–1494 D.

33. Macy, p. 42.

34. See Mark C. Poster, *Erring* (Chicago: University of Chicago Press, 1984), for a discussion of representational functions in theology.

35. See Saint Anselm, *Monologion, Patrologiae,* 158:169 CD–173 C. See also Saint Anselm, *A New, Interpretative Translation of St. Anselm's Monologion*

and Proslogion, ed. and trans. Jasper Hopkins (Minneapolis, MN: Arthur J. Banning Press, 1986), chaps. 20–21.

36. "Therefore, O God, not only are You that than which a greater cannot be thought, but You are also something greater than can be thought" (Saint Anselm, *Proslogion, Patrologiae,* 158:235 C). See also Saint Anselm, *St. Anselm's Proslogion,* translated with an introduction and philosophical commentary by M. J. Charlesworth (Oxford: Clarendon Press, 1965), pp. 136–37; *A New, Interpretive Translation,* p. 245.

37. Saint Anselm, *A New, Interpretive Translation,* p. 121; *Monologion, Patrologiae,* 158:176 AB.

38. Saint Anselm, *A New, Interpretive Translation,* p. 79; *Monologion, Patrologiae,* 158:154 C.

39. See Michel Foucault, *The Order of Things: An Archaeology of the Human Sciences* (New York: Random House, 1973), chap. 3.

40. Saint Anselm, *A New, Interpretive Translation,* p. 145; *Monologion, Patrologiae,* 158:188 B.

41. Saint Anselm, *A New, Interpretive Translation,* pp. 145–46; *Monologion, Patrologiae,* 158:189 AB.

42. In the twelfth century, the concept of the *cognitio Dei* was further transformed to accommodate the heightened interest in divine creation. Philosophy, biblical study, and the visual arts recorded a shift of emphasis from the universality of *logos* to the reciprocal dialectic of *theosis* (a mystical conjunction of the ascending individual with the descending god). See R. W. Hanning, "'Ut enim faber . . . sic creator': Divine Creation as the Context for Human Creativity in the Twelfth Century," *Word, Picture, and Spectacle,* ed. Clifford Davidson (Kalamazoo, MI: Medieval Institute Publications, Western Michigan University, 1984), pp. 95–149.

43. Saint Augustine, *The Confessions of Saint Augustine,* trans. E. M. Blaiklock (Nashville, TN: Thomas Nelson, 1983), bk. 10, chap. 11, pp. 250–51.

44. "There all things are stored, each under its proper head, in accordance with its delivery, each through its proper gate—light, for example, and all colours and corporeal shapes by way of the eyes, through the ears, too, all kinds of sound, and all scents by the nose's ingress, and tastes through that of the mouth, by the sense of touch all things hard or soft, hot or cold, smooth or rough, heavy or light, whether within or without the body. All this that huge storage place of memory, with its unimaginable secret nooks and indescribable corners, receives, to be recollected and brought back at need. They all enter by the appropriate gate and are there laid up. The things themselves, however, do not go in, but only images of things perceived" (Saint Augustine, *The Confessions of Saint Augustine,* bk. 10, chap. 8, pp. 246–47).

45. See chaps. 8–20 in Saint Benedict, *The Rule of Saint Benedict,* trans. Dom Justin McCann (England: Stanbrook Abbey Press, 1937), or trans. John Baptist Hasbrouck (Kalamazoo, MI: Cistercian Publications, 1983).

46. Anselm's definition of meditation is closely related to the concept of memory. According to Mary Carruthers, medieval memory advice stressed synesthesia in making a memory image. The images were supposed to be seen and felt and to have taste or tactile qualities. The process of recollection was a process of remembering the places where each "bit" of knowledge was stored. These places (*loci, sedes*) were to be properly lighted, moderate in size, different from one another in shape, and not too crowded. See Mary Carruthers, *The Book of Memory: A Study of Memory in Medieval Culture* (Cambridge: Cambridge University Press, 1990), chaps. 1–2.

47. Quoted in Southern, *Saint Anselm*, p. 97.

48. Quoted in ibid., p. 102. See also Saint Anselm, *The Prayers and Meditations of Saint Anselm with the Proslogion*, translated with an introduction by Sister Benedicta Ward, with a foreword by R. W. Southern (London: Penguin Books, 1973).

49. Southern, *Saint Anselm*, p. 102.

50. Saint Anselm, *Monologion, Patrologiae*, 158:145A. See also Brian Stock, *The Implications of Literacy: Written Language and Models of Interpretation in the Eleventh and Twelfth Centuries* (Princeton, NJ: Princeton University Press, 1983), pp. 329–62, for discussion of Saint Anselm's philosophy and, specifically, of the concept of the text, the uses of the text, and their relation to the word.

51. Saint Anselm, *A New, Interpretive Translation*, pp. 85–87; *Monologion, Patrologiae*, 158:159 D–160 A.

52. Saint Anselm, *A New, Interpretive Translation*, p. 91; *Monologion, Patrologiae*, 158:161 B.

53. Saint Anselm, *Monologion, Patrologiae*, 158:187 B–188 C.

54. See, for example, Saint Anselm, *A New, Interpretive Translation; Why God Became Man*, trans. Joseph M. Colleran (Albany, NY: Magi Books, 1969); *St. Anselm's Proslogion*. See also Saint Aelred of Rievaulx, *The Mirror of Love, The Medieval Mystics of England*, ed. Eric Colledge (New York: Charles Scribner's Sons, 1961), pp. 105–21.

55. This argument, which was grounded in Plato's *Timaeus* and received a meticulous (Christian) gloss in the works of William of Conches and Gilbert of Poitiers as well as in Bernard Silvestris's *Cosmographia* in the first half of the twelfth century. See, for example, Bernard Silvestris, *Cosmographia*, ed. Peter Dronke, Textus Minores 53 (Leiden: E. J. Brill, 1978).

56. Allan John MacDonald, *Lanfranc* (London: Oxford University Press, 1926), p. 64; Frank Barlow, *The English Church, 1000–1066* (London: Longman, 1979), pp. 302–10.

57. Lanfranc, *The Letters of Lanfranc Archbishop of Canterbury*, ed. Helen Clover and Margaret Gibson (London: Oxford University Press, 1979), epis. 1, p. 31. This collection of letters supersedes the collection in *English Historical Documents*, vol. 2.

58. Lanfranc was consecrated by William, bishop of London, Walchelin of Winchester, Remigus of Dorchester or Lincoln, Siward of Rochester, Herfast of Elmham or Thetford, Stigand of Selsey, Hermann of Sherborne, and Giso of Wells. See Lanfranc, "Memorandum on the Primacy of Canterbury," *Letters,* pp. 39–41.

59. *Letters,* epis. 1, p. 33.

60. Lanfranc, *Letters,* epis. 2, pp. 35–39.

61. See Lanfranc, "Memorandum on the Primacy of Canterbury," *Letters,* pp. 39–41, for details.

62. Lanfranc, *Letters,* epis. 11, p. 75.

63. Ibid., pp. 75–77.

64. Ibid., p. 77.

65. Ibid., p. 77.

66. Ibid., p. 79.

67. *Councils and Synods with Other Documents Relating to the English Church,* ed. Dorothy Whitelock, Martin Brett, and Christopher Brooke, 2 vols. (Oxford: Clarendon Press, 1981), 2:619.

68. Lanfranc, *Letters,* epis. 11, p. 79.

69. MacDonald, *Lanfranc,* p. 112.

70. *Councils and Synods,* 2:619.

71. Ibid., pp. 575–76, 605–7.

72. "I have come to our estate of Freckenham, near St. Edmund's abbey, where on the king's orders and under pressure of ill health I have decided to undergo a regime. That is why I am detaining Abbot Baldwin, to whom the king has personally commended my case, even though he has entered into a lawsuit with Richard at this assembly over certain matters in dispute between them. But since the abbot has been excused this journey by both you and Richard himself, I urgently recommend that the case itself be deferred until we can all meet on another occasion and by our united efforts conclude the affair without partiality to anyone" (Lanfranc, *Letters,* epis. 44, p. 141).

73. Consider the following text:

Abbot Baldwin's clerk and servant Berard brought you our letter about his affairs. As he himself affirmed to me later, you made a coarse joke about it; you uttered cheap and unworthy remarks about me in the hearing of many; and you declared with many an oath that you would give me no assistance in that matter. There will be another time and another place to speak of these things.

But my immediate instructions are these: that you lay no claim to the property of St. Edmund unless you can give indisputable proof that it was claimed by your predecessors and that you discharge the aforesaid Berard without any fine or threat of punishment, until the case comes into our own court and can be rightly concluded according to canon law and our own ruling as judge.

Give up the dicing (to mention nothing else) and the world's amusements, in which you are said to idle away the entire day: read Scripture and above all set yourself to master the decrees of the Roman pontiffs and the canons of the holy councils. . . . In the papal decrees we read as follows: "Let every province always look to its own metropolitan for direction in all affairs." . . . In the councils of Toledo: "Thus it is the right that every man look to the bishop from whom he received the honour of consecration for direction in his manner of life. So according to the decrees of our fathers that see which is a man's mother in the priesthood shall instruct him in his conduct as a churchman." And a little further on: "Anyone infringing these decrees shall spend six months with his metropolitan bishop, excluded from communion, under a penitential regime." . . . No reasonable man can think that I am rashly encroaching on a jurisdiction that is not mine, for by God's mercy it is agreed that this whole island called Britain is within the undivided jurisdiction of our one church.

Banish the monk Hermann, whose life is notorious for its many faults, from your society and your household completely. It is my wish that he live according to a rule in an observant monastery, or—if he refuses to do this—that he depart from the kingdom of England. (Lanfranc, *Letters,* epis. 47, pp. 151–53)

74. MacDonald, *Lanfranc,* p. 117.

75. Lanfranc, *Letters,* epis. 43, p. 139.

76. Ibid., epis. 51, p. 163.

77. Ibid., epis. 53, p. 167; epis. 59, p. 175.

78. Ibid., epis. 61, p. 179.

79. Ibid., epis. 41, p. 135.

80. Ibid., epis. 46, p. 149.

81. Eadmer, *Historia novorum in Anglia, et opuscula duo de vita Sancti Anselmi et quibusdam miraculis ejus,* ed. Martin Rule, *Rerum Britannicarum medii aevi scriptores, or Chronicles and Memorials of Great Britain and Ireland during the Middle Ages,* 99 vols. (London: Longman, 1884), 81:12, 17; Eadmer, *History of Recent Events in England,* trans. Geoffrey Bosanquet (London: Cresset Press, 1964), pp. 13, 17–18.

82. Eadmer, *Historia novorum in Anglia,* p. 13; *History of Recent Events in England,* p. 13.

83. Quoted in MacDonald, *Lanfranc,* pp. 137–38.

84. Lanfranc, *Letters,* epis. 61, p. 179.

85. *Lanfranc,* p. 143.

86. "On the night following the resurrection of our Lord, while the three women were seeking the body of the Lord, our saviour, a lame man, with his own tendons crying out, stretched himself out, and, erect on his feet, he stood healthy and straight" (*Memorials of Saint Dunstan, Archbishop of Canterbury,* ed. William Stubbs, *Rerum Britannicarum medii aevi scriptores, or Chronicles and Memorials of Great Britain and Ireland during the Middle Ages,* 99 vols. [London: Longman, 1874], 63:231). This passage, however, introduces more questions than the answers it provides. When did this miracle happen? Did it happen

during the Easter Mass that was attended by lay population? If so, does it mean that the celebration of the Resurrection was moved from the night office? Or did it happen during the night office?

87. See Richard W. Pfaff, "Lanfranc's Supposed Purge of the Anglo-Saxon Calendar," *Warriors and Churchmen in the High Middle Ages: Essays Presented to Karl Leyser,* ed. Timothy Reuter (London: Hambledon Press, 1992), pp. 95–108; T. A. Heslop, "The Canterbury Calendars and the Norman Conquest," *Canterbury and the Norman Conquest: Churches, Saints, and Scholars, 1066–1109,* ed. Richard Eales and Richard Sharpe (London: Hambledon Press, 1995), pp. 53–85. Both authors address one of the most poignant issues regarding the change in the Anglo-Norman calendars, that is, the extent to which the Norman takeover may or may not have had consequences for the feats of major local saints.

88. *The Monastic Constitutions of Lanfranc,* trans. David Knowles (London: Thomas Nelson and Sons, 1951), p. 1. Subsequent references to the *Constitutions* are to pages in this volume and will be cited by page numbers in parentheses in the text.

89. Saint Benedict, *The Rule of Saint Benedict,* trans. Dom Justin McCann, pp. 31–34.

90. Of the offering of a child to the monastery, the *Constitutions* stipulates: "If a child is to be offered to the monastery he shall be tonsured, and then, bearing in his hands a host and chalice with wine in it, as is the custom, he shall be offered by his parents after the Gospel to the priest celebrating Mass. When his offering has been received by the priest, his parents shall wrap the child's hands in the cloth which covers the altar and which hangs down in front, and then the abbot shall accept them. When this is done the parents shall straightway promise before God and his saints that the child shall never abandon the monastic life through their agency or that of anyone representing them, and that they will never knowingly give him anything that might lead to his ruin. This promise shall have been previously written down and witnessed, and now they shall make it verbally and then place it on the altar" (110–11). Then, the abbot blessed a cowl. While taking a piece of garment off the boy, the abbot said, "May the Lord strip thee of the old man." While placing the cowl on the boy, the abbot said, "May the Lord clothe thee with the new man" (111). With the pronouncement of these words, the obligation to manifest the structural and spiritual belonging became a verbal description of the general status, since a monk's profession, or, in other words, a monk's obligation to manifest his structural and spiritual belonging, did not take place until he reached a certain age. The boy was taken to be shaved and clothed with the habit of the order. The *Constitutions* then stipulates, "When he is grown up and is to make his profession, all is done as described previously for the case of one coming into the monastery from the world, save the part which has been done already should not be repeated" (111).

The process of initiation to the monastic life followed a set formula regardless of whether a novice was an outsider or an older boy who had already spent time at the monastery. A man was brought to the guest house. After the abbot or prior questioned him, he was introduced to the chapter house, where, after the act of obeisance, he made a formal statement that he had a desire to become a monk. According to the *Constitutions,* "Then he shall be bidden to rise and shall be told of all things hard and harsh which those who wish to live a devout and regular life endure in this estate, as well as the things harder and harsher which may befall them if they bear themselves disorderly" (105). If he still persisted in his desire, he was taken to the nave of the church. At the end of the Chapter, the novice master took him to be tonsured, shaved, and robed in the regular habit without the cowl. During the novitiate, he was not forbidden to communicate with other monks; instead, he was to observe their life, listen to their teachings, and make frequent confessions. "When many days have passed," reads the *Constitutions,* "if the brethren approve of his behavior and he of their way of life" (107), the profession took place. The rules were read to him again. The warning about the difficulty of the monastic life was given. The *Constitutions* stipulates that upon his agreement to endure all of these things, "[t]hen the novice shall go to the feet of the abbot, or of him who is superior at the time if the abbot is away; then returning to where he stood, and keeling, he shall humbly bow in front and to the right and left, giving thanks to the brethren for their kind prayers on his behalf" (107). The novice did not become a full member of the community, however, until he was given permission to speak at a Chapter meeting. From that moment, not only his spiritual self but also all his earthly possessions belonged to the order.

When a brother was near death and requested to be anointed, the brethren came to him after the Chapter. They stood around him. The dying man was sprinkled with holy water, and after the psalms, *Kyrie eleison,* the chapter, and the collects, he made his confession and was absolved by all present. He absolved them in return. Then he was anointed. Lanfranc wrote, "When the anointing is done the priest shall wash his hands and the water shall be thrown on the fire, or into the *sacrarium*" (121). The priest then went into the church for the sacrament. Lanfranc wrote, "When it is brought, the sick man, after washing his mouth, receives Communion, unless he shall by chance have already received Communion that day" (121). When there was an indication that the brother was nearing death, two brethren remained with him reading the Passion and other parts of the gospels to him as long as he stayed conscious. Lanfranc wrote: "When his senses fail, they shall recite the psalter. . . . When the sick man is in his agony and at the very point of death, if God so wills, then the servant in charge shall unfold a sackcloth and lay on it ashes in the form of a cross from edge to edge of the sackcloth, and set the dying brother thereon. . . . When he sees him now in the agony of passing, he shall take the board in his hand and run to the door of the cloister and beat the board there with sharp and rapid blows until he is sure the community have heard" (122). Special formularies were sung. After the washing of the body and the vigil, the body was buried. So long as the body remained unburied, the community was obliged to keep silent, save for the saying of the prayers during the religious and other duties.

91. Michel de Certeau, *The Writing of History,* trans. Tom Conley (New York: Columbia University Press, 1988), p. xv.

92. There is evidence that, when carried to new foundations, the *Regularis concordia* did not always contain all the observances. For example, in a post-1004 letter, Aelfric recommended that the monks at Eynsham observe the regulations of the consuetudinary. His abbreviated version of the *Regularis concordia* recommends, however, not the celebration of the night office as specified in the tenth-century code but a monastic one. See "Aelfrici Abbatis Epistula," *Consuetudinum Saeculi x/xi/xii Monumenta Non-Cluniacensia,* ed. Kassius Hallinger, Corpus Consuetudinum Monasticarum, t. 7, pars. 3 (Siegburg: Franz Schmitt, 1984), p. 174.

93. Arnold William Klukas, "The Architectural Implications of the *Decreta Lanfranci,*" *Anglo-Norman Studies,* vol. 6: Proceedings of the Battle Conference, ed. R. Allen Brown (Woodbridge, Suffolk: Boydell Press), pp. 140–44.

Chapter 3

1. Throughout, I cite the works of Honorius Augustodunensis as they appear in *Patrologiae Cursus Completus, Series Latina,* ed. Jacques Paul Migne, 221 vols. (Paris: Garnier Fratres, 1895), vol. 172.

2. Honorius Augustodunensis, *Gemma animae, Patrologiae,* 172:555 A.

3. Ibid., 172:570 BC.

4. Honorius Augustodunensis, *Eucharisticon, Patrologiae,* 172:1254 A–1255 B. For the illuminating analysis of Honorius's treatment of the body of Christ in the Eucharist, see Caroline Walker Bynum's reading of select passages in *Elucidarium,* in Caroline Walker Bynum, *The Resurrection of the Body in Western Christianity, 200–1336* (New York: Columbia University Press, 1995), pp. 147–53.

5. See O. B. Hardison, Jr., *Christian Rite and Christian Drama in the Middle Ages: Essays in the Origin and Early History of Modern Drama* (Baltimore, MD: Johns Hopkins University Press, 1965), pp. 39–46.

6. Gary Macy, *The Theologies of the Eucharist in the Early Scholastic Period: A Study of the Salvific Function of the Sacrament according to the Theologians c. 1080–1220* (Oxford: Clarendon Press, 1984), p. 76.

7. Guibert of Nogent-sous-Coucy, *De sanctis et eorum pignoribus, Patrologiae,* 156:629 D–630 B, 643 D.

8. Baldwin of Canterbury, *De sacramento altaris, Le sacrament de l'autel,* ed. John Morson, Sources chrétiennes 94 (Paris: Editiones du Cerf, 1963), p. 246.

9. Peter the Venerable, *Contra Petrobrusianos hereticos,* ed. James Fearns,

Corpus christianorum: Continuatio mediaevalis 10 (Turnhout: Typographi Brepols Editores Pontificii, 1968), pp. 119–20; Macy, p. 92.

10. *The Medieval Mystics of England,* ed. Eric Colledge (New York: Charles Scribner's Sons, 1961), pp. 5–7.

11. *The Mirror of Love, The Medieval Mystics of England,* p. 105. Subsequent citations in parentheses in text refer to page numbers in this edition.

12. Macy, pp. 112–13.

13. Ibid., p. 116.

14. Ibid., pp. 119–20.

15. See Peter Browe, *Die eucharistischen Wunder des Mittelalters* (Breslau: Verlag Müller and Seiffert, 1938); Édouard Dumoutet, *Le désir de voir l'hostie* (Paris: Gabriel Beauchesne, 1926); idem, *Corpus Domini aux sources de la piete eucharistique medievale* (Paris: Gabriel Beauchesne, 1942).

16. Guitmund of Aversa, *De corporis et sanguinis Christi veritate in eucharistia, Patrologiae,* 149:1449 D–1450 A; Macy, p. 87.

17. Browe, pp. 151–52.

18. See, for example, Gerard G. Grant, "The Elevation of the Host: A Reaction to Twelfth-Century Heresy," *Theological Studies* 1 (1940): 228–50; V. L. Kennedy, "The Moment of Consecration and the Elevation of the Host," *Medieval Studies* 6 (1944): 121–50.

19. See Macy, pp. 91–92, for a critical analysis of the theories as well as for the sources.

20. Albert Mirgeler, *Mutations of Western Christianity,* trans. Edward Quinn (London: Burns and Oates, 1964), pp. 111–20.

21. Dumoutet, *Le désir,* pp. 126–34.

22. See, for example, George Zarnecki, *Art of Medieval World* (New York: Harry N. Abrams, 1975).

23. Saint Anselm, *Why God Became Man,* trans. Joseph Colleran (Albany, NY: Magi Books, 1969); *Cur Deus Homo, Patrologiae,* 158:359 C–432 B.

24. Saint Anselm, *Why God Became Man,* bk. 1, chap. 11, pp. 84–85; *Cur Deus Homo, Patrologiae,* 158:376 B–377 A.

25. Saint Anselm, *Why God Became Man,* bk. 1, chap. 22, p. 111; *Cur Deus Homo, Patrologiae,* 158:395 B.

26. Saint Anselm, *Why God Became Man,* bk. 1, chap. 23, p. 112; *Cur Deus Homo, Patrologiae,* 158:396 AB.

27. Saint Anselm, *Why God Became Man,* bk. 2, chap. 1, p. 120; *Cur Deus Homo, Patrologiae,* 158:401 C.

28. Saint Anselm, *Why God Became Man,* bk. 2, chap. 7, p. 125; *Cur Deus Homo, Patrologiae,* 158:404 D–405 A.

29. Saint Anselm, *Why God Became Man,* bk. 2, chap. 8, p. 128; *Cur Deus Homo, Patrologiae,* 158:406 C–407 A.

30. Saint Anselm, *Why God Became Man,* bk. 2, chap. 19, p. 160; *Cur Deus Homo, Patrologiae,* 158:427 AB.

31. Saint Anselm, *The Prayers and Meditations of St. Anselm with the Proslo-*

gion, translated with an introduction by Sister Benedicta Ward, with a foreword by R. W. Southern (London: Penguin Books, 1988), p. 95.

32. Ibid., p. 96.

33. This aspect of the sacred-human history of the life of Christ is discussed at length by Gillian Evans, who asserts: "few of those who had written about the Incarnation in the years between the completion of Anselm's *Cur Deus Homo* and the Abelardian statement of the *Commentary on Roman* had been content to stop where Anselm stopped. Bruno of Segni had asked himself Anselm's question and answered it along the same line, but even he had paused to dwell on the fact that Christ ate, drank, hungered, wept and did other things which men do, and to meditate upon his burial in intimate detail. Anselm's successor's show a new concern for a better understanding of the sheer humanity of Christ, an urge to discuss the details of his ordinary life, to see him perhaps first of all as a man" (Gillian Rosemary Evans, *Anselm and a New Generation* [Oxford: Clarendon Press, 1980], p. 163).

34. For a general index of the twelfth-century versions of the *Quem quaeritis* see Hardison, p. 310.

35. Richard Axton, *European Drama of the Early Middle Ages* (London: Hutchinson, 1974), p. 69.

36. For the Latin and English texts see Karl Young, *The Drama of the Medieval Church,* 2 vols. (Oxford: Clarendon Press, 1933), 1:678–81; Axton, pp. 69–70; Hardison, pp. 240–44, 301–4.

37. Michel de Certeau, "Mystic Speech," *Heterologies: Discourse on the Other,* trans. Briam Massumi, with a foreword by Wlad Godzich (Minneapolis, MN: University of Minnesota Press, 1986), p. 91.

38. In 1175, Guibert of Gembloux (also know as Wibert), a Benedictine monk, wrote to Hildegard when he heard about her unique charismas. Since he was a cloistered monk and, thus, was not allowed to visit her personally, he wanted her to answer some of his questions concerning the practical aspect of her visions: Were they in German or in Latin? Did they show her knowledge of the Bible or were they the action of the Holy Spirit? When he received no answer, Guibert wrote again. This time, Hildegard answered him with a letter, the text of which is quoted in parts here. Guibert was at Rupertsberg when Hildegard died on September 17, 1079. After her death, Guibert edited some of her works. See Hildegard of Bingen, *Book of Divine Works,* edited with an introduction by Matthew Fox (Santa Fe, NM: Bear and Co., 1987), pp. 347–51.

39. Hildegard of Bingen, *Scivias,* trans. Bruce Hozeski (Santa Fe, NM: Bear and Co., 1986), p. 3. See also, Hildegard von Bingen, *Scivias,* trans. Mother Columba Hart and Jane Bishop (New York: Paulist Press, 1990). Subsequent references are to page numbers in the Hozeski edition.

40. This reference to the "real" recalls Roland Barthes's statements that "our entire civilization has a taste for the reality effect . . . whose sole pertinent feature is precisely to signify that the event represented has *really* taken place."

According to Barthes, historical discourse supposes, on the one hand, that the referent is detached from the discourse and, on the other hand, that the referent enters into direct relation with the signifier: "In other words, in 'objective' history, the 'real' is never anything but an unformulated signifier, sheltered behind the apparent omnipotence of the referent" (Roland Barthes, *The Rustle of Language*, trans. Richard Howard [New York: Hill and Wang, 1986], pp. 127–28, 141–48).

41. Michel de Certeau, *The Practice of Everyday Life*, trans. Steven Rendall (Berkeley, CA: University of California Press, 1984), p. xi.

42. Michel de Certeau, *The Mystic Fable*, trans. Michael B. Smith (Chicago: University of Chicago Press, 1992), 2.

43. Richard of Saint Victor, *In Apocalypsim Joannis, Patrologiae*, 196: 686 D.

44. See, for example, Valerie Lagorno, "The Medieval Continental Women Mystics: An Introduction," *An Introduction to the Medieval Mystics of Europe*, ed. Paul E. Szarmach (Albany, NY: State University of New York Press, 1984); Barbara Newman, *Sister of Wisdom: St. Hildegard's Theology of the Feminine* (Berkeley, CA: University of California Press, 1987); Sabina Flanagan *Hildegard of Bingen, 1098–1179: A Visionary Life* (London and New York: Routledge, 1989); Elizabeth Dreyer, *Passionate Women: Two Medieval Mystics* (New York: Paulist Press, 1989); Mary Ford-Grabowsky, "Angels and Archetypes: A Jungian Approach to Saint Hildegard," *The American Benedictine Review* 41.1 (March 1990): 1–19; Karma Lochrie, "The Language of Transgression: Body, Flesh, and Word in Mystical Discourse," *Speaking Two Languages: Traditional Disciplines and Contemporary Theory in Medieval Studies*, ed. Allen J. Frantzen (Albany, NY: State University of New York Press, 1991); *The Ordo Virtutum of Hildegard of Bingen*, ed. Audrey Ekdahl Davidson (Kalamazoo, MI: Medieval Institute Publications, Western Michigan University, 1992); Ingeborg Ulrich, *Hildegard of Bingen: Mystic, Healer, Companion of Angels*, trans. Linda M. Maloney (Collegeville, MN: Liturgical Press, 1993). See also Kathryn Kirby-Fulton, "A Return to the 'First Dawn of Justice': Hildegard's Vision of Clerical Reform and the Eremitical Life," *American Benedictine Review* 40.4 (December 1989): 383–407; Helen J. John, "Hildegard of Bingen: A New Twelfth-Century Woman Philosopher?" *Hypatia: A Journal of Feminist Philosophy* 7.1 (winter 1992): 115–23; Ulrike Wiethaus, "Cathar Influences in Hildegard of Bingen's Play *Ordo Virtutum*," *American Benedictine Review* 38.2 (June 1987): 192–203. These studies describe Hildegard of Bingen's milieus (historical, cultural, monastic, social), the contexts for her works (literary, musical, dramatic), and her idiosyncratic capacities (mental, emotional, erotic, spiritual); she is considered in relation to the construction of categories (feminine, woman, and mother) by the male, patriarchal, or patristic culture in the Middle Ages and in relation to medieval constructions of the female body as fissured flesh, sealed body, or abject body.

45. De Certeau, *The Writing of History,* trans. Tom Conley (New York: Columbia University Press, 1988), p. 4.

46. Hugh of St. Victor quoted in de Certeau, *The Mystic Fable,* p. 93.

47. Bruce Hozeski, "*Ordo Virtutum:* Hildegard of Bingen's Liturgical Morality Play," *Annuale Medievale* 13 (1972): 45–69. There are different editions of *Ordo Virtutum.* The Latin text is easily available in Peter Dronke, *Poetic Individuality in the Middle Ages* (Oxford: Clarendon Press, 1970), pp. 180–92. The English version of the text can be found in, for example, Hozeski, 45–69. See also the performing edition, edited by Audrey Ekdahl Davidson (cited in n. 44). Subsequent references are in parentheses in text and are to Hozeski's translation.

48. See *Scivias,* part 3, visions 2 and 3, pp. 189–205.

49. See Potter's "The *Ordovirtutum:* Ancestor of the English Moralities?", "Sheingorn's" "The Virtues of Hildegard's *Ordo Virtutum;* or, it *was* a Woman's World," and Julia Bolton Holloway's "The Monastic Context of Hildegard's *Ordo Virtutum,*" *The Ordo Virtutum of Hildegard of Bingen,* pp. 31–41, 43–62, 63–77.

50. There are numerous editions of the *Jeu d'Adam,* which is also called *Ordo Representacionis Adae, The Play of Adam,* or *Le Mystère d'Adam.* See, for example, *The Service for Representing Adam, Medieval Drama,* ed. David Bevington (Boston, MA: Houghton Mifflin Co., 1975); *Le jeu d'Adam,* ed. Wolfgang van Emden (Edinburgh: British Rencesvals Publication, 1996); *The Play of Adam,* ed. Carl J. Odenkirchen (Brookline, MA: Classical Folia Editions, 1976); *Le jeu d'Adam,* ed. Willem Noomen (Paris: Champion, 1971).

51. See E. K. Chambers, *The Medieval Stage,* 2 vols. (London: Oxford University Press, 1903); Hardin Craig, *English Religious Drama of the Middle Ages* (Oxford: Clarendon Press, 1955); Hardison; Grace Frank, *The Medieval French Drama* (Oxford: Clarendon Press, 1954), pp. 74–84; Kenneth Urwin, "The 'Mystère d'Adam': Two Problems," *Modern Language Review* 34 (1939): 70–72; William Calin, "Structural and Doctrinal Unity in the *Jeu d'Adam,*" *Neophilologus* 46.4 (1962): 249–54; Joseph Dane, "Clerical Propaganda in Anglo-Norman *Adam,*" *Philological Quarterly* 62.2 (spring 1983): 241–51; Wendy Morgan, "'Who Was Then the Gentleman?': Social, Historical, and Linguistic Codes in the *Mystère d'Adam,*" *Studies in Philology* 79.2 (spring 1982): 101–21; Stephen Justice, "The Authority of Ritual in the *Jeu d'Adam,*" *Speculum* 62.4 (1987): 851–64.

52. Ibid., p. 851.

53. Ibid., p. 852.

54. Ibid., p. 852.

55. For scholarship referring to the staging of the *Jeu d'Adam* see Grace Frank, "The Genesis and Staging of the *Jeu d'Adam,*" *PMLA* 59 (1944): 7–17; Bruce McConachie, "The Staging of the *Jeu d'Adam,*" *Theatre Survey* 20.1 (May

1979): 27–42; Lynette Muir, *Liturgy and Drama in Anglo-Norman Adam* (Oxford: Basil Blackwell, 1973).

56. Bevington, 80; Odenkirchen, 43. Subsequent references to *Jeu d'Adam* will be indicated in parentheses in text by page numbers in these two volumes. The translations are quoted from Bevington's collection.

57. Morgan, p. 105.

58. Justice, p. 855.

59. *Decrees of the Ecumenical Councils,* ed. Norman P. Tanner, 2 vols. (London: Sheed and Ward, 1990), 1:224.

60. Morgan, p. 118.

61. Justice, p. 859.

62. See, for example, Calin, p. 250; Odenkirchen, p. 25.

63. Justice, p. 860.

64. Ibid., p. 861.

65. Ibid., p. 863.

66. *Scivias,* pp. 207–23.

67. Ibid., p. 207.

68. Ibid., p. 209.

Chapter 4

1. *Decrees of the Ecumenical Councils,* ed. Norman P. Tanner, 2 vols. (London: Sheed and Ward, 1990), 1:245. Subsequent citations refer to page numbers in this volume.

2. See chapters 1, 67–70, and [71]. On the contribution of the Fourth Lateran Council to defining the dogma of transubstantiation, there is disagreement among scholars. For example, Philip Schaff, Francis Dvornik, and Hubert Jedin imply that the council gave, for the first time, the ecclesiastical sanction to the term *transubstantiation,* whereas Gary Macy, using the works of Darwell Stone, Hans Jorrison, and James McCue for his support, suggests that chapter 1 offered no definition of the term and merely included terminology commonly used to assert the real presence of Christ in the Eucharist against the claims of the Cathars. For detailed discussion see Philip Schaff, *History of the Christian Church* (New York: Charles Scribner's Sons, 1910), pp. 174–79; Francis Dvornik, *The General Councils of the Church* (London: Burns and Oates, 1961), p. 55; Hubert Jedin, *Ecumenical Councils of the Catholic Church: An Historical Outline* (New York: Herder and Herder, 1960), pp. 78–80; Gary Macy, *The Theologies of the Eucharist in the Early Scholastic Period: A Study of the Salvific Function of the Sacrament according to the Theologians c. 1080–1220* (Oxford: Clarendon Press, 1984), p. 140.

3. See also *Patrologiae Cursus Completus, Series Latina,* ed. Jacques Paul Migne, 221 vols. (Paris: Garnier Fratres, 1894), 216:824 B.

4. Chapter 1 is a new profession of faith; chapters 2–3 deal with heretics

and contain dogmatic statements that would later justify the actions of the Inquisition; chapter 4 discusses the pride of Greeks toward Latins; chapter 5 deals with the dignity of patriarchs. Chapters 6–13 discuss the church's disciple; 14–22, the reform of clerical morals; 23–32, episcopal elections and the administration of benefices; 33–34, exaction of taxes; 35–49, canonical suits; 50–52, matrimony; 53–61, tithes; 62, saints' relics; 63–66, simony; 67–70, Jews.

5. For an insightful analysis of place and space see Michel de Certeau, *The Practice of Everyday Life,* trans. Steven Rendall (Berkeley, CA: University of California Press, 1984), pp. 115–30.

6. Michel de Certeau, *The Mystic Fable,* trans. Michael B. Smith (Chicago: University of Chicago Press, 1992), p. 16.

7. Macy, pp. 140–41.

8. *Gemma animae, Patrologiae,* 172:570 A; Saint Aelred of Rievaulx, *The Mirror of Love, The Medieval Mystics of England,* ed. Eric Colledge (New York: Charles Scribner's Sons, 1961); Hildegard of Bingen, *Scivias,* trans. Bruce Hozeski (Santa Fe, NM: Bear and Company, 1986) or trans. Mother Columba Hart and Jane Bishop (New York: Paulist Press, 1990).

9. James McCue, "The Doctrine of Transubstantiation from Berengar through the Council of Trent," *Lutherans and Catholics in Dialogue,* ed. Paul C. Empie and T. Austin Marphy, 3 vols. (Minneapolis, MN: Augsburg Publishing House, n.d.), 3:93.

10. See Michal Kobialka, "*Corpus Mysticum et Representationem:* Hildegard of Bingen's *Scivias* and *Ordo Virtutum,*" *Theatre Survey* 37.1 (May 1996): 1–22.

11. For the general information regarding the feast of Corpus Christi see Miri Rubin, *Corpus Christi: The Eucharist in Late Medieval Culture* (Cambridge: Cambridge University Press, 1991), chap. 3 and especially pp. 164–76.

12. See Peter Browe, *Die eucharistischen Wunder des Mittelalters* (Breslau: Verlag Müller and Seiffert, 1938), pp. 44–47. See also a groundbreaking study by Caroline Walker Bynum, *Fragmentation and Redemption: Essays on Gender and the Human Body in Medieval Religion* (New York: Zone Books, 1991), pp. 119–50, which illustrates the significance of women in the development of the eucharistic piety and devotion in the thirteenth century.

13. See, for example, Miri Rubin, "Corpus Christi: Inventing a Feast," *History Today* 40 (July 1990): 16.

14. For information about the Beguine communities see Rubin, *Corpus Christi,* pp. 167–69; Walter Simons, "Reading a Saint's Body: Rupture and Bodily Movement in the *Vitae* of Thirteenth-Century Beguines," *Framing Medieval Bodies,* ed. Sarah Kay and Miri Rubin (Manchester: Manchester University Press, 1994), pp. 10–23. The Beguine way of life was criticized in decree 16 of the Council of Vienna (1311–12): "We have heard from trustworthy sources that there are some Beguines who seem to be led by a particular insanity. They argue and preach on the holy Trinity and the divine essence, and express opinions contrary to the catholic faith with regard to the articles of faith

and the sacraments of the church. These Beguines thus ensnare many simple people, leading them into various errors. They generate numerous other dangers to souls under the cloak of sanctity. . . . With the approval of sacred council, we perpetually forbid their mode of living and remove it completely from the Church of God. We expressly enjoin on these and other women, under pain of excommunication to be incurred automatically, that they no longer follow this way of life under any form, even if they adopted it long ago, or take it up anew. . . . Of course we in no way intend by the foregoing to forbid any faithful women, . . . from living uprightly in their hospices, wishing to live a life of penance and serving the Lord of hosts in a spirit of humility. This they may do, as the Lord inspires them" (*Decrees of the Ecumenical Councils,* 1:374).

15. *Textus antiqui de festo Corporis Christi,* ed. Peter Browe (Münster: Typis Aschendorff, 1934), pp. 21–23; Rubin, *Corpus Christi,* p. 174.

16. See Dvornik, p. 66.

17. See *Textus antiqui de festo Corporis Christi,* p. 31; the English version can be found in V. A. Kolve, *The Play Called Corpus Christi* (Stanford, CA: Stanford University Press, 1966), p. 45.

18. Kolve, p. 46; Rubin, *Corpus Christi,* p. 185.

19. E. K. Chambers, *The Mediaeval Stage,* 2 vols. (Oxford: Clarendon Press, 1903); Hardin Craig, "The Corpus Christi Procession and the Corpus Christi Play," *Journal of English and Germanic Philology* 13 (1914): 589–602; O. B. Hardison, Jr., *Christian Rite and Christian Drama in the Middle Ages: Essays in the Origin and Early History of Modern Drama* (Baltimore, MD: Johns Hopkins University Press, 1965); Martin Stevens, "The York Cycle: From Procession to Play," *Leeds Studies in English* 6 (1972): 37–61; Margaret Dorrell, "Two Studies of the York Corpus Christi Play," *Leeds Studies in English* 6 (1972): 63–111; Stanley Kahrl, *Traditions of Medieval English Drama* (London: Hutchinson, 1974); Peter Travis, *Dramatic Design in the Chester Cycle* (Chicago: University of Chicago Press, 1982); Mervyn James, "Ritual, Drama, and Social Body in the Late Medieval English Town," *Past and Present* 98 (February 1983): 3–29; idem, *Society, Politics, and Culture: Studies in Early Modern England* (Cambridge: Cambridge University Press, 1986); Rubin, Corpus Christi; Theresa Coletti, "A Feminist Approach to the Corpus Christi Cycles," *Approaches to Teaching Medieval English Drama,* ed. Richard Emmerson (New York: Modern Language Association of America, 1990), pp. 78–89; idem, "Purity and Danger: The Paradox of Mary's Body and the Engendering of the Infancy Narrative in the English Mystery Cycles," *Feminist Approaches to the Body in Medieval Literature,* ed. Linda Lomperis and Sarah Stanbury (Philadelphia, PA: University of Pennsylvania Press, 1993), pp. 65–95; Alexandra Johnston, "All the World Was a Stage," *The Theatre of Medieval Europe,* ed. Eckehard Simon (Cambridge: Cambridge University Press, 1991); Ruth Evans, "Body Politics: Engendering Medieval Cycle Drama," *Feminist Readings in Middle English Literature: The Wife of Bath and All Her Sect,* ed. Ruth Evans and Lesley Johnson (London and New York: Routledge, 1994), pp. 112–39; Sarah Beckwith, "Ritual, Theater, and

Social Space in the York Corpus Christi Cycle," *Bodies and Disciplines: Intersections of Literature and History in Fifteenth-Century England,* ed. Barbara A. Hanawalt and David Wallace (Minneapolis, MN: University of Minnesota Press, 1996), pp. 63–86.

20. Rubin, "Corpus Christi: Inventing a Feast," p. 21. In response to the challenges posed to the sacrament of the Eucharist, session 13 of the Council of Trent (October 11, 1551) was devoted to establishing the decrees on the presence of Christ in the Sacrament that prohibited "all Christians from venturing to believe, teach or preach otherwise concerning the most holy eucharist than as has been explained and defined in the present decree." The following eight chapters of the session 13 of the Council of Trent discuss such matters as, for example, the real presence of Christ in the Sacrament, the reasons for its institution, its excellent qualities, transubstantiation, and the worship and reverence to be shown to this sacrament. Because, as it is stated, "it is not enough to declare the truth," the eight chapters are followed by the eleven canons so "all may understand which heresies they must guard against and avoid." See *Decrees of the Ecumenical Councils,* 2:693–98.

21. See Hardison, pp. 309–11, for the listing of the *Quem quaeritis* forms.

22. The Latin text of this Prague version of the *Quem quaeritis* can be found in Karl Young, *The Drama of the Medieval Church,* 2 vols. (Oxford: Clarendon Press, 1933), 1:403–4.

23. See Jean Leclerq, "Influence and Noninfluence of Dionysius in the Western Middle Ages," *Pseudo-Dionysius: The Complete Works,* trans. Colm Luibheid, with foreword, notes, and translation collaboration by Paul Rorem (New York: Paulist Press, 1987), pp. 25–32; de Certeau, *The Mystic Fable,* p. 9; Paul Rorem, *Pseudo-Dionysius: A Commentary on the Texts and an Introduction to Their Influence* (New York: Oxford University Press, 1993).

24. See *The Celestial Hierarchy, Pseudo-Dionysius: The Complete Works,* p. 145. Subsequent citations refer to page numbers in this volume.

25. See ibid., p. 199. Subsequent citations refer to page numbers in this volume.

26. See, for example, Suger of Saint-Denis, *On the Abbey Church of St.-Denis and Its Art Treasures,* edited, translated, and annotated by Erwin Panofsky (Princeton, NJ: Princeton University Press, 1946); Edward Foley, "St.-Denis Revisited: The Liturgical Evidence," *Revue Bénédictine* 100 (1990): 532–49; *Abbot Suger and Saint-Denis,* ed. Paula Gerson (New York: Metropolitan Museum of Art, 1986); Christopher Wilson, *The Gothic Cathedral* (London: Thames and Hudson, 1990), pp. 31–45.

27. Andrzej Piotrowski, "Architecture as Space of Representation," *Medieval Practices of Space,* ed. Barbara Hanawalt and Michal Kobialka (Minneapolis: University of Minnesota Press, forthcoming). In his investigation of the function of light in the mosaics of the church Hosios Loucas (Greece), Piotrowski suggests that light and space in this monastic house represent an ideological paradox. The mosaics depicting the biblical scenes translate the

sacred space into a conceptual one and define it in terms of physical matter; at the same time, all that which can be understood as matter loses its degree of materiality when light moves through it and, thus, creates the possibility for anagogical illumination.

28. Rubin, *Corpus Christi,* p. 37.

29. McCue in *Lutherans and Catholics in Dialogue,* pp. 101–2.

30. Please note that, with the focus on what is possible to be thinkable and expressed within a field, this investigation does not concern itself with the dominant interpretations of the emergence of medieval drama and theater that are grounded in the historical typology of Christ's passion. While interesting in their own right, they bring forth the notion of the dramatic representations of the Passion events that was triggered by the scriptural and liturgical dialogue of the angel and the Marys at the empty tomb. This is precisely what is not a guiding principle in these investigations.

31. See Foucault, *The Order of Things: An Archaeology of the Human Sciences* (New York: Random House, 1973), chap. 2, for a detailed discussion of the concept of resemblance.

Selected Bibliography

Manuscript Collections

British Library. MS ADD 37517 (Bosworth Psalter, ca. 980).
———. MS ADD 49598 (*Benedictional of St. Aethelwold,* ca. 973).
———. MS Arundel (Psalter, ca. 1060).
———. MS Cotton Caligula A XIV (Hereford Troper, ca. 1050).
———. MS Cotton Faustina B III (*Regularis concordia,* 970x973).
———. MS Cotton Tiberius A III (*Regularis concordia,* second half of the eleventh century).
———. MS Cotton Titus D XXVI and D XXVII (New Minster, 1023–35).
———. MS Cotton Vespasian A VIII (New Minster Charter, ca. 966).
———. MS Stowe 2 (Psalter, 1050–75).
———. MS Stowe 944 (New Minster Register, ca. 1031).

Articles in Journals

Aers, David. "Rewriting the Middle Ages: Some Suggestions." *Journal of Medieval and Renaissance Studies* 18 (1988): 221–40.

Badir, Patricia. "Representations of the Resurrection at Beverley Minster circa 1208: Chronicle, Play, Miracle." *Theatre Survey* 38.1 (May 1997): 9–41.

Bjork, David A. "On the Dissemination of the *Quem quaeritis* and the *Visitatio Sepulchri* and the Chronology of Their Early Sources." *Comparative Drama* 14 (spring 1980): 46–69.

Brown, Elizabeth. "The Tyranny of a Construct: Feudalism and Historians of Medieval Europe." *American Historical Review* 79 (October 1974): 1063–88.

Burr, D. "Scotus and Transubstantiation." *Medieval Studies* 34 (1972): 336–50.

Calin, William. "Structural and Doctrinal Unity in the *Jeu d'Adam.*" *Neophilologus* 46.4 (1962): 249–54.

Cambell, Thomas P. "Liturgy and Drama: Recent Approaches to Medieval Theatre." *Theatre Journal* 33 (October 1981): 289–301

Chadwick, Henry. "Ego Berengarius." *Journal of Theological Studies,* n.s., 40.2 (October 1989): 414–48.

Craig, Hardin. "The Corpus Christi Procession and the Corpus Christi Play." *Journal of English and Germanic Philology* 13 (1914): 589–602.

Dane, Joseph. "Clerical Propaganda in Anglo-Norman *Adam.*" *Philological Quarterly* 62.2 (spring 1983): 241–51.

Davril, Anselme. "Johan Drumbl and the Origin of the *Quem quaeritis:* A Review Article" *Comparative Drama* 20 (spring 1986): 65–75.

Deshman, Richard. "*Christus rex et magi reges:* Kingship and Christology in Ottonian and Anglo-Saxon Art." *Frühmittelalterliche Studien* 10 (1976): 367–405.

Dorrell, Margaret. "Two Studies of the York Corpus Christi Play." *Leeds Studies in English* 6 (1972): 63–111.

Evans, Paul. "Some Reflections on the Origin of the Trope." *Journal of the American Musicological Society* 14 (1961): 119–31.

Flanigan, C. Clifford. "Comparative Literature and the Study of Medieval Drama: Review of Scholarship." *Yearbook of Comparative and General Literature* 35 (1986): 56–104.

———. "The Liturgical Context of the *Quem quaeritis* Trope." *Comparative Drama* 8 (spring 1974): 45–62.

———. "The Liturgical Drama and Its Tradition: A Review of Scholarship, 1965–75." *Research Opportunities in Renaissance Drama* 18 (1975): 81–102; 19 (1976): 109–36.

Fleming, Robin. "Rural Elites and Urban Communities in Late Anglo-Saxon England." *Past and Present* 141 (November 1993): 26–29.

Foley, Edward. "St.-Denis Revisited: The Liturgical Evidence." *Revue Bénédictine* 100 (1990): 532–49.

Ford-Grabowsky, Mary. "Angels and Archetypes: A Jungian Approach to Saint Hildegard." *American Benedictine Review* 41.1 (March 1990): 1–19.

Frank, Grace. "The Genesis and Staging of the *Jeu d'Adam.*" *PMLA* 59 (1944): 7–17.

Frazee, Charles A. "Late Roman and Byzantine Legislation on the Monastic Life from the Fourth to the Eighth Centuries." *Church History* 51.3 (September 1982): 263–79.

———. "The Origin of Clerical Celibacy in the Western Church." *Church History* 41.2 (June 1972): 149–67.

Gamer, Helena. "Mimes, Musicians, and the Origin of the Medieval Religious Play." *Deutsche Beitrage zur geistigen Überlieferung* 5 (1965): 9–28.

Gibson, James M. "*Quem quaeritis in prespere:* Christmas Drama or Christmas Liturgy." *Comparative Drama* 15 (winter 1981–82): 343–65.

Goldstein, Leonard. "On the Origin of Medieval Drama." *Zeitschrift für Anglistik und Amerikanistik* 29 (1981): 101–15.

Gransden, Antonia. "Traditionalism and Continuity during the Last Century of Anglo-Saxon Monasticism." *Journal of Ecclesiastical History* 40.2 (April 1989): 159–207.

288

Grant, Gerard G. "The Elevation of the Host: A Reaction to Twelfth-Century Heresy." *Theological Studies* 1 (1940): 228–50.

Hozeski, Bruce. "*Ordo Virtutum:* Hildegard of Bingen's Liturgical Morality Play." *Annuale Medievale* 13 (1972): 45–69.

James, Mervyn. "Ritual, Drama, and Social Body in the Late Medieval English Town." *Past and Present* 98 (February 1983): 3–29.

Jeffrey, David L. "Franciscan Spirituality and the Rise of Early English Drama." *Mosaic* 8 (summer 1975): 17–46.

John, Eric. "The King and the Monks in the Tenth-Century Reformation." *Bulletin of the John Rylands Library* 42.1 (September 1959): 61–87.

———. "Some Latin Charters of the Tenth Century Reformation in England." *Revue Bénédictine* 70.2 (1960): 333–59.

———. "The Sources of the English Monastic Reformation: A Comment." *Revue Bénédictine* 70.1 (1960): 197–203.

John, Helen J. "Hildegard of Bingen: A New Twelfth-Century Woman Philosopher?" *Hypatia: A Journal of Feminist Philosophy* 7.1 (winter 1992): 115–23.

Justice, Stephen. "The Authority of Ritual in the *Jeu d'Adam.*" *Speculum* 62.4 (1987): 851–64.

Kennedy, V. L. "The Moment of Consecration and the Elevation of the Host." *Medieval Studies* 6 (1944): 121–50.

Kirby-Fulton, Kathryn. "A Return to the 'First Dawn of Justice': Hildegard's Vision of Clerical Reform and the Eremitical Life." *American Benedictine Review* 40.4 (December 1989): 383–407.

Klukas, Arnold William. "The Architectural Implications of the *Decreta Lanfranci.*" *Anglo-Norman Studies* 6 (1984): 136–71.

Kobialka, Michal. "*Corpus Mysticum et Representationem:* Hildegard of Bingen's *Scivias* and *Ordo Virtutum.*" *Theatre Survey* 37.1 (May 1996): 1–22.

———. "Theatre History: The Quest for Instabilities." *Journal of Dramatic Theory and Criticism* (spring 1989): 239–52.

Linke, Hansjürgen. "Drama und Theater des Mittelalters als Feldinterdisziplinarer Forschung." *Euphorion* 79 (1985): 43–65.

Marrow, James. "*Circumdederunt me canes multi:* Christ's Tormentors in Northern European Art of the Late Middle Ages and Early Renaissance." *Art Bulletin* 59 (June 1977): 167–81.

McConachie, Bruce. "The Staging of the *Jeu d'Adam.*" *Theatre Survey* 20.1 (May 1979): 27–42.

McGee, Timothy J. "The Liturgical Placement of the *Quem quaeritis* Dialogue." *Journal of the American Music Society* 29 (1976): 1–29.

Morgan, Wendy. "'Who Was Then the Gentleman?': Social, Historical, and Linguistic Codes in the *Mystère d'Adam.*" *Studies in Philology* 79.2 (spring 1982): 101–21.

Norton, Michael L. "Of 'Stages' and 'Types' in *Visitatione Sepulchri.*" *Comparative Drama* 21 (spring and summer 1987): 34–61, 127–41.

Pascal, R. "On the Origin of Liturgical Drama in the Middle Ages." *Modern Language Review* 36 (July 1941): 369–87.

Patterson, Lee. "On the Margin: Postmodernism, Ironic History, and Medieval Studies." *Speculum* 65.1 (January 1990): 87–108.

Payen, Jean-Charles. "Théâtre medieval et culture urbane." *Revue d'historie du théâtre* 35 (1983): 233–50.

Rankin, Susan. "Musical and Ritual Aspects of *Quem quaeritis.*" *Münchener Beitrage zur Mediavistik und Renaissanceforschung* 36 (1985): 181–92.

Roach, Joseph R. "Slave Spectacles and Tragic Octoroons: A Cultural Genealogy of Antebellum Performance." *Theatre Survey* 33.2 (November 1992): 167–87.

Robinson, J. W. "The Late Medieval Cult of Jesus and the Mystery Plays." *PMLA* 80 (1965): 508–14.

Rubin, Miri. "Corpus Christi: Inventing a Feast." *History Today* 40 (July 1990): 16.

Scolari, Massimo. "Elements for a History of Axonometry." *Architectural Design* 55.5/6 (1985): 72–78.

Sheerin, Daniel J. "The Dedication of the Old Minster in 980." *Revue Bénédictine* 88.3 (1978): 261–73.

Shrader, Charles R. "The False Attribution of an Eucharistic Tract to Gerbert of Aurillac." *Medieval Studies* 35 (1973): 178–204.

Stevens, Martin. "The York Cycle: From Procession to Play." *Leeds Studies in English* 6 (1972): 37–61.

Stiefel, Tina. "The Heresy of Science: A Twelfth-Century Conceptual Revolution." *Isis* 68.243 (September 1977): 347–62.

Sticca, Sandro. "Drama and Spirituality in the Middle Ages." *Medievalia and Humanistica* 4 (1973): 69–87.

Symons, Dom Thomas. "Sources of the *Regularis concordia.*" *Downside Review* 59 (January 1941): 14–36; 59 (April 1941): 143–70; 59 (July 1941): 264–89.

Urwin, Kenneth. "The 'Mystère d'Adam': Two Problems." *Modern Language Review* 34 (1939): 70–72.

Warning, Rainer. "On the Alterity of Medieval Religious Drama." *New Literary History* 10 (1979): 265–92.

Wiethaus, Ulrike. "Cathar Influences in Hildegard of Bingen's Play *Ordo Virtutum.*" *American Benedictine Review* 38.2 (June 1987): 192–203.

Woerdeman, Jude. "The Source of the Easter Play." *Orate Fratres* 20 (April 1946): 262–72.

Books

Abulafia, David, Franklin, Michael, and Rubin, Miri, eds. *Church and City: 1000–1500.* Cambridge: Cambridge University Press, 1992.

Aers, David. *Community, Gender, and Individual Identity*. London and New York: Routledge, 1988.

———. *Medieval Literature: Criticism, Ideology, and History*. Brighton, Sussex: Harvester Press, 1986.

———, ed. *Culture and History: 1350–1600*. Hemel Hempstead, Great Britain: Harvester Wheatsheaf, 1992.

Ambrose, Saint. *De sacramentis*. Vol. 16:435–74. *Patrologiae Cursus Completus, Series Latina*. Ed. Jacque Paul Migne. 221 vols. Paris: Garnier Fratres, 1884.

Andersen, Flemming F., ed. *Medieval Iconography and Narrative*. Odense, Denmark: Odense University Press, 1980.

Anderson, Mary Desiree. *Drama and Imagery in English Medieval Churches*. Cambridge: Cambridge University Press, 1963.

Anglo-Norman Studies. Vol. 6: Proceedings of the Battle Conference. Ed. R. Allen Brown. Vol. 6. Woodbridge, Suffolk: Boydell Press, 1984.

Anglo-Saxon England. Ed. Michael Lapidge et al. Vols. 21 and 24. Cambridge: Cambridge University Press, 1992, 1995.

Anselm, Saint. *Cur Deus Homo*. Vol. 158:359–432. *Patrologiae Cursus Completus, Series Latina*. Ed. Jacque Paul Migne. 221 vols. Paris: Garnier Fratres, 1884.

———. *The Letters of Saint Anselm of Canterbury*. Translated and annotated by Walter Fröhlich. 2 vols. Kalamazoo, MI: Cistercian Publications, 1993.

———. *Monologion*. Vol. 158:169–223. *Patrologiae Cursus Completus, Series Latina*. Ed. Jacque Paul Migne. 221 vols. Paris: Garnier Fratres, 1884.

———. *A New, Interpretative Translation of St. Anselm's Monologion and Proslogion*. Ed. and trans. Jasper Hopkins. Minneapolis, MN: Arthur J. Banning Press, 1986.

———. *The Prayers and Meditations of Saint Anselm with the Proslogion*. Translated with an introduction by Sister Benedicta Ward, with a foreword by R. W. Southern. London: Penguin Books, 1988.

———. *Proslogion*. Vol. 158:223–38. *Patrologiae Cursus Completus, Series Latina*. Ed. Jacque Paul Migne. 221 vols. Paris: Garnier Fratres, 1884.

———. *St. Anselm's Proslogion*. Translated with an introduction and philosophical commentary by M. J. Charlesworth. Oxford: Clarendon Press, 1965.

———. *Why God Became Man*. Trans. Joseph Colleran. Albany, NY: Magi Books, 1969.

Aristotle. *The Complete Works of Aristotle*. Ed. Jonathan Barnes. Princeton, NJ: Princeton University Press, 1984.

Aronowitz, Stanley. *Science as Power*. Minneapolis, MN: University of Minnesota Press, 1988.

Asser. *Alfred the Great*. Ed. and trans. Simon Keynes and Michael Lapidge. Harmondsworth, Middlesex: Penguin, 1983.

———. *Life of King Alfred*. Trans. Albert S. Cook. London: Ginn, 1906.

Augustine, Saint. *The Confessions of Saint Augustine*. Trans. E. M. Blaiklock. Nashville, TN: Thomas Nelson, 1983.

Axton, Richard. *European Drama of the Early Middle Ages.* London: Hutchinson, 1974.

Aylett, John F. *In Search of History.* London: Edward Arnold, 1985.

Bachrach, Bernard S., and Nicholas, David, eds. *Law, Custom, and the Social Fabric in Medieval Europe.* Kalamazoo, MI: Western Michigan University, 1990.

Bailey, Mark. *A Marginal Economy.* Cambridge: Cambridge University Press, 1989.

Barlow, Frank. *The English Church, 1000–1066.* London: Longman, 1979.

Barrol, J. Leeds, III, ed. *Medieval and Renaissance Drama in England: An Annual Gathering of Research, Criticism, and Reviews.* New York: AMS Press, 1984.

Barstow, Anne Llewellyn. *Married Priests and the Reforming Papacy.* New York: E. Mellen Press, 1982.

Barthes, Roland. *The Rustle of Language.* Trans. Richard Howard. New York: Hill and Wang, 1986.

Baumstark, Anton. *Comparative Liturgy.* English edition by F. L. Cross. London: A. R. Mowbray and Co., 1958.

Beckwith, Sarah. *Christ's Body: Identity, Culture, and Society in Late Medieval Writing.* London and New York: Routledge, 1993.

Bellamy, John. *Crime and Public Order in the Late Middle Ages.* London: Routledge and Kegan Paul, 1973.

Benedict, Saint. *The Rule of Saint Benedict.* Trans. Dom Justin McCann. England: Stanbrook Abbey Press, 1937.

———. *The Rule of Saint Benedict.* Trans. John Baptist Hasbrouck. Kalamazoo, MI: Cistercian Publications, 1983.

Benson, Robert L., and Constable, Giles, eds. *Renaissance and Renewal in the Twelfth Century.* Cambridge, MA: Harvard University Press, 1982.

Bettenson, Henry, ed. *Documents of the Christian Church.* London: Oxford University Press, 1963.

Bevington, David, ed. *Medieval Drama.* Boston, MA: Houghton Mifflin Co., 1975.

Biddick, Kathleen. *The Other Economy.* Berkeley, CA: University of California Press, 1989.

Biddle, Martin. *Object and Economy in Medieval Winchester.* 2 vols. Oxford: Clarendon Press, 1990.

———, ed. *Winchester in the Early Middle Ages.* Oxford: Clarendon Press, 1976.

Binns, Alison. *Dedications of Monastic Houses in England.* Woodbridge, Suffolk: Boydell Press, 1989.

———. *An Introduction to Anglo-Saxon England.* Cambridge: Cambridge University Press, 1977.

Blakiston, John Milburn George. *Winchester Cathedral.* Winchester: Friends of Winchester Cathedral, 1970.

Blatchford, Ambrose N. *Church Councils and Their Decrees.* London: Philip Green, 1909.

Bloch, Marc. *Feudal Society.* Chicago: University of Chicago Press, 1962.

Bloch, R. Howard, and Nichols, Stephen G., eds. *Medievalism and the Modernist Temper.* Baltimore, MD: Johns Hopkins University Press, 1996.

Bolton, James Lawrence. *The Medieval English Economy: 1150–1500.* London: J. M. Dent, 1980.

Bourdieu, Pierre. *Distinction: A Social Critique of the Judgement of Taste.* Trans. Richard Nice. Cambridge, MA: Harvard University Press, 1984.

Boussard, Jacques. *The Civilization of Charlemagne.* New York: McGraw-Hill Book Co., 1968.

Boyd, Catherine. *Titles and Parishes in Medieval Italy.* Ithaca, NY: Cornell University Press, 1952.

Briscoe, Marianne G., and Coldewey, John C. *Contexts for Early English Drama.* Bloomington, IN: Indiana University Press, 1989.

Brockett, Oscar G. *History of the Theatre.* 7th ed. Boston, MA: Alleyn and Bacon, 1982.

Brooke, Christopher Nugent Lawrence. *Medieval Church and Society.* New York: New York University Press, 1972.

———. *The Structure of Medieval Society.* London: Thames and Hudson, 1971.

Browe, Peter. *Die eucharistischen Wunder des Mittelalters.* Breslau: Verlag Müller and Seiffert, 1938.

Brown, Peter. *The Rise of Western Christendom: Triumph and Diversity, A.D. 200–1000.* Cambridge, MA: Blackwell, 1996.

Brownlee, Kevin, Brownlee, Marina, and Nichols, Stephen G., eds. *The New Medievalism.* Baltimore, MD: Johns Hopkins University Press, 1991.

Bryan, George. *Ethelwold and Medieval Music-Drama at Winchester.* Bern: Peter Lang, 1981.

Burns, James Henderson, ed. *The Cambridge History of Medieval Political Thought.* Cambridge: Cambridge University Press, 1988.

Bussby, Frederick. *Winchester Cathedral.* Southampton: Paul Cave, 1979.

Butler, James H. *The Theatre and Drama of Greece and Rome.* San Francisco, CA: Chandler Publishing Co., 1972.

Bynum, Caroline Walker. *Fragmentation and Redemption: Essays in Gender and the Human Body in Medieval Religion.* New York: Zone Books, 1991.

———. *The Resurrection of the Body in Western Christianity, 200–1336.* New York: Columbia University Press, 1995.

Cabaniss, Allen. *Liturgy and Literature.* University City, AL: University of Alabama Press, 1970.

Campbell, James. *The Anglo-Saxons.* Ithaca, NY: Cornell University Press, 1982.

Cantor, Norman F. *Inventing the Middle Ages.* New York: William Morrow and Co., 1991.

Cargill, Oscar. *Drama and Liturgy.* New York: Octagon Books, 1969.

Carolingian Chronicles: Royal Frankish Annals and Nithard's Histories. Trans. Bernhard Walter Scholz. Ann Arbor, MI: University of Michigan Press, 1970.

Carruthers, Mary. *The Book of Memory: A Study of Memory in Medieval Culture.* Cambridge: Cambridge University Press, 1990.

Cartularium Saxonicum: A Collection of Charters Relating to Anglo-Saxon History. Ed. Walter de Gray Birch. 3 vols. London: Charles J. Clark, 1893.

Chambers, E. K. [Edmund Kerchever]. *The Mediaeval Stage.* 2 vols. Oxford: Clarendon Press, 1903.

Chance, Jane. *Gender and Text in Later Middle Ages.* Gainsville, FL: University Presses of Florida, 1996.

Chapman, T. *Time: A Philosophical Analysis.* Dordrecht, Holland: D. Reidel Publishing Co., 1982.

Chartier, Roger. *Cultural History.* Ithaca, NY: Cornell University Press, 1988.

Chenu, Marie Dominique. *Nature, Man, and Society in the Twelfth Century.* Chicago: University of Chicago Press, 1968.

Chronicon Monasterii de Abington. Ed. Joseph Stevenson. Vol. 2. *Rerum Britannicarum medii aevi scriptores, or Chronicles and Memorials of Great Britain and Ireland during the Middle Ages.* 99 vols. London: Longman, 1858.

Claster, Jill N. *The Medieval Experience: 300–1400.* New York: New York University Press, 1982.

Clemoes, Peter, ed. *Anglo-Saxon England.* Cambridge: Cambridge University Press, 1974.

Clogan, Paul Maurice, ed. *Medievalia et Humanistica.* Cambridge: Cambridge University Press, 1975.

Cohen, Gustave. *La théâtre en France au moyen âge.* Paris: Reider, 1931.

Colledge, Eric, ed. *The Medieval Mystics of England.* New York: Charles Scribner's Sons, 1961.

Constable, Giles. *Medieval Monasticism: Bibliography.* Toronto: University of Toronto Press, 1976.

Consuetudinum Saeculi x/xi/xii Monumenta non-Cluniacensia. Ed. Kassius Hallinger. Corpus Consuetudinum Monasticarum, t. 7 pars. 3. Siegburg: Franz Schmitt, 1984.

Craig, Hardin. *English Religious Drama.* Oxford: Clarendon Press, 1955.

Crawford, Samuel John, ed. *Byrhtferth's Manual.* London: Oxford University Press, 1929.

D'Ancona, Alessandro. *Origini del teatro italiano.* 2 vols. Turin: Ermanno Loerscher, 1891.

Davidson, Audrey Ekdahl, ed. *The Ordo Virtutum of Hildegard of Bingen.* Kalamazoo, MI: Medieval Institute Publications, Western Michigan University, 1992.

Davidson, Clifford. *Illustrations of the Stage and Acting in England to 1580.* Kalamazoo, MI: Medieval Institute Publications, Western Michigan University, 1991.

———, ed. *Word, Picture, and Spectacle.* Kalamazoo, MI: Medieval Institute Publications, Western Michigan University, 1984.

Davidson, Clifford, and Stroupe, John H., eds. *Drama in the Middle Ages: Comparative and Critical Essays.* New York: AMS Press, 1991.

Davis, R. H. C., and Wallace-Hadrill, J. M., eds. *The Writing of History in the Middle Ages.* Oxford: Clarendon Press, 1981.

Day, John. *The Medieval Market Economy.* Oxford: Basil Blackwell, 1987.

Deansley, Margaret. *History of the Medieval Church.* 8th ed. London: Methuen, 1954.

———. *The Pre-Conquest Church in England.* London: A. and C. Black, 1963.

de Boor, Helmut. *Die Textgeschichte der lateinischen Osterfeiern.* Tübingen: Niemeyer, 1967.

de Certeau, Michel. *Heterologies: Discourse on the Other.* Trans. Brian Massumi, with a foreword by Wlad Godzich. Minneapolis, MN: University of Minnesota Press, 1986.

———. *The Mystic Fable.* Trans. Michael B. Smith. Chicago: University of Chicago Press, 1992.

———. *The Practice of Everyday Life.* Trans. Steven Rendall. Berkeley, CA: University of California Press, 1984.

———. *The Writing of History.* Trans. Tom Conley. New York: Columbia University Press, 1988.

Delany, Sheila. *Medieval Literary Politics: Shapes of Ideology.* Manchester: Manchester University Press, 1990.

Deleuze, Gilles. *The Deleuze Reader.* Edited with an introduction by Constantin V. Boundas. New York: Columbia University Press, 1993.

Diller, Hans-Jürgen. *Redeformen des englischen Misterienspiels.* Munich: Fink, 1973.

Dolan, Diane. *Le drame liturgique de Paques en Normandie et en Anglettere au moyen âge.* Paris: Presses Universitaires de France, 1975.

Dreyer, Elizabeth. *Passionate Women: Two Medieval Mystics.* New York: Paulist Press, 1989.

Dronke, Peter. *Poetic Individuality in the Middle Ages.* Oxford: Clarendon Press, 1970.

Drumbl, Johann. *Quem quaeritis: Teatro sacro dell'alto medioevo.* Roma: Bulzoni, 1981.

Duby, Georges. *The Early Growth of the European Economy.* London: Weidenfeld and Nicolson, 1974.

Duchesne, Louis Marie Olivier. *Christian Worship: Its Origin and Evolution.* Trans. M. L. McClure. London: Society for Promoting Christian Knowledge, 1903.

Dumoutet, Édouard. *Corpus Domini aux sources de la piete eucharistique medievale.* Paris: Gabriel Beauchesne, 1942.

———. *Le désir de voir l'hostie.* Paris: Gabriel Beauchesne, 1926.

Dunn, E. Catherine. *The Gallican Saint's Life and the Late Roman Dramatic Tradition.* Washington, DC: Catholic University of America Press, 1989.

Dunne, John Scriber. *Time and Myth.* London: University of Notre Dame, 1975.

Durand of Troarn. *De corpore et sanguine Domini.* Vol. 149:1375–1424. *Patrologiae Cursus Completus, Series Latina.* Ed. Jacque Paul Migne. 221 vols. Paris: Garnier Fratres, 1884.

Dvornik, Francis. *The General Councils of the Church.* London: Burns and Oates, 1961.

Eadmer. *Historia novorum in Anglia, et opuscula duo de vita Sancti Anselmi et quibusdam miraculis ejus.* Ed. Martin Rule. Vol. 81. *Rerum Britannicarum medii aevi scriptores, or Chronicles and Memorials of Great Britain and Ireland during the Middle Ages.* 99 vols. London: Longman, 1884.

———. *History of Recent Events in England.* Trans. Geoffrey Bosanquet. London: Cresset Press, 1964.

———. *The Life of Saint Anselm.* Ed. Richard William Southern. London: Thomas Nelson and Sons, 1962.

Eales, Richard, and Sharpe, Richard, eds. *Canterbury and the Norman Conquest: Churches, Saints, and Scholars, 1066–1109.* London: Hambledon Press, 1995.

Elder, Rozanne, ed. *The Spirituality of Western Christendom.* Kalamazoo, MI: Cistercian Publications, 1976.

Eliade, Mircea. *The Myth of the Eternal Return.* Trans. Willard Trask. New York: Pantheon Books, 1954.

Else, Gerald. *The Origin and the Early Form of Greek Tragedy.* Cambridge, MA: Harvard University Press, 1967.

Emden, Wolfgang van, ed. *Le jeu d'Adam.* Edinburgh: British Rencesvals Publication, 1996.

Emilsson, Eyjólfur Kjalar. *Plotinus on Sense Perception.* Cambridge: Cambridge University Press, 1988.

Emmerson, Richard, ed. *Approaches to Teaching Medieval English Drama.* New York: Modern Language Association of America, 1990.

Empie, Paul C., and Marphy, T. Austin, eds. *Lutherans and Catholics in Dialogue.* 3 vols. Minneapolis, MN: Augsburg Publishing House, n.d.

Enders, Jody. *Rhetoric and the Origins of Medieval Drama.* Ithaca, NY: Cornell University Press, 1992.

English Historical Documents. Vol. 1: *500–1042.* Ed. Dorothy Whitelock. London: Eyre and Spottiswoode, 1955.

English Historical Documents. Vol. 2: *1042–1189.* Ed. David C. Douglas. London: Eyre and Spottiswoode, 1953.

Eusebius Bruno. *Ad Berengarium Magistrum, de sacramento Eucharistiae.* Vol. 147:1201–4. *Patrologiae Cursus Completus, Series Latina.* Ed. Jacque Paul Migne. 221 vols. Paris: Garnier Fratres, 1884.

Evans, Gillian Rosemary. *Anselm and a New Generation.* Oxford: Clarendon Press, 1980.

Evans, Joan. *Monastic Life at Cluny, 910–1157.* London: Oxford University Press, 1931.

Evans, Ruth, and Johnson, Lesley, eds. *Feminist Readings in Middle English Literature: The Wife of Bath and All Her Sect.* London and New York: Routledge, 1994.

Flanagan, Sabina. *Hildegard of Bingen, 1098–1179: A Visionary Life.* London and New York: Routledge, 1989.

Fletcher, Collins. *The Production of Medieval Church Music-Drama: A Repertory of Complete Plays.* Charlottesville, VA: University Press of Virginia, 1972.

Folz, Robert. *The Coronation of Charlemagne.* Trans. J. E. Anderson. London: Routledge and Kegan Paul, 1974.

Foucault, Michel. *The Archaeology of Knowledge and the Discourse on Language.* Trans. A. M. Sheridan Smith. New York: Random House, 1972.

———. *The Order of Things: An Archaeology of the Human Sciences.* New York: Random House, 1973.

Frank, Grace. *The Medieval French Drama.* Oxford: Clarendon Press, 1954.

Frantzen, Allen J., ed. *Speaking Two Languages: Traditional Disciplines and Contemporary Theory in Medieval Studies.* Albany, NY: State University of New York Press, 1991.

Frappell, L. D., ed. *Principalities, Powers, and Estates.* Adelaide: Adelaide University Press, 1979.

Furley, John Sampson. *City Government of Winchester.* Oxford: Clarendon Press, 1923.

Gardiner, Harold. *Mysterie's End.* New Haven, CT: Yale University Press, 1946.

Gasquet, Francis Aidan. *Monastic Life in the Middle Ages.* London: Bell and Sons, 1922.

Gem, Harvey S. *An Anglo-Saxon Abbot, Aelfric of Eynsham.* Edinburgh: T. and T. Clark, 1912.

Gerson, Paula, ed. *Abbot Suger and Saint-Denis.* New York: Metropolitan Museum of Art, 1986.

Gibson, Gail McMurray. *The Theater of Devotion: East Anglian Drama and Society in the Late Middle Ages.* Chicago: University of Chicago Press, 1989.

Gibson, Margaret. *Lanfranc of Bec.* Oxford: Clarendon Press, 1978.

Gilchrist, Roberta, and Mytum, Harold, eds. *The Archaeology of Rural Monasteries.* British Series 203. Oxford: British Archaeological Reports, 1989.

Gilson, Etienne Henry. *History of Christian Philosophy in the Middle Ages.* New York: Random House, 1955.

Godfrey, John. *The Church in Anglo-Saxon England.* Cambridge: Cambridge University Press, 1962.

Goodman, Arthur Worthington. *Chartulary of Winchester Cathedral.* Winchester: Warren and Son, 1927.

Greenblatt, Stephen, and Gunn, Giles, eds. *Redrawing the Boundaries: The Transformation of English and American Literary Studies.* New York: The Modern Language Association of America, 1992.

Grosz, Elizabeth. *Space, Time, and Perversion: Essays on the Politics of Bodies.* London and New York: Routledge, 1995.

Guibert of Nogent-sous-Coucy. *De sanctis et eorum pignoribus.* Vol. 156:607–80. *Patrologiae Cursus Completus, Series Latina.* Ed. Jacque Paul Migne. 221 vols. Paris: Garnier Fratres, 1884.

Guitmund of Aversa. *De corporis et sanguinis Christi veritate in eucharistia.* Vol. 149:1427–94. *Patrologiae Cursus Completus, Series Latina.* Ed. Jacque Paul Migne. 221 vols. Paris: Garnier Fratres, 1884.

Haddan, Arthur West, and Stubbs, William. *Councils and Ecclesiastical Documents Relating to Great Britain and Ireland.* 3 vols. Oxford: Clarendon Press, 1869–78.

Hamelin, Jeanne. *Le théâtre chretien.* Paris: Librairie A. Fayard, 1967.

Hanawalt, Barbara A., and Wallace, David, eds. *Bodies and Disciplines: Intersections of Literature and History in Fifteenth-Century England.* Minneapolis, MN: University of Minnesota Press, 1996.

Hanning, Robert. *The Vision of History in Early Britain.* New York: Columbia University Press, 1966.

Hardison, O. B. [Osborne Bennett], Jr. *Christian Rite and Christian Drama in the Middle Ages: Essays in the Origin and Early History of Modern Drama.* Baltimore, MD: Johns Hopkins University Press, 1965.

Harrison, Jane Ellen. *Themis: A Study of the Social Origins of Greek Religion.* Cambridge: Cambridge University Press, 1912.

Hart, C. R. *The Early Charters of Northern England and the North Midlands.* Studies in Early English History 6. Leicester: Leicester University Press, 1975.

Harvey, Barbara. *Monastic Dress in the Middle Ages.* Canterbury: Trustees of the William Urry Memorial Fund, Chapter Library of Canterbury Church, 1988.

Haslam, Jeremy, ed. *Anglo-Saxon Towns in Southern England.* Chichester, Sussex: Phillimore, 1984.

Hegel. *Philosophy of Mind.* Foreword by J. N. Findlay. Oxford: Clarendon Press, 1971.

Herrin, Judith. *The Formation of Christendom.* Princeton, NJ: Princeton University Press, 1987.

Hildegard of Bingen. *Book of Divine Works.* Edited with an introduction by Matthew Fox. Santa Fe, NM: Bear and Co., 1987.

———. *Scivias.* Trans. Bruce Hozeski. Santa Fe, NM: Bear and Co., 1986.

———. *Scivias.* Trans. Mother Columba Hart and Jane Bishop. New York: Paulist Press, 1990.

Hilton, Rodney. *Class Conflict and the Crisis of Feudalism.* London: Hambledon Press, 1985.

Historians of the Church of York and Its Archbishops. Ed. James Raine. Vol. 71. *Rerum Britannicarum medii aevi scriptores, or Chronicles and Memorials of Great Britain and Ireland during the Middle Ages.* 99 vols. London: Longman, 1879.

Hodkin, Robert Howard. *History of the Anglo-Saxons.* 2 vols. London: Oxford University Press, 1935.

Hollister, C. Warren. *The Twelfth-Century Renaissance.* New York: John Wiley and Sons, 1969.

Honorius Augustodunensis. *Elucidarium.* Vol. 172:1109–76. *Patrologiae Cursus Completus, Series Latina.* Ed. Jacque Paul Migne. 221 vols. Paris: Garnier Fratres, 1884.

———. *Eucharisticon.* Vol. 172:1249–58. *Patrologiae Cursus Completus, Series Latina.* Ed. Jacque Paul Migne. 221 vols. Paris: Garnier Fratres, 1884.

———. *Gemma animae.* Vol. 172:541–738. *Patrologiae Cursus Completus, Series Latina.* Ed. Jacque Paul Migne. 221 vols. Paris: Garnier Fratres, 1884.

Hughes, Andrew. *Medieval Manuscripts for Mass and Office.* Toronto: University of Toronto Press, 1982.

Hunningher, Benjamin. *The Origin of the Theatre.* New York: Hill and Wang, 1961.

Hunt, Noreen. *Cluny Under Saint Hugh: 1049–1109.* London: Edward Arnold, 1967.

Hunter Blair, Peter. *An Introduction to Anglo-Saxon England.* Cambridge: Cambridge University Press, 1962.

James, Mervyn. *Society, Politics, and Culture: Studies in Early Modern England.* Cambridge: Cambridge University Press, 1986.

Jedin, Hubert. *Ecumenical Councils of the Catholic Church: An Historical Outline.* New York: Herder and Herder, 1960.

John, Eric. *Orbis Brittanniae and Other Studies.* Leicester: Leicester University Press, 1966.

Jungmann, Joseph A. *The Mass of the Roman Rite.* 2 vols. New York: Bonzinger Bros., 1950.

Kahrl, Stanley. *Traditions of Medieval English Drama.* London: Hutchinson, 1974.

Kay, Sarah, and Rubin, Miri, eds. *Framing Medieval Bodies.* Manchester: Manchester University Press, 1994.

Keene, Derek. *Survey of Medieval Winchester.* 2 vols. Oxford: Clarendon Press, 1985.

Kitto, Humphrey Davy Findley. *Greek Tragedy.* London: Methuen, 1954.

Knowles, David. *The Christian Centuries.* 2 vols. New York: McGraw-Hill Book Co., 1968.

———. *The Evolution of Medieval Thought.* London: Longman, 1962.

———. *The Monastic Order in England.* Cambridge: Cambridge University Press, 1950.

———. *The Religious Houses of Medieval England.* London: Sheed and Ward, 1940.

———, trans. *The Monastic Constitutions of Lanfranc.* London: Thomas Nelson and Sons, 1951.

Knowles, David, and Hadcock, Neville R. *Medieval Religious Houses: England and Wales.* London: Longman, 1971.

Knudsen, Hans. *Deutsche Theatergeschichte.* Stuttgart: Alfred Kroner Verlag, 1959.

Kolve, V. A. *The Play Called Corpus Christi.* Stanford, CA: Stanford University Press, 1966.

Kratzmann, Gregory, and Simpson, James, eds. *Medieval English Religious and Ethical Literature.* Cambridge: D. S. Brewer, 1986.

Kuttner, Stephen. *The History of Ideas and Doctrines of Canon Law in the Middle Ages.* London: Variorum Reprints, 1980.

———. *Medieval Councils, Decretals, and Collections of Canon Law.* London: Variorum Reprints, 1980.

Laing, Lloyd Robert, and Laing, Jennifer. *Anglo-Saxon England.* London: Routledge and Kegan Paul, 1979.

Lanfranc. *De corpore et sanguine domini.* Vol. 150:407–42. *Patrologiae Cursus Completus, Series Latina.* Ed. Jacque Paul Migne. 221 vols. Paris: Garnier Fratres, 1884.

———. *The Letters of Lanfranc, Archbishop of Canterbury.* Ed. Helen Clover and Margaret Gibson. Oxford: Oxford University Press, 1979.

Lapidge, Michael, Gneuss, Helmut, and Clemoes, Peter, eds. *Learning and Literature in Anglo-Saxon England.* Cambridge: Cambridge University Press, 1985.

Lawrence, Clifford Hugh. *Medieval Monasticism.* London: Longman, 1989.

Lea, Henry Charles. *History of Sacerdotal Celibacy in the Christian Church.* New York: University Books, 1966.

Levison, W. *England and the Continent in the Eighth Century.* Oxford: Clarendon Press, 1946.

Lipphardt, Walther. *Lateinische Osterfeiern und Osterspiele.* 6 vols. Berlin and New York: Walter de Gruyter, 1975–81.

Lomperis, Linda, and Stanbury, Sarah, eds. *Feminist Approaches to the Body in Medieval Literature.* Philadelphia, PA: University of Pennsylvania Press, 1993.

Loyn, Henry Royston, and Percival, John. *The Reign of Charlemagne: Documents on Carolingian Government and Administration.* New York: St. Martin's Press, 1975.

Luard, Henry Richard, ed. *Annales Monastici.* 5 vols. London: Rerum Britannicarum Mediiaevi Scriptores, 1958.

Lyotard, Jean-François. *The Postmodern Condition: A Report on Knowledge.* Trans. Geoff Bennington and Brian Massumi, with a foreword by Frederic Jameson. Minneapolis, MN: University of Minnesota Press, 1988.

———. *The Differend: Phrases in Dispute.* Trans. Georges van den Abbeele. Minneapolis, MN: University of Minnesota Press, 1990.

———. *Postmodern Fables.* Trans. Gerges van den Abbeele. Minneapolis, MN: University of Minnesota Press, 1997.

MacDonald, Allan John. *Lanfranc.* London: Oxford University Press, 1926.

———. *Berengar and the Reform of Sacramental Doctrine.* London: Longman, 1930.

Macy, Gary. *The Theologies of the Eucharist in the Early Scholastic Period: A Study of the Salvific Function of the Sacrament according to the Theologians c. 1080–1220.* Oxford: Clarendon Press, 1984.

Mann, Horace K. *The Lives of the Popes in the Early Middle Ages.* 18 vols. London: Kegan Paul, Trench, Trubner, 1906–32.

Marenbon, John. *Early Medieval Philosophy.* London: Routledge and Kegan Paul, 1983.

Markus, R. A. [Robert Austin]. *Gregory the Great and His World.* Cambridge: Cambridge University Press, 1997.

Marrow, James H. *Passion Iconography in Northern European Art.* Belgium: Van Ghemmert, 1979.

Mayo, Janet. *A History of Ecclesiastical Dress.* London: B. T. Batsford, 1984.

McGinn, Bernard, and Meyendorff, John, eds. *Christian Spirituality: Origins to the Twelfth Century.* New York: Crossroad, 1985.

McIntyre, John. *Saint Anselm and His Critics.* Edinburgh: Oliver and Boyd, 1954.

Medieval Art and Architecture at Winchester Cathedral. British Archaeological Association Conference Transactions for the Year 1980. Leeds: W. S. Maney and Son, 1983.

Memorials of St. Dunstan, Archbishop of Canterbury. Ed. William Stubbs. Vol. 63. *Rerum Britannicarum medii aevi scriptores, or Chronicles and Memorials of Great Britain and Ireland during the Middle Ages.* 99 vols. London: Longman, 1874.

Milgeler, Albert. *Mutations of Western Christianity.* Trans. Edward Quinn. London: Burns and Oates, 1964.

Miller, Edward, and Hatcher, John. *Medieval England: Rural Society and Economic Change, 1086–1348.* London: Longman, 1978.

Monastic Agreement of the Monks and Nuns of the English Nation, The. Translated with an introduction and notes by Dom Thomas Symons. London: Thomas Nelson and Sons, 1953.

Monumenta Annonis. Ed. Anton Legner. Cologne: Greven and Bechtold, 1975.

Morrison, Karl F. *History as a Visual Art in the Twelfth-Century Renaissance.* Princeton, NJ: Princeton University Press, 1990.

Morson, John, ed. *Le sacrament de l'autel.* Sources chrétiennes 94. Paris: Editiones du Cerf, 1963.

Mourret, Fernand. *A History of the Catholic Church.* 8 vols. St. Louis, MO: B. Herder Book Co., 1946.

Murdoch, John Emery, and Sylla, Edith Dudley. *The Cultural Context of Medieval Learning.* Dordrecht: D. Reidel Publishing Co., 1975.

Muir, Lynette. *The Biblical Drama of Medieval Europe.* Cambridge: Cambridge University Press, 1995.

————. *Liturgy and Drama in Anglo-Norman Adam.* Oxford: Basil Blackwell, 1973.

Nagler, Alois M. *The Medieval Religious Stage.* New Haven, CT: Yale University Press, 1976.

Newman, Barbara. *Sister of Wisdom: St. Hildegard's Theology of the Feminine.* Berkeley, CA: University of California Press, 1987.

Nichols, Stephen. *Romanesque Signs: Early Medieval Narrative and Iconography.* New Haven, CT: Yale University Press, 1983.

Noble, Thomas, and Contreni, John, eds. *Religion, Culture, and Society in the Early Middle Ages.* Kalamazoo, MI: Medieval Institute Publications, 1987.

Noomen, Willem, ed. *Le jeu d'Adam.* Paris: Champion, 1971.

Novick, Peter. *That Noble Dream: "The Objectivity Question" and the American Historical Profession.* Cambridge: Cambridge University Press, 1988.

Odenkirchen, Carl J., ed. *The Play of Adam.* Brookline, MA: Classical Folia Editions, 1976.

Oosthout, Henri. *Modes of Knowledge and the Transcendental.* Amsterdam: B. R. Grüner, 1991.

Ordo Romanus Primus. With introduction and notes by George Cuthbert. London: Alexander Morning, 1905.

Panofsky, Erwin. *Architecture and Scholasticism.* Cleveland, OH: World Publishing Co., 1968.

Parry, David. *Households of God: The Rule of Saint Benedict with Explanations for Monks and Lay-people Today.* London: Darton, Longman, and Todd, 1980.

Parsons, David, ed. *Tenth-Century Studies: Essays in Commemoration of the Millennium of the Council of Winchester and Regularis concordia.* London: Phillimore, 1975.

Paschasius Radbertus. *De corpore et sanguine domini.* Ed. Beda Paulus. Corpus christianorum: Continuatio mediaevalis 16. Turnhout: Typographi Brepols Editores Pontificii, 1969.

————. *De corpore et sanguine domini.* Vol. 120:1255–1350. *Patrologiae Cursus Completus, Series Latina.* Ed. Jacque Paul Migne. 221 vols. Paris: Garnier Fratres, 1884.

Patterson, Lee. *Negotiating the Past: The Historical Understanding of Medieval Literature.* Madison, WI: University of Wisconsin Press, 1987.

Pelikan, Jaroslav Jan. *The Christian Tradition.* 4 vols. Chicago: University of Chicago Press, 1971–84.

Peter the Venerable. *Contra Petrobrusianos hereticos.* Ed. James Fearns. Corpus christianorum: Continuatio mediaevalis 10. Turnhout: Typographi Brepols Editores Pontificii, 1968.

Pfaff, Richard William. *Medieval Latin Liturgy.* Toronto: University of Toronto Press, 1982.

Pickering, Frederick P. *Essays on Medieval German Literature and Iconography.* Cambridge: Cambridge University Press, 1980.

Planchart, Alejandro. *The Repertory of Tropes at Winchester.* 2 vols. Princeton, NJ: Princeton University Press, 1977.

Plotinus. *The Enneads.* Trans. Stephen MacKena. London: Faber and Faber, n.d.

Postan, Michael Moissey. *The Medieval Economy and Society.* London: Weidenfeld and Nicolson, 1972.

Poulet, George. *Studies in Human Time.* Trans. Elliott Coleman. Baltimore, MD: Johns Hopkins University Press, 1956.

Powell, James, ed. *Medieval Studies.* Syracuse, NY: Syracuse University Press, 1976.

Prosser, Eleanor. *Drama and Religion in the English Mystery Plays: A Re-Evaluation.* Stanford, CA: Stanford University Press, 1961.

Pseudo-Dionysius: The Complete Works. Trans. Colm Luibheid, with foreword, notes, and translation collaboration by Paul Rorem. New York: Paulist Press, 1987.

Rancière, Jacques. *The Names of History: On the Poetics of Knowledge.* Trans. Hassan Melehy. Minneapolis, MN: University of Minnesota Press, 1994.

Rankin, Susan. "The Music of the Medieval Liturgical Drama in France and England." Ph.D. dissertation, University of Cambridge, 1981.

Ratramnus. *De corpore et sanguine domini.* Ed. J. N. Bakhuizen van den Brink. Verhandelingen der Koninklijke Nederlandt se Akademie van Wetenschappen, Afd. Letterkunde; nieuwe recks; deel 87. Amsterdam: North-Holland, 1974.

Redmond, James, ed. *Themes in Drama: Drama and Religion.* Cambridge: Cambridge University Press, 1983.

Reuter, Timothy, ed. *Warriors and Churchmen in the High Middle Ages: Essays Presented to Karl Leyser.* London: Hambledon Press, 1992.

Rey-Flaud, Henri. *Le cercle magique.* Paris: Gallimard, 1973.

———. *Pour une dramaturgie du moyen âge.* Paris: Presses Universitaires de France, 1980.

Richard of Saint Victor. *In Apocalypsim Joannis.* Vol. 196:683–887. *Patrologiae Cursus Completus, Series Latina.* Ed. Jacque Paul Migne. 221 vols. Paris: Garnier Fratres, 1884.

Robertson, Agnes Jane, ed. *Anglo-Saxon Charters.* Cambridge: Cambridge University Press, 1939.

———, ed. *The Laws of the Kings of England from Edmund to Henry I.* Cambridge: Cambridge University Press, 1925.

Robinson, J. Armitage. *The Times of Saint Dunstan.* Oxford: Clarendon Press, 1923.

Rorem, Paul. *Pseudo-Dionysius: A Commentary on the Texts and an Introduction to Their Influence.* New York: Oxford University Press, 1993.

Rossum, Gerhard Dohrn-van. *History of the Hour.* Trans. Thomas Dunlap. Chicago: University of Chicago Press, 1996.

Round, John Horace, ed. *Ancient Charters, Royal and Private prior to A.D. 1200*. London: Pipe Roll Society, 1888.

Rubin, Miri. *Corpus Christi: The Eucharist in Late Medieval Culture*. Cambridge: Cambridge University Press, 1991.

Sawyer, Peter Hayes, ed. *Anglo-Saxon Charters*. London: Royal Historical Society, 1968.

Sayles, George Osborne. *The Medieval Foundations of England*. London: Methuen, 1977.

Schaff, Philip. *History of the Christian Church*. 8 vols. New York: Charles Scribner's Sons, 1910.

Schnusenberg, Christine. *The Relationship between the Church and the Theatre*. Lanham, MD: University Press of America, 1988.

Sepet, Marius. *Le drame religieux au moyen âge*. Paris: Blaud, 1890.

———. *Les prophetes du Christ: Etude sur les origines du théâtre au moyen âge*. Paris: Didier, 1878.

Silvestris, Bernard. *Cosmographia*. Ed. Peter Dronke. Textus Minores 53. Leiden: E. J. Brill, 1978.

Simon, Eckehard, ed. *The Theatre of Medieval Europe*. Cambridge: Cambridge University Press, 1991.

Smith, Lucy Margaret. *The Early History of the Monastery of Cluny*. London: Oxford University Press, 1920.

Somerville, Robert. *Papacy, Councils, and Canon Law in the Eleventh–Twelfth Centuries*. Aldershot, Great Britain: Variorum, 1990.

Southern, Richard William. *The Making of the Middle Ages*. New Haven, CT: Yale University Press, 1953.

———. *Saint Anselm*. Cambridge: Cambridge University Press, 1990.

———. *Saint Anselm and His Biographer*. Cambridge: Cambridge University Press, 1963.

Speaight, Robert. *The Christian Theatre*. London: Burns and Oates, 1960.

Steinbach, Rolf. *Die deutschen Oster- und Passionsspiele des Mittelalters*. Cologne: Bohlau, 1970.

Stemmler, Theo. *Liturgische Feiern und geistliche Spiele*. Tübingen: Niemeyer, 1970.

Stenton, Frank Merry. *Anglo-Saxon England*. Oxford: Clarendon Press, 1943.

Stevens, John. *Words and Music in the Middle Ages*. Cambridge: Cambridge University Press, 1986.

Sticca, Sandro. *The Latin Passion Play: Its Origin and Development*. Albany, NY: State University of New York Press, 1970.

———, ed. *The Medieval Drama*. Albany, NY: State University of New York Press, 1972.

Stock, Brian. *The Implications of Literacy: Written Language and Models of Interpretation in the Eleventh and Twelfth Centuries*. Princeton, NJ: Princeton University Press, 1983.

Straw, Carole. *Gregory the Great: Perfection in Imperfection.* Berkeley, CA: University of California Press, 1988.

Suger of Saint-Denis. *On the Abbey Church of St.-Denis and Its Art Treasures.* Edited, translated, and annotated by Erwin Panofsky. Princeton, NJ: Princeton University Press, 1946.

Szarmach, Paul E., ed. *An Introduction to the Medieval Mystics of Europe.* Albany, NY: State University of New York Press, 1984.

————. *Sources of Anglo-Saxon Culture.* Kalamazoo, MI: Medieval Institute Publication, Western Michigan University, 1986.

Tanner, Norman P., ed. *Decrees of the Ecumenical Councils.* 2 vols. London: Sheed and Ward, 1990.

Taylor, Jerome, and Nelson, Alan H., eds. *Medieval English Drama.* Chicago: University of Chicago Press, 1972.

Temple, Elzbieta. *Anglo-Saxon Manuscripts, 900–1066.* London: Harvey Miller, 1976.

Textus antiqui de festo Corporis Christi. Ed. Peter Browe. Münster: Typis Aschendorff, 1934.

Theoduin of Liège [Deoduinus]. "Contra Brunonem et Berengarium." Vol. 146:1439 B. *Patrologiae Cursus Completus, Series Latina.* Ed. Jacque Paul Migne. 221 vols. Paris: Garnier Fratres, 1884.

Thompson, Bard. *Liturgies of the Western Church.* Cleveland, OH: Meridan Books, 1961.

Thompson, James. *Feudal Germany.* Chicago: University of Chicago Press, 1928.

Thorpe, Benjamin, ed. *Ancient Laws and Institutions of England.* London: George, Eyre, and Andrew Spottiswoode, 1840.

Titow, Jan Zbigniew. *Winchester Yields: A Study of Medieval Agricultural Prod tivity.* Cambridge: Cambridge University Press, 1972.

Tolhurst, J. B. L., ed. *The Monastic Breviary of Hyde Abbey, Winchester.* 6 vols. London: Harrison and Sons, 1933.

Travis, Peter. *Dramatic Design in the Chester Cycle.* Chicago: University of Chicago Press, 1982.

Two Lives of Charlemagne. Trans. Lewis Thorpe. Harmondsworth: Penguin, 1969.

Tydeman, William. *The Theatre in the Middle Ages.* Cambridge: Cambridge University Press, 1978.

Ullmann, Walter. *The Papacy and Political Ideas in the Middle Ages.* London: Variorum Reprints, 1976.

Ulrich, Ingeborg. *Hildegard of Bingen: Mystic, Healer, Companion of Angels.* Trans. Linda M. Maloney. Collegeville, MN: Liturgical Press, 1993.

Ure, James. *The Benedictine Office.* Edinburgh: Edinburgh University Press, 1957.

Vattimo, Gianni. *Transparent Society.* Trans. David Webb. Baltimore, MD: Johns Hopkins University Press, 1992.

Vircillo, Carmela, ed. *Early Monastic Rules.* Collegeville, MN: Liturgical Press, 1982.

Walker, Williston. *A History of the Christian Church.* New York: Charles Scribner's Sons, 1985.

Warner, George Frederic, and Wilson, Henry Austin, eds. *The Benedictional of St. Aethelwold.* Oxford: Privately printed for presentation to the members of the Rorburghe Club, 1910.

White, Hayden. *Tropics of Discourse.* Baltimore, MD: Johns Hopkins University Press, 1978.

White, Lynn, Jr. *Medieval Religion and Technology.* Berkeley, CA: University of California Press, 1978.

Whitelock, Dorothy, Brett, Martin, and Brooke, Christopher, eds. *Councils and Synods with Other Documents Relating to the English Church.* 2 vols. Oxford: Clarendon Press, 1981.

Wickham, Glynne. *Early English Stages: 1300–1660.* 2 vols. London: Routledge and Kegan Paul, 1963.

———. *The Medieval Theatre.* London: St. Martin's Press, 1974.

Wilson, Christopher. *The Gothic Cathedral.* London: Thames and Hudson, 1990.

Woolf, Rosemary. *Art and Doctrine.* London: Hambledon Press, 1986.

Wormald, Francis. *The Benedictional of St. Aethelwold.* London: Faber and Faber, 1959.

———. *English Kalends before A.D. 1100.* Woodbridge, Suffolk: Boydell Press, 1988.

———. *The Winchester Psalter.* London: Miller and Medcalf, 1973.

Wormald, Patrick, ed. *Ideal and Reality in Frankish and Anglo-Saxon Society.* Oxford: Blackwell, 1983.

Wulfstan of Winchester. *Life of St. Aethelwold.* Ed. Michael Lapidge and Michael Winterbottom. Oxford: Clarendon Press, 1991.

Yorke, Barbara, ed. *Bishop Aethelwold: His Career and Influence.* Woodbridge, Suffolk: Boydell Press, 1988.

Young, Karl. *The Drama of the Medieval Church.* 2 vols. London: Oxford University Press, 1933.

Zacour, Norman P. *Medieval Institutions.* New York: St. Martin's Press, 1976.

Zarnecki, George. *Art of the Medieval World.* New York: Harry N. Abrams, 1975.

Index

DATE DUE

APR 1 2 2001			
			Printed in USA